The Netherlands and the Rise of Modern Imperialism
Maarten Kuitenbrouwer

Whereas numerous studies on British, French and German imperialism have been undertaken, which are available in English, the Dutch case is relatively unexplored. Does it fit the general pattern of nineteenth-century European imperialism? This is one of the major questions in the historical debate on the colonial past of the Netherlands. Most specialists have given a negative answer. This study challenges the traditional view. For the English-speaking reader, it offers the most comprehensive and substantial analysis of Dutch colonialism and the most thorough response to the rise of modern imperialism to date. The author combines a chronological approach with a topical one and reaches important conclusions by comparing the Dutch case with those of Britain, Belgium and Portugal, thus relating to international patterns of modern imperialism.

Maarten Kuitenbrouwer is Lecturer in the Department of the History of International Relations, University of Utrecht.

The Netherlands and the Rise of Modern Imperialism

Colonies and Foreign Policy, 1870–1902

Maarten Kuitenbrouwer

Translated from the Dutch by
Hugh Beyer

BERG

New York / Oxford

Distributed exclusively in the US and Canada by
St. Martin's Press, New York

English edition first published in 1991 by
Berg Publishers Limited
Editorial Offices:
165 Taber Avenue, Providence R.I. 02906, USA
150 Cowley Road, Oxford OX4 1JJ, UK

Originally published as *Nederland en de opkomst van het moderne imperialisme. Koloniën en buitenlandse politiek 1870–1902*, De Bataafsche Leeuw 1985. © Maarten Kuitenbrouwer 1985
English translation © Maarten Kuitenbrouwer 1991

Library of Congress Cataloging-in-Publication Data
Kuitenbrouwer, M.
    [Nederland en de opkomst van het moderne imperialisme. English]
    The Netherlands and the rise of modern imperialism : colonies and foreign policy, 1870–1902 / Maarten Kuitenbrouwer : translated from the Dutch by Hugh Beyer.
    p. cm.
    Translation of: Nederland en de opkomst van het moderne imperialisme.
    Includes bibliographical references.
    Includes index.
    ISBN 0–85496–681–1
    1. Netherlands—Foreign relations—1830–1898. 2. Netherlands—Foreign relations—1898–1948. 3. Netherlands—Colonies. 4. Netherlands—Foreign relations—Indonesia. 5. Indonesia—Foreign relations—Netherlands. I. Title.
    DJ261.K8413 1991
    949.2'06—dc20   90–36901
                                                              CIP

British Library Cataloguing in Publication Data
Kuitenbrouwer, Maarten
    The Netherlands and the rise of modern imperialism : colonies and foreign policy, 1870–1902.
    1. Dutch imperialism, history
    I. Title II. Nederland en de opkomst van het moderne imperialisme. *English*
    325.3209492
    ISBN 0–85496–681–1

Printed in Great Britain by
Billing & Sons Ltd, Worcester

Contents

Contents

Preface to the English Edition

This book is mainly about Dutch relations with the overseas world during the rise of modern imperialism. In particular, it is about the Dutch pattern of expansion and reaction which emerged from these relations. In the introduction I have outlined the theoretical framework of my analysis as well as my points of departure. Chapters one to three are mainly descriptive and focus on Dutch relations with the Indonesian Archipelago and South Africa. The conclusion of the book is that the Netherlands developed its own variant of modern imperialism in the Indonesian Archipelago, partly for internal and partly for external reasons. This conclusion is further elaborated in a comparative analysis of the Dutch position during this period with those of Britain, Portugal and Belgium.

The book is a complete and unabridged translation of my doctoral thesis for the University of Amsterdam in 1985. Any new literature on modern imperialism which has appeared since then has therefore not been used. The translation has been made possible by a generous subsidy from the *Nederlandse organisatie voor wetenschappelijk onderzoek* (Dutch Organisation for Scientific Research). I would also like to express my special thanks to the translator, Hugh Beyer, for his elegant translation, particularly as regards the difficult nineteenth century quotations.

Maarten Kuitenbrouwer

Introduction

Imperialism is one of those polemical terms of nineteenth century politics which has acquired a more respectable and scholarly meaning in the course of the twentieth century, but without losing its original meaning completely. Around the middle of the nineteenth century imperialism still had specifically European overtones. At that time it stood for a personal desire for power and was synonymous with Napoleon's or Caesar's power politics, as Koebner showed in his history of the word *imperialism*.[1]

Through Disraeli's *Imperial Policy*, after 1870, the term imperialism came to be linked with colonial expansion overseas. But it wasn't until 1900 that the word acquired its modern, general and impersonal meaning. Under the influence of the Spanish–American War and the Boer War it began to be widely used as a critical, anti-capitalist term. And although its analytical, scholarly meaning has since then become more distinct from its political connotations, it has always remained a loaded term. 'Imperialism is no word for scholars', said the British colonial historian W. K. Hancock scornfully in 1940.[2] The powerful revival of academic interest in the term during the sixties and seventies cannot therefore be seen independently of the political discussion of those years.

However, in spite of these permanent ideological connotations, it still seems to be a useful – and sometimes even an enlightening – term for studying the nineteenth and twentieth centuries. I will therefore give a brief overall view of the most significant developments in the historiography of imperialism, both internationally and with particular reference to the Netherlands. Finally, against this background, I will relate the basic issues of this study to the emergence of modern imperialism in general.

1. Koebner and Schmidt, *Imperialism*, chapter 1.
2. Cited by Etherington, *Theories*, p. 220.

1

Modern Imperialism

Terminology and Historical Periods

Until recently the definition, chronological division and explanation of imperialism has mainly been a discussion point between Marxist theoreticians and non-Marxist specialist historians. The radical authors who opened the debate around the year 1900 narrowed the term imperialism down to the endeavours of the great Western powers at that time to secure new fields for investment, if necessary by force.

This aggressive capitalist striving for expansion was, according to Hobson, Hilferding, Luxemburg and Lenin, a relatively recent phenomenon that was not exclusively aimed at overseas territory and which did not necessarily appear in the form of colonialism. Etherington has rightly pointed out that their theories were not so much meant to explain the preceding colonial expansion, as to predict the future distribution and redistribution of world territory.[3] However, as soon as the First World War was over, theories of imperialism were increasingly understood as economic explanations of colonialism: first by a new generation of Marxist authors who looked at the problem within the framework of the anti-colonial struggle; then also by non-Marxist historians such as Hancock who tried to show in his historical research that colonial 'guardianship' was motivated, not by a capitalist desire for profit, but by political and humanitarian considerations. From this poi⸲ : of view, the scramble for colonies was soon seen as the most typical episode in the period of modern imperialism, as the time between 1870 and 1914 came to be known.[4]

After the Second World War and the period of decolonisation, this emphasis on formal, territorial domination as the main criterion of imperialism was no longer understood in quite such absolute terms. Both Marxists and non-Marxists began to show more interest in informal and economic forms of domination during the pre- and post-colonial phases of imperialism. In 1953 two British colonial historians, R. Robinson and J. Gallagher, introduced the concept of an informal imperialism of free trade, which they said had brought forth formal, colonial imperialism.[5] Their theory of continuity was

3. Ibid., pp. 263–7.
4. Ibid., chapters 10 and 11.
5. Gallagher and Robinson, 'Imperialism', taken over by Louis, *Imperialism*, pp. 53–73.

limited, first and foremost, to British expansion overseas. Above all, they objected to the usual distinction that was made by British historians between mid-Victorian anti-imperialism and imperialism during the late Victorian period. According to Robinson and Gallagher, it was only the means of British policy that changed, not the aims. Having maintained its overseas supremacy by means of free trade and gunboat diplomacy during a large part of the nineteenth century, Britain increasingly had to establish its formal, colonial domination, due to local conflicts and growing competition with other European powers. And so the transition from informal to formal imperialism was gradual and often 'reluctant'. Robinson and Gallagher summarised the continuity in British overseas expansion like this: 'British policy followed the principle of extending control informally if possible and formally if necessary'.[6]

Since then Robinson and Gallagher's continuity theory has been questioned by a number of British historians. Free trade was enforced less systematically by the British government than Robinson and Gallagher maintained, whereas colonial expansion under Disraeli was no longer quite as 'reluctant'.[7] Although the continuity thesis was partly intended as a critique of the Marxist concept of 'new' imperialism, it was actually taken up quite eagerly by neo-Marxists in particular. However, they interpreted the term so widely that there was almost no distinction at all between normal economic relations and imperialism. Neo-Marxist theorists showed a strong tendency towards generalisation and the abstract, sometimes stretching the term imperialism so far that it covered several centuries of 'North–South' relations. As a result, neo-Marxist analysis seemed far removed from the original Marxist theories, which concentrated on the specific pattern of capitalist expansion and world politics around the year 1900.[8]

Ultimately, these anachronistic applications of the term imperialism have brought to light very few facts and have not contributed to a more adequate interpretation of those that are known already, thus lending support to the argument that, in historical research, one should avoid definitions that are too wide. In this instance, modern imperialism as a historical category should be reserved

6. Ibid., p. 67.
7. For the criticism by O. Macdonagh and D. C. M. Platt, see ibid., pp. 14–24; cf. Eldridge, *Victorian Imperialism*, pp. 74–80.
8. Etherington, *Theories*, pp. 238–63; cf. Mommsen, *Theories*, pp. 113–42.

above all for the period between 1870 and 1914.[9]

In my analysis I have decided to define imperialism as the effort to establish formal or informal political control over another society. This working definition yields an analytical distinction between imperialism on the one hand and on the other mere verbal manifestations of expansionism or genuine forms of expansion which are not aimed at political control but at economic exchanges, such as trade. The distinction between colonial expansion (or colonialism) and imperialism is above all historical. The Western powers did not begin to step up their efforts at colonial expansion until after 1870, whereas colonialism after the First World War was no longer aimed at territorial gains but rather at maintaining one's political power. Modern imperialism can be understood in this context as a historical process, resulting – intentionally or unintentionally – from the efforts of Western powers to establish their rule over non-Western societies. it seems to me pointless, therefore, to try to find a general formula that would set a chronological limit on modern imperialism. For the European powers which had established their formal and informal control outside Europe at the beginning of the nineteenth century, the transition to a purposeful colonial expansionism was generally more gradual than for newcomers at the end of the century. From 1880 onwards, international relations were dominated to a large extent by their competitive struggle for colonies. Around 1900 a new, violent phase started in modern imperialism, when a number of powerful Western nations no longer directed their aggressive expansionist efforts merely at the last unoccupied territories in Africa and Asia, but also at small 'white' states, such as the Boer Republics in South Africa, or the existing colonies of weaker European countries, such as Spain and Portugal.

This aggressive phase was to a considerable extent dominated by economic considerations and interests. Etherington therefore maintains that modern imperialism did not start until 1895 and that it ended in 1920, with the territorial redrawing of political boundaries in the aftermath of the First World War.[10] Such a chronological demarcation certainly serves to bring certain things sharply into focus and therefore has its value. It rightly corrects the anachronistic tendency to pre-date modern imperialism far back into the nine-

9. Mommsen, *Imperialismus*, pp. 213–14; cf. Etherington, *Theories*, pp. 267–73 and 280–4.
10. Ibid., pp. 273–80.

teenth century, or even into the late eighteenth century. But Etherington's concept cannot yield full explanation because it is too closely tied to the one-sided economic doctrines of the original theories of imperialism.

Explanations in Terms of Western Causes

According to these theories, the causes of contemporary imperialism must be seen almost exclusively in terms of economics, particularly in the urge to find new opportunities for investing the growing capital surplus of Western capitalist enterprises. The notion of an overseas outlet for surplus capital was originally put forward by American imperialists during the Spanish–American War in 1898. It was through the publications of the colourful capitalist and socialist H. G. Wilshire that this idea reached J. A. Hobson and, later, Lenin.[11]

It was the Boer War which had given rise to Hobson's influential study of imperialism. According to this progressive British liberal, however, it did not necessarily follow that a growing capital surplus should automatically lead to imperialism. Rather, he maintained, this surplus had been caused by the low level of consumption among the working classes. Wage rises, social welfare measures and other reforms could, according to Hobson, take the most significant motive force out of imperialism in the future.[12] But according to Marxist theorists such as Hilferding, Rosa Luxemburg and Lenin it was already too late for such reforms to offer a way out. They saw capital surplus as a necessary consequence of falling profits in home investment during the final phase of capitalism. Monopolist capitalism simply had to take refuge in imperialism. However, as overseas investment opportunities were also running out, it was inevitable that wars should break out between the most powerful imperialist countries, wars which would eventually lead to the breakdown of capitalism. On the eve of the First World War, the German social democrat Karl Kautsky still thought that it was possible for the main Western powers to achieve a joint, peaceful exploitation of overseas territories. Lenin believed that the imperialist world war would herald the beginning of the socialist world revolution.[13]

After the First World War, when most revolutionary attempts

11. Ibid., chapters 1 and 2.
12. Ibid., chapters 2 and 3; cf. Mommsen, *Theories*, pp. 11–17.
13. Ibid., pp. 29–58; cf. Etherington, *Theories*, chapters 6–7.

had failed and Western capitalism had recovered, there was growing scepticism of the economic explanation of modern imperialism. The Austrian socialist J. Schumpeter developed an alternative explanation: he saw imperialism not as the latest stage of capitalism, but simply as a form of 'atavism' which had its origins in the pre-capitalist period. The driving force, he said, must be seen in the traditional, militarist aristocracy and its efforts to compensate for a diminishing influence in Europe by seeking possessions abroad.[14] The political explanations that were developed by historians during the inter-war period were also directed – explicitly or implicitly – against Marxist theories of imperialism. The American historian W. Langer believed that modern imperialism had its roots in the sphere of international relations – especially in the disturbance of the balance of power in Europe after 1890.[15] British colonial historians explained overseas expansion mainly in terms of political strategies and humanitarian concerns, but they rejected the term imperialism. After the Second World War, however, their successors did use this term, but encapsulated it in alternative theories of 'informal', 're-luctant' or 'peripheral' imperialism. In particular, D. K. Fieldhouse was extremely critical of the economic explanations which had been offered by Hobson and Lenin.

Fieldhouse was indeed able to provide convincing statistical evidence that British capital export during the period of modern imperialism had gone mainly to the United States, the white dominions and other growing nuclei within the capitalist world, and only to a lesser extent to the old and new colonies in Africa and Asia. French capital export had been following a similar pattern, with a large number of small-scale entrepreneurs and rentiers who preferred to invest their savings in Russia rather than in the African tropics – much to the despair of Ferry and other advocates of colonial expansion.[16] Moreover, the formation of monopolies, which was pointed out so emphatically by Lenin, had not progressed very far in British and French capitalism around the year 1900. According to Fieldhouse, financiers and other capitalist pressure groups did not generally exert much influence on colonial policies. After some detailed research into archives, Robinson and Gallagher came to the conclusion that the British 'official mind' had been motivated above all by political and strategic considerations in

14. Ibid., pp. 151–65; cf. Mommsen, *Theories*, pp. 18–28.
15. Cf. Langer, *Diplomacy*, chapter 3.
16. Fieldhouse, 'Imperialism'; cf. Brunschwig, *Mythes*, pp. 79f.

the division of Africa – particularly by security interests in India. This is why British expansion was at first rather reluctant in character, though towards the end of the nineteenth century it was increasingly dominated by nationalist sentiments. According to Henri Brunschwig, French colonialism after 1871 had been motivated from the very beginning by a desire for national prestige.[17] When Fieldhouse attacked the 'Hobson–Lenin thesis' in 1961, he concluded: 'it is clear that imperialism cannot be explained in simple terms of economic theory and the nature of finance capitalism. In its mature form it can best be described as a sociological phenomenon with roots in political facts.'[18]

In the meantime it has become rather obvious that a purely political explanation of modern imperialism in terms of international power politics or mass nationalism is even less satisfactory. In their attempts to disprove Hobson and Lenin's original theories, the critics were often in danger of overshooting their target by denying any form of economic influence on modern imperialism. Indeed, as Etherington has pointed out,[19] the historical research of these critics was concerned with nineteenth-century colonial expansion, so that their results hardly even touched those theories – theories which were aimed primarily at the dynamics of imperialist world politics in the early twentieth century.

Nevertheless, when we reject a one-sided economic explanation, this does not mean that we should now affirm a one-sided political explanation of modern imperialism. When assessing the relative significance of economic causes, it is not so important whether the new colonies really were profitable, but rather whether they were expected to become profitable after a period of consolidation. Recent studies have shown that the division of Africa was indeed guided by the anticipation of economic advantages and that these certainly did play an important part, side by side with power politics and nationalism. It is worth noting that on the eve of the Boer War as much as one-tenth of British capital exports was invested in South Africa.[20] Mommsen, in particular, pointed out that the sharp distinction between political and economic factors, which the 'Rankeans' had taken over from their Marxist opponents,

17. Cf. Robinson and Gallagher, *Africa*; Brunschwig, *Mythes*.
18. Fieldhouse, 'Imperialism', p. 209.
19. Etherington, *Theories*, pp. 267–8.
20. Edelstein, *Overseas Investment*, p. 303. Cf. Hopkins, *Economic History*, pp. 135–67; Hynes, *Economics*, pp. 5–6.

had obscured any insight into the continuous interaction between these factors which modern imperialism showed in practice.[21]

Meanwhile, during the sixties, there was a surge of interest in Marxist theories of imperialism. However, the original doctrines were applied in such an abstract and ahistorical way that there were very few tangible points of contact between them and historical research into modern imperialism. This became particularly clear at the Oxford seminar in 1969, where both Marxist and non-Marxist theoreticians took part. One exception was the Marxist-inspired contribution by H.-U. Wehler on the role of social imperialism in the colonial expansion of Germany. Previously, the term social imperialism had been used by the British historian B. Semmel to describe the ideas of Chamberlain as well as others who thought along similar lines, and Wehler now adapted it to describe the colonial policies of Bismarck.[22] However, he also expanded this theory to give a new explanation of modern imperialism in general.

Wehler understood social imperialism as the effort of the elites in industrialised countries to avoid domestic crises by means of overseas expansion and thus to maintain the social status quo within their own societies. This was achieved both by obtaining new markets to avert the danger of over-production and by deflecting internal social tensions to the outside. Seen against the background of the Great Depression between 1873 and 1896, says Wehler, such a manipulation of domestic relations provided a very significant motivation for imperialism in the majority of capitalist countries. But he maintains that in large countries, such as Germany and the United States, where industrialisation developed especially quickly, social imperialism was ever the most important force. Traditionally, and particularly in connection with these countries, the basis for a political explanation of modern imperialism had been the 'primacy of foreign politics'. According to Wehler, however, this should be replaced by the 'primacy of domestic politics'.[23]

Wehler's approach is certainly more than just another variation of an attempt to explain modern imperialism in economic terms. He

---

21. Mommsen, *Imperialismus*, pp. 56–7. Mommsen maintains that many political explanations of modern imperialism are derived from Ranke's concept of a continuous power struggle between the great powers; cf. *Theories*, p. 74.

22. Wehler, 'Industrial Growth'; cf. the introduction by Owen and Sutcliffe, *Studies*. See also Wehler, *Bismarck*, and Semmel, *Imperialism*.

23. Cf. Wehler, *Bismarck*, pp. 486–503; *Kaiserreich*, pp. 182–5; *Aufstieg*, pp. 37–43.

himself claimed to offer a synthesis of a Marxist-inspired perspective of capitalist development and recent insights from social sciences into the behaviour of elite groups and their ideological consensus. But it is not always very easy to distinguish the most important points in his complicated and eclectic approach. Mommsen has pointed out that the relationship between 'substructure' and 'superstructure', between objective and subjective factors remains rather vague in Wehler's analysis of social imperialism. Moreover, as a historical explanation of Bismarck's colonial politics, his analysis seems to be rather questionable. It was not until the turn of the century that social imperialism was to play an important role, both in Germany's *Weltpolitik* and in British imperial policies.[24]

The most important causes which have been postulated since the year 1900 to explain modern imperialism can be summarised as follows:

1. External political causes, resulting from the dynamics of international relations;
2. Internal political causes, in the form of more or less spontaneous nationalism or manipulated social imperialism;
3. Economic causes, which may be commercial, industrial or financial, depending on their origins.

These causes can obviously be understood and applied in a variety of ways: in an objective sense as general, impersonal factors; or in a subjective sense as personal motives.[25] It seems that for a historical analysis of modern imperialism the most relevant level is an intermediate stage of institutions and organisations with overseas involvement. We could add a whole host of cultural, demographic, military, technological and other causes to the ones listed above. However, such endless analytical hair splitting is unlikely to yield any fruitful results. Once Wehler's theory of social imperialism has been added, it seems that, for the time being, the possibilities for explaining modern imperialism in terms of Western causes have been exhausted. Historians have therefore diverted their attention from the West in recent years and are now concentrating, above all, on the 'local factor', that is on non-Western causes.

---

24. Mommsen, *Imperialismus*, p. 80; cf. *Theories*, pp. 93–100. See also Baumgart, *Imperialismus*, pp. 99–100 and 118–27; cf. Wehler, *Kaiserreich*, pp. 172–9.
25. For the theoretical and methodological aspects see Reynolds, *Modes*, chapter 6.

Explanations in Terms of Local Causes

This shift of historical emphasis must be seen within the wider context of an increasing interest in Third World countries after the Second World War and decolonisation. In historiography, this has led to a sensible broadening of perspective. Traditional colonial history, which was mainly dominated by a Euro-centric viewpoint, has been replaced by new perspectives that do more justice to the relative autonomy of Asian, African and Latin American history. For the study of modern imperialism – always understood as the climax of Europe's power in the world – this shift of perspective certainly means a rehabilitation of those groups which, until recently, were regarded only as 'agents' or 'victims' and were therefore assigned a relatively instrumental role in imperialism; the roles of local administrators and indigenous elites, in particular, have been re-evaluated. When the idea of Europe as the centre of power was questioned by post-war historiographers, this more critical attitude could now strike a chord both with administrative and proto-nationalist traditions. Inevitably, however, despite the consolidation of these new perspectives, the old antithesis between the two traditions continued to prevail. Such a development can be seen very clearly in the work of Robinson and Gallagher who made a significant contribution to the post-war shift of emphasis in the historiography of modern imperialism, writing mainly from the administrative point of view.[26]

As for their interpretation and timing of imperialism, Robinson and Gallagher are now giving considerably more precedence to local, non-Western circumstances and groups. They have been doing so ever since the appearance of their article on the free trade empire, in which they already understood the transition from informal to formal control as a consequence of local developments, especially the weakening of the 'collaborating' elites and the emergence of 'pseudo-nationalist' resistance movements.[27] In their study of the partition of Africa they gave a further analysis of collaboration and resistance, to which they also added the 'sub-imperialism' of European colonisers, missionaries and adminis-

26. In an interview with *Itinerario* (1977, no. 1, pp. 20–1), Robinson frankly expressed this colonial, administrative point of view. The term 'collaboration' was met with vehement criticism, especially by African and Asian historians; cf. Louis, *Imperialism*, pp. 36–7.
27. Ibid., pp. 25, 68–9.

Introduction

trators. Indigenous resistance to increasing British penetration –
particularly in Egypt and South Africa – was a direct cause of
colonial expansion. The restored collaboration of traditional elites
then formed the basis of the colonial rule that followed.[28]

At the well-known Oxford seminar in 1969 Robinson gave a
general summary of these insights in his 'sketch of a theory of
collaboration',[29] pleading for an 'excentric' approach to imperialism. This involved thinking of it in geographic terms as the overlap-
ping of Europe's expanding circle and the smaller circles around the
power centres outside Europe. 'It ought to be commonplace',
Robinson stated in this context,

> that from beginning to end imperialism was a product of interaction
> between European and non-European politics. European economic and
> strategic expansion took imperial form when these two components
> operated at cross purposes with the third and non-European component
> – that of indigenous collaboration and resistance; the missing key to a
> more historical theory is perhaps to be found in this third element.'[30]

Since then an increasing number of historians have adapted their
research to this new paradigm, with a significant amount of emphasis on the 'turbulent frontier', that is the local power vacuum as the
cause of imperialism.[31] However, economic factors are also regarded as significant. It is certainly true to say that the shift of
historical interest towards the non-European world has helped to
break down the antithesis between economic and political interpretations, thus bridging a gap which used to hinder the development
of historiography while it was still centred upon Europe.

This applies particularly to Fieldhouse who seems to be more
aware of the role of economic interests and pressure groups in a
non-European context than he used to be when he was still concentrating mainly on Europe. In his recent work he has considerably
modified the significance of European causes in relation to 'peripheral' factors. Fieldhouse's ideas are based on Robinson and
Gallagher's continuity thesis. In about 1830 trade links between
Europe and the non-European world gradually began to increase,

28. See also 'The partition of Africa', originally in 1962 as a contribution to *New Cambridge Modern History*, but also in Louis, *Imperialism*, pp. 73–128; cf. the criticism ibid., pp. 27–36.
29. Robinson, 'Non-European foundations', pp. 117–43.
30. Ibid., 119–20.
31. Cf. Eldridge, *Victorian Imperialism*, pp. 138–42.

11

with the result that a form of co-operation emerged between European traders and the traditional elites. Around the year 1880 a series of conflicts led to a general crisis in this co-operation, which then forced the European governments to adopt a policy of intervention and annexation. Economic expansion, according to Fieldhouse, thus led to imperialism only indirectly, via these local crises on the periphery.[32]

Of the different local factors which have been put forward in these new approaches, we can certainly regard the expansionist urge of European traders, missionaries and administrators as an autonomous cause that led to imperialism. However, it is difficult to see how the collaboration or the resistance of indigenous elites could have had this effect – at least not if imperialism is understood as the purposeful and active effort to control another society. Nevertheless, I do feel that the new approaches are valuable in so far as they direct our attention firmly towards the active role which was played by indigenous elites in the process of European expansion. Fieldhouse maintains that the new paradigm is still too general to pass as a special historical explanation of modern imperialism.[33] So far it has been based above all on negative arguments, that is the denial of Western causes. For a more positive explanation, the necessary research is indeed still lacking.

Because of its general character, the new paradigm can quite easily lead to a confusion of cause and effect or of cause and motive. What was it that disrupted the co-operation between local Europeans and indigenous elites? Just the immanent effects of gradually growing trade between different cultural groups? Why was it precisely around 1880 that local unrest led to European intervention throughout the world? Where was it that the decisions of annexation really were made – in the colonial outposts or in the European capitals? Until now, neither Fieldhouse nor any other adherents of the new paradigm have been able to answer such questions satisfactorily.[34]

Comparison and Synthesis

Apart from new empirical research it seems that, as far as the theoretical side is concerned, the study of modern imperialism

32. Fieldhouse, *Economics*, parts I and IV.
33. Ibid., p. 8.
34. For some critical comments on the new paradigm see Eldridge, *Victorian*

would benefit most from a comparative analysis. This would then help to determine more accurately the relative significance of different causes for specific countries and areas.

The Leiden Centre for the History of European Expansion has taken a number of initiatives in this context which are of great international importance. Wesseling and Emmer have expressed their hope that these series of comparative studies can contribute to the development of an interdisciplinary approach and a common terminological apparatus, though it still remains to be seen how the Centre can achieve these objectives.[35] The publication *Expansion and Reaction*, which was the starting point of the series, certainly showed that there are problems of epistemology and methodology involved. The general character of the central concepts of expansion and reaction, the relative lack of structure in the comparative framework and the tendency of several writers to distance themselves from the traditional image of Europe as the centre of modern imperialism – all this seems to have contributed to a rather negative result:

> No expansion in British or French Black Africa, little in China and India, some expansion in North Africa and the East Indies; as for reactions, they were rather effects, side-effects of widely different types. If some expansion did occur, then it was for the most part unintentional, undesired and uncontrolled . . . The question arises once more: has European expansion ever really existed?[36]

This question, however, was finally answered in the affirmative by Wesseling. He rightly pointed out the historical importance of modern imperialism, which he understood as the consequence of the 'mutual penetration of state and society' in Europe for international relations outside Europe. This is a sensible concept, even though it is centred upon Europe.[37] As we still do not have a new interdisciplinary approach or a common terminological apparatus, such ideas are indeed indispensable. Meanwhile, however, even the most old-fashioned history of ideas can be relevant for the study of modern imperialism. This can be seen, for instance, in Gollwitzer's

Imperialism, pp. 144–6; Wehler's contribution in Louis, *Imperialism*, pp. 208–11; à Campo, 'Orde', pp. 156–60.
35. Wesseling and Emmer, 'Overseas History', p. 16.
36. Wesseling, 'Expansion', p. 16.
37. Ibid., pp. 13–14.

extensive study of *weltpolitisches Denken* (world political thinking).[38] For the period of modern imperialism Gollwitzer distinguished a number of general tendencies in contemporary thinking about world politics, such as social Darwinism, international power politics, striving for economic expansion and ethical imperialism. He then discussed the national viewpoints of England, France, Germany, Russia and the United States, paying particular attention to navalism and other geopolitical notions. Finally he discussed the thoughts about world politics of internationalists and anti-imperialists. But although Gollwitzer's extensive and varied insights cover a large area, they contain very few explicit comparisons. The study by W. Baumgart of British and French imperialism, on the other hand, does offer a systematic comparison, though rather summary and schematic in character.[39]

Baumgart took four general areas of analysis as his starting point: power politics, socio-psychological factors, economic factors and socio-economic factors. He maintained that the evolution of power politics was the most significant cause of modern imperialism, both in Britain and France. However, he conceived this evolution so widely that also the continuity of colonial expansion, technological development and the 'absorbency' of the power vacuum outside Europe were all regarded as part of the central 'historical and political' explanation. Nevertheless, at the heart of it he sees both international conflicts and agreements between England, France and other European powers, which are treated by him from the viewpoint of the European balance of power.[40] Nationalism and other socio-psychological factors also had an important role, lending support and legitimacy to British and French imperialism. In France, nationalism sometimes even played the most decisive role in the decision-making process, which can be seen, for example, in the influence of public opinion on the ratification of the Brazza Macoco Agreement of 1882.[41]

Baumgart expresses himself rather less favourably about economic and socio-economic factors. Like many other critics, he casts his economic explanation in the same mould that Hobson and Lenin had fashioned at the same time. Thus he adapts their theories to British and French colonial expansion, though only to reject them

38. Gollwitzer, *Geschichte*, pp. 17f.
39. Baumgart, *Imperialismus*.
40. Ibid., pp. 8f.
41. Ibid., pp. 33f.

again in the light of new evidence, that is capital export, trade and the role of pressure groups. However, 'Eldorado ideas' about the supposedly lucrative nature of the colonies are understood by Baumgart as part of the political and historical explanation, rather than the economic explanation.[42] As we have seen, there are difficulties in such a denial of economic factors. In his criticism of Wehler's socio-economic explanation of modern imperialism Baumgart is considerably more convincing. In Germany social imperialism did not begin to play an important role until the time of the Emperor Wilhelm II. It was certainly not the most dominant factor for Bismarck. Furthermore, British social imperialism was more concerned with strengthening the Empire through domestic reforms than detracting from internal tensions by means of imperialist adventures.[43] In his comparative analysis Baumgart puts more emphasis on the common points of British and French imperialism than on their differences. He maintains that colonial expansion was in both countries mainly motivated by power politics and nationalism, while economic and social factors were largely of secondary importance. Even so, they played a greater role in England than in France, where industrial development was less advanced.[44]

Quite apart from its one-sided emphasis on political factors, Baumgart's comparative analysis does not deal sufficiently with the process-like character of modern imperialism – the continuous interaction between the powers involved with their often unintentional consequences, as well as the interaction between internal and external factors. Paul Kennedy's study of the rise of Anglo–German antagonism before the First World War is much more successful in this respect.[45] In this book Kennedy alternated between a comparative analysis of the political and socio-economic structures of the two countries and a chronological description of their mutual relations from 1860 onwards. Although these diachronic chapters are scarcely integrated with the synchronic, comparative parts of Kennedy's study, the study has nevertheless clarified a number of points. His insight into the relationship between internal modernisation and international rivalry is particularly relevant for the analysis of modern imperialism. The formation of the political system in the two countries, their industrialisation and their col-

42. Ibid., pp. 64f.
43. Ibid., pp. 96f.
44. Ibid., pp. 127f.; cf. Mommsen, *Theories*, p. 75.
45. Kennedy, *Rise*.

15

onial expansion had proceeded at different speeds, and Britain therefore generally reacted more defensively to their mutual rivalry than Germany. Ideological currents in which the interaction between internal and external factors showed itself especially clearly – such as social Darwinism, nationalism and social imperialism – were therefore more moderate in Britain than in Germany. Kennedy saw the outburst of jingoism during the Boer War as a relatively superficial and therefore non-permanent phenomenon.[46] So far as Germany is concerned, Kennedy's analysis forms an attractive alternative to Wehler's one-sided emphasis on domestic factors.

In his diachronic description of Anglo–German relations and his synchronic comparison of the two societies Kennedy gives a well-founded and convincing synthesis of many research data as well as different historiographic ideas. A similar synthesis of modern imperialism is offered in a study of Raymond Betts, though in more general terms and less definitively.[47] In his survey – which Betts himself calls an example of *haute vulgarisation* – he combines also a chronological and a thematic approach. After presenting a historical summary of European expansion from the Napoleonic Wars to the First World War, he gives an in-depth discussion of the political, economic and cultural aspects of the expansion process, concentrating mainly on European tendencies, but not only from a European perspective. Betts puts a great deal of emphasis on the continuity of expansion of countries which had already been established overseas at the beginning of the nineteenth century, particularly Britain and France. Between 1815 and 1870 Anglo–French rivalry led to the gradual expansion of colonial territories as well as informal spheres of influence in Africa and the Far East, and a similar pattern had emerged in Central Asia with regard to British–Russian rivalry.[48] Expansion was further stimulated by technological developments, with the opening of the Suez Canal as the first major event.[49]

Using the terms *pre-emption* and *contiguity*,[50] Betts gives an original and illuminating analysis of the transition to modern imperialism. The mechanism of contiguity, of geographically adjacent areas, points to a European expansion which – so far as the old

---

46. Ibid., chapter 18; cf. his introduction in Kennedy and Nicholls, *Movements*.
47. Betts, *False Dawn*.
48. Ibid., pp. 35f.; cf. Gillard, *Struggle*, pp. 7f.
49. Betts, *False Dawn*, pp. 6–7; cf. Headrick, *Tools*, pp. 9–10.
50. Betts, *False Dawn*, pp. 71–2.

colonial powers are concerned – was steady, continuous, and generally proceeded from established bases that already existed. The 'local factor' continued to play an important role in this context. But with the emergence of new great powers, such as Germany and Italy, expansion increased drastically after 1870 and eventually resulted in a real scramble for colonies. It is this discontinuity which is denoted by the word *pre-emption*.[51] According to Betts, the new colonial occupations and the extension of the old ones had a strongly anticipatory and preventive character. The desire to be there before others was caused by the tense political situation and the economic crisis in Europe. It was reinforced by ideological currents such as nationalism and social Darwinism. The new mood was aptly expressed by Lord Rosebery's famous phrase of 'pegging out claims for the future'. The result was that colonial rivalry acquired a rather autonomous character, with a tendency to grow stronger. Modern imperialism, according to Betts, was to a large extent pre-emptive, although contiguity continued to play a role.

The Position of the Netherlands

The Netherlands: a Special Case?

While there has grown a wide diversity of approaches, they all seem to agree on one point, that modern imperialism was mainly a tendency of large countries and not of small ones. Explanations of the phenomenon in terms of international power politics even appear to exclude the possibility that small countries could have engaged in imperialism at all. 'Imperialist politics', wrote Gollwitzer, 'is only possible on the basis of a large state. Despite its large colonial possessions, one cannot count the Netherlands, for instance, among the imperialist powers.'[52]

Whenever the Netherlands is mentioned in the general literature on modern imperialism, it is mainly in connection with its pre-imperialist colonial position. Betts merely listed the Netherlands under two entries in his index: 'loss of colonial empire', and 'employs "culture system" in Java'.[53] Baumgart mentioned Dutch expansion in the Indonesian Archipelago after 1850 as an example of

51. The term *pre-emption* was suggested to Betts by Langer, ibid., p. 81.
52. Gollwitzer, *Geschichte*, p. 19.
53. Betts, *False Dawn*, p. 266.

Introduction

administrational 'sub-imperialism'.[54] This characterisation corresponds to Schöffer's assessment of Dutch expansion in his contribution to the comparative volume *Expansion and Reaction*.[55] According to Schöffer, Dutch expansion was very reluctant and reactive in character. It was the result of Dutch interaction with other Western states or with indigenous states within the Indonesian Archipelago. Very few political and economic impulses ever came from the Netherlands. The pacification of the Archipelago, according to Schöffer, was only superficially akin to the imperialism of other Western states. Instead, it was a matter of completing an internal colonial expansion process within relatively stable international borders.

This is why Schöffer put Dutch expansion in inverted commas in the title of his contribution to the comparative volume. According to Robinson and Brunschwig, however, French and British expansion in Africa was even less significant, and they claimed that the power there was entirely in the hands of local administrators and indigenous elites. And so we are left to conclude – with a measure of irony – that in the East Indies there was some and in Africa no expansion at all.[56]

But apart from the problems of conceptualisation, comparative analysis and historical revision in this first, general volume of a continuing series, it nevertheless seems that Dutch expansion has only taken a marginal place in the recent international historiography on modern imperialism. A non-imperialist image is presented which is mainly based on rather dated literature about Dutch colonial history, much of it written before the war.[57] Indeed, Van Goor has pointed out correctly that the term imperialism has been studiously avoided in the writing of Dutch colonial history. Dutch expansion in the Indonesian Archipelago between 1870 and 1914 was called 'rounding of the state' by Colenbrander and 'the establishment of Dutch authority in its Outer Regions' by Stapel, while Vlekke spoke of the 'unification of Indonesia'.[58]

54. Baumgart, *Imperialismus*, p. 30.
55. Schöffler, 'Dutch "Expansion"', pp. 78–85.
56. Wesseling, 'Expansion', p. 10. Cf. Brunschwig, 'French Expansion'; Robinson, 'European Imperialism'.
57. Cf. the bibliographical reference on Dutch colonial policy in *Modern European Imperialism: a Bibliography of Books and Articles 1815–1972*, J. P. Halstead and S. Porcari eds (Boston 1974) I, pp. 270–90. In Wehler's *Bibliographie zum Imperialismus* (Göttingen, 1977), the Netherlands are not mentioned at all.
58. Van Goor, *Kooplieden*, p. 135. Cf. Colenbrander, *Koloniale Geschiedenis*,

18

Vlekke's book, which was initially only published in the United States in 1942, was still far too blunt in the eyes of some colonial officials. Later, Vlekke gave quite an interesting account of the pressure that was exerted on him to delete an entire chapter on the Acheh War from the proofs, 'because it is not really important and will only give a false impression'.[59] Only the conservative historian Gerretson was willing to use the term *empire*, although he felt that the 'second empire' was considerably less impressive than the first, for which the heroic governor-general of the *VOC*, Jan Pieterszoon Coen, had laid the foundation in the Indonesian Archipelago in the early seventeenth century.[60] The rejection of the term imperialism for the Netherlands was all the more remarkable because the colonial expansion of other countries was in fact described as such. However, there was no mention of the Netherlands or the East Indies in Bartstra's general *Geschiedenis van het moderne imperialism* (History of Modern Imperialism).[61]

This duplicity originally arose because of a comparison, made by contemporary Dutch socialists, between the Boer War and the pacification of Acheh, which will be discussed below. This parallel led to vehement nationalist reactions: after all, there was a close kinship with the Boer Republics, whereas Acheh was only an uncivilised 'pirates' den'; and of course the Netherlands was not a cynical great power like Britain.

The contrast with other countries was further reinforced by growing international legalism in the Netherlands and the introduction of the so-called 'ethical policy' in the East Indies. It was said that the borders of the East Indies had already been defined internationally before the emergence of modern imperialism, and within these borders the Dutch government was bringing order, welfare and civilisation. But even the socialist authors, who had opened the discussion around 1900, had difficulties in using the term imperialism with any consistency. In the Netherlands, for instance, hardly anything existed that approached monopoly capitalism – a fundamental condition of imperialism, according to Marxist theories abroad. However, according to Roland Holst and De Leeuw, a form of Dutch imperialism did exist, albeit with

---

chapter 22; Vlekke, *Nusantara*, chapter 10.
    59. Vlekke, 'Indonesië', pp. 404–5.
    60. Henssen, *Gerretson*, p. 30.
    61. Bartstra, *Geschiedenis*; cf. Colenbrander, *Koloniale Geschiedenis*, vol. I, pp. 210f.

'numerous features of its own',[62] in particular 'territorial saturation'.

After the Second World War and decolonisation there was a long period of silence in the Netherlands on subjects such as imperialism. In 1960, Coolhaas's English-language bibliography was almost exclusively confined to pre-war literature on the 'Pacification of the Outer Districts'.[63] Indirectly, the traditional self-image of the Netherlands as a non-imperialist nation became even more plausible when a number of new ideas emerged in the writing of Dutch history, and several authors emphasised the special position of the Netherlands in other, related, areas. As was pointed out above, international power politics generally formed an important motivating factor for imperialism. According to Boogman, however, Dutch foreign policy had always been dominated by the 'tradition of Holland', with its 'maritime and commercial tendencies' such as neutrality, a rejection of power politics, free trade and territorial contraction. Boogman even suggested that the absence of an imperialist mentality with regard to colonies was suitable evidence of the lasting influence of 'the tradition of Holland'.[64]

It was said that, in other countries, nationalism may well have been an important domestic cause for imperialism, while the Netherlands was just then experiencing a process of so-called 'pillarisation' (that is the formation of religious and ideological subcultures with corresponding organisations). And although this political and cultural pluralism, according to Lijphart, certainly did not prevent a feeling of national identity, it was hardly able to promote modern mass nationalism. In this context, Daalder and Schöffer have pointed to the gradual and moderate character of political changes in the Netherlands.[65] In most capitalist countries, imperialism was directly or indirectly stimulated by the process of industrialisation.

However, De Jonge has convincingly shown that Dutch industrialisation did not really take off until the end of the nineteenth century, and even then on a rather small scale.[66] Considering that

62. De Leeuw, *Nederland*, p. 14; cf. Roland Holst, *Kapitaal* I, pp. 151f.; ibid., vol. II, pp. 20f.
63. See W. P. Coolhaas, *A Critical Survey of Studies on Dutch Colonial History* (The Hague, 1960).
64. Boogman, 'Tradition', p. 103; cf. 'Netherlands'; 'Achtergronden'.
65. Lijphart, *Verzuiling*, pp. 85–8. Cf. Daalder, 'Netherlands', pp. 207–13; Schjöffer, 'Bestel', pp. 632–6.
66. De Jonge, *Industrialisatie*, pp. 339–67.

political and socio-economic development was so gradual in the Netherlands, one might have expected an even less fertile soil for social imperialism. These ideas of a special Dutch position considerably coloured the historiographic context in which the international discussion of modern imperialism was received.

Imperialism and Expansion in the Archipelago

These new ideas about modern imperialism were discussed in detail at the conference organised by the Dutch Historical Society in 1970 on 'Dutch Expansion in the East Indies at the Time of Modern Imperialism, 1870–1914'. At the conference B. W. Schaper gave a historiographic introduction in which he first dealt with the well-known political and economic explanations and then, among other approaches, Robinson and Gallagher's continuity thesis, Fieldhouse's 'periphery' approach, and Wehler's theory of social imperialism.[67] According to Schaper, the recent international discussion showed clearly that modern imperialism as a historical category must be understood in a pluralist sense – as the convergence of different forces and trends in a certain period. He maintained, though with some reservations, that both in its phases and its overall character

> Dutch imperialism was part of modern European imperialism. There had, however, always been some hesitation, due to the Dutch policy of neutrality, so that the Dutch version was a typical form of 'reluctant imperialism', with a preference for a more informal character. In the Netherlands itself . . . it seems that this hesitation was not overcome until the end of the nineteenth and beginning of the twentieth centuries.[68]

The use of the term imperialism for Dutch expansion in the Archipelago was treated with even more caution in the various historical papers at the conference. It was pointed out by a number of contributors that certain motivating factors for modern imperialism were all but missing in the case of the Netherlands. Pluvier maintained that, after the outbreak of the Acheh War, international rivalry no longer played an important role in Dutch expansion. By the time modern imperialism started, the territorial framework of the expansion had already been fixed in its broad outlines, particu-

67. Schaper, 'Nieuwe opvattingen'.
68. Ibid., p. 8.

21

larly as a result of treaties with Britain in 1824 and 1871. Between 1871 and 1914, according to Pluvier, colonial issues decreased 'quickly and noticeably' in Dutch foreign affairs.[69] And Van der Wal believed that impulses from domestic affairs in the Netherlands were equally weak. On the contrary, both the government and Parliament in The Hague continually urged 'abstention' in the 'Outer Regions', while the Batavian administration and the local administrators tended to be in favour of intervention. Expansion was always initiated by Batavia or the overseas outposts, whereupon The Hague followed mostly with reluctance. Although Van der Wal did not actually use the term 'periphery', this was implicit in his analysis.[70] Approaching the question from a completely different perspective, Van 't Veer emphasised the pre-imperialist, colonial character of the Acheh War; strong economic and ethical impulses of a nationalist kind did not arise in the Netherlands until around the year 1900.[71] This division into periods was foremost in virtually all contributions to the conference, and it was felt that Dutch expansion in the Archipelago only began to show traits of imperialism in the 1890s.

According to Van Tijn, this division into phases was a result of the 'capitalist growth dynamics' in the Netherlands. Unlike Schaper, he felt it was sensible and indeed possible to set up a hierarchy of causes within modern imperialism. The development of capitalism in this context was seen by Van Tijn as the most significant 'general driving force', and the absence of powerful political causes – either domestic or foreign – indicated that the decisive factors in the case of the Netherlands were of an economic kind. He supported his view by positive evidence, such as the growth of Dutch investment in the Outer Regions around 1900.[72]

The conference of the Dutch Historical Society took place at a time when there had been a general increase of interest in phenomena such as 'imperialism' in the Netherlands. In the 1960s, as soon as the Dutch had come to terms with their own 'trauma of decolonisation', a broad protest movement began to gain ground in the Netherlands which was directed against American involvement in Vietnam and other Third World countries. Indirectly, the protest against American imperialism led to a renewed interest in similar

69. Pluvier, 'Internationale aspekten'.
70. Van der Wal, 'Nederlandse expansie'.
71. Van 't Veer, 'Machthebbers'.
72. Van Tijn, 'Nabeschouwing'.

elements in their own colonial past, such as the excessive violence of 'police action' in Indonesia during decolonisation and, longer ago, the Acheh War. In 1969, two important studies were published on this subject: one in Dutch by Van 't Veer, and another in English by the Australian historian Reid.[73] In an article on 'counter-insurgency research' at the turn of the century, the radical sociologist Wertheim even claimed that there was a direct parallel with American intervention in Vietnam.[74] However, in the historical research on Dutch expansion that followed the conference, such topical political considerations hardly played any role at all.

Of the various factors that were discussed at the conference, economic and 'peripheral' factors were given particular attention. Fasseur applied Van der Wal's analysis to Dutch expansion between 1830 and 1870.[75] He showed conclusively that the colonial administration had indeed been of importance in Dutch expansion, with local administrative officials continually trying to intervene in the Outer Regions. Such initiatives were often supported by the administration in Batavia which then presented the Dutch government with a *fait accompli*. In fact, according to Fasseur, this pattern formed the basis of the Acheh War in 1873. However, he says, this war dragged on so much that it rather reduced any scope for 'frontier imperialism' of local administrators. Nevertheless, at the end of the war, the 'man on the spot' certainly played an important role again.[76] Van Goor, in particular, has pointed out that the Indonesian elites had their own autonomous position in the process of expansion. In large parts of the Archipelago, he said, it was only at the end of the nineteenth century that the colonial administration began to dominate decisively. Until then, it was to a large extent dependent on the behaviour of Indonesian princes, who followed their own strategies of co-operation and resistance.[77] Van Goor had borrowed this perspective mainly from Robinson's analysis and the studies of the Indonesian historian Resink. Resink maintained that the *de facto* independence of most Indonesian states before 1900 was recognised – even formally – by The Hague and Batavia, and he believes that only foreign relations with European countries were

---

73. Cf. Van 't Veer, *Atjeh-oorlog*; Reid, *Contest*. See also Wesseling, 'Post-imperial Holland', pp. 138–41.
74. Wertheim, 'Counter-insurgency research'.
75. Fasseur, 'Koloniale paradox'.
76. Both Van Heutsz and Snouck Hurgronje; Van 't Veer, *Atjeh-oorlog*, pp. 186f.
77. Van Goor, *Kooplieden*, pp. 135–40; cf. Ricklefs, *History*, p. 126.

subject to certain restrictions.[78] Other Indonesian historians, on the other hand, feel that the Dutch presence in the Archipelago was far less unobtrusive – especially with regard to the *Parang Belanda*, the Dutch war against Acheh.[79]

The economic interpretation of Dutch expansion has also taken different forms. Based on Van Tijn's theory, Van den Broeke has examined the role of two large mining companies, the Royal Dutch Oil Company and the Billiton Tin Mining Company, which were both involved in oil and tin production. The Royal Dutch in particular extended its activities around the year 1900, among other places in parts of Sumatra, which had been pacified not long before, often at the request of the company. However, it is not entirely clear how far the policy of pacification was influenced by such pressure, because Van den Broeke did not examine the process of political decision making.[80]

Jobse's examination of the notorious tin expeditions to Flores, on the other hand, shows clearly that the colonial administration had its own economic expectations with regard to profit.[81] According to Tichelman, however, 'capitalist growth dynamics' cannot provide a sufficient basis for explaining Dutch imperialism. Following Roland Holst, he pointed out that certain 'structural' conditions for imperialism were missing in the Dutch economy.[82] Furthermore, according to à Campo, there was a discrepancy between current economic interpretations of modern imperialism and the actual capacity for Dutch economic expansion.[83] At the same time he felt that this discrepancy could be overcome if one considered the radically different positions held by the Netherlands and the East Indies within the world economy. The subjection and development of the Outer Regions went hand in hand with the increasing economic independence of the East Indies. On the level of decision making, this process has been examined just as little as the unmistakable increase in Dutch investment.

While economic and local aspects received a considerable amount of interest, international and domestic factors have been examined very little in recent studies. And yet there are clear indications that

---

78. Resink, *Indonesia's History*, pp. 109f., pp. 267f.
79. Cf. Alfian, 'Acheh Sultanate'; Abdullah, 'Impacts'.
80. Van den Broeke, *Koninklijke*, pp. 12–14.
81. Jobse, 'Tin-expeditions', pp. 15f.
82. Tichelman, 'Stagnatie, pp. 135f.
83. à Campo, 'Orde'.

such political aspects do in fact deserve more attention. The existing literature suggests that supposed or actual threats from outside, once the Acheh War had started, definitely played a role in the establishment of colonial administration in Borneo and New Guinea.[84] Domestic nationalism certainly manifested itself very powerfully in the Lombok expedition.[85] In my own research, I have therefore concentrated mainly on domestic and foreign political relations. However, rather than limiting myself to colonial matters, I have also taken other overseas relations into account. The relevant literature points also to a pattern of expansion and reaction in this respect, though it is not identical with the colonial pattern.

Between Neutrality and Imperialism

Wels, in particular, has shown that during the emergence of modern imperialism overseas relations had an important place in Dutch foreign affairs.[86] During the period of 1871–1907, colonial topics alone constituted about a quarter of the official documents published by Woltring and Smit, and indeed often more than half if other overseas issues are included. Wels has pointed out that in many of these issues colonial matters played a role, either directly or indirectly. This observation has its parallel in Vandenbosch's thesis that the Netherlands' position as a small European state was 'complicated' by its extensive colonial territories outside Europe.[87] Such 'complications' occurred whenever the Netherlands took part in the international endeavours of the greater powers, such as the Berlin Conference, the Suez Convention and the intervention during the Boxer Rebellion in China. In the latter case Van Dongen has noted a characteristic ambivalence 'between neutrality and imperialism' in the Dutch attitude.[88]

Around 1900 there was pressure from various sides that the Netherlands should establish colonial bases in China; this pressure came from, among others, the local Dutch representative and some politicians in the Netherlands. This was motivated by large-scale colonial interests in connection with Chinese contract labour in the East Indies. But, in view of the rivalry between the great powers,

84. Cf. Irwin, *Borneo*, pp. 191f.; Van der Veur, *Search*, pp. 61f.
85. Van Goor, *Episode*, pp. 15f.
86. Wels, *Aloofness*, pp. 102.
87. Vandenbosch, *Foreign Policy*, pp. 191f.
88. Von Dongen, *Neutraliteit*, pp. 347–54.

142534 25

the Dutch secretary of foreign affairs decided to adhere strictly to
the principle of neutrality and to reject territorial aspirations out of
hand. However, the Netherlands did take part in the international
intervention by the great powers during the Boxer Rebellion, albeit
with the necessary reserve. Dutch relations with Venezuela often
displayed a similar ambivalence between neutrality and imperialism;
here, it was its colonial interests in Curaçao that occasionally
motivated the Netherlands to intervene.[89] Nevertheless, one question that deserves further attention is the extent to which Dutch
aloofness in China, Venezuela and other overseas territories was
dictated by the principle of neutrality or by more pragmatic
considerations.

When we look at modern imperialism as an international
phenomenon, Dutch relations with Africa are particularly interesting. On the eve of the partition in 1872, the Netherlands ceded its
last African territories to Britain. However, Dutch withdrawal from
Elmina was closely connected with the effort to expand in Sumatra,
although it is not yet entirely clear how close the connection was.[90]
Also, there continued to be lively trade relations with the west coast
of Africa, especially around the Congo estuary, and this was in fact
the reason why the Netherlands was represented at the Berlin
conference in 1884. Wesseling gave a very clear analysis of the
Dutch position at this conference. To protect Dutch trade interests
in the Congo, careful support was given to the principle of free
trade, and particular attention was paid to the scope of international
agreements at the conference. What gave rise to a great deal of
concern was the definition of a colony in terms of effective occupation. After all, large parts of the Dutch overseas territories in the
East Indies either did not fulfil this criterion at all or only to a very
small extent.[91] Meanwhile, Dutch trade interests had come under a
fair amount of pressure in the Leopold Congo Free State.[92] The
consequences of the partition of Africa for Dutch trade have not
been systematically examined yet. The defeat of the South African
Boer Republics by the British certainly put an end to Dutch
expansionism going much further in that area than mere trade
interests.

Dutch expansion in South Africa had its roots in nationalist

89. Cf. Goslinga, *Curaçao*; Smit, *Nederland*, pp. 208f.
90. Cf. Van 't Veer, *Atjeh-oorlog*, pp. 32–6; Reid, *Contest*, pp. 69–73.
91. Wesseling, 'Nederland'.
92. Cf. Miers, *Britain*, pp. 286–93.

interests towards the Boers, who were historically related to the Dutch. These nationalist feelings were aroused by the first Boer War in 1880–1, and in the course of the 1880s and 1890s quite a few Dutch acquired strong positions in the administration, in education and in the railway system of the Transvaal. Although the presence of the Dutch had partly come about at the request of Kruger, it did develop – according to several authors – a number of clear imperialist traits. Schutte uses the word 'cultural imperialism' in this context, while Kröll sees a resemblance between Dutch nationalist expansionism and the imperialism of the great powers.[93]

The value of these theses is in directing our attention to an interesting possibility. Nationalism, it seems, may well have been a domestic cause of Dutch expansion, though not primarily in the Indonesian Archipelago but chiefly in South Africa. However, Blom is right to point out that these ideas need to be elaborated and tested further.[94] Whatever the case may be, there can be no question of formal imperialism. The Dutch government maintained a strictly neutral position throughout the two Boer Wars and carefully abstained from supporting the Dutch Transvaal Movement during the intervening period. Again, this raises the question to what extent Dutch policies were dictated by the principle of neutrality rather than pragmatic considerations, such as their dependence on Britain with regard to colonial affairs.[95]

Starting Points of the Analysis

In 1971, Tichelman observed that a book on Dutch imperialism was still to be written.[96] Wesseling came to the same conclusion in 1979 and added a number of other interesting observations, maintaining that it was actually doubtful whether there had ever been any Dutch imperialism:

> The position of the Netherlands is paradoxical, in so far as it has been both the most imperialistic nation, in the sense of economic exploitation and *mise en valeur*, and the least imperialistic, because it did not follow a policy of formal expansion, and even abandoned its last possessions in

---

93. Cf. Schutte, *Hollanders*, pp. 21f.; Kröll, *Buren-Agitation*, pp. 64–5 and 160.
94. J. C. H. Blom, discussion of Kröll, *Buren-Agitation*, in TvG 88 (1975), pp. 128f.
95. Cf. Smit, *Nederland*, pp. 51f.
96. F. Tichelman, 'Het Nederlandse imperialisme', *NRC-Het Handelsblad*, 9 July 1971.

Africa shortly before the final partition of that continent. Consequently, the history of Dutch imperialism would be difficult to incorporate into the general discussion about European imperialism, which is strongly dominated by the problems surrounding the partition of Africa and by international rivalries, or to put it more generally, the problems of international relations.[97]

According to Wesseling, an analysis of Dutch imperialism should pay greater attention to concepts such as 'informal' and 'peripheral' imperialism as well as to Marxist economic categories.

In my analysis I have, in part, used other starting points. In the first place, I have not concentrated on Dutch imperialism in the Archipelago alone, but also on Dutch expansionism elsewhere. Also, I have systematically considered the Dutch reaction to the imperialism of other nations, both in connection with the Archipelago and in other places. It seems to me that such a broad approach is appropriate and justified when dealing with a small European power that had already established itself in various parts of the overseas world before the emergence of modern imperialism. The analysis of international relations fulfils a strategic function that lends coherence to the analysis, though without anticipating international rivalry as a factor of imperialism in the case of the Netherlands. Nor have 'peripheral' or economic factors been neglected. But in view of the current state of research, most attention has been paid to political factors, both foreign and domestic.

Apart from secondary literature, the primary sources on which this study is based are mainly related to the formation of opinions and actual policies in the Netherlands. For the decision making at the level of government I have made use of published sources, particularly the *Bescheiden betreffende de buitenlandse politiek* (Official documents on foreign affairs), as well as unpublished ones, such as the private correspondence of colonial secretaries and governor-generals. For parliamentary decision making I have systematically gone through the relevant official reports. Interestingly, it has turned out that not only Colonial Reports but also Consular Reports contain a large amount of new data on Dutch overseas relations. As for the role of pressure groups – on the borderline between the formation of opinions and political decision making – I have mainly confined myself to published sources, such

97. Wesseling, 'Dutch historiography', pp. 138–9; cf. *idem*, *Myths*, pp. 4–9.

as the annual reports of the Chambers of Commerce in Amsterdam and Rotterdam. Furthermore, I have systematically examined a number of magazines between 1870 and 1902. Inevitably, newspapers had to be studied more selectively; however, I have aimed at covering a fair spread of the most relevant political and ideological currents in the Netherlands.

The book which is the outcome of this analysis is meant as a historical synthesis. Broadly speaking, it is about Dutch overseas relations during the emergence of modern imperialism. More specifically, it is about the pattern of expansion and reaction that emerged from these relations. Chronologically, the main topic is limited by the Anglo–Dutch treaties about the Gold Coast, Sumatra and Surinam around 1870 and the debate on imperialism around 1900 in connection with the Boer War and the pacification of Acheh. Dutch relations with Acheh and the Transvaal both form the key to the intervening period. As for the well-known dilemma between a chronological and a thematic approach, I have tried to find a workable interim solution. The different topics have been dealt with in relation to one another, roughly for each decade, although a certain amount of overlap has of course been inevitable.

After three chronological, mainly descriptive chapters, the study will be related to the most important theoretical and historiographic approaches mentioned in this introduction. These final observations will be concluded with an analysis in which the position of the Netherlands is compared with those of Britain, Portugal and Belgium during the rise of modern imperialism.

1

Trade and Colonies (1870–1880)

In the history of imperialism the 1870s are generally regarded as a transition period – a transition from the reluctant and often informal expansion of a limited number of European states during most of the nineteenth century to the time after 1880 when more and more countries were involved, and when colonial expansion accelerated and increased. The latter is known as modern imperialism.[1]

On the one hand, overseas expansion around the year 1870 was still mainly a matter of commercial interests rather than new colonies. The colonial powers themselves were even considering the abolition of existing colonies, and there was controversy as to whether new ones should be established. On the other hand, the first symptoms of modern imperialism were already beginning to show, both in Europe and outside it. The Franco–German War, the unification of both Germany and Italy and the consolidation of the United States had led to new political relations. Insecurity and rivalry had been further increased by economic depression. The repercussions of this development could also be felt outside Europe and America. In the 1870s there was an increasing interest in the world outside Europe, thus giving a new meaning to the activities of European adventurers and explorers as well as to conflicts with non-European states which had often been going on for years. Whereas the new powers had hardly taken any active steps to win colonies, the older colonial states were increasingly beginning to adopt a policy of expansion as a precautionary measure – an expansion of colonial possessions that was primarily aimed at consolidating what they owned already.

As a small European state with considerable commercial and colonial interests overseas, the Netherlands did not fail to be di-

---

1. Cf. Betts, *False Dawn*, pp. 72–5; Baumgart, *Imperialismus*, pp. 8–10; Eldridge, *Victorian Imperialism*, pp. 89–119; fieldhouse, *Economics*, pp. 145f. and 234f.

rectly affected by this new situation in the seventies. Around 1870, the Netherlands, too, was more concerned with extending its trade than acquiring colonies. Indeed, it was one of the few colonial powers that actively renounced existing possessions. However, the underlying aim of this reduction was the simultaneous consolidation of other possessions. Subsequently, the government in The Hague and the administration in Batavia over-reacted, so that their strategic intervention led to the annexation of an independent state and a long, drawn-out war overseas. We can therefore state that, for the Netherlands, the period of modern imperialism started with the Acheh War, as early as 1873.

The Netherlands and the World Overseas

Overseas Relations (1814–1870)

The relations between the Netherlands and the overseas world around the year 1870 was still largely the outcome of its first phase of expansion, caused by the big trade companies of the seventeenth century. By 1870 the Netherlands had lost contact with many of the territories it had acquired in the seventeenth century. Dutch outposts in North America and Brazil had already been lost in the seventeenth century. In the course of the Napoleonic Wars all possessions fell into British hands for shorter or longer periods, although the Netherlands received the most important ones back again in the treaty of 1814. Nevertheless, it did lose its outposts in South Africa, Guyana and Ceylon.[2] In the Anglo–Dutch Treaty of 1824 it renounced its claims on the remaining posts in India and Malacca.

In those areas where the Netherlands had lost its sovereignty, its other interests also became diluted. It continued to maintain what were its closest ties with the Cape and the Boers, who had travelled from there after 1834, especially in the areas of religion and culture.[3] Commercially, however, Dutch interests in the first half of the nineteenth century concentrated increasingly on the remaining colonies, particularly the East Indies, to a lesser extent the West Indies and only to a very small degree its possessions on the Gold Coast in Africa.

2. See also the contributions on the seventeenth and eighteenth centuries in the publication *Overzee*.
3. Cf. Van Winter, *Hollanders* I, pp. 19–22; Schutte, *Hollanders*, pp. 9–17.

A further narrowing of overseas relations took place in 1830, with the introduction of the Javanese system of forced cultivation by the state. It stipulated that Javanese villages should produce at least one-fifth of their crops for the European market as a form of taxation. Thus Java directly provided considerable advantages for the Netherlands, in the form of colonial profits for the Dutch treasury,[4] and the colonial rule and economic exploitation concentrated more and more on Java. With regard to the so-called Outer Regions in the East Indies, the Conservative Minister of the Colonies J. Van den Bosch, introduced the policy of 'abstention', (*onthouding*), except for Sumatra, where the Islamic resistance movement of the Padris was crushed during the 1830s. 'Most of the outer territories', said his Conservative successor J. C. Baud in 1845, 'have always been liabilities; by wanting too much all at once, there would be more and more disadvantages from one year to the next.'[5] Also, in the West Indies and Africa, which had ceased to be assets when the slave trade was abolished, policies were mainly determined by financial considerations.[6]

The system of consignment, whereby goods were only consigned to Dutch shipping companies, and other protective measures meant that Dutch trade and industry profited greatly from this 'late mercantilist' governmental policy. At the same time, however, they became increasingly dependent on it. King William I's ambitious plans to acquire new markets in Asia and South America with the help of semi-governmental institutions such as the Netherlands Trading Company failed very quickly. Trade contacts in South America were mainly restricted to colonies in the West Indies and local trade between Curaçao and Venezuela. China and Japan, where trade links date back to the time of the Dutch East Indian Company, were only visited sporadically now. Merchants regularly stopped off in Africa, at the Cape of Good Hope, on their way to Java. But straightforward trade with Africa was more and more neglected. The horizon of the Dutch merchants was indeed becoming rather limited during the first half of the nineteenth century.[7]

During this time, history-conscious Dutch people looked back to earlier periods of power and wealth, while at the same time they saw the current development as a warning. After 1713 the Republic had

---

4. Cf. Fasseur, *Kultuurstelsel*; Burger, *Geschiedenis* I, pp. 93f.
5. [Colijn], *Politiek beleid* I, pp. 43–4; cf. Fasseur, 'Koloniale paradox', pp. 165–6.
6. Fasseur, 'Suriname', pp. 194–6.
7. Brugmans, *Paardenkracht*, pp. 103f. and 136f.

ceased to be a great power, and William I's ambitions in that direction finally became totally unrealistic in 1830, after Belgium had separated from the Netherlands. Characteristically, both in the eighteenth and the nineteenth centuries, the loss of power led to a turning away from European power politics.[8] Dutch foreign affairs after 1830 bore the mark of strict aloofness. From then onwards, the Netherlands was a second-rate power within Europe; this position was certainly compensated for by being, outside Europe, the greatest colonial power after Britain.[9] Indeed, Britain occupied a key position for the Netherlands, both in Europe and outside. In both areas, after 1814, the Netherlands was to a considerable extent dependent on British protection, even though this relationship had never been established formally.

Before then, the two countries had been both rivals and allies. In the nineteenth century, their relations were mainly friendly, even though the old rivalry occasionally reappeared. At the time of the 1814 treaty they were on rather good terms with each other, despite their great difference in power. However, the Netherlands had ceded Berbice, Demerary and Essequibo, with a great deal of reluctance.[10] With the arrival of Raffles in the Indonesian Archipelago, there were soon new points of friction.

In 1824 a new treaty was signed which was to bring an end to these problems. Territorial and commercial relations in the Archipelago could again be dealt with in a friendly manner. The Netherlands renounced its claim on Singapore and gave up its posts in India and Malacca, in exchange for British posts in Sumatra. According to section 14 of the new treaty, the territory north of Singapore was to become British, and that to the south of it Dutch. Economically, the treaty mainly provided for free trade in the Archipelago. Not everything that was agreed between Britain and the Netherlands was laid down in the treaty. The independence of the Sultanate of Acheh in north Sumatra, that produced half of the world's consumption of pepper during the 1820s, was guaranteed by an exchange of notes between the British and Dutch negotiators and then added to the treaty. The Netherlands undertook 'to regulate its relations with *Acheen*, in such a manner that the State, without losing anything of its independence, may offer both to the

8. Goudsblom, 'Nederlandse samenleving', pp. 19–21. Cf. Boogman, 'Netherlands', pp. 487–90; Wels, *Aloofness*, pp. 29–45.
9. Ibid., pp. 99–100.
10. Fasseur, 'Suriname', p. 194.

sailor and the merchant that constant security which can only be established by the moderate exercise of European influence.'[11]

The Anglo–Dutch treaty of 1824 continued to be important for the rest of the nineteenth century, even though it did not put an end to mutual conflicts on colonial territories. In retrospect, the text was interpreted in the Netherlands in such a way that the exchange of territories really meant the rejection of 'mixed possessions'. However, nobody went quite as far in 1824. When the areas north and south of Singapore were marked off, only the islands directly surrounding it were named explicitly. Moreover, the Dutch negotiators had promised solemnly not to aim at political domination or any trade monopoly in the Archipelago.

However, after the separation of Belgium, Anglo–Dutch relations rather cooled down again. And so it was in fact the Netherlands which went straight against the spirit of the treaty. As part of its new colonial system in Java, it introduced a series of protectionist measures which hit British commerce and shipping the hardest. As a counter-measure, Britain adopted a more benevolent attitude towards the requests of local princes who had long been asking for support against the Netherlands. Colonial relations reached their lowest point when the British government recognised the enterprising James Brooke as its official representative in northern Borneo and annexed the area of Labuan in 1846. Britain rejected Dutch protest based on the 1824 treaty. After all, this treaty did not make any explicit mention of Borneo, and Labuan was north of Singapore.[12] Because of this supposed British threat in the Archipelago, the Dutch government temporarily departed from its policy of abstention during the 1840s. Baud wrote to the colonial administration in Batavia to take measures 'for the consolidation of our supreme territorial and political authority in the Indian Archipelago and to ensure our rights of sovereignty'.[13] Batavia responded by concluding treaties with a large number of Indonesian rulers in the Outer Regions, which established Dutch 'supreme authority' in their relations with foreign countries, but recognised their authority in internal affairs. Three successive military expeditions to enforce Dutch 'supreme authority' on the Balinese princes all failed miserably. When it seemed that the dreaded British intervention was not

11. Marks, *Contest*, pp. 261f.
12. Tarling, *British Policy*, pp. 86f. and 183f.; cf. Goedeman, *Indië*, passim.
13. [Colijn], *Politiek beleid* I, p. 34; cf. pp. 27–8.

going to happen, The Hague went back to its traditional policy of abstention again.

Formally, abstention and aloofness continued to be the key to the 1850s and 1860s, both for Dutch relations with the local Archipelago states and also for other overseas interests. However, as Fasseur has pointed out, this policy was often set aside by active colonial officials and military commanders, both locally and in Batavia. Apart from maintaining Dutch prestige, it was personal ambition which acted as an important factor here. Administrative sub-imperialism reached its climax in the 1850s, with the bloody wars against Bandjarmasin in south Borneo and Bone in Celebes.[14] But after the formal annexation of the old Sultanate of Bandjarmasin and the appointment of a new prince in Bone the colonial army returned to Batavia, leaving only a token force behind. The fear that there might be another Brooke also continued to play a role. In 1858 the colonial administration intervened in north-east Sumatra at the request of the Sultan of Siak, who seemed to be threatened by an outpost of British adventurers. The Sultan of Siak continued in office under Dutch protection, but without any permanent administrative or military presence. Subsequently, foreigners were refused entry and Dutch entrepreneurs were encouraged to come and grow tobacco in the area around Deli. Prompted by the Straits settlements in nearby Malacca, the British government repeatedly protested against these and other obstructions of British trade. Finally, in 1857, a 'treaty of friendship' was signed with the Sultan of Acheh, who incidentally had some border conflicts with the Sultan of Siak, to guarantee the safety of commerce and shipping in the area around Acheh, after there had been repeated requests for the Straits.[15] After repeated complaints from the Straits the British government had asked for an implementation of the notes to the 1824 treaty.

However, after 1850, a number of new factors became important in the Archipelago. These were domestic: political and economic. In 1848, the Dutch Parliament and public opinion were given more influence on colonial policies, and in the Second Chamber a 'colonial opposition' was formed, which consisted of Liberals under the leadership of W. R. van Hoëvell, a former Protestant minister in Batavia. In his first speech he argued fervently in favour of strong action against piracy in the Archipelago, in the interests of the local

14. Fasseur, 'Koloniale paradox', pp. 174–84; cf. Van Goor, *Kooplieden*, pp. 148–50.
15. Reid, *Contest*, pp. 25–30.

population and of Dutch trade.[16] The wars against Bandjarmasin and Bone attracted more attention in the Netherlands than previous expeditions.[17]

This increasing interest also had an economic dimension. Dutch entrepreneurs began to develop tentative activities outside Java. In 1850, a concession for tin mining on the island of Billiton near Sumatra was requested and was granted two years later. In 1860, the Billiton Company was founded which soon turned out to be a great success.[18] Furthermore, both the government and the colonial administration gave some support to agricultural enterprises. Before then, Van den Bosch and Baud had already wanted to reserve Sumatra for certain forms of private agriculture, to supplement the system of forced cultivation in Java. Now there was a growing interest among businessmen, especially with regard to Deli, where tobacco was promising to be very successful. In 1869, the Deli Company was founded in Amsterdam with the financial support of the powerful Netherlands Trading Company; it was the first modern cultivation company in the Outer Regions.[19]

However, the political and economic impulses for expansion that came from the Netherlands were too weak to lead to any change in the Dutch policy of abstention. The petition of F. H. van Vlissingen to the king shows this very clearly. In 1857, Van Vlissingen and a number of Liberal businessmen and scientists advocated the colonisation of the Outer Regions. The government then appointed a committee under the chairmanship of the former governor-general J. J. Rochussen, who rejected the idea of large-scale colonisation but wholeheartedly supported the opening of the Outer Regions to Dutch enterprise. The committee made a series of recommendations to the government, suggesting how the conditions might be created. They came to the conclusion that a selective, carefully considered extension of Dutch control was inevitable, 'even though some of the occupied areas must be regarded as future liabilities'.[20] Shortly afterwards, however, when Rochussen became Minister of the Colonies, he was in no hurry to put the committee's recommendations into practice.

16. *Handelingen Tweede Kamer* (Parliamentary Reports of the Second Chamber), 15 December 1849, pp. 150–3.
17. Fasseur, 'Koloniale paradox', p. 178.
18. Kemp, *Tinnen soldaat*, pp. 38–45.
19. Broersma, *Oostkust*, pp. 23ff.; cf. Mansvelt, *Geschiedenis* I, pp. 376 and 369–81.
20. Somer, *Korte Verklaring*, p. 106.

His Liberal successors, J. Loudon and I. D. Fransen van de Putte, were equally reluctant to accept any effort in the Outer Regions that might incur additional costs. 'I see every extension of our authority in the Archipelago as a step towards our fall', wrote Loudon to the governor-general in 1861, 'and all the more so because we have already outgrown our strength in this respect.'[21] As before, he prescribed a strict policy of abstention to the colonial administration with regard to Borneo and Celebes, which was observed by Batavia very strictly throughout the 1860s. In Sumatra, on the other hand, colonial control was further intensified on the west and south coast.[22] The more Dutch Liberals became involved in government, the more they too were affected by financial considerations. The opening of Java to private cultivation was given priority in the 1860s over the further opening of the Outer Regions.[23] For the time being, however, many Liberal opponents of state cultivation in Java did not want to do without the transfer of the East Indian budget surplus to the Dutch treasury. The East Indian surplus contributed to a number of Liberal policies, like the abolition of slavery in the West Indies and the modernisation of infrastructure in the Netherlands. Some Liberal MPs even felt that unprofitable colonies, such as Curaçao and Elmina on the Gold Coast, should be sold off.[24] By 1870, in the Indonesian Archipelago, the Netherlands was in formal, direct control of Java and Madura, the small islands of Ambon, the main source of indigenous, Christian soldiers for the colonial army, Riau, Bangka, Biliton and Nias, some coastal enclaves in Celebes and Borneo, and the west and south-east coasts of Sumatra. A far more informal and indirect form of control had been established with the sultanates of Pontianak and Sambas in west Borneo, of Ternate and Tidore in the Moluccas, and of Jambi and Siak covering most of the east coast of Sumatra.

The Netherlands had also begun to show more interest in overseas areas outside the colonies. It was concerned, first and foremost, with trade. The general revival of international trade and the liberalisation of trade relations, in which the Netherlands had followed Britain since the abolition of the Navigation Acts in 1848, now also affected Dutch trade in all areas. Between 1850 and 1870, the overall

21. [Colijn], *Politiek beleid*, I, p. 81.
22. Reid, *Context*, pp. 30–5.
23. Cf. *Bijlagen Handelingen Tweede Kamer* (Parliamentary Reports of the Second Chamber, Appendices) 1864–5, p. 371.
24. Cf. Goslinga, *Curaçao*, p. 85; Coombs, *Gold Coast*, pp. 36 and 41.

import and export figures tripled, reaching nearly 655 and 539 million guilders respectively. Trade was mainly directed towards Europe, in particular Britain and Prussia. Between 1865 and 1870, about 30 per cent of all imports came from Britain, 25.5 per cent from Prussia, 16.7 per cent from Java and 3.9 per cent from the remaining non-Western countries; 35.5 per cent of Dutch exports went to Prussia, 27.2 per cent to Britain, 9.6 per cent to Java and 2 per cent to other non-Western areas.[25] However, with the gradual disappearance of artificial protective measures, there was a further decline in colonial trade. The lowering of differential rights in Fransen van de Putte's new East Indian tariff law, which came into force in 1865, was an important step in this direction.[26] Dutch shipping companies, in particular, had difficulties adapting to the new situation. Between 1850 and 1870, the Netherlands sank from the fourth to the eighth position among the world's merchant navies. Overseas shipping, in particular, which was still almost entirely undertaken with sailing boats, was difficult to maintain.[27]

Indeed, overseas markets outside the colonies were more important for the Dutch economy than one might gather from the trade statistics. After 1850, old ties with the Far East and with South America were revived again, and new ones were started, for example by the Netherlands Trading Company in British India.[28] One initiative that seemed to be particularly successful was the Congo estuary trade. This was started in 1857 by the Rotterdam firm Kerdijk & Pincoffs, which became a limited liability company called the African Trade Association in 1868.[29]

According to the Consular Reports, published annually from 1865, there were more lucrative openings for the Netherlands in the non-Western world. However, Dutch trade and shipping companies were already finding it rather difficult to cope with the existing export volume. At regular intervals, the Consular Reports told of cases where Dutch goods were traded by foreign companies in Asia, Africa and Latin America via London, Hamburg and

25. P. N. Muller, 'De handel von Nederland in de laatste vijf en twintig jaar, 1847–1871', *De Economist* (1875) I, pp. 1–37; cf. Wanjon, *Geschiedenis*, pp. 77–8.
26. See also the entries 'Scheepvaart en handel' (Shipping and trade) and 'Rechten' (Rights) in the *ENI*.
27. See also the report of the parliamentary fact-finding committee about the state of the Dutch merchant navy, *Bijlagen Handelingen*, 1874–5, no. 7.1., 4–5.
28. Mansvelt, *Geschiedenis* I, pp. 376–9 and 381–3.
29. Wesseling, 'Nederland', pp. 561–3; cf. Oosterwijk, *Vlucht*, pp. 38f.

Antwerp.[30] The reverse was also true, for example in the Congo trade where Rotterdam firms mainly traded British products.[31] In general, however, it was mainly Dutch products – especially textiles, alcohol and dairy products – that were exported to overseas markets via foreign countries and on foreign ships. Naturally, this type of export went down in the trade statistics as European, rather than non-European, trade. Even contemporaries found it difficult to estimate the value of these 'hidden exports'.

Non-European relations were not the most important point in Dutch foreign affairs. Throughout the 1860s, Dutch diplomacy was increasingly concerned with maintaining Dutch neutrality and independence in Europe.[32] In the area of foreign trade, priority was given to European and colonial relations.[33] But whenever there was any interest in the non-European world, the Dutch foreign secretaries were less inclined to strict aloofness than they were in Europe. Even a small European power such as the Netherlands clearly had more scope in this area. And so neutrality applied mainly in those cases where relations with a greater European power were indirectly at issue, particularly with Britain. This explains why it was so uncommonly difficult to establish diplomatic relations with the South African Republic, the former Transvaal, which had become independent of Britain in 1852. Again and again, a number of foreign affairs secretaries had to make sure that Britain had no objections to such relations. Although this was never the case and the Dutch Parliament regularly urged the government to recognise the South African Republic, diplomatic relations were not established until 1869 and, even then, no diplomatic representation was sent for the time being.[34]

In 1863, diplomatic and commercial relations with China were initiated very calmly and inconspicuously, after the great powers had used force to break through China's isolation from the rest of the world.[35] In Japan, however, the Netherlands played a far more active role. Having kept in the background during the opening of

30. Dutch exports via foreign channels were reported regularly by consuls in China (Shanghai and Hong Kong), Japan (Kanagawa), Egypt (Alexandria), Aden, Brazil (Rio de Janeiro) and Argentina (Buenos Aires); cf. *Consulaire verslagen* (Consular Reports) (1868–78) *passim*.

31. Wesseling, 'Nederland', p. 568.

32. Tamse, *Nederland*, pp. 103–19.

33. Ibid., pp. 87–91.

34. Pelzer, 'Erkenning', pp. 49–59.

35. Van Dongen, *Neutraliteit*, pp. 41–3.

Japan in the 1850s, it took part in a punitive expedition of European powers in the sixties. This was directed against a vassal of the Shogun who had opened fire on European ships – including Dutch ones – near Shimonoseki. In 1864, the Netherlands also signed a convention of the same name in which Japan was made to pay damages. This direct action was taken not so much on behalf of Dutch trading interests, which had already been secured in the 1858 treaty, but 'because this is a genuine offence against our flag', as Minister Cremers declared. It was of course also significant that the Netherlands acted together with the great powers, rather than on its own.[36]

Although the confiscation of ships and goods in Venezuela in 1870 did not lead to military action, this was nevertheless threatened.[37] Even the relatively peaceful custom of 'showing the flag' was emphatically used by the Netherlands as a 'display of power' in several areas of unrest, such as the Persian Gulf in 1869. However, the use or even the threat of force was the exception rather than the rule in overseas relations during the 1850s and 1860s. The means for such purposes were correspondingly limited, and the Dutch navy had great difficulties fulfilling its defence tasks at home and in the East Indies.[38]

Government and Parliament

As we have seen, the Netherlands – as a small power – was only to varying degrees both able and prepared to direct the course of its overseas relations. Whenever it did, the decision-making process was determined by formal as well as informal relations. The formal framework had been fixed in the 1848 constitution. The royal prerogative which, until then, used to have priority in colonial administration and foreign affairs, was limited in both areas by the revision of the constitution. Although the 'supreme government' of the colonial possessions and foreign relations was still in the hands of the king, he no longer had an exclusive say in the matter. The new constitution stipulated that the main guidelines for colonial rule, as laid down in government regulations, and also control over colonial finance had to be legally defined. Furthermore, the government was

---

36. *Handelingen Tweede Kamer* (Parliamentary Reports of the Second Chamber), 14 May 1864, p. 650. Cf. Van Kleffens, *Betrekkingen*, pp. 204f.
37. Goslinga, *Curaçao*, pp. 10–15.
38. Cf. Spanjaard, *Bescherming*, pp. 132–8.

now obliged to give a detailed annual report on the state of the colonies.

In 1854, a government regulation for the East Indies came into force, followed by the accountability law in 1865, after the government had already started publishing its annual reports.[39] In the administration of foreign relations, parliamentary control was extended quite considerably, as well, through the introduction of ministerial responsibility and the establishment of an annual budget. However, there were relatively few formal changes in other areas. Declaring war and signing treaties continued to be the king's prerogative. Treaties resulting in alterations of territorial boundaries within or outside Europe required parliamentary consent. As for other treaties, until the constitutional revision of 1887, the king was only obliged to notify Parliament.[40]

The 1848 constitution left a lot of scope for personal influence and *de facto* power relations in the decision-making process. This was especially true for the king. Despite his limited constitutional powers, it seemed, at first sight, that he had a considerably powerful position. This was due both to the popularity of the House of Orange among the Dutch population, and his relations with foreign dynasties. However, King William III made use of these opportunities in such a capricious and rude manner that his influence on the decision-making process remained limited. The ministers, for example, deliberately kept the minutes of the Council of Ministers very short and vague to prevent the king from gaining any concrete information. And in fact King William III showed hardly any interest in overseas relations. Only certain appointments and military matters attracted his attention from time to time.[41]

His brother, Prince Henry Fredrick William – 'Henry the Seafarer' – was far more interested and indeed more influential than the king himself. His concern for overseas matters included not only shipping and science, but also business matters. For example, he was involved as one of the most important active members and shareholders in the formation of the Billiton Company and the Netherlands Steamshipping Company. Indeed, it was not expedient for a Minister of the Colonies to ignore a request for a concession that

39. Cf. De Louter, *Handleiding*, pp. 81f.
40. Asser, *Bestuur*, pp. 100f.
41. Tamse, *Nederland*, pp. 94–9. Cf. Van 't Veer, *Majesteit*, pp. 48f.; Van Raalte, *Staatshoofd*, pp. 101f.

had the backing of the prince.[42] But apart from the royal family and household, there were also numerous members of the Privy Council – the highest advisory body – who acted behind the scenes and considerably influenced the decision making about overseas affairs. In 1862, a number of new members were appointed to the Council who had given evidence of their expertise or at least interest in this area: the Calvinist Anti-Revolutionaries Ae. Mackay and P. J. Elout van Soeterwoude, as well as the Liberals Van Hoëvell and P. J. Bachiene.[43]

The Ministry of the Colonies was considered to be more important than that of Foreign Affairs. 'After all,' it said self-confidently in the explanatory memorandum on the 1870 East Indian budget, 'the Netherlands is a considerable power because of the Dutch East Indies.' The possession of colonies was so fundamental to the Dutch political system that it affected not only the colonies but also other departments, particularly the navy, defence and foreign affairs.[44] Indeed, it was customary to involve the Minister of the Colonies in the decision making on such related matters. As for foreign affairs, this was mainly a matter of direct colonial questions and relations with the Middle and Far East. However, the Minister of the Colonies was even involved in matters such as the recognition of the South African Republic.[45] Of the two ministries, the Ministry of the Colonies was already much larger: in 1869, apart from the secretary-general, it employed 35 civil servants, as compared to 11 in the Ministry of Foreign Affairs.[46]

After the Minister of the Colonies, the most important functionary in carrying out policies was the governor-general of the East Indies. A secret instruction of 1855, which followed the new governmental regulation, stipulated that the governor-general had to obey the 'king's orders' as communicated to him through the Minister of the Colonies.[47] However, the governor-general was responsible for the day-to-day administration of the East Indies, so

42. Hofdijk, *Prins Hendrik*, pp. 126–7, 142–4, 147–9. Cf. notes 18, 87 and 91.
43. Cf. Fasseur, *Kultuurstelsel*, pp. 112, 174, 191 and 230; Kuitenbrouwer, 'Afschaffing', pp. 82, 87–8 and 90–1.
44. For a summary of budget items for the navy, defence, domestic affairs, foreign affairs and justice that came directly from colonial possessions, see also the explanatory memorandum for the 1870 Indian Budget, *Bijlagen Handelingen Tweede Kamer* (Parliamentary Reports of the Second Chamber, Appendices) 1869–70, nos. 4 and 7.
45. Cf. Pelzer, 'Erkenning', pp. 50–1.
46. Cf. *Staats-Almanak* (1870), pp. 47f. and 642f.
47. Boon, *Van Lansberge*, pp. 8–19.

that – in practice – he had a considerable amount of scope. As we saw above, quite a few of them succeeded in applying their limited authority widely and actively, particularly with regard to the Outer Regions, and the minister would then have great difficulties reversing such initiatives. It is worth noting that those who served both as ministers and as governor-generals were generally more inclined towards expansion when they were governor-generals. This was true of Rochussen, C. F. Pahud, and particularly of Loudon, who displayed the greatest discrepancy between his functions as a minister (1861–2) and a governor (1872–5), whereas the Conservative P. Mijer strictly adhered to a policy of abstention, both as a minister (1856–8, 1866), and as governor-general (1866–72).[48]

It was ironic that Mijer of all people should have served under ministers who – in Sumatra, at least – advocated expansion, particularly De Waal and Van Bosse, whereas Loudon found that Fransen van de Putte was a minister who was more in favour of abstention. All these Liberal ministers were in fact important figures: E. de Waal, who had occupied high offices in Batavia, was considered to be a close confidant of the Liberal Prime Minister J. R. Thorbecke; P. P. van Bosse had regularly acted as Minister of Finance and occupied an important independent position among Dutch Liberals; finally, Fransen van de Putte, who had been a navigation officer in the Dutch merchant navy and had made his fortune as a sugar contractor in Java, became, after his return, the leader of the Young Liberals in the Netherlands.

As Minister of the Colonies, Van de Putte pursued the abolition of all state cultivation, forced labour and communal landowning in Java, and the limitation of the transfers from the East Indian to the Dutch budget. In this radical aim he failed, having antagonised the leader of the Old Liberals, the former law professor Thorbecke. But when he became Minister of the Colonies for the second time in 1872, Van de Putte was still regarded as a prominent Liberal leader. His main objectives were the stimulation of private landowning among the Javanese, the reform of the local administration by the aristocracy and the extension of lower and higher education. With regard to the Outer Regions, however, he was to meet his match in Governor-general Loudon, who had proved to be an active and authoritarian provincial governor of south Holland. Moreover,

48. Cf. [Colijn], *Politiek beleid* I, pp. 179f.; Somer, *Korte Verklaring*, p. 92; Fasseur, 'Koloniale paradox', p. 179.

Loudon had been Van de Putte's patron at the beginning of his promising career as sugar contractor in Java.[49]

While the colonial department was largely manned by political and administrative heavyweights with clear Conservative or Liberal leanings, the Ministry of Foreign Affairs often formed the least important item in the formation of a government. And so Liberal governments preferred to find their foreign affairs secretaries in Roman Catholic circles, in order to broaden the domestic basis of the cabinet. Among these, the Groningen aristocrat E. J. J. B. Cremers had been a dedicated Liberal. The experienced diplomat J. L. H. A. Gericke van Herwijnen and the north Brabant notable P. J. A. M. van der Does de Willebois, on the other hand, were considered to be somewhat colourless politically. In fact, political continuity was to a large extent determined by the Dutch diplomatic service – a small group, which consisted mainly of the nobility and was relatively closed. The number of diplomatic representatives abroad was small, too: 15 in 1870, four of them outside Europe.[50] Dutch diplomats preferred to leave the promotion of trading interests to the consular service. The number of consuls fluctuated around 200 during the 1850s and 1860s; most of them were foreigners and no more than 15 drew a full or part-time salary. The functioning of the consular service therefore came under growing criticism, as it gradually became obvious that free trade necessitated the active promotion of trade. In Parliament, this criticism of the Liberals was coupled with growing scepticism of the use of traditional diplomatic representation.[51]

Parliamentary control over colonial and foreign affairs was mainly based on its budgeting rights. The influence of Dutch MPs showed itself particularly in the annual budget debates. If the length of these debates and the degree of participation are anything to go by, MPs also generally regarded colonies as more important than foreign affairs. During the 1860s, both colonial and diplomatic questions had led to a sharp polarisation of Conservatives and Liberals. But in relations with the Outer Regions and other overseas territories there had been far more consensus during those years. Conservative and Liberal ministers as well as MPs were mainly

---

49. For the relations between Van de Putte and Loudon, see Fasseur, 'Suikercontractant', pp. 333–55. Cf. Loudon's anti-riot action in 1868, Loudon 'Memoirs', Loudon Collection (ARA) pp. 260–3.

50. Wels, *Aloofness*, pp. 124–6; cf. Jurriaanse, *Ministers*, pp. 113f.

51. Wels, *Aloofness*, pp. 193–4; cf. Tamse, 'Consular service'.

inclined towards restraint. In fact, Dutch historians have been rather sceptical about the significance of Parliament and the parliamentary parties, especially with regard to the colonies. Inasmuch as Van der Wal regarded Parliament as important, he sought its significance in colonial experts, the so-called 'East Indian specialities'. These MPs, according to Van der Wal, were united by their common experiences in the East Indies and therefore formed a relatively closed and like-minded group, regardless of their party-political affiliations.[52]

Although we are anticipating the results of this analysis, it seems worth noting that colonial issues in the 1860s and the Acheh affair in the 1870s unquestionably brought party-political differences to light. Such issues involved not only colonial experts but also other politicians. Furthermore, the influence of figures such as Van Hoëvell, Fransen van de Putte and – later – O. van Rees did not remain limited to colonial politics. On the other hand, there was also a colonial expert like De Waal who repeatedly declined a seat in Parliament because he felt that he was not experienced enough outside colonial matters.[53]

As for the influence of Parliament, it is sufficient for our purposes to say that the constitutional crisis after the acceptance of the Keuchenius motion in 1866 was finally resolved in favour of parliamentary democracy. A number of contemporaries even maintained that the colonies had become too much of a 'party political issue' in the 1860s. When Loudon was appointed in 1871, the vice-president of the Privy Council, Mackay, for instance, expressed his hope that the 'gravitational centre of East Indian politics' would from then onwards be Batavia rather than The Hague.[54]

The degree of stagnation in parliamentary decision making around 1870 was above all caused by considerable discord among the Liberal majority. In the 1850s and 1860s, the Dutch parties were still in the making, and no genuine parliamentary fractions had emerged, perhaps with the exception of the Calvinist Anti-Revolutionaries. Recent research has shown the importance in the Second Chamber of networks that were formed around a number of prominent politicians.

The 'East Indian Club' must be mentioned in this context – it was

52. Van der Wal, 'Nederlandse expansie', pp. 51f.; cf. Van 't Veer, *Atjeh-oorlog*, pp. 71–2.
53. N. P. van den Berg, 'E de Waal', *Levensberichten* (1906) p. 89.
54. Mackay to Loudon, 22 July 1871, Loudon Collection.

a group of seven Young Liberal MPs who supported Fransen van de Putte in the 1860s and 1870s. But even within this small, informal group, there were differing viewpoints, which can be seen in the votes on the East Indian surplus and the Acheh affair. It therefore seems certain that the 'East India Club' was to some extent a personal projection of the Zeeland delegate D. van Eck (1849–84), who was continually at variance with Van de Putte and who criticised him and his supporters for putting East Indian interests above those of the Netherlands.[55] Though with some exaggeration, one could say that Van Eck himself formed a one-man West Indian club, because of his connections with the Curaçao trading house of J. A. Jesurun. Again and again, whenever the interests of this firm were endangered in turbulent Venezuela, Van Eck would condemn the country in the Dutch Parliament and accuse it of attacking Dutch sovereignty and international law.[56]

A number of MPs, mostly ex-army and navy officers, had first-hand knowledge of overseas territories and the Outer Regions. Lieutenant General J. van Swieten, who served as Liberal MP for Amsterdam from 1864 to 1866, had acquired a good deal of experience as commander of various expeditions, governor of the west coast of Sumatra and supreme commander of the East Indian Army. Similarly, the conservative MPs J. L. Nierstrasz and G. Fabius had traversed the Archipelago several times when they were naval officers. And their Conservative colleague, Rear Admiral F. F. de Casembroot, had in fact distinguished himself as commander of the Dutch squadron in the Shimonoseki expedition in Japan.

Apart from Java, there were not many MPs with vested interests overseas. Members of Parliament from Amsterdam, Rotterdam and Twente, on the other hand, were generally more inclined to take such interests into account. Van Eck, for example, had vested interests in relations between Curaçao and Venezuela; L. Pincoffs, the big man behind the Congo trade, held a Liberal seat in the First Chamber from 1872 onwards. The Anti-Revolutionary member of the Second Chamber and delegate for Rotterdam, M. A. F. H. Hoffman, had traded with China. However, between 1868, when L. W. C. Keuchenius left Parliament, and 1879, when he came back again, there was no real 'colonial speciality' among the Calvinist

55. Tamse, *Memoires*, p. 43.
56. *Handelingen Tweede Kamer* (Parliamentary Reports of the Second Chamber), 19 November 1872, p. 385. Van Eck was a lawyer and barrister of Jesurun in the Netherlands; cf. Goslinga, *Curaçao*, pp. 38, 44 and 81.

Anti-Revolutionary group. The first Roman Catholic colonial expert, H. A. des Amorie van der Hoeven – who had been a free-thinking Liberal solicitor and journalist in Java until his conversion to Catholicism in 1869 – was not to take a seat in the Second Chamber until 1875.[57]

Interest Groups and Public Opinion

The composition of the Dutch Parliament meant that there was a close connection between Parliamentary decision making and extra-parliamentary interests and the formation of opinions with regard to overseas relations. On the whole, the growing gulf between the 'realm of the law' and the 'realm of reality', as Tamse described it around 1870, caused fewer problems in the area of foreign and colonial affairs than in domestic matters.[58] It was generally seen as sensible and fair that those Dutch people who took an interest in overseas affairs should be heard at an early phase in the decision-making process. Whenever matters were far-reaching and complicated, such as the abolition of West Indian slavery or the colonisation of the Outer Regions, state committees were appointed which consisted of a wide variety of members. Also, the Second Chamber could make use of its right of enquiry. This happened, for instance, in 1874, when an enquiry was held into the state of Dutch shipping and the shipbuilding industry. If there were specifically economic issues in the sphere of colonial or foreign affairs, the relevant minister usually asked the Chambers of Commerce for advice. Whenever this did not happen or not sufficiently, there was always the option of sending a petition to the king, a minister or the two Chambers of Parliament. This was indeed a very common method by which interested individuals or groups of people tried to exert some influence on the decision-making process. As we shall see, some petitions were taken quite seriously.

As yet, however, there was hardly any sign of permanently organised pressure groups or orchestrated press campaigns. The institutions and publications that might have played such a role were far too small and exclusive. Where colonial issues were con-

---

57. These and the following biographical data have been taken from common reference books such as the *Nieuw Nederlandsch-Biografisch Woordenboek* and the *ENI*, supplemented with data from recent literature, in particular: Tamse, *Memoires*,; Taal, *Liberalen*; De Vries, *Herinneringen*.
58. Tamse, 'Liberale ministeries', pp. 418–20.

cerned, the various societies and periodicals tried to maintain a balance in their activities between general information and political pressure. One periodical with an outspoken political approach was the *Tijdschrift voor Nederlandsch-Indië* (*TNI*), which – from 1867 onwards – acted as the mouthpiece of the colonial reformers. Its new editors were the Liberal MPs Fransen van de Putte, C. van Heukelom and C. J. F. Mirandolle, as well as the Rotterdam merchant H. Muller and the Leiden ethnologist P. J. Veth. Other progressive Liberals, such as General Van Swieten and the Amsterdam banker and economist N. G. Pierson, contributed regular articles to the magazine. After the solution of the 'colonial question' (that is the abolition of state cultivation in Java) in 1870, its influence was gradually reduced, and after 1871 the editorial office was increasingly managed by only one person, the Liberal ex-civil servant, G. H. van Soest.[59] Also, the East Indian Society, founded in 1854 by a number of moderate Liberal 'specialities' in order to promote impartial information on colonial issues, took a political, Van de Putte-style turn during the 1860s. When the society gave up the anonymity of discussions in its publications and when motions were accepted at its meetings, it came to be known as The East Indian Pre-Parliament. In fact, of about two hundred members, the majority consisted of Liberal Dutch politicians, scientists, businessmen and only a few ex-civil servants and other colonial experts.[60]

In the 1860s, when the system of forced cultivation was being abolished in Java, the society began to discuss the economic development of the Outer Regions quite regularly. The Liberal physician and zoologist P. Bleeker fervently pleaded for fast and powerful expansion in the Archipelago, and a more conservative ex-civil servant from time to time expressed himself very strongly in opposition to this idea. However, most members identified with their chairman, Van Swieten, who favoured peaceful and gradual expansion as well as a system of indirect rule that had been applied so successfully in Siak while he was governor in Sumatra.[61] Van Swieten was chairman from 1867 to 1873, and after that time he had opportunity to try out his ideas in practice as government commissioner in Acheh.

59. Kuitenbrouwer, 'Pierson', p. 7.
60. De Roo de la Faille, 'Herdenking', pp. 16–21. Cf. the members' list of the *Handelingen van het Indisch Genootschap* (Reports of the East Indian Society).
61. Ibid., meetings of 27 January 1865, pp. 193–219; 27 February 1866, pp. 39–77; 27 March 1866, pp. 79–108; 13 April 1866, pp. 109–47, particularly pp. 144–7 for Van Swieten's conclusion.

After 1870 even the East Indian Society lost its political edge again, although it was to retain its predominantly Liberal character. Around the year 1870, the Royal Institute of Philology, Geography and Ethnology, founded by Baud in 1851, had lost its outspoken political and conservative character. As a result, there developed something like a personal union between the leaders of the Royal Institute and the East Indian Society, and a fusion of the two was discussed at regular intervals.[62] Similarly, the Geographic Society, founded in 1873, soon came to be dominated by the same people. Around 1870, a small, mainly Liberal elite had come into being, which encompassed the most important governmental functions of institutions in colonial and overseas affairs. These included, among others, Veth, Bleeker, Van Soest, Privy Councillor Bachiene, the MP W. T. Gevers Deynoot and the geographer and historian P. J. B. C. Robidé van der Aa.

The activities of Roman Catholic and Protestant missionary organisations were largely outside this Liberal sphere – except for the Bible Society where Veth served on the committee. The Roman Catholic mission towards the end of the nineteenth century was hierarchically managed from Rome and Batavia and concentrated mainly on Flores and Timor, where Catholicism had already been established by the Portuguese. From 1859, Dutch Jesuits also participated in this limited missionary effort.[63]

The modern Protestant mission in the Netherlands had begun with the foundation of the Dutch Missionary Society in 1797. In the 1850s, this largely liberal society was torn to pieces by vehement religious controversies. Traditional mission fields in the Moluccas and Timor had to be abandoned. Under the inspired leadership of the former schoolteacher J. C. Neurdenburg, who was the director of the Mission House in Rotterdam from 1865 to 1895 and editor-in-chief of its publication *Mededelingen* (Announcements), the society gradually managed to overcome this setback. After 1870, missionary activities in the Archipelago increased again, particularly in Celebes, with the traditional mission field of Minahassa as its basis.[64]

Another organisation which was equally active in the Outer

---

62. De Roo de la Faille, 'Herdenking', pp. 1–13 and 21–2.

63. Mulders, *Missie*, pp. 79–84.

64. J. Craandijk, 'Johan Christiaan Neurdenburg', *Levensberichten* (1896), pp. 219–55; cf. 'Een enkele blik achterwaarts geslagen en dan weder voorwaarts', *Mededeelingen* (1872), pp. 1–10.

Regions and also independent in its approach was the Dutch Bible Society, founded in 1814.[65] Of the orthodox breakaway groups that had separated from the Missionary Society, only the Utrecht Missionary Association (1859) was active in Java. From 1862 onwards, missionaries were sent to New Guinea and its neighbouring islands. Among these various organisations, the Missionary Society was particularly active as a pressure group within the Netherlands. Using sermons, brochures and petitions, it sought to influence the government, the Dutch Parliament and public opinion in order to obtain more support for its missions. One of the aims of the society was the removal of restrictions for missionaries in the Outer Regions, the subsidising of missionary training and – as a long-term objective – legal equality of Christian 'natives' and 'Europeans'.[66] The *Berigten* (Reports) of the Utrecht Missionary Association sounded a very introverted, non-political note. Even subscribers who wanted to get something 'for their money and their prayers', and who were especially interested in the number of converts among the Papuans, were told off in no uncertain terms.[67]

There were no separate Dutch organisations for the promotion of economic interests in the colonies or elsewhere overseas. Instead, as we have already seen such functions were regularly undertaken by the Chambers of Commerce, especially in Amsterdam, Rotterdam and Twente. Around 1870, there were no clashes between the various interests they represented, though the differences between them were quite significant. The world of trade in Amsterdam was still rather strongly oriented towards colonial interests, which were connected with the systems of consignment and of forced cultivation in Java as well as plantation agriculture in Surinam, where slavery had only been abolished in 1863.

In the Chamber of Commerce, as in Amsterdam politics in general, there was a fierce controversy in the 1860s between Liberals and Conservatives about the current economic system in the colonies and in trade politics. This argument was not resolved until 1870, when it ended in favour of the Liberals.[68] Rotterdam traders, on the other hand, concentrated less one-sidedly on the colonies and the Liberals managed to carry their point sooner. Apart from Java,

65. Swellengrebel, *Leydeckers voetspoor* I, pp. 21–6 and 142f.
66. Craandijk, 'Neurdenburg', p. 149; cf. 'Het standpunt van ons Genootschap', *Mededeelingen* (1870), pp. 97–123.
67. See the testimony of 'Brother Woelders' in *Berigten* (1872), p. 27.
68. Van Tijn, *Twintig jaren*, pp. 328f., cf. Quack, *Herinneringen*, pp. 89f.

Curaçao and Elmina, Rotterdam had also established trade relations with other parts of Asia, Africa and South America. The Chamber of Commerce and local politics in the 1860s were already dominated by Pincoffs, Muller and other Liberal representatives of the Rotterdam world of trade.[69] This liberalisation also showed itself in the management of the Netherlands Trading Company where Muller soon made a significant contribution to its renewal and reorientation from 1868 onwards.

The Chamber of Commerce in Twente had been mainly Liberal in orientation since the 1850s. In the 1860s textile exports had spread not only to Java but also to China and other new overseas markets. A large part of it, however, went through foreign trade and shipping companies, via Hamburg and London. This explains why the majority of Twente industrialists were in favour of free trade.[70] The Association of Dutch Industrialists and their weekly magazine *De Nederlandsche Industrieel*, on the other hand, strongly advocated the principle of reciprocity as well as preferential treatment by the Dutch government for the beginning of industry. These industrialists, who came mainly from the small industrial centres outside Amsterdam, Rotterdam and Twente, even adopted the name 'protectionists', which was originally given to them as a derogatory term by Liberal journalists.[71]

Also, a look at the most important magazines in the Netherlands shows that the growing interest in the overseas world was mainly Liberal in orientation. The leading magazine *De Gids* often contained articles on colonial matters by Veth who was one of its editors from 1844 to 1876.[72] And the outspoken Liberal magazine *De Economist* also gave a considerable amount of attention to colonial matters and trade politics. While J. K. W. Quarles van Ufford, who worked as a senior civil servant in the Colonial Department until 1871, was in charge of the widely read *Koloniale Kroniek* (Colonial Chronicle) in the *Economist*,[73] P. N. Muller, the Amsterdam-based brother of the Rotterdam trader, regularly wrote about colonial matters both in *De Gids* and *De Economist*.[74] Articles in these Liberal magazines were considered to be authoritative and

69. Cf. Muller, *Muller*, pp. 215f.; Mees, *Man, passim*; Oosterwijk, *Vlucht*, pp. 57f.
70. Verkade, *Thorbecke*, pp. 241f.; cf. Mees, *Man*, pp. 350f.
71. Cf. *Nederlandsche Industrieel*, 24 July 1870.
72. Cf. Van de Lith, 'Veth', *passim*.
73. O. J. H. van Limburg Stirum, 'Jhr. J. K. W. Quarles van Ufford', *Levensberichten* (1904), pp. 112–31.
74. Dyserinck, *Muller*, pp. 17f. and 36f.

influential – at least among those 10 per cent of male Dutch adults who paid enough tax to be entitled to vote. Before 1870, the 'people behind the voter' were hardly affected by big colonial matters and foreign affairs.

Indeed, it is worth noting that such topics were given a great deal of attention in national papers, such as the *Nieuwe Rotterdamsche Courant* (New Rotterdam Daily) and the Amsterdam-based *Algemeen Handelsblad*. Until the abolition of the newspaper tax in 1869, the number of papers, their size and circulation were rather limited.[75] But in the course of the 1870s the number of newspapers doubled and, apart from the 'respectable' nationwide press there was now also an extensive local and indeed 'popular' press. Among these cheap newspapers, the Amsterdam-based *Nieuws van den Dag* (News of the Day) achieved a circulation of 25,000 at that time, compared with some 9,000 of the *N.R.C.* and the *Algemeen Handelsblad*, 2,500 of the Hague paper *Vaderland* (Fatherland) and 1,500 of the *Arnhemsche Courant* (Arnhem Journal).[76] These were the most important Liberal dailies, with the *N.R.C.*, representing the political right and the *Vaderland* the political left of the Liberal spectrum.

One particularly radical paper was *De Amsterdammer*, which started as a weekly magazine in 1877 and became a daily paper in 1883. As a weekly, in 1880, it had a circulation of 4,000 copies. The mouthpiece of Dutch Conservatives was the *Dagblad van Zuid-Holland en 's Gravenhage* (Daily News of South Holland and 's Gravenhage), with the same circulation of 4,000. This was also the size of the nation-wide Roman Catholic papers, the Amsterdam *Tijd* (Time) and the Rotterdam *Maasbode* (Meuse Messenger). The Calvinist Anti-Revolutionaries started their own nation-wide paper in 1872, *De Standaard*, with their new leader, the young Amsterdam minister A. Kuyper, as editor-in-chief and an initial circulation of 2,500.

With these circulation figures, the Netherlands had managed to catch up with other countries. The development of the telegraph and other modern media of communication meant that the supply of daily news in the Netherlands became increasingly important for the formation of opinions and policies on overseas affairs. The rise

75. In 1866, there was one newspaper per 22,000 inhabitants in the Netherlands, compared with 16,500 in Britain in 17,000 in Belgium; Schneider and Hemels, *Nederlandse krant*, p. 178.
76. Cf. Hemels, *Bres*, appendix XIV.

of modern imperialism in general and the Acheh War in particular were to give many examples of this.

The Situation around 1870

The year 1870 is an important point in Dutch historiography. It was the beginning of a new period, marked by the Franco–Prussian War, the formation of the German empire in foreign affairs, the opening of the Suez Canal, the Dutch agrarian laws and the Anglo-Dutch colonial treaties in colonial affairs. The Netherlands was also on the threshold of a new period in domestic affairs.

But, as the preceding paragraphs have shown, concerning overseas policies and the formation of opinion, there was not only an awareness of change but also of continuity in the Netherlands. The year 1870 therefore does not form an absolute starting point for our study but a relative one, a year of transition when a number of issues came to the fore and others disappeared into the background. This development was almost certainly accelerated by the dramatic events of that year, though the transition was generally smooth and relatively autonomous.

When the system of forced cultivation was gradually abolished in 1870, other colonial problems emerged. Apart from his agrarian laws, De Waal presented a parliamentary bill whereby the East Indian contribution to the Dutch treasury would have been limited to a fixed amount and a separate department for the Outer Regions would have been set up in Batavia. The Dutch Second Chamber was above all relieved that the 'colonial question' had finally been solved and its members were still rather reluctant to endorse experiments with the Dutch credit balance and the policy of abstention. The fixed amount was therefore rejected by a large majority.[77] The other proposal, however, was accepted – though by a narrow majority – because many MPs felt that such a department for the Outer Regions would help to avoid 'expensive expeditions and lengthy wars'.[78]

Nevertheless, in the same year – 1870 – the Netherlands came closer to its most expensive and protracted war in the Archipelago. On 24 June De Waal instructed the Batavian colonial administration

77. *Handelingen Tweede Kamer* (Parliamentary Reports of the Second Chamber), 8 November 1869, p. 287.
78. Ibid., p. 114. The actual establishment of the department, incidentally, never took place.

to take stronger action against Acheh-based piracy and slave trade, taking care, 'for the present', not to violate the sovereignty of Acheh, as laid down in the 1824 treaty. It was pointed out, though, that 'from now on, this should be no reason for abstention where interference is necessary'.[79]

With growing Dutch influence in north Sumatra there was an increasing conviction in The Hague that the 1857 Friendship Treaty with Acheh offered an insufficient guarantee for the protection of commerce and shipping and that it did not exclude foreign influence. In 1865, Fransen van de Putte had already suggested to his foreign affairs colleague that the terms of the 1824 Acheh notes should be revised. The opening of the Suez Canal, which was expected to lead to a considerable increase in commerce and shipping around north Sumatra, seemed to make the whole matter even more urgent. Together with the Foreign Minister T. M. Roest van Limburg, De Waal therefore took concrete measures to obtain the necessary revision from Britain.

De Waal's successor Van Bosse was clearly convinced that, in colonial matters, important changes had taken place under his predecessor. Referring to the exchange of views with the Second Chamber, he wrote to the newly appointed governor-general Loudon that 'the "agrarian property" element' had become irrelevant: 'I am now more concerned with the "financial element and the Outer Regions".' The shift of interest from Java to Sumatra and from sugar and coffee to tobacco and minerals was, according to Van Bosse, also noticeable outside the Chamber. He therefore pointed out to Loudon that there had been a request for a concession to exploit the rich coalfields of Ombilin in Sumatra, which had been discovered in 1868; this request had attracted considerable interest in the Netherlands and was supported by Prince Henry. '*On veut battre monnaie!*' (They want to make money!) wrote Van Bosse.[80]

Around 1870, as soon as the most important colonial question – the system of state cultivation – had been solved, a whole series of overseas issues became problematic, in addition to the Outer Regions and the financial contribution of Java, which had also become colonial issues. During 1870, after the Dutch intervention, Venezuela opened negotiations with a view to normalising relations. However, the damages claimed by Jesurun and other Curaçao

---

79. *Officieele bescheiden*, p. 30. Cf. Reid, *Contest*, p. 55; Fasseur, 'Nederland', p. 175.

80. Van Bosse to Loudon, 13 May to 23 October 1871, Loudon Collection.

trading houses towards Venezuela offered sufficient ground for new conflicts.[81] In Surinam in 1873 the ten-year state supervision of the emancipated slaves, which had started in 1863, was to run out. The Surinam plantation owners and those with a vested interest in Amsterdam were already beginning to press, in advance, for the immigration of new contract workers from China and British India.[82] On the Gold Coast, the mutual territorial exchanges between Britain and the Netherlands, which had been agreed in 1867, had disastrous effects on relations with and between the African tribes.

The Netherlands was now faced with the choice of extending its military and administrative presence quite considerably or ceding its entire possessions to Britain.[83] The problems on the Gold Coast gave De Waal an opportunity to widen the negotiations with Britain concerning the Siak question in Sumatra to reach a more general settlement on colonial matters, including Acheh. The Siak issue was closely connected with the restrictions imposed by the Netherlands on British commerce and shipping in the Archipelago. Also, on a more general level, a fundamental choice in trade politics became imminent in 1870. After all, in 1872 the East Indian Tariff Law of 1865 was to run out. After the lowering of differential rights, which had already taken effect at the time, a choice between maintaining protectionism and its complete abolition seemed inevitable.

Many contemporaries felt that the urgency of these colonial and trade political issues was underlined by two events which had made a deep impact around the year 1870: the opening of the Suez Canal and the Franco–Prussian War. Both had of course been predicted for some time. From 1859 onwards there had been continuous progress in the construction of the Suez Canal. Dutch commerce and shipping, however, were particularly slow in responding. Although there were regular warnings about the consequences of the canal on world-wide traffic, the Dutch continued to use sailing vessels, whereas other countries made increasing use of steamships. Initiatives to establish a regular steamship link with the East Indies had failed, mainly due to a lack of co-operation on the part of Amsterdam traders who did not dare to risk their vested interest in sailing vessels.

In 1870, a year after the ceremonial opening of the Suez Canal,

81. Goslinga, *Curaçao*, pp. 27–8.
82. Cf. Willemsen, *Koloniale politiek*, pp. 98f.; Kuitenbroùwer, 'Afschaffing', pp. 86–9.
83. Coombs, *Gold Coast*, pp. 44f.; cf. Baesjou, *Asante Embassy*, pp. 28–34.

the Rotterdam and Amsterdam Chambers of Commerce finally entered into negotiations, through the mediation of Prince Henry, and the Netherlands Steamshipping Company was founded.[84] The order for the first large steamships was placed in England, amidst the protests of the Dutch shipbuilding and engineering industries, which were hardly prepared for such a task at this point.[85] The opening of the canal meant a considerable shortening of the link with the East Indies. The average journey, which used to take about 120 days by sailing vessel via the Cape, now only took about 40 days by steamship via Suez. The link with the East Indies was further improved in 1871, when a telegraph line was established from Sumatra to Singapore, which had already been linked to the existing transcontinental line.[86]

After 1870 it was generally assumed that the opening of the Suez Canal would have a radical effect on Dutch colonial and commercial relations, with a significant increase in overseas trade, though the Netherlands would also be exposed to increasing foreign competition. An observer such as Prince Henry therefore still expressed concern for the future, even after the establishment of the Netherlands Steamshipping Company. Should the Netherlands lose its historical share of overseas trade, said the prince, 'this would also mean the loss of great resources for the Netherlands and our independence among the nations would be jeopardised more than from any other cause'.[87] Now that the Suez Canal had become a fact, it was pointed out on various sides that new initiatives were necessary and that these should be supported by the government. Reports of the Chambers of Commerce as well as the articles in the *Nederlandsche Industrieel* and *De Economist*, for example, insisted on a reform and extension of the consular service; international regulations that would protect private property at sea; more showing of the flag in foreign waters; and the appointment of Dutch representatives in China, South Africa and other non-European countries with which relations had recently been established.[88] The

84. *Verslag KvK-Amsterdam* (Report of the Amsterdam Chamber of Commerce) 1869, pp. 8–9, appendix A; ibid. (1870), pp. 140–1. Cf. Verslag *KvK-Rotterdam* (Report of the Rotterdam Chamber of Commerce), 1869, pp. 31–2.

85. *Nederlandsch Industrieel*, 6 and 20 March 1970.

86. See the entries 'Reisgelegenheden' (Means of transport), 'Scheepvaart en handel' (Shipping and trade) and 'Post en telegraafdienst' (Postal and telegraphic service) in the *ENI*.

87. Prince Hendrik to Loudon, 12 August 1871, Loudon Collection.

88. *Verslag KvK-Amsterdam* (Report of the Amsterdam Chamber of Commerce)

foundation of the Dutch Geographic Society in 1873 was also in line with this new energetic mentality. 'Geography is a practical science *par excellence*,' said Veth, the first chairman, in his opening speech, 'and should generally be of special interest to a trading nation that is constantly trying to find new ways and means of establishing profitable relations.' And there was indeed a good deal of interest. In 1874 the society already counted 360 members, with 80 from the world of commerce, shipping and industry.[89]

The Franco–Prussian War had some repercussions on the position of the Netherlands within Europe. The war itself and the preceding complications had given rise to great concern in the Netherlands about the way in which small states could preserve their independence. The situation prompted the Netherlands to seek support from Britain, although neither country felt that a formal alliance would be desirable.[90] Apart from the Luxemburg issue, Dutch diplomacy had survived the ensuing crises rather well. However, trust in the diplomatic service had not exactly been promoted among the Dutch bourgeoisie either. 'Diplomacy is *en déclin*,' concluded the Liberal *NRC* in 1871. According to this paper, the spirit of the time was against the practice whereby 'small countries spent a fortune just to taste the satisfaction of being represented abroad by an ambassador who spends his days in a *dolce far niente*.' The closing of the Papal embassy by the Second Chamber that year formed a climax, for the time being, of this sceptical attitude.[91]

Historians have found that Dutch anxiety about a possible annexation of the Netherlands subsided as soon as the new relations in Europe had become stabilised after 1871.[92] However, these worries came back whenever the chances of a new European war seemed to increase. The concern for the destiny of the smaller states in power politics was undoubtedly sublimated by a growing preoccupation with international law as a guarantee for peace and security. The foundation of the General Dutch Peace Alliance in 1871, under the

---

1869, pp. 149f.; *Verslag KvK-Rotterdam* (Report of the Rotterdam Chamber of Commerce), 1869, pp. 32f. Cf. *Nederlandse Industrieel*, 11 July, 8 and 29 August 1869; A. Plate, 'De eischen von den vrijen handel', *De Economist* (1870) I, pp. 401f.

89. *TAG* (1876) I, pp. 13–14 and 89.

90. Tamse, *Nederland*, pp. 86–7.

91. *NRC*, 2 May 1871; cf. *Handelingen Tweede Kamer* (Parliamentary Reports of the Second Chamber), 17 November 1871, p. 252.

92. Anxiety about a possible German annexation prevailed more in public opinion

chairmanship of Van Eck, was one of the first signs. It attracted 2,500 members in 1871. This interest in international law was also given substance on a policy level, when the well-known specialist in international law T. M. C. Asser was appointed adviser of the Minister for Foreign Affairs in 1876.[93]

The European wars had also given rise to the fear that the Netherlands might lose the East Indies – a fear which was to continue with the emergence of modern imperialism. In 1870 there were two different views with regard to defending the colony. One assumed that a possible attack would come mainly from those continental powers which did not have a fleet with which they could conquer the East Indies directly. 'The keys of our East Indian possessions are in Amsterdam', said the Liberal MP, J. K. H. de Roo van Alderwerelt, who was also the most prominent representative of this view. De Roo therefore advocated a further reduction of the defence budget for the East Indies and more spending on the defence of the Netherlands itself.[94] The other point of view was that the danger of an attack on the East Indies lay not with France or Prussia but with Britain, which had, after all, become master of the Dutch colonies during the Napoleonic Wars. Furthermore, it was necessary to reckon with the expansion of the United States in the Pacific – the 'Romans of the New World'. 'The first shot that is fired in the Netherlands on our eastern and southern borders', wrote the Liberal colonial magazine *TNI*, Fransen van de Putte's mouthpiece, in response to De Roo's statements, 'is also the sign that we can expect the British or American fleet in our East Indian harbours any day.'[95] For that matter, most participants in this discussion agreed that the long stretch of Archipelago could hardly be defended by a small country like the Netherlands. Many Liberals therefore saw the complete opening of the East Indies to foreign trade and capital as the best guarantee for its security. 'With a decent trade tariff we can keep all enemies from Europe out of the East

---

than among Dutch diplomats, though; cf. Woltring, *Bescheiden* I, no. 302; ibid. II, nos 4–4a, 325, 341, 353, 425. S.a. Von der Dunk, *Niederlande*, pp. 10–12; Tamse, *Nederland*, p. 322.

93. Wels, *Aloofness*, pp. 60f.; cf. Kamphuis, *Vredebond*, chapters 2 and 3.

94. *Handelingen Tweede Kamer* (Parliamentary Reports of the Second Chamber), 12 November 1869, pp. 186–7; cf. J. K. H. de Roo van Alderwerelt, 'Het Indisch Budget van Oorlog', *De Gids* (1868) III, pp. 522f.

95. L. E. Gerdessen, 'Het Indisch leger tegenover een buitenlandsche vijand', *TNI* (1871) I, pp. 414–15.

Indies', Minister Van Bosse wrote in a private letter to Loudon.[96]

Around the year 1870 there was an attitude of defensive expansion in the Netherlands with regard to the overseas world. This leads to questions about the general state of Dutch society 'on the threshold of a new age'. The importance of maintaining aloofness and neutrality had, for the time being, pushed all other tendencies in foreign affairs into the background. But under the pressure of trade and Parliament, the government soon began to take an interest in trade politics again, though aloofness and neutrality remained as underlying aims.

Public opinion now displayed a much greater tendency towards moralising and legalism than before.[97] The events around 1870 had considerably sharpened national conscience in this respect. On the other hand, there was still very little modern mass nationalism in the Netherlands. It seems unlikely that this was due to the process of religious and political 'pillarisation' which had hardly started at all in 1870.[98] More likely, it reflected the Netherlands' position as a small power at a time when small powers seemed to be having great difficulty in holding their own. It may also be a consequence of that general backwardness in the modernisation of Dutch society, which, according to Van Tijn, was apparent in comparison with other countries.[99]

The theory that the Netherland was slow to become modernised because it lacked strong industrial development has, however, been disputed recently, especially as regards the time around 1870. Bos maintains that, compared with Britain, the Netherlands had a rather modern economic system, even though it was less industrialised. Its infrastructure, educational system and communicational links had already been renewed quite significantly. Its production was varied and it had a technology which was sufficiently competitive for the time. Certain industries, such as textiles, were in fact highly industrialised. Other industries such as shipping, however, did indeed initially lag behind the economic development at home and abroad.[100] With this in mind, it is not surprising that Dutch overseas relations during the 1870s showed impulses both for expansion

96. Van Bosse to Loudon, 12 March 1869, Loudon Collection.
97. In 1874 minister Gericke van Herwijnen described the Netherlands as 'a power of the second rank for which it is desirable always and in all places, whenever possible, to stay neutral'; Woltring, *Bescheiden* I, no. 510.
98. Stuurman, *Verzuiling*, p. 136–9.
99. Cf. Van Tijn, 'Drempel'.
100. Bos, *Brits–Nederlandse handel*, pp. 78–93; cf. Nusteling, *Rijnvaart*, pp. 399f.

and for concentration – a pattern that was repeated in colonial as well as trade politics.

Overseas Expansion and Concentration

The Anglo–Dutch Treaties

The conclusion of treaties on colonial issues between Britain and the Netherlands at the end of 1870 and the beginning of 1871 has been described in detail by Coombs, Reid and Van 't Veer.[101] Broadly speaking, the treaties contained the following agreements. Firstly, Britain agreed to recognise Dutch sovereignty over Siak and other parts of Sumatra which were to be modelled after Siak. At the same time the Netherlands was to abolish restrictions on British trade, shipping and other enterprises in those parts. Secondly, the Netherlands ceded its Gold Coast possessions to Britain. The third ruling concerned the recruitment and emigration of contract labour in British India for Surinam. Both contemporaries and historians paid a lot of attention to the question of who exactly had taken the initiative and in how far there was a link between the three treaties.

In the meantime it has been proved conclusively that both British and Dutch governmental circles had in fact long anticipated the achieved results, but that De Waal put forward the decisive proposal in autumn 1869. The presentation as a comprehensive whole seems to have been partly a matter of tactics. It gave both governments the opportunity to point out the quid pro quo – the advantages and disadvantages – to their respective domestic opponents. When this obvious purpose was threatening to fail in the first instance, the interdependence of the three treaties was somewhat toned down again.

However, apart from formal implications, the link between the treaties also meant that the Netherlands consciously reorganised its colonial priorities. At the time, De Waal was primarily concerned with discharging Dutch commitment on the Gold Coast while at the same time achieving more freedom of movement with regard to Acheh. In the long term, he felt that opportunities for development were doubtful in Africa, but extremely promising in the Archipelago, particularly in Sumatra. Subsequently, though, De Waal was to deny that the cession of Elmina resulted in a free hand in

---

101. Cf. Coombs, *Gold Coast*, pp. 57f.; Reid, *Contest*, pp. 60f.; Van 't Veer, *Atjeh-oorlog*, pp. 32f.

Sumatra.[102] However, after De Waal had left office at the beginning of 1871, the new Liberal ministry under the leadership of Thorbecke stated in a detailed memorandum that 'the cession of our posts on the coast of Guinea should not proceed except in conjunction with the assurance of our sovereignty and our influence in the East Indies.' In this context, the removal of restrictions with regard to Acheh were pointed out in particular. These had given the Netherlands the freedom to extend its sovereignty in Sumatra, 'that most important island'. The new ministry was therefore willing to accept the treaties with Britain and to submit three separate bills to the Second Chamber.[103]

The Privy Council, however, was far less favourably inclined towards these treaties, and its final report, which had been drafted by Mackay, included serious objections both to form and content. If there was really a connection between the three treaties, why were they not submitted to the Chambers together, within a single bill? If a free hand in Sumatra was seen as the most important compensation for the cession of African possessions, why was British recognition of the Dutch treaty with the Sultan of Siak of 1858 chosen as the starting point, and why was Acheh only mentioned in the exchanged notes? The Privy Council therefore denied that this was satisfactory compensation. After all, the Siak Convention had already lifted the restrictions on British trade and shipping. The Council asked whether the 1824 treaty might not be repealed so that British recognition of Dutch sovereignty would include the entire Archipelago, especially Borneo. It was felt that the cession of the African possessions should not be taken lightly: 'It may be true that we can also trade without colonial possessions, but such an assumption would lead to giving up all our colonies. And what would the Netherlands be without colonies?'[104] This suggestion was completely rejected by the government.

In their reply, the Minister of the Colonies, Van Bosse, and the Foreign Minister, Gericke van Herwijnen, argued forcefully against any reopening of negotiations with Britain. Quite apart from the fact that Britain was sure to expect even more concessions from the Netherlands in the event of a repeal of the 1824 treaty, the extension of colonial rights and obligations in the entire Archipelago would be beyond the limited powers of the Netherlands. The two ministers

102. De Waal, *Indische Financiën* I, pp. 67–73.
103. Woltring, *Bescheiden* I, no. 15.
104. Ibid., no. 54.

felt that the duty which the Netherlands already had in Sumatra 'and which it might well have towards Acheen in the future, cannot be taken lightly'.[105] On 23 April 1871 the two treaties were submitted to the Second Chamber.[106]

Meanwhile, the intended cession of the insignificant African possessions had given rise to a great deal of turmoil both inside and outside Parliament. Opposition came mainly from Conservatives and – partly – from Liberals. The Conservative paper *Dagblad* branded the cession as a 'suicidal and short-sighted policy', which could lead to the enforced cession of possessions in the West Indies, the East Indies and 'possibly even the cession of parts of our Fatherland'.[107] Even some Liberals opposed the cession on historical and nationalist grounds, while other Liberals also pointed out the potential economic significance of the African possessions.

The Liberal opposition to the scheme came from a rather limited and clearly recognisable centre, that is from Rotterdam, especially from Muller, the most prominent Gold Coast trader, who explained his objections in the *NRC*.[108] Other Liberal papers were therefore rather sceptical towards objections from Rotterdam.[109] All the more so because Robidé van der Aa had shown quite convincingly that, a long time before then, the Rotterdam firm had already diverted a large portion of the Gold Coast trade to other parts of the west coast of Africa, particularly Liberia.[110] In the *Algemeen Handelsblad* the cession was defended for reasons of principle. The paper pointed out that the general attitude towards colonial possessions had undergone changes recently. On the one hand, commerce now had to be regarded as more important than colonies; and, on the other hand, the possession of colonies currently imposed more obligations than before. The Netherlands was for example unable to educate the local population of Elmina properly, and such a task could be accomplished more effectively by Britain.[111]

The intended cession of Elmina was discussed especially promi-

105. Ibid., no. 60; cf. no. 57.

106. *Bijlagen Handelingen Tweede Kamer* (Parliamentary Reports of the Second Chamber, Appendices) 1870–1, pp. 125f.

107. *Het Dagblad von Zuid-Holland en 's Gravenhage*, 21–3 May 1871.

108. *NRC*, 20–6 May 1871; cf. Muller, *Muller*, pp. 195f.

109. Cf. 'Koloniale kroniek', *De Economist* (1872) I, pp. 267f.; *TNI* (1871) II, pp. 109–10.

110. Robidé van der Aa, *Afrikaansche Studiën*, pp. 73–6.

111. *Het Handelsblad*, 5–6 May 1871.

nently by the general public. Correspondingly, a great deal of attention was given in the Second Chamber to the Siak Convention, which was regarded as compensation for the cession. The detailed exchange of ideas which followed the submission of the bills already showed quite clearly that the majority of MPs were extremely sceptical about this point. As the diplomatic notes on the Siak agreement were never actually produced, there also remained a number of uncertainties with regard to Acheh.[112] However, in the public discussion of the treaties on 5, 6, and 7 July 1871, those MPs who knew more about the whole matter made it quite clear that they had no more reservations with regard to Acheh's independence. Former Minister for Foreign Affairs Cremers thought it was very important that the Netherlands could now take strong measures against 'one of the most barbarian states, where human flesh is still regarded as a delicacy'.[113] Fransen van de Putte, too, felt it was 'a great advantage' that the Netherlands would now have more freedom of movement towards Acheh.[114] Other Liberals, such as Mirandolle, thought that the treaty offered too little compensation for the cession of the Gold Coast. They would have preferred a general repeal of the 1824 treaty. Also, they felt that the modelling of the future expansion in Sumatra on the example of Siak was unacceptable.[115]

Conservative spokesmen, too, were against the Siak agreement, though for totally different reasons. In the first place they felt that future Dutch economic interests would be harmed by giving British economic interests free access to Sumatra. But in the second place they saw a dangerous tendency towards expansion in the treaty. Nierstrasz, who had once visited Acheh as a navy officer, warned emphatically against possible plans to stir up such a 'hornets' nest': 'We have no business there . . . It will only cost a lot of money and human lives. The further we keep away from it . . . the better.'[116]

112. *Bijlagen Handelingen Tweede Kamer* (Parliamentary Reports of the Second chamber, Appendices) 1870–1, pp. 1783f., 1815f., 1859f.

113. *Handelingen Tweede Kamer* (Parliamentary Reports of the Second Chamber), 6 July 1871, p. 1107. All kinds of unfavourable qualities were ascribed to the local population of Acheh by the Dutch, such as religious fanaticism, cruelty and 'immorality'; this charge of cannibalism, however, was exceptional. Cremers may well have confused Acheh with the animalist Batak area, where such practice may possibly have occurred.

114. *Handelingen Tweede Kamer* (Parliamentary Reports of the Second Chamber), 7 July 1871, p. 1127.

115. Ibid., 5 July, p. 1098.

116. Ibid., 7 July, p. 1142.

The cession of Elmina, on the other hand, was strongly opposed by Conservatives. It was pointed out that the Netherlands had a national and historic obligation, and Africa was seen as the 'land of the future'.[117] Britain's willingness to take over these possessions was looked at with great suspicion, and the Drente Conservative Liberal L. Oldenhuis Gratama repeatedly referred to Britain as 'the cunning and perfidious Albion'.[118]

Those who favoured the cession reacted to such arguments with a good deal of scepticism. 'Where are they – those Dutch Livingstones – who will risk their lives and property in the course of Africa's development and civilisation?' the Amsterdam MP E. H. 's Jacob said sarcastically, defending the cession with a fiery speech on the advantages of free trade and the disadvantages of colonial possessions.[119] Nor did Fransen van de Putte have any 'unsurmountable objections' to abandoning the Gold Coast, even though he represented Rotterdam in the Second Chamber.[120]

In their final speeches, Van Bosse's and Gericke's main thrusts were on the importance of a better understanding with Britain on colonial matters.[121] The treaty whereby the Netherlands ceded its African possessions was subsequently carried by a majority of 34 to 30. The Siak agreement, on the other hand, was defeated, with 36 votes to 28. Most Conservative, Anti-Revolutionary and Catholic MPs had voted against both bills; most Liberals had voted for both of them. A fifth of all Liberals, including Mirandolle, had voted for the cession of the Gold Coast and against the Siak agreement.[122] The so-called 'Coolie Treaty', which regulated the recruitment and emigration of contract workers from British India to Surinam, was then carried by a large majority, despite the problem that Britain was only willing to permit a contract period of five rather than ten years.[123]

The defeat of the Siak Convention greatly embarrassed the Dutch government. Gericke instructed Count Ch. M. E. G. van Bylandt, the new ambassador in London, to assure the British Foreign Minister, Lord Granville, that the rejection of the treaty should not

117. Ibid., 5 July, pp. 1089f.
118. Ibid., p. 1091; 7 July, p. 1141.
119. Ibid., 6 July, p. 1116.
120. Ibid., p. 1125.
121. Ibid., 7 July, pp. 1128f.; pp. 1145f.
122. Ibid., p. 1146.
123. Ibid., 15 December 1871, p. 249.

be understood as an unfriendly act towards Britain.[124] Although Lord Granville did not contradict this statement, he nevertheless showed very little enthusiasm – according to Van Bylandt – for any further concessions to the Netherlands in the Archipelago. Van Bylandt had the impression that the British government would be quite pleased once the cession of the Gold Coast had proceeded as planned and the solution to the Siak question was shelved for the time being.[125] The Dutch government, however, was not at all keen. The cession bill was not to be passed to the First Chamber until a new treaty had been reached over Sumatra. Nor was the suggestion of the British ambassador, Vice-Admiral Harris, carried out whereby such an arrangement might have been linked to the planned repeal of the East Indian tariff.[126] Especially at the Department of Colonies there was rather a lot of anxiety about further British claims in this direction in case the Netherlands should propose a general revision of the 1824 treaty. 'The broader the repeal,' said a civil servant of this department, 'the more Dutch feathers will be flying.'[127]

Finally Granville opened the door for a resumption of negotiations by announcing via Harris on 29 August that the British government would be pleased to receive new proposals from the Dutch side.[128] Meanwhile, Van Bylandt had already conferred with The Hague and drafted a new text for a treaty, describing clearly, in two clauses, the political and economic relations in Sumatra. The first clause guaranteed Dutch sovereignty in the whole of Sumatra, without mentioning the example of Siak any more and with an explicit repeal of the reservations regarding Acheh. According to the second clause, British and Dutch trade, shipping and other enterprises were to be given equal status in Sumatra. There were still some difficulties over the precise formulation of the second clause, as both sides were concerned about hidden advantages in each other's texts. But, on the whole, negotiations proceeded smoothly and in a good spirit. On 2 November 1871 the new Sumatra Treaty was signed.[129]

The new treaty was received quite favourably by the Second Chamber, although the revision was more a matter of form than

124. Woltring, *Bescheiden* I, no. 101.
125. Ibid., nos 106–7, 113, 122.
126. Ibid., nos 101–2; cf. 112.
127. Ibid., no. 103.
128. Ibid., no. 132; cf. 118.
129. Ibid., nos 113, 135–6, 156–7.

content.[130] During the public debate on 15 December, attention was further focused on the consequences of the treaty for relations with Acheh. The Liberal MP A. van Naamen van Eemnes regarded it as an improvement that the new treaty gave 'complete freedom of action' in this respect. Mirandolle expressed himself in a similar way.[131] However, Conservative speakers – particularly J. Heemskerk – felt that this treaty was an even more obvious manifestation of 'the desire for annexation'. Nierstrasz made it known that he would nevertheless vote in favour of the treaty, 'so that there can finally be an end to the bickering between us and Britain over Sumatra'.[132] Van Bosse emphatically denied on behalf of the government that annexation was the aim: it was merely a matter of 'having the opportunity for more leverage when this becomes necessary'.[133] Feeling more or less reassured by this statement, the Chamber passed the Sumatra Treaty by a large majority of 54 to 13.[134] Subsequently, several attempts were made to move the Conservative majority of the First Chamber to prevent the cession of Elmina. A spokesman of the local population went specially to The Hague for this purpose.[135] The Conservative Utrecht lecturer C. W. Vreede began to collect petitions at the last minute.[136] But despite a lot of criticism, all three treaties were finally passed by the First Chamber – the Gold Coast Agreement by 29 to 6 and the other two unanimously.[137]

It is worth noting that when the treaties were discussed in Parliament, a good deal of attention was paid to Acheh, both by advocates and opponents. This is all the more remarkable because in recent literature the impression has been given that MPs approved the Sumatra Treaty rather carelessly.[138] Nor can it be said, however, that Fransen van de Putte, Van Bosse and other influential Liberals

130. *Bijlagen Handelingen Tweede Kamer* (Parliamentary Reports of the Second Chamber, Appendices) 1871–2, pp. 914f., 918f.

131. *Handelingen Tweede Kamer* (Parliamentary Reports of the Second Chamber), 15 December 1871, pp. 640 and 643.

132. Ibid., pp. 644–5.

133. Ibid., p. 646.

134. Ibid., p. 648.

135. Baesjou, *Asante Embassy*, pp. 43–4; for the petitions of the population of Elmina to the government and the Dutch Parliament, see documents nos 46, 65, 117.

136. For the petitions, see Vreede, *Hoofdartikelen*, pp. 104–5.

137. *Handelingen Eerste Kamer* (Parliamentary Reports of the First Chamber), 17 January 1872, p. 220; ibid., 18 January, pp. 228 and 230.

138. Van der Wal, 'Nederlandse expansie', p. 49; cf. Van 't Veer, *Atjeh-oorlog*, p. 34; Reid, *Contest*, pp. 71–3.

were consciously aiming at a war with Acheh. They preferred, by far, a gradual expansion modelled on Siak.

Mirandolle and other Liberals, on the other hand, did not want to see the future expansion in Sumatra linked to the relatively peace-loving model of Siak. Van Bosse sensed a rather aggressive attitude towards Acheh, even among his own civil servants. 'As regards our guardianship of Acheen, they are pushing rather hard at the Department', he wrote to Loudon. 'I will keep it in check, though I would like you to be aware of it, because the whole matter is sure to get into your hands.[139] Loudon took this advice to heart. The result, which is now well known, had not at first been envisaged, but several MPs had already warned of it during the discussions of the Anglo-Dutch treaties.

Overseas Trade

One particular question which had always played a part in the background of the Anglo-Dutch treaties, but which came to the fore in a number of issues at the beginning of the 1870s, was whether overseas trade ought to follow the Dutch flag or whether it should be aimed at new markets outside the colonies. This question assumed a central position in the revision of the East Indian tariff laws. Although this revision was finally carried out along Liberal lines, Dutch traders had more difficulties with it than with the cession of the unimportant African possessions. The initiative therefore came from Batavia, where the Chamber of Commerce advocated the abolition of differential rights and all export rights as early as 1870. Entrepreneurs in Java were beginning to feel concerned about their future links with the world market after the opening of the Suez Canal and once the system of forced cultivation had been abolished.[140] At the time, Dutch trade and shipping had difficulties adapting to the changing circumstances. As his first parliamentary bill, Minister van Bosse did indeed achieve the total abolition of differential rights, but he maintained the tariffs at reduced levels, for financial reasons, at a level of 10 per cent for import and 3 to 6 per cent for export.

The Dutch Chambers of Commerce which had been consulted by

---

139. Van Bosse to Loudon, 2 May 1871, Loudon Collection.
140. Cf. Boon, *Van Lansberge*, pp. 87–8. For the advice given by the Batavian Chamber of Commerce to the governor-general, see the entry 'Rechten (in-, uit- en doorvoer)' (Rights (imports, exports and transit)) in the *ENI*.

Van Bosse reacted to this Liberal bill with mixed feelings. One single Chamber – the Groningen one – whole-heartedly supported the abolition of any kind of protection.[141] Of the Chambers that were more involved with colonial trade, the Amsterdam Chamber of Commerce was most negative in its judgement. With 9 votes to 5, they passed a motion advising the Dutch Parliament that the abolition must be regarded as 'highly unfavourable', warning that, due to the threat of British competition, it would lead to 'unpredictable disadvantages for our trade and industry'. The *Nederlandsche Industrieel* (Dutch Industrialist) and the Chambers of Commerce in the smaller towns expressed themselves in similar terms.[142] The Rotterdam Chamber and the management of the Netherlands Trading Company approved of the abolition of differential rights in principle but suggested a gradual introduction of free trade for a period of six years. They felt that since Dutch trade and industry had been under protection in the colonies for such a long time, they were insufficiently prepared for the sudden abolition of all protectionist policies.[143]

A gradual introduction of free trade was also advocated by the Twente Chamber of Commerce. Manufacturers in Twente even suggested a further lowering of rights for the textiles that were imported to the East Indies.[144] However, Van Bosse went ahead with his original proposals. In his memorandum of his parliamentary bill, which he submitted to the Second Chamber on 18 October 1871, he explained that the introduction of free trade was a 'demand of the time' and would become even more painful if it were postponed any further.[145] He found support in the Liberal press. The *Handelsblad* and *De Economist* described the criticism of the Chambers of Commerce as rather exaggerated and pessimistic.[146] In

141. Cf. *Nederlandsche Industrieel*, 26 February 1871.
142. *Verslag KvK Amsterdam* (Report of the Amsterdam Chamber of Commerce) 1871, pp. 132f. For the petitions of the Association of Dutch Industrialists and the advice of the Brabant Chamber of Commerce, see *Nederlandsche Industrieel*, 23 April and 16 December 1871.
143. Cf. ibid., 19 March 1871.
144. Cf. ibid., 6 November 1870, 12 and 19 February, 7 March 1871, for the advice from the Almelo and Enschede Chambers of Commerce as well as the petitions from Twente industrialists.
145. Cf. *Bijlagen Handelingen Tweede Kamer* (Parliamentary Reports of the Second Chamber, Appendices) 1871–2, pp. 500f.
146. H. A. Wijnne, 'Herziening van het Indisch tarief van in- en uitvoerregten', *De Economist* (1871) II, pp. 893f.; *Het Handelsblad*, 17 and 18 March. The introduction of free trade was also applauded at a meeting of the East India Society on 25 April: *Handelingen*, pp. 87f.

the Second Chamber, the bill was also received quite favourably at the committee level. Apart from economic arguments, the interim report also emphasised the political reasons for abolishing trade protection which Van Bosse had put forward in his confidential correspondence: free trade meant that other countries would feel 'less inclined to envy our beautiful overseas possessions'.[147]

After Van Bosse, his successor Fransen van de Putte took over the bill, though with one significant modification. In accordance with the wishes of the Twente industrialists, he lowered the import rights for manufactured goods further, bringing them down to 6 per cent.[148]

At the open debate in October 1872 there were only a few MPs who still opposed the abolition of differential rights on grounds of principle. The Amsterdam delegate 's Jacobs, who had spoken so highly of free trade at the cession of Elmina, now rejected it as being in conflict with the interests of commerce, industry and the treasury.[149] A number of Liberal MPs from Twente and the surrounding area still proposed a gradual introduction of free trade. However, their amendment was rejected.[150] Kappeyne van de Coppello's proposal, which would have abolished export rights completely, was equally unsuccessful.[151] The entire bill was finally carried by a narrow majority of 38 to 36.[152] On 15 November it was also passed by the First Chamber, with 21 to 14 votes. In this Chamber, the Twente industrialist C. T. Stork made a remarkable plea for the abolition of protectionism in colonial trade. 'No country in the world is in a better position for commerce and . . . industry than ours', he stated.

> But what we don't have is connections with the foreign regions. Except for our overseas possessions, there are no Dutchmen in Asia or America. Everywhere there are Germans, Swiss and English. We are therefore served less well or more expensively than other trading nations. This can be different and it *must* be different.[153]

147. *Bijlagen Handelingen Tweede Kamer* (Parliamentary Reports of the Second Chamber, Appendices), 1871–2, p. 1372; cf. note 96 above.
148. *Bijlagen Handelingen Tweede Kamer* (Parliamentary Reports of the Second Chamber, Appendices), 1872–3, no. 57.
149. *Handelingen Tweede Kamer* (Parliamentary Reports of the Second Chamber), 9 October 1872, pp. 88f.
150. With 51 votes to 21, ibid., 10 October, p. 140.
151. With 46 votes to 24, Ibid., 14 October, p. 163.
152. Ibid., 15 October, p. 168.
153. *Handelingen Eerste Kamer* (Parliamentary Reports of the First Chamber), 15 November 1872, pp. 88–9.

During the same few years, therefore, initiatives were developed on several different sides that were aimed at improving the position of the Dutch abroad. In a petition to the king, in 1871, the Amsterdam Chamber of Commerce demanded that the Netherlands should take the initiative and press for a further reform of international maritime law. In particular, it was felt that private property at sea should be protected more and that contraband goods should be defined more narrowly than had been done at the Paris Conference in 1856.[154] The government decided to explore this possibility, and to sound out the ground Gericke wrote to the ambassadors in the big European capitals. When it turned out that Britain continued to be opposed to any further reform, the minister dropped the matter again, despite insistence from the Chamber of Commerce.[155] A number of circles also demanded that the Dutch navy should resume the showing of the flag in overseas waters. In 1869 ships were withdrawn from the auxiliary squadron in the East Indies and sent to Japan, Turkey and the Persian Gulf. In the course of the 1870s, warships were sent to foreign ports regularly, particularly when trade problems seemed imminent.[156]

However, the most significant contribution to the strengthening of the Dutch position outside Europe was seen in the expansion and reform of the Dutch consular service. In the first place, both within the Second Chamber and outside it, there were proposals for more salaried consulates to be established. Secondly, it was felt that Dutch nationals ought to be appointed to such posts.[157] The appointment of W. H. Read, an Englishman, as the Dutch consul-general in Singapore in 1871 must have been quite a thorn in the flesh for many people. And when Minister Roest van Limburg submitted a proposal to the Chamber which was aimed at extending the legal competence of consuls abroad, a number of general complaints about the functioning of the consular services were brought forward. The reorganisation of consular jurisdiction itself was

154. *Verslag KvK-Amsterdam* (Report of the Amsterdam Chamber of Commerce), 1871, pp. 119–24.
155. See Gericke's circular of 13 February 1871 and the reactions of the ambassadors: Woltring, *Bescheiden* I, nos 23, 26, 30–3, 38–9, 44. Cf. *Handelingen Tweede Kamer* (Parliamentary Reports of the Second Chamber), 19 November 1872, pp. 383f.
156. *Nederlandsche Industrieel*, 11 July 1869, 11 March 1877. For the showing of the flag in the Middle East during the Turkish–Russian War, see Woltring, *Bescheiden* II, no. 197 and 200–200A.
157. *Bijlagen Handelingen Tweede Kamer* (Parliamentary Reports of the Second Chamber, Appendices) 1868–9, pp. 587, 602–3.

greatly applauded and passed with an overwhelming majority.[158]

Subsequently, in 1874, minister Gericke prepared a consular service reform that was to go even further, though he felt that a lot of the criticism was exaggerated. With the appointment of ten to twelve salaried consuls, preferably Dutchmen, it was hoped that the Netherlands would reach the same level as other countries again. The minister made nearly 100,000 guilders available for this purpose, to be financed from the consular levies for Dutch trade and shipping. He also started training prospective consuls and improving the consular examinations.[159] However, these innovations were carried out with little enthusiasm after Gericke's retirement. Of the ten to twelve planned consulates, only four were actually created – that is newly established or extended – in Aden, Rio de Janeiro, Bangkok and Penang, whereas the consulate-generals in Tripoli and Elmina were reduced to unsalaried consulates.

Both the Dutch Parliament and the world of commerce therefore remained dissatisfied with the government's effort to promote Dutch overseas interest.[160] Indeed, the trade figures showed that Dutch trade in the East Indies had declined since the introduction of the new tariff law in 1874, while trade with the rest of the overseas world had hardly increased at all. The share of the East Indies in the Netherlands' exports had only dropped slightly: from 7.9 per cent in 1870 to 7.4 per cent in 1880. The reduction of imports was far more dramatic: from 15.9 per cent in 1870 to 6.7 per cent in 1880. The share of the other overseas territories, on the other hand, had increased a little: from 4.4 per cent to 5.4 per cent; while their export share had been reduced: from 2.2 to less than 1 per cent. In reality, however, export was greater, because many Dutch products were shipped via foreign ports. In the 1870s, this was probably done to an even greater extent than before, due to the decline of Dutch shipping in the overseas world.[161] In some circles, these figures obviously gave rise to a triumphant reiteration of their earlier warning against the introduction of free trade in the colonies. In the

---

158. Ibid., pp. 858f.; ibid., 1869–70, pp. 637f.; cf. *Handelingen Tweede Kamer* (Parliamentary Reports of the Second Chamber), 26 November 1871, pp. 990f.; ibid., 27 November, p. 1018.

159. *Bijlagen Handelingen Tweede Kamer* (Parliamentary Reports of the Second Chamber, Appendices) 1873–4, no. 156; cf. *Handelingen Tweede Kamer* (Parliamentary Reports of the Second Chamber), 24 March 1874, pp. 1186f.

160. Ibid., 8 December 1880, p. 593f. Cf. W. N. van Hamel, 'Ons consulaatwezen', *De Economist* (1876) II, pp. 1149f.; P. N. Muller, 'Verre Handelsvrienden', *De Gids* (1879) iv, pp. 163f.

161. *Statistiek* (1881) II. Cf. appendix 3.

Nederlandsche Industrieel it was even argued that unless protection was quickly introduced again, 'it would be more advantageous to sell the colonies at a good price or to hand them over on condition that Dutch trade companies can continue to establish themselves there in the same way as the British, German and other companies.' Even in *De Economist* there was a note of regret in view of the sudden and total abolition of differential rights.[162]

In general, however, the disappointing results were not ascribed to free trade, but to the long period of protectionism that had preceded it. This was also the conclusion of the parliamentary committee which, in 1874, had conducted an inquiry into the poor state of Dutch shipping.[163] Furthermore, one could point out a number of other impediments in overseas trade. Firstly, after the speculation crisis of 1873, there was a 'lull' in the European economy which had already led to an intensification of foreign competition with Dutch exports to overseas markets. Secondly, imports had suffered particularly when Javanese sugar exports had been shifted to Britain, which had abolished its excise duty on sugar in 1874. Finally, it was also felt that Dutch industrialists were generally not adventurous enough, that there was 'little enthusiasm among young traders and industrialists to establish themselves in foreign parts, particularly in the Dutch East Indies'.[164] However, the decline of the Netherlands might have been worse. The textile industry managed to maintain its sales very well in Java and other overseas markets. The loss of Javanese sugar was at least partly compensated for by tin and tobacco from Sumatra. And so the advice of the Liberal press that one should pursue the present path as before sounded quite realistic.[165]

---

162. *Nederlandsche Industrieel*, 27 April 1879, Cf. M. G. J. Rive, 'Onze handelsbelangen naar aanleiding van de Enquête', *Economist* (1876) I, p. 136.

163. Committee report of the 17 March 1875, *Bijlagen Handelingen Tweede Kamer* (Parliamentary Reports of the Second Chamber, Appendices) 1874–5, nos 7.1 and 10f. Cf. Muller, 'Handelsvrienden', p. 169; J. D. Veegens, 'Consignatiestelsel en handelsvloot', *Vragen des Tijds* (1876) I, pp. 231f.

164. Review of J. A. C. van Leeuwen, *Neêrland's Jongelingschap en Neêrland's Handel*, Amsterdam 1876, in *De Economist* (1876) I, p. 613.

165. Cf. N. G. Pierson, 'De crisis van 1873', ibid. I, pp. 837f.; *idem*, 'Kapitaalsbehoeften en internationaal verkeer', ibid. (1876) I, pp. 1f.; Muller, 'Handelsvrienden', pp. 69f.; S. van Houten, 'Onze Handelspolitiek', *Vragen des Tijds* (1879) II, pp. 322f. Cf. Bos, *Brits–Nederlandse handel*, pp. 83f., 252f.; De Jonge, *Industrialisatie*, pp. 30f., 110f.

Asia: the New Path to the East

Searching for new trade relations and markets, the Dutch industry was initially interested, above all, in Asia. As was noted in the report of the Amsterdam Chamber of Commerce in 1870, 'the opening of the Suez Canal obviously means that more attention is being paid to the East.'[166] In as far as the Dutch government was actively involved in promoting overseas trade relations, it concentrated mainly on Asia during the 1870s. From the very beginning, the developments around the Suez Canal were followed very closely by the secretaries of the colonies and of foreign affairs, because of the great economic and strategic significance of the canal for relations with the East Indies.

The international conference in Constantinople on the regulation of ship measurements and the levying of tolls, which started in 1874 and continued for many years, was given a large amount of attention. The Dutch delegate was M. H. Jansen, a retired naval officer and nautical scientist who became a member of the Privy Council in 1875. He was instructed by Gericke to co-operate as much as possible with the British delegate at the conference, because British interests in the French canal society were seen as 'largely identical' with Dutch interests. Both wanted to achieve inexpensive and unimpeded transit.[167] After Britain had acquired the majority holding of the canal society, concluded a treaty with the society on the sizes of ships and the levying of tolls and alluded to an occupation of the canal during the Russian–Turkish War in 1877, the Netherlands became more independent in its policies and began to promote a neutral, international status for the canal.[168] Careful steps were taken to ensure that the rights of all users would be recognised in the treaty on ship measurements and tolls. But when it became obvious that the British government was not very enthusiastic about this Dutch initiative, Minister van Lynden van Sandenburg decided in 1879 to 'let the matter rest, at least for the time being'.[169]

Meanwhile it had become obvious that, despite a difficult start, the Netherlands was making more and more use of the canal. In

166. *Verslag KvK Amsterdam* (Report of the Amsterdam Chamber of Commerce) 1871, p. 12.
167. Woltring, *Bescheiden* I, no. 447.
168. Ibid., II, nos 101, 167, 269–71, 283.
169. Ibid., no. 442, cf. nos 406 and 413.

1876 Dutch ships were the third most frequent vessels in the canal, after Britain and France.[170] At first, it did indeed look as if the increasing use of the canal would lead to an intensification of trade relations with the Middle East. But by the end of the 1870s it had become obvious that Dutch vessels using the canal were mainly on the way to the East Indies. In 1869 the Dutch consul-general in Alexandria had already pointed out the potential significance of the Arabic world after the opening of the Suez Canal.[171] Dutch traders, too, showed some interest at first. However, actual initiatives were limited to a small number of isolated commercial transactions.[172] According to the consul in Jeddah, a financially secure company would be necessary for profitable and lasting trade, following the example of the African Trade Association in Rotterdam. He developed detailed plans for Dutch trade in the Arabic countries, with vessels from the East Indies calling at Jeddah on the return journey and delivering Javanese pilgrims.[173]

The Consular Reports show that Dutch tobacco and alcoholic liquor were particularly popular in the Middle East, although they were hardly ever supplied by Dutch ships. The new consul-general in Alexandria, J. W. Anslijn, therefore said it was 'inexplicable' that in 1879 only a single Dutch vessel had called at the harbour, while 69 Dutch ships had passed through the Suez Canal that year and considerable quantities of Dutch and Egyptian goods had been sold in both directions via London and Liverpool.[174] The consul-general at Aden expressed himself in a similar vein.[175] And although trade with British India was already quite substantial, it could – according to local consuls – be far more effective if Dutch ships were involved more directly rather than going mainly via England.[176] The same view was held with regard to Dutch trade in China and Japan. Indeed, in the case of these large empires with millions of potential

---

170. Of a total of 1,461 ships which passed through the Suez Canal, 1,092 sailed under the British flag, 89 under the French flag and 59 under the Dutch flag: *Consulaire verslagen* (Consular Reports) 1877, p. 302.

171. Ibid., 1869 I, p. 156.

172. *Verslag KvK Amsterdam* (Report of the Amsterdam Chamber of Commerce), 1870, pp. 12f.; cf. N. J. den Tex, 'Onze handel in de Perzische golf en de Roode Zee', *De Economist* 19 (1871) I, pp. 1f. and 148f.

173. *Consulaire verslagen* (Consular Reports) 1874 I, pp. 515–44.

174. Ibid. 1880, pp. 258–9.

175. Ibid. 1876, pp. 13–15; ibid. 1877, p. 19; ibid. 1880, pp. 16–17.

176. Cf. the reports of the Dutch consuls in Bombay, Calcutta, Karachi and Colombo, ibid. 1877, *passim*.

buyers, such a view did not fail to make an impression in the Netherlands.

Relations with China had become the centre of interest around 1870, in connection with a rather odd conflict between the Foreign Minister, Roest van Limburg, and the Second Chamber. In the 1870 budget, Roest had assigned a certain amount for a full-scale embassy in China. The delicate nature of relations with Chinese government functionaries, said the minister, made it desirable to have a diplomatic representative. Many Liberal MPs thought differently. Since commerce formed the more important part of relations with China, they felt that a consulate was by far the most adequate type of Dutch representation, and indeed it was much cheaper. The MP for Deventer, G. Dumbar – known as the 'diplomat killer' who also initiated the abolition of the Dutch embassy at the Vatican in 1871 – submitted an amendment whereby the budget item of the embassy in China would be deleted. He was supported by MPs who referred to trade statistics, arguing that commerce with China had been relatively insignificant, with import figures of about one million guilders and export of about half a million over the preceding years. Even Hoffmann, the Anti-Revolutionary MP, who had himself traded with China in the 1840s, expected very little for the future, considering that most protective measures in overseas trade and shipping had been lifted. In reality, though, the Chinese market was far more significant than could be gathered from the trade statistics, especially for Dutch export. However, even the minister was not really aware of this, as could be gathered from his feeble reaction to the Chamber's criticism. The amendment was carried by 37 votes to 35.[177]

The world of commerce and particularly the textile industry reacted quite vehemently to this decision of the Second Chamber. In the first Chamber, Stork stated that at least four million guilders worth of textiles were exported from Twente to China via London and Hamburg each year.[178] The Rotterdam Chamber of Commerce initiated a petition movement, urging the Foreign Minister to establish diplomatic representation as soon as possible. The Almelo Chamber of Commerce argued in their petition that 'a quarter, if

177. Cf. *Handelingen Tweede Kamer* (Parliamentary Reports of the Second Chamber), 2 December 1869, pp. 413f.

178. *Handelingen Eerste Kamer* (Parliamentary Reports of the First Chamber), 12 January 1870, p. 133.

not a third, of our manufactured goods are exported to China.'[179] The minister subsequently submitted a new bill for the establishment of an embassy in China. This proposal, too, was rejected, though this time with only 35 votes to 34.[180] Finally, in the 1872 budget, Minister Gericke followed a suggestion that had been made by the Conservative MP W. van Goltstein as early as 1869, that there should be a consul-general in China with the diplomatic status of a chargé d'affaires, as in Venezuela and Japan. This proposal was passed by the Second Chamber without a roll-call vote.[181]

The first Dutch representative to be appointed was J. H. Ferguson, a former naval officer and the last Dutch governor of the Gold Coast. After his appointment in 1872, he pursued every avenue to raise his diplomatic status. He succeeded in 1884, when he was reappointed as 'envoy and consul-general'. For the promotion of commerce, which the members of the Chamber apparently regarded as important, diplomatic status did indeed seem to be indispensable.[182]

Ferguson certainly tried very actively to find new opportunities for Dutch commerce. In a detailed report on 'China's agriculture, industry and trade'; he stated that Dutch commerce did indeed proceed to a large extent via other countries. The Netherlands itself sold large quantities of textiles to China and received Chinese tea in return, though the extent and value of this indirect trade was impossible to determine. Dutch shipping was obviously deficient in this respect.[183] To put an end to 'such an odd phenomenon that a mainly seafaring nation should export the products of its industry . . . through foreign soil', he suggested opening a regular government-sponsored steamship service to China and Japan – via the East Indies, which had always had intensive trade relations with the Far East. Ferguson felt that such a step was urgent, because increasing British and American competition was threatening to push the

179. *Bijlagen Handelingen Tweede Kamer* (Parliamentary Reports of the Second Chamber, Appendices) 1869–70, p. 1423.

180. *Handelingen Tweede Kamer* (Parliamentary Reports of the Second Chamber), 13 May 1870, p. 1398. The petitions of the Chambers of Commerce of Rotterdam, Amsterdam, Almelo and Leiden as well as the Twente Association for the Promotion of Industry and Commerce had been added to the bill as appendices; cf. *Bijlagen Handelingen Tweede Kamer* (Parliamentary Reports of the Second Chamber, Appendices) 1869–70, pp. 1421f.

181. *Handelingen Tweede Kamer* (Parliamentary Reports of the Second Chamber), 15 November 1871, p. 255; cf. ibid., 2 December 1869, p. 414.

182. Cf. van Dongen, *Neutraliteit*, p. 51f.

183. Cf. *Consulaire verslagen* II (Consular Reports II) 1874, pp. 1109–52. Cf. ibid. (1876), pp. 303–5.

Dutch textile industry out of the Chinese market. This was also the result of the lax attitude of many Twente manufacturers: 'Only very few of them take the trouble to work regularly for this market, and most . . . manufacturers only turn to China when times are bad for other markets.'[184]

The government followed Ferguson's advice. The 1879 colonial budget included a 100,000-guilder subsidy to the Netherlands Steamshipping Company for the opening of a regular link with the Far East. This initiative, however, was received with considerable scepticism in the Second Chamber. Several Liberal MPs questioned the subsidy on the principle of private enterprise. They were supported by some Conservative MPs, such as W. Wintgens, who were concerned about 'an influx of Chinese' into the East Indies. The subsidy was rejected by 36 votes to 35.[185] The following year, though, a subsidy was given to a different company, and with 40,000 guilders the Dutch East Indian Steamship Company – which was in fact partly British – was helped to provide a regular service between the East Indies and China.[186]

In Japan Dutch shipping had declined even further, and during the 1870s the market share of the Dutch textile industry was almost lost completely, even though – according to the Consular Reports – there continued to be a clear demand for certain Dutch materials, such as turkey reds from Twente and Leiden.[187] Diplomatic relations with Japan were dominated by negotiations to repeal the Shimonoseki Convention. These talks had been initiated by the new Imperial government. The Japanese delegation which visited America and Europe during 1872–3 in order to find out Western views, also came to the Netherlands in 1873. Apart from trade relations, Minister Gericke also took the opportunity to bring up the situation of Japanese Christians.[188]

In the negotiations that followed in Japan, the Netherlands initially pursued the same line as the more powerful countries,

184. Ibid., pp. 1006f.; cf. ibid. (1876), p. 796.

185. *Handelingen Tweede Kamer* (Parliamentary Reports of the Second Chamber), 28 November 1878, p. 166.

186. *Handelingen Tweede Kamer* (Parliamentary Reports of the Second Chamber), 23 October 1879, pp. 238. Cf. Brugmans, *Chinavaart*, pp. 26–7.

187. Cf. reports of the consuls in Kanagawa, Yokohama and Nagasaki, *Consulaire Verslagen* I (Consular Reports I) 1869, pp. 142–59, II, 9–23; ibid., 1879, pp. 528–38.

188. Cf. report of the talks between Gericke and the Japanese delegation on 4 March 1873, Woltring, *Bescheiden* I, no. 354; cf. nos 174, 176, 181, 212, 232, 285. For the journey of the Japanese delegation and the subsequent negotiations, see Araki, *Geschichte*, pp. 85f.

aiming at a remission of Japan's financial obligations in exchange for the opening of new harbours and a lowering of tariffs. However, the Dutch representative in Japan, E. W. F. Wttewaal van Stoetwegen (a name that became relevant again around 1900), wanted to cling to the extra-territorial rights which the Netherlands had acquired under Shogun's rule. 'After all, it cannot be denied', commented the diplomat, 'that we are dealing here with ignorant and uncivilised heathens whose concepts of all sorts of things are so widely different from ours that one cannot possibly grant them the right to pass laws which will then be binding for us and which they might even force us to obey.'[189]

In 1880 the Japanese government declared Wttewaal *persona non grata*, claiming that he had leaked confidential information of the negotiations to the English-speaking press. Wttewaal gladly accepted his untimely transfer, although he felt that the Japanese government deserved 'severe chastisement'. He was alluding to the Dutch warship which had been sent to Japanese waters for the purpose of showing the flag and on which he was to travel back. However, Minister Van Lynden made it quite plain that there was nothing demonstrative about the showing of the flag, and so far as he was concerned, Wttewaal might just as well travel back by mail-boat.[190]

Africa: Trade without Colonies

During the debates on the Anglo–Dutch treaties, minister Gericke and some MPs had argued forcefully against the view that Africa was the continent of the future. However, Dutch trade in the 1870s turned out to be comparatively more successful in Africa than in Asia, where expectations had at first been so much higher. At the time, Gericke had thought of Africa as a scene of 'barbarity, continuous war, murder and arson'.[191] The wars, however, which ravaged the Gold Coast during the 1870s were to a large extent

189. Woltring, *Bescheiden* II, no. 544; cf. nos 410–13, 429, 523. For a memorandum of the second (trade-political) section of 1878 on following the course of the European powers, see no. 375A.

190. Ibid., nos 505–51; cf. 535, 539. However, Van Lynden stated in a letter to the Naval Defence Secretary that 'the presence of a Dutch warship would remind the Japanese population and government that even the Netherlands disposes of the means to defend, if required, the interests of its subjects at the most remote points of the globe and to give emphasis to its demands'; cf. note 1 of no. 550A.

191. *Handelingen Tweede Kamer* (Parliamentary Reports of the Second Chamber), 7 July 1871, p. 1128.

caused by the cession of Elmina and the hasty withdrawal of the Dutch in 1872. The Elmina population strongly resisted the arrival of the new British rulers who had traditionally protected their enemies, the Fante. Their resistance was supported by their traditional allies, the powerful Ashanti. In 1873, the British broke local resistance by force and a year later started their first large-scale expedition against the Ashanti.[192] In the Netherlands, these bloody events gave rise to bitter Conservative criticism of the government, which was accused of neglecting Dutch responsibilities towards the Elminese population. The Liberal press, on the other hand, generally showed itself relieved that the Netherlands had finally got rid of these duties.[193] After the disorderly transfer, the government was only interested in whether or not it could continue to recruit soldiers for the East Indies in Elmina.[194] Once the colonial administration had been transferred, Dutch trade on the Gold Coast was indeed soon ousted by British trade, as Muller had predicted. His firm, incidentally, was not hit very hard by the cession of Elmina, because in the 1870s trade with Liberia was expanding considerably.[195]

The trade of the Rotterdam-based African Trade Association (Afrikaansche Handelsvereeniging, AHV) in the Congo area was even more important and successful. The AHV continue to grow throughout the 1870s until it became the biggest European establishment in that area, with about fifty factories. As mentioned above, the AHV at first sold mainly British goods, though the spirits which, after manufactured goods, formed the largest part of the turnover, were definitely of Dutch origin. In 1870 about half of the export to the Congo – goods to the value of about 1.2 million guilders – came from the Netherlands. Imports, which consisted mainly of palm oil, amounted to 1.6 million guilders.[196] Despite fluctuations, the turnover of the AHV increased steadily throughout the 1870s. At least on paper, profits were quite impressive, and a

192. Cf. Baesjou, *Asante Embassy*, pp. 34–6; Coombs, *Gold Coast*, pp. 98f.

193. Cf. G. H. van Soest, 'Hoe een kolonie te loor gaat', *TNI* (1875) I, pp. 204f.; W. J. Knoop, 'Iets over ons krijgswezen', *Die Gids* (1874) 38 iv, pp. 89–91; *Het Dagblad von Zuid-Holland en 's-Gravenhage*, 15 July 1874.

194. Cf. Baesjou, *Asante Embassy*, nos 101 and 137; Woltring, *Bescheiden* II, nos 199, 288, 331.

195. *Consulaire verslagen* (Consular Reports) 1876, pp. 217–22; ibid., 1879, pp. 531–4.

196. Robidé van der Aa, *Afrikaansche Studiën*, pp. 129–30. Cf. Anstey, *Britain*, pp. 30–1; Wesseling, 'Nederland', pp. 562–3.

dividend of around 10 per cent was often achieved. Again, Prince Henry was involved in this successful business, and from 1877 onwards he was honorary chairman of the association.

One of the most important shareholders of the AHV, M. Mees explained the secret behind the great success in a letter to Stork in 1875. In his view, this was mainly due to its modern form of organisation as a limited liability company as well as its having the courage to develop new initiatives on the new, though risky, African market. He also gave a diagnosis of the disappointing results of Dutch commerce in Asia and South America: 'The main error of the firms which I have seen languishing recently has been that they keep to the same terrain which has long been exploited already and where the owners of existing businesses have all the advantages on their side.'[197] Although in 1879 success seemed to be based largely on the ingenious malversation of Pincoffs, the most important basis of trade must have been sound. After Pincoffs had fled to America and his company had gone into liquidation, the New African Trade Company Ltd was founded, mainly due to Muller's efforts, and when it continued its trade with the Congo, it achieved even better results.[198]

With the success of Dutch trade, the Dutch public also became increasingly interested in the activities of explorers and missionaries in 'the dark continent'. The Geographical Society attached great significance to the opening of the Congo basin – a project that seemed promising both from an economic and scientific point of view. In 1876, at King Leopold's request, Veth took part in the international geographic conference which was held in Brussels with this aim in mind. Veth and other committee members, such as C. M. Kan and W. F. Versteeg, worked enthusiastically on the formation of the Association Internationale Africaine in 1877. Having indignantly rejected the accusation that King Leopold also had non-humanitarian aims, Veth saw the association as something that could 'increase the glory of the nation' and 'promote patriotic interests'.[199] The AHV also showed interest in Leopold's initiatives. The Dutch section of the association was under the chairmanship of

197. Mees, *Man*, pp. 527–8.
198. Ibid., 418f.; cf. Oosterwijk, *Vlucht*, pp. 138f.; Muller, *Muller*, pp. 303f. and 321f.
199. *TAG* (1879), pp. 80f. The popular illustrated magazines *Eigen Haard* (Own Home) and *De Aarde en haar Volken* (The Earth and its Peoples) also gave a considerable amount of attention to Africa and voyages of exploration.

Prince Henry, and its most prominent members were Veth, Kan, Pincoffs and Kerdijk. Pincoffs seems to have succeeded in persuading King Leopold that priority should be given, for the time being, to the scientific exploration of the Congo basin, rather than opening one's own trade companies.[200]

The Dutch Missionary Society also showed interest in Africa during the 1870s, even though no active initiatives were made. Within the framework of general missionary theory, as advocated by Neurdenburg, Africa took an important place as a field for experiments. If the most 'barbarian' races of the world should be open to christianisation and civilisation, then missionary work could succeed anywhere. He believed that Africa was ideal for 'regular' commerce, but he firmly opposed trade in arms, gunpowder and strong liquor, which were also sold to Africa by the Rotterdam companies. He saw this as the most important source of the slave trade and tribal warfare which was hampering African progress. Secular academic disciplines, particularly human geography and ethnography, also had an important place in Neurdenburg's concept of modern missionary work.[201] Virtually all observers, incidentally, agreed that it was important for trade, science and missions to work together in the development of the black continent. Colonial possessions were not regarded very highly in this context, and the association was welcomed so enthusiastically in the Netherlands precisely because of its non-colonial character.

The first symptoms of Africa's approaching partition, of which Leopold's association was one, were not followed up immediately by Dutch diplomats. Indeed, Dutch foreign policies even showed reserve when direct commercial interests were at issue – an attitude for which there were good reasons. In 1876, there was a conflict between the Dutch consul in Liberia, who was also the general agent of Muller's company at the time, and the Liberian government. Although Muller advocated powerful action, the Dutch Foreign Office commissioned the consul-general of Elmina to hold an inquiry in Liberia. This showed that Muller had indeed used his consular privileges rather liberally in the interests of his own busi-

200. Cf. Wesseling, 'Nederland', pp. 565–6; Oosterwijk, *Vlucht*, pp. 143f.
201. J. C. Neurdenburg, 'Wat heeft de aanraking met christenen geleerd omtrent de vatbaarheid der niet-christenen voor het Christendom?' *Madedeelingen* (1876) pp. 91–3. Cf. E. H. Lasonder, 'Het wederkeerig belang der zending en der taal-, land- en volkenkunde', ibid., pp. 209f.; J. van Loenen, 'Zending en onderwijs', ibid. (1878) pp. 211–14.

ness. The matter was then settled amicably with the Liberian government – a result that did not satisfy Muller at all. According to a departmental note, he would have preferred an ultimatum of the kind: 'Do as H. H. Muller & Co. demand, or we'll bomb Monrovia.'[202]

However, when the Portuguese government was trying to extend its sovereignty around the Congo estuary from Angola, the Dutch Foreign Office showed more sympathy for the complaints of the Dutch trading interests, the *AHV*. The Portuguese colonial administration had a particularly bad name among traders, because of its high tariffs and other obstacles which it imposed on commerce. Minister Van der Does de Willebois shared this view, but he preferred to contact the British government first before taking any direct action against Portugal. And after British traders, too, had voiced their protest, the British government started to exert pressure on the Portuguese government so that the latter decided not to link its claim on the Congo estuary with practical consequences.[203]

When the first results of Disraeli's 'Imperial Policy' were reported from London by Van Bylandt, the Dutch secretaries of foreign affairs reacted with great caution. The focal points of Britain's new policy were in North and South Africa. As we have seen before, the position of the Suez Canal was taken particularly seriously in The Hague, but more because of its potential implications for Asia rather than Africa. Therefore, when Britain was threatening to occupy the canal during the Russian–Turkish War in 1877, Dutch diplomats mainly expressed an interest in the unimpeded passage of troops heading for the Acheh War.[204] And when Britain annexed the South African Republic in 1877, the Dutch government carefully avoided all comment and distanced itself as much as possible from the protests of public opinion and also from the attempts of the Transvaal deputation which tried to seek support from the Netherlands in 1878. Indeed, according to Van Bylandt, 'the desire to turn that part of South Africa which is suited for colonisation

202. Cf. the summary of the meeting of the Second Sub-department on 31 December 1882, Woltring, *Bescheiden* III, no. 261; cf. ibid. II, nos 207–207A, 327, 360–360A.

203. Van der Does to Van Bylandt, 20 November 1876; ibid., no. 206. Cf. nos 208, 210, 217–18, 222, 232; Anstey, *Britain*, pp. 40f. See also A. Jansen, 'Het Portugeesch koloniaal bestuur', *De Economist* (1879) II, pp. 94f.

204. Woltring, *Bescheiden* II, nos 255, 258, 263, 269–71, 276, 286. Cf. Anderson, *Eastern Question*, pp. 200f.

into an exclusively British possession is natural and in order.'[205]

During the 1870s interest in South Africa increased in the Netherlands. It was regularly pointed out that there were opportunities for emigration and commerce, though in practice not many people made use of them.[206] Nevertheless, quite a few Dutch emigrants had acquired important positions as Protestant ministers or civil servants in the two Boer republics. Indeed, in 1872 the Dutch minister Th. F. Burgers, who was a liberal both politically and in his religion, was elected president of the South African Republic. In 1875–6 he visited the Netherlands in order to find support for his plans to develop the Transvaal by laying a railway line to Delagoa Bay in Mozambique. He even succeeded in obtaining a loan from the world of finance in Amsterdam. His secretary, Th. M. Tromp, gave lectures on the importance of railway links for the future relations between the Netherlands and the Transvaal, among others for the Dutch Geographical Society.[207] At Burgers's request, a trade and friendship treaty between the Netherlands and the South African Republic was signed in 1876.[208]

When, in 1877, the news of the British annexation became known in the Netherlands, reactions varied. Vreede made a fierce protest to the British government as well as an appeal to the British people, asking for a repeal of the annexation. At the same time, he criticised the Dutch government sharply for its lax attitude.[209] There were also some critical voices from liberal academic circles, though the response was limited.[210] In the Anti-Revolutionary *Standaard* the annexation was only condemned, to some extent, by Kuyper and his friend F. Lion Cachet who, as a fundamentalist minister, had been one of Burgers's most vehement opponents in South Africa.[211]

205. Woltring, *Bescheiden* II, no. 396; cf. nos 194, 300, 305, 381. For the British annexation, see also Schreuder, *Scramble*, pp. 13f.

206. The consul-general in Cape Town noted that there was still very little trade with the Boer republics or immigration into them; cf. *Consulaire verslagen* (Consular Reports) 1871 II, pp. 252–5; ibid. (1876), pp. 217–22.

207. *TAG* (1877) pp. 336f.; cf. W. A. van Rees, 'Onze Hollandsche Broeders in Zuid-Afrika', *De Gids* 40 (1876) I, pp. 331f. For Burgers's visit see also Van Winter, *Hollanders* I, pp. 12f.; Schutte, 'Nederland', pp. 570–1.

208. *Bijlagen Handeligen Tweede Kamer* (Parliamentary Reports of the Second Chamber, Appendices) 1876–7, no. 156; cf. Woltring, *Bescheiden* II, no. 108.

209. Vreede, *Hoofdartikelen*, pp. 288–302.

210. Vreede's Utrecht petition was also signed by the Liberal lecturers C. M. Kan and P. Harting, while a Leiden petition was supported, among others, by R. Fruin, H. Kern, P. A. van der Litz and J. T. Buys; cf. Van Cittert-Eymers and Kipp, *Herinneringen*, pp. 134–5; Vreede, *Hoofdartikelen*, p. 292.

211. Van Koppen, *Kuyper*, pp. 18–19, 64f.

In Christian circles, there was certainly no general sympathy for the Boers. Because of their callous treatment of the black populations, they had been condemned quite sternly by the Anti-Revolutionary revival movement during the 1840s and 1850s. Neurdenburg now more or less demanded a better treatment of the blacks as a condition for supporting South Africa's aspirations to independence.[212] The liberal *Handelsblad* no longer rejected the annexation out of hand, either. The confused and bankrupt situation of the South African Republic during the last year of Burgers's presidency had failed to make a very good impression on the business world of Amsterdam.[213] When, after the annexation, the government laconically withdrew its bill for a friendship treaty, the Second Chamber also refrained from commenting. Only the Conservative MP Wintgens emphatically expressed his desire that 'a single word of profound, heartfelt sympathy for our brothers, the Dutch in South Africa, should be spoken in the Dutch Parliament'.[214]

South America: Colonies without Trade

During the period of modern imperialism, European interest was not, in the first place, directed towards South America. Very little was still expected of the 'old' colonies, which used to be exploited by means of slaves, although plantation economy was continued with Indian and Chinese contract labour. The Monroe Doctrine was fully respected after Napoleon III's Mexican adventure in order to prevent formal imperialism from coming from the European side. Trade relations with the turbulent Latin American countries were to a large extent dominated by Britain, although competition with the United States and Germany was increasing.

In the 1870s Dutch policies towards South America were mainly directed at consolidating the existing position of the Netherlands. This had already become obvious in the organisation of emigration to Surinam, which Van Bosse had carried out without much enthusiasm to ensure at least the continuation of plantation economy.[215] It was to become even more apparent in the conflict

---

212. J. C. Neurdenburg, 'De oorlog in de Transvaal', *Mededeelingen* (1877) pp. 53–5.

213. *Het Handelsblad*, 2 May 1877.

214. *Handelingen Tweede Kamer* (Parliamentary Reports of the Second Chamber), 9 May 1877, p. 1345.

215. Cf. Willemsen, *Koloniale politiek*, pp. 99–100; Tinker, *System*, pp. 112–13.

with Venezuela, when the Dutch government was even prepared to risk a war, if necessary, in order to keep Curaçao and maintain Dutch interests in Venezuela.

Dutch involvement in Venezuela, which continually dominated Dutch foreign politics during the 1870s, has been described in detail by Goslinga, so that it is sufficient here to give a brief survey of the most important points.[216] The traditional components of the conflict consisted, in the first place, of friction between each successive Venezuelan government and Curaçao trading houses such as Jesurun, which took an active part in the turbulent domestic affairs, including the smuggling of weapons. Secondly, the delicate position of Curaçao as a place of exile for political refugees from Venezuela also played an important part. And finally, the Netherlands, too, had its part in Venezuela's international financial debt, which regularly gave rise to conflicts with its creditors concerning the repayments. A new element came into play with the emergence of an expansionist nationalism in Venezuela, embodied in the person of President A. Guzman Blanco whose most important prominent aspiration was the annexation of Curaçao. The Dutch, on the other hand, were now beginning to be concerned about a possible intervention by the great powers, especially the United States and Germany.

After diplomatic relations had been resumed in 1870, irritation over economic, financial and political problems increased considerably. In 1875, the Dutch government decided to send a squadron to Venezuela which was to lend forceful emphasis to its demand that confiscated ships and goods from Curaçao should be returned. According to his instructions, the squadron commander was empowered to use force in the event that 'Dutchmen and Dutch interests' were further touched or if Venezuela would really undertake an armed attack on Curaçao.[217] Guzman Blanco gave in and sent an ambassador to The Hague in order to try to solve the dispute in a peaceful way. The Foreign Minister, Van der Does de Willebois, however, showed very little sympathy for the Venezuelan point of view. Relations subsequently deteriorated very quickly, and diplomatic relations were broken off again by Venezuela at the end of 1875.[218] Meanwhile, the Dutch press and Second Chamber

---

216. Goslinga, *Curaçao*; cf. Hood, *Gunboat Diplomacy*, chapters 5 and 6.
217. See the instruction with explanations by Van der Does, Woltring, *Bescheiden* II, nos 28–28A; cf. Goslinga, *Curaçao*, pp. 30f.
218. Woltring, *Bescheiden* II, nos 63, 72, 88–90, 94.

had become rather alarmed. At the end of 1875, ex-minister Cremers made it quite clear to the minister that the Second Chamber was seeking, 'without exception', a peaceful solution to the conflict.[219] A year later, Dutch–Venezuelan relations were still so tense that only Van Eck could muster any appreciation for the minister's policies. Cremers felt that Van der Does was personally responsible for the deadlock which the conflict had reached. Des Amorie van der Hoeven wondered whether Dutch Curaçao – 'that barren rock' – should not perhaps be ceded to Venezuela voluntarily, 'in order to prevent such complications in the future'.[220]

However, Van der Does and his successors were still determined to keep Curaçao, both out of national pride and also because of the international implications which another cession of colonial territory might have. Although the danger of a Venezuelan invasion was felt to be rather small in view of the country's limited military power, there were rumours outside the Netherlands that Venezuela had been buying armoured naval vessels, and these allegations were investigated quite thoroughly.[221] Also, Guzman's peaceful offer to buy Curaçao or exchange it for territory near Surinam was categorically rejected. Dutch prestige did not allow such a transaction.[222]

Van der Does seems to have been even more concerned about offers from the United States and Germany to act as mediators in the conflict. In both cases, he was inclined to take rumours seriously that these powers were trying to obtain Curaçao or some other part of the Dutch West Indian colonies. However, the Dutch ambassador in Washington rather felt that the United States was hardly prepared to enforce the Monroe Doctrine south of Panama. Moreover, when asked, the American administration made it clear that Venezuelan requests for mediation or support would be rejected, if the Netherlands was against it.[223] Nor was there any evidence for Germany's supposed desire to annex West Indian territories. Nevertheless, when Germany put forward its ideas for mediation or arbitration, Van der Does still expressed himself rather suspiciously about German intentions: 'Germany's expectations with regard to

219. *Handelingen Tweede Kamer* (Parliamentary Reports of the Second Chamber), 30 November 1875, p. 520.

220. Ibid., 1 December 1876, pp. 395–403.

221. Woltring, *Bescheiden* II, nos 99, 125, 144, 189, 474, 493.

222. See the aide-mémoires of Van der Does and his *chef de cabinet*, Van Karnebeek, ibid., nos 150, 174, 295A. Cf. Goslinga, *Curaçao*, pp. 85f.

223. Woltring, *Bescheiden* II, nos 111, 127–30, 152, 174, 236, 315. For the Monroe Doctrine see Ibid., no. 69.

transatlantic possessions allow quite a few conjectures.'[224] In 1877, after Guzman Blanco's presidency had come to an end, tensions between the Netherlands and Venezuela gradually eased again, although diplomatic relations were not resumed. However, a latent fear continued to persist in The Hague that some great power might interfere, particularly in Curaçao.[225]

The extent to which Dutch foreign affairs were dominated by political considerations in the conflict with Venezuela can be gathered from the low trade volume with Curaçao and indeed also Venezuela.[226] Once the Venezuelan ports were open again, the Dutch consuls stated that Dutch commerce and shipping no longer showed much interest, although Dutch goods continued to sell abroad in the usual way.[227] The consular reports from the other Latin American countries with which the Netherlands maintained relations displayed the same pattern which we also saw in Asia. For example, about half the sugar, gin, cheese and candles that were sold in Argentina each year came from the Netherlands. These goods, however, were mainly sold via foreign trade companies in Antwerp and Hamburg. Dutch shipping to Argentina still consisted almost entirely of sailing vessels and was reduced even further during the 1870s.[228] The same happened to direct trade and shipping with Brazil.[229] Nevertheless, the consuls generally felt optimistic about the future prospects of Dutch commerce. If one considered the improvement which had taken place since the middle of the century, despite a large number of civil wars and *coups d'état*, 'what will be the situation', asked the Dutch consul in Buenos Aires, 'when these countries have settle down to some peace and quiet?'[230]

224. Ibid., no. 240; cf. nos 112–17, 120–8, 130, 133, 245.
225. Ibid., nos 382, 386; cf. Goslinga, *Curaçao*, pp. 92f.
226. Exports to Curaçao in 1871 were 250,000 guilders, imports 135,000 guilders. Exports to Venezuela were 'stopped completely' in 1871, and imports were 26,000 guilders. However, the share of the Netherlands in Venezuela's international debts doubled between 1873 and 1879 from 10 to 20 per cent; cf. Goslinga, *Curaçao*, pp. 78 and 100.
227. *Consulaire verslagen* (Consular Reports) 1880, pp. 620 and 334–5.
228. Ibid. (1876) pp. 253–8; ibid. (1877) pp. 196–200; ibid. (1879) pp. 798–809.
229. Ibid. (1876) pp. 233–9; ibid. (1878) pp. 44–63; ibid. (1881) pp. 106–19.
230. Ibid. (1881) p. 99.

Annexation and Abstention in the Archipelago

The Origins of the Acheh War

When we look at the entire development of overseas relations in the 1870s, we have very little occasion to speak of imperialism in connection with the Netherlands. However, the withdrawal from the Gold Coast and the reserve which characterised Dutch overseas policies throughout this period went hand in hand with an expansionist urge in the Indonesian Archipelago that does indeed deserve to be called imperialist. The Venezuelan problem had already shown that Dutch policies could be aggressive at times, when the protection of colonial interests in relation to a non-Western state was connected with the fear that Western powers might intervene. Such a pattern was even more clearly noticeable when the Netherlands declared war on Acheh, an independent Indonesian sultanate with half a million inhabitants on the north coast of Sumatra.

The origins of the Acheh War have been documented extensively since 1873. For a long time, Dutch historiography was dominated by the official Dutch position which claimed that Acheh itself must be held responsible for the war, pointing that it had become inevitable when, after a long period of 'piracy' and other hostile acts, Acheh began to seek active support from Turkey, the United States and other foreign powers.[231] In recent historiography, though, this picture has changed radically. Not Acheh, but the Netherlands is held responsible for the outbreak of the war – or rather the Dutch East Indian colonial administration under the impulsive leadership of Governor-General Loudon.

Nevertheless, a number of issues still allow a variety of different interpretations. In the first place, there is the question in how far the Acheh War can actually be regarded as an instance of modern imperialism. According to Van 't Veer, the war still displayed a pre-imperialist, colonial character when it started. In Fasseur's view, the occurrence of the war can be seen as a local, 'peripheral' form of imperialism, even though he does not actually use this term.[232] As for the decision-making process, Reid sees the policies of the Dutch Minister of the Colonies, particularly of Fransen van

231. Cf. De Klerck, *Atjeh-oorlog*, pp. 343–4; Somer, *Korte Verklaring*, pp. 181–2. In a more moderate form, this interpretation can also be found earlier in Vlekke, *Nusantara*, pp. 318f.

232. Van 't Veer, *Atjeh-oorlog*, p. 55; 'Machthebbers', pp. 44–5. Cf. Fasseur, 'Koloniale paradox', pp. 179–80 and 184–5.

de Putte, as powerful support for Loudon's aggressive actions, whereas Fasseur maintains that Van de Putte tried to restrain Loudon and prevent a war.[233] The significance of foreign threats is therefore also assessed differently in this context. Reid sees it merely as a pretext by which The Hague and Batavia tried to conceal their expansionist efforts. According to Fasseur, the quick-tempered Loudon, in particular, was really motivated by his fear of foreign intervention.[234]

As for the role of Acheh, there is currently very little doubt remaining. Reid, in particular, has shown that Acheh's 'treachery' in 1873 was not a cause but a result of Dutch aggression. Under the sultanate of Ibrahim Mansur Shah (1857–70), internal stability had increased considerably and the sea around Acheh had in fact become less dangerous. And yet, as early as in the 1860s, there were moves in The Hague to prepare for the subjection of Acheh. After 1870, these efforts were undoubtedly corroborated by the political disintegration and growing unrest under the sultanate of the young and inexperienced Mahmud Shah (1870–1874). The manner and frequency of Acheh piracy, incidentally, still needs a considerable amount of research. Reid may have rather a rosy view of it as a local form of commercial conflict, though the ideas of Dutch contemporaries who saw Acheh as a barbarian 'pirates' den' were rather exaggerated. Moreover, among the very few convincing cases of piracy documented by the official report of 1874, not one Dutch vessel or trader was involved.[235] The Dutch colonial administration in Batavia and the rulers of Acheh have therefore been among the most significant parties to receive attention lately, whereas the role of the Dutch government, Parliament and public opinion has only been dealt with superficially and rather fragmentally. In discussing the causes of the Acheh War we shall therefore start with developments inside the Netherlands itself, without, however, losing sight of Dutch interaction with the East Indies, Acheh and other foreign powers. Finally, after an assessment of the various factors, we shall return to the pertinent literature on the subject.

One of the most important conditions inside the Netherlands which set the whole development in motion and finally led to the declaration of war was the Sumatra Treaty. As we have noted, De

233. Ibid., pp. 179–80; cf. Reid, *Contest*, p. 89.
234. Ibid., pp. 21 and 95; cf. Fasseur, 'Koloniale paradox', p. 179.
235. Reid, *Contest*, pp. 16–17, 79–83. For the Dutch definition of piracy in the Archipelago, see Van Goor, *Kooplieden*, 141–4.

Waal's aim at the Siak Convention was that Britain should repeal its guarantee of Acheh's independence. In a letter to the king in 1870, he had referred to Acheh as 'this state ... which for political reasons will have to become Dutch', pointing out that Acheh's independence would entail local and international risks. Even before the Siak Convention was well and truly signed, he called upon the governor-general to take 'a stronger line' towards Acheh.[236] The Siak Convention was subsequently rejected by the Second Chamber, though certainly not due to any feeling that the Netherlands should refrain from extending its sphere of influence to Acheh. In fact, a number of Liberal MPs wanted to see this option specially emphasised in any arrangement with Britain. The Sumatra Treaty, which made allowances for such a desire, was therefore accepted by a large majority. At this stage neither the new Minister of the Colonies, Van Bosse, nor the Liberal majority in the Second Chamber were actually aiming at war with Acheh. They did, however, want to see to it that Acheh was well under Dutch control, in order to put an end to piracy and other 'evil deeds' – particularly now that the Sumatra Treaty re-emphasised their full obligation to protect commerce and shipping, which the Netherlands had already taken upon itself in the 1824 treaty. Like his predecessor, Van Bosse already wrote regularly to the colonial administration in the East Indies with this in mind, even before the Sumatra Treaty officially took effect on 17 March 1872.[237]

The rather aggressive tenor which was thus added to the Sumatra Treaty by the Netherlands was further corroborated by two further general circumstances which we have already come across: the increasing interest in the economic exploitation of the Archipelago, especially Sumatra, together with a definite fear of foreign intervention or even an attack on the East Indies. During the preparations for the Siak Convention De Waal had pointed out both the opportunities for economic development in Sumatra and the extension of British, French and American influence in the vicinity of the Archipelago.[238] Both circumstances were also taken into consideration by Van Bosse, though with a certain matter of factness which was characteristic of this Dutch Liberal. The main reason that he paid any attention to Sumatra's minerals, for instance, was because there was a considerable amount of interest in the Netherlands. He

236. De Klerck, *Atjeh-oorlog*, pp. 326 and 329.
237. De Klerck, *Atjeh-oorlog*, p. 338.
238. Ibid., pp. 304–5.

seems to have felt much more strongly about the cultivation of tobacco in Deli. When, in the course of 1872, European plantations were threatened by 'disturbances', he 'unreservedly' supported strong action on the part of the colonial administration – especially because he felt that 'Atcheen was behind it all'.[239]

In so far as Van Bosse took seriously speculations about a foreign attack on the East Indies, he felt that a liberalisation of the East Indian tariffs was the best form of protection. While he was waiting for Parliament to deal with the relevant bill, which he had submitted with such an aim in mind, he gave Loudon the following sober advice: 'Watch out for *coups de main*, but don't dream of a seven-year war with a European power.' After all, Britain was no longer very interested in acquiring new territories.[240] However, Van Bosse did express a good deal of concern about Acheh's attempts to find foreign support. Although Britain had 'most loyally' rejected such attempts in 1872, Acheh was now 'going to turn its eyes towards Berlin or Washington'. 'Action', he said, commenting on the Dutch policy towards Acheh, 'now seems far more to my taste than those continuous delays.'[241] Such opinions of government officials like Van Bosse, which were expressed in private, found their echo in the Dutch press. The *Arnhemsche Courant*, for instance, wrote: 'Sumatra must become what Java has already become for us – an area that has undeniably and entirely been made subject to our rule, and this must become obvious to the whole world.'[242]

Until the turn of 1871–2, when Loudon finally arrived in Batavia as the new governor-general, the impulses for more forceful action against Acheh had mainly come from the Netherlands. When Loudon's Conservative predecessor Mijer had given his advice with regard to the Siak and Sumatra treaties, he had already shown himself particularly apprehensive about the possible consequences of more extensive interference with Acheh. Even the majority of the East Indian Council, the highest advisory body of the governor-general, advocated a policy of abstention.[243] In August 1871, after he had ignored several approaches, Mijer finally gave in to The Hague's impatient demands that the Netherlands should show its flag to Acheh, and so he sent a warship to Acheh, with a representa-

239. Van Bosse to Loudon, 4 July 1872, Loudon Collection.
240. Van Bosse to Loudon, 12 March 1872, Loudon Collection.
241. Van Bosse to Loudon, 25 March 1872, Loudon Collection.
242. *Arnhemsche Courant*, 22 April 1872.
243. Cf. Klerck, *Atjeh-oorlog*, pp. 341–2.

tive of the colonial administration on board. After some delay, the delegation was received quite politely by the young Sultan of Acheh. Although the discussion of Dutch complaints did not yield any tangible results, it was hoped in Batavia that this mission would guarantee good relations with Acheh for the time being.

The report of the trip reinforced Van Bosse's impression that 'Acheen's power is no more than a shadow'.[244] Still waiting for the development of the mission, he told the colonial administration on 12 September 1871 to grant possible requests for support from disloyal vassals of the sultan, especially in the unsafe border areas torn by conflict. 'In each case', said Van Bosse, 'the result will be that the unlawful influence of Acheh will be repelled while ours increases.'[245] In the new governor-general he had found someone who would put this strategy enthusiastically into practice. Loudon sent Dutch warships to break up Acheh's blockade of disloyal vassal states, and at the beginning of 1872 this led to another argument with Acheh.

From March onwards, when the Sumatra Treaty officially took effect, Loudon seems to have taken it more and more for granted that a violent subjection of the actual sultanate would eventually be inevitable. When the East Indian Council made a plea for a peaceful arrangement, respecting the sovereignty and integrity of the sultanate, he brushed this aside as mere 'illusions'. He found the official political line of the minister 'rather more liberal in its concept and more noble in principle than the one which was intended to keep the Asian despot in power at the cost of development and the common good'.[246] Conversely, Loudon was also supported by Van Bosse, who encouraged him to keep firm against the 'foolish advice' of the Council which he should reject in no uncertain terms.[247]

Meanwhile, the Acheh government had become well aware of the cloud hanging over it. Throughout 1872, envoys went to Singapore and Constantinople in order to win foreign support. These attempts obviously did not pass unnoticed and were sooner or later bound to meet with Dutch countermeasures. In April 1872, the Dutch Foreign Minister Gericke had already asked Dutch ambassadors to increase their alertness.[248] The critical developments which finally led to the

244. Van Bosse to Loudon, 25 March 1872, Loudon Collection; cf. De Klerck, *Atjeh-oorlog*, pp. 344f.
245. Ibid., pp. 343–54.
246. Ibid., pp. 375ff.
247. Ibid., pp. 359–61.
248. See Gericke's circular letter of 30 April 1872, Woltring, *Bescheiden* I, no. 239.

war therefore seem to have taken place during that period which was determined by hard-liners, both in Batavia and The Hague – from Loudon's appearance in January 1872 until Van Bosse's retirement in July.

The new Minister of the Colonies, Fransen van de Putte, soon showed himself very concerned about the turn which the Acheh affair had taken. He realised, to his dismay, 'that V. Bosse's messages had indeed given quite some occasion for rather aggressive actions'. But from then onwards, this was to be avoided as much as possible. 'I believe that aggression on our part is irresponsible and that we should only protect trade and resist slavery and piracy', he told Loudon in November.[249] Loudon replied: '*I will not stir up that hornets' nest* if it is not necessary, but Acheh may well force us to do so.'[250] Now that relations had been disturbed considerably and Acheh had sent envoys abroad, Loudon obviously saw his expectations confirmed.

At this point, the familiar pattern of colonial decision making seems to have shown itself again – a governor-general striving for expansion and a Minister of the Colonies trying, in vain, to prevent this development. Such a statement, however, needs some further explanation. Although Van de Putte consistently urged that a peaceful settlement should be pursued, he did not believe that a war must be avoided at all costs. The difference of opinion with Loudon was not so much about the aims of the Acheh policies but the manner in which they were carried out. Van de Putte, too, wanted to establish Dutch supremacy over Acheh. Like the East Indian Council and quite a few local government officials, however, he preferred a settlement that followed the Siak model, whereby Dutch influence could spread peacefully and gradually while the sultanate continued to exist. 'Let the pear get ripe and overripe', he advised the impatient Loudon, 'until it falls off by itself.'[251] As for a war with Acheh, Van de Putte felt that it was undesirable from a 'general political point of view', because it would give the Netherlands a bad name in Europe. He therefore suggested an interim solution, should a settlement like the one in Siak not be manageable: 'If we were to spread our rule or sovereignty by means of blockades or – better – at the

---

Cf. Reid, *Contest*, pp. 90–1; 'Indonesian Diplomacy', pp. 80f.

249. Fransen van de Putte to Loudon, 7 November 1872, Loudon Collection.

250. Loudon's 'Memoirs', p. 330, Louden Collection.

251. Fransen van de Putte to Loudon, 21 November 1872, Loudon Collection.

request of the small states themselves in order to resist obstructions to trade . . . or slavery . . . then it will all appear less odious than it does at the moment.' This proposal was indeed not very far removed from Van Bosse's original political line.[252]

Loudon, in turn, was still prepared to make just one single attempt to achieve a *rapprochement* with Acheh, without threats. However, when new negotiators were sent to Acheh during the second half of 1872, this only led to new misunderstandings and tensions.[253] Loudon had now reached the point where hardly anything could stop him from taking up arms against Acheh. Such action was suggested all the more forcefully when Consul-General Read sent a dramatic telegram from Singapore on 15 February 1873 informing Loudon of 'very important intrigues' between envoys from Acheh and American and Italian consuls.[254]

The background and consequences of Singapore's supposed 'treachery' have already been described quite extensively by Reid and Van 't Veer, so we can limit ourselves to the most important points.

When Read claimed that foreign intervention was imminent in the Acheh conflict, it was at first taken very seriously by everyone. When Loudon received a report claiming that Italian and American warships were already on their way to Acheh, he sent it on to The Hague without further investigation, recommending that the relevant governments should immediately be 'called upon to give a counter-order for abstention'.[255] The Dutch government in The Hague was already well aware that the Acheh was trying to obtain support from the Sultan of Turkey.[256] Also, there had long been rumours about the attempts of American and Italian agents to acquire footholds in the Archipelago. Moreover, there was indeed an American squadron in Hong Kong, and Italian warships were operating from Singapore.[257] The cabinet immediately decided to find out in Washington and Rome if the consuls in Singapore had acted on behalf of their governments.[258] Awaiting further develop-

252. Cf. De Klerck, *Atjeh-oorlog*, pp. 368–74.
253. *Officieele bescheiden*, p. 43.
254. Cf. Reid, *Contest*, pp. 91–7; Van 't Veer, *Atjeh-oorlog*, pp. 43–57.
255. Loudon to Fransen van de Putte, 16 February 1873, *Officieele bescheiden*, p. 43.
256. Woltring, *Bescheiden* I, nos 294 and 319.
257. On 5 December 1872 Fransen van de Putte himself had told Loudon to 'keep a close eye on the movements, behaviour and actions of adventurers from Europe and elsewhere' who were operating from Singapore; ibid. I, no. 310.
258. Minutes of the Cabinet Council, 18 February 1873, ibid., no. 332.

ments, the governor-general was then given the go-ahead to send an armed expedition to Acheh, with the purpose of demanding 'an explanation', asking Acheh to 'account' for its conduct and obtaining a satisfactory 'arrangement of relations between the Netherlands and Acheh'. However, following the advice of the circumspect privy councillor Elout van Soeterwoude, Fransen van de Putte made one important reservation: 'Unless you have reason to doubt the correctness of the report from the consul of Singapore, any delay will be considered unlawful.'[259]

Loudon, however, had very little doubt – probably because he had heard through a 'reliable source' that the American squadron was now on the point of moving from Hong Kong to Acheh. Loudon therefore saw the entire development as part of an even greater plot in which Russia, Germany and America were dividing the world between them. 'Woe to the small states and our colonies', he wrote to Fransen van de Putte.[260] On 4 March Loudon gave the instruction to the vice-president of the Council of the East Indies, J. F. N. Nieuwenhuyzen, who was to accompany the expedition to Acheh as government commissioner, to declare war unless the sultan recognised Dutch 'supreme authority' within 24 hours.[261] Fransen van de Putte objected to this ultimatum.

Meanwhile it had turned out that the Italian government wanted to have nothing to do with the Acheh conflict.[262] No clear answer had been received from the American government, which Van de Putte did not find reassuring at all. Unlike Minister for Foreign Affairs Gericke, Van de Putte found it hard to believe that the American consul could have acted without any authorisation from Washington.[263] But it was precisely because of the uncertainty of the international context of the conflict that he felt a war should definitely be avoided. Sovereignty, in his view, should not be presented as an ultimatum, but ought to be the outcome of negotiations. Again, however, he did not make this entirely clear. 'We

259. Fransen van de Putte to Loudon, 18 February 1873, *Officieele bescheiden*, p. 40; cf. Elout van Soeterwoude to Fransen van de Putte, 18 February 1873, Fransen van de Putte Collection.

260. Quoted by Fasseur, 'Koloniale paradox', p. 179. For the rumour from Hong Kong, see Loudon, 'Memoirs', p. 335; cf. Loudon to Fransen van de Putte, 4 March, *Officieele bescheiden*, p. 79.

261. For the instruction, see *Officieele bescheiden*, pp. 81–2.

262. Cf. Woltring, *Bescheiden* I, nos 336 and 353.

263. Fransen van de Putte even feared that, if it turned out that the American consul had acted without authority, Washington would still support him for reasons of prestige. Fransen van de Putte to Loudon, 6 March 1873, Loudon Collection.

cannot and do not wish to tie your hands by means of prohibitions', he assured Loudon, and if the other side should obstinately refuse to negotiate, he agreed that war was inevitable. This rather irritated Loudon, and so he asked what demands he should actually make, whereupon Van de Putte finally replied that he objected not so much to the content of the instruction but rather 'the way it was introduced and its form'. Apart from the suggestion to replace 'sovereignty' with a demand to 'render account' as the primary ultimatum, the instruction remained unchanged.[264]

By 8 March, the American Foreign Secretary had made it quite clear that the US consul in Singapore had indeed acted without authority.[265] As soon as Van de Putte received this report, he informed Loudon, though he saw no reason to cancel the expedition, which was to leave Batavia on 22 March, or even to change radically the government commissioner's instruction. Now that the Acheh question had reached such an advanced stage, Van de Putte probably thought – despite his objections – that it was much better if the entire matter were settled as quickly as possible.[266] Even after Washington's reassurances, there was still some anxiety in The Hague concerning foreign intervention. On his way to Japan, F. W. H. von Weckherlin, the new Dutch envoy to Japan (and future ambassador to the United States), was asked to hold a thorough inquiry into the general development in Singapore. He found that there was plenty of reason to mistrust the American consul's actions.[267] Later, in Tokyo, he affirmed in a letter to Loudon that 'the government in Washington was aiming, sooner or later, to extend its influence in East Asia.' Moreover, Loudon remained firmly convinced of the 'necessity of a *fait accompli*, so that foreign claims would be excluded once and for all'.[268] This is why he did not bother to communicate this latest American declaration to Nieuwenhuyzen, who had already travelled to Penang, ahead of the expedition, on 7 March.

When Nieuwenhuyzen arrived before Acheh on 22 March, he

264. Cf. the exchange of telegrams and letters between 4 and 12 March, *Officieele bescheiden*, pp. 46–50, 62–7 and 79–86.

265. Cf. Woltring, *Bescheiden* I, no. 358.

266. Cf. the telegrams and letters of 7, 9 and 12 March, *Officieele bescheiden*, pp. 48 and 63. On 20 March Van de Putte still conveyed the king and the cabinet's agreement with 'your strong action'; Loudon Collection.

267. Von Weckherlin to Fransen van de Putte, 13 April 1873, Fransen van de Putte Collection; cf. Woltring, *Bescheiden* I, no. 371.

268. Von Weckherlin to Fransen van de Putte, 10 June and 29 November 1873. Cf. Weckherlin to Loudon, 5 May 1874, Loudon Collection.

began to ask the sultan to account for his 'treachery' in Singapore. When, in his view, no sufficiently satisfactory answer was forthcoming, he finally declared war on Acheh on 26 March. The Dutch troops who subsequently landed on the Acheh coast met with unexpectedly fierce resistance. On 20 April, after the death of the Dutch commander, the expedition was terminated.[269] The war had become a fact, but Dutch 'sovereignty' was far from being established in Acheh.

After this failure, Van de Putte reminded Loudon again and again of their previous exchange of ideas on the government commissioner's instruction. Loudon sneeringly attributed this grieved reaction to the minister's growing 'claustrophic fear of the Second Chamber'.[270] This was because, on 4 April, Van de Putte had been interpellated by the Conservative MP Nierstrasz about the declaration of war before it had been officially made known. At the time, he was in a rather awkward position. It was impossible to deny the Reuter report, but the actual declaration of war could not be made without contradicting his former reassurances to the Chamber.[271] At the end of 1872 he had declared in connection with the Dutch intervention in Deli: 'It is *neither the wish nor the aim* of the Dutch government to promote an extension of our authority in Sumatra.'[272] He had repeated these words on 27 February, in reply to some concerned questions about the course of events in Acheh.[273] He now had to report to the Chamber that he could not make any statement about the war until he had received a progress report from Batavia.

At his instigation, a large report on the relations between the Netherlands and Acheh from 1824 onwards was then set up, emphasising Acheh's attempts to gain foreign support. When this was discussed by the Chamber at the end of April, the disastrous course of the expedition had already become known. The military preparation of the expedition was sharply criticised from different sides. However, only the Conservatives felt that the war was unjustified

269. For the exchange of correspondence between Nieuwenhuyzen and the sultan, the declaration of war and the suspension of the expedition, see *Officieele bescheiden*, pp. 113–29.

270. Fransen van de Putte to Loudon, 10 and 24 April 1873; cf. Loudon, 'Memoirs', p. 349, Loudon Collection.

271. *Handelingen Tweede Kamer* (Parliamentary Reports of the Second Chamber), 4 April 1873, pp. 1362–6.

272. Ibid., 26 October 1872, pp. 346–7.

273. Ibid., 27 February 1873, p. 970.

and should be stopped as quickly as possible. The most important Liberal speakers – Van Rees, Cremers and De Roo – believed that the declaration of war had been inevitable and pointed out that it was necessary to avenge the setback.[274] The Chamber did not give its final verdict until a year later, behind closed doors. By then the political controversy concerning the Acheh question had become considerably sharper. However, at the outbreak of the war, Fransen van de Putte still had the support of a large majority in the Chamber and of public opinion, even though his presentation of his policy had not come across very well.

Even outside the Dutch Parliament, the war had already been discussed for quite some time before it actually broke out. In October 1872, the famous writer Multatuli, a humanitarian former colonial civil servant, had already predicted the war in his *Brief aan den Koning* (Letter to the king), which later became quite notorious.[275] Considering the Sumatra Treaty as a 'rat trap', the Conservative press, too, had repeatedly pointed out the danger of a war. Once it had broken out, however, the Conservative paper *Dagblad* was the only one to criticise it sharply.[276] Although the Liberal press did not regard the war as desirable, it nevertheless saw it as fully justified. As before, the *Arnhemsche Courant* went furthest in this. 'Our right in the East Indies', was the social Darwinist conclusion of this paper, 'is the right of the strongest.' It argued: 'Like all colonial powers, like Britain in British India, like France in Algeria, like North America towards the American Indian tribes, like Russia in Asia . . . the Netherlands sometimes has to play the role of the conqueror in order to hold its own.'[277] In the *Nieuwe Rotterdamsche Courant*, which was closely linked to Van de Putte and his faction, the war was regarded as a justified anticipation, because of the danger of foreign intervention.[278] Later, the *Handelsblad* was to

274. Ibid., 28, 29 and 30 April 1873, pp. 1375–423; cf. Bijlagen 1872–3, no. 141.
275. Multatuli, *Verzameld werk* V, pp. 681–4; cf. Van 't Veer, *Atjeh-oorlog*, pp. 38–9.
276. *Het Dagblad van Zuid-Holland en 's-Gravenhage*, 4 and 7 March, 6, 7, 22, 25 and 28 April 1873. There were also protests against the declaration of war in the circles of the First International, though these protests attracted very little interest; cf. Giele, *Eerste internationale*, p. 219.
277. This conclusion was explained as follows: 'It is a general law of nature that the strong live at the expense of the weak'; *Arnhemsche Courant*, 24 April 1873; the same paper had already urged the violent subjection of Acheh on 6 January.
278. Cf. *NRC*, 'De Atchineesche verwikkelingen', 18 March, 3, 4 and 5 April 1873.

express itself in a similar vein.[279]

Only the *Vaderland* showed a considerable amount of sympathy for the difficult position of Acheh after the Sumatra Treaty: 'How would the Belgians feel, we ask, if France and Britain decided to destroy the treaty that guarantees Belgium's neutrality and if in one of their parliaments the issue were discussed in the same way as Acheen in ours?' This left-wing Liberal paper saw the war as a sad but inevitable collision between Acheh's justified endeavour to maintain independence and the Netherlands' equally justified attempt to prevent the intervention of third parties.[280] In the popular paper *Nieuws van den Dag* (News of the Day), on the other hand, the Acheh population was called 'proud, murderous, treacherous, dishonest and immoral'.

The denomination press initially described these new Muslim enemies in similar terms. Both the Roman Catholic *Tijd* (Time) and the Calvinist Anti-Revolutionary *Standaard* felt that a continuation of the war was necessary for maintaining Dutch prestige in the Archipelago, though they did not – for the time being – consider the legal basis of the war. 'Taking a strong line', said the *Standaard*, 'and doing so calmly, earnestly and inexorably is the only remedy at present.'[282]

The rather unfavourable image of Acheh and its inhabitants was reinforced by the findings of the scholar Veth who published a topical study, though with a scientific aim, on the occasion of the war. Unfortunately, his hopeful prediction in part one that the Netherlands would quickly subjugate the degenerate Acheh was disproved by the facts even before the publication of part two. The knowledge of Acheh's general topography and history in the Netherlands was in fact rather nicely illustrated by the map which Veth had included in his study. It showed a 'very mountainous but completely unknown interior'.[283]

So much for my own version of the origins of the Acheh War. But how do they relate to the existing literature? Fasseur has rightly raised the question in how far the declaration of war can be regarded as 'the improvised beginning of a policy of expansion, inspired by

279. *Het Algemeen Handelsblad*, 26, 27 and 28 April 1873. Liberal magazines also approved of the war; cf. *TNI* (1873) I, pp. 321–3; *De Economist* (1873) I, pp. 420–3.
280. *Het Vaderland*, 5 March 1873; cf. 3 and 4 March, 26 and 28 April.
281. *Het Nieuws van den Dag*, 7 March 1873; cf. 8 March and 28 April.
282. *De Standaard*, 21 April 1873, cf. 22 and 24 April; the same leading articles had probably been written by Kuyper. See also *De Tijd*, 22 April 1873.
283. P. J. Veth, *Atchin* I, pp. 2–3.

"the new imperialism"'. Insofar as Fasseur accepted the term imperialism in this context he applied it to Loudon's actions in Batavia, which showed the continuity with the preceding expansion.[284] However, unlike the other Indonesian states in the Archipelago, Acheh was a completely independent state with regard to international law. But what seems to me even more important is the observation that Loudon's aggressiveness, which did indeed play an important part in the last phase, had been prepared and made possible by the Netherlands itself. The Sumatra Treaty, the ambition to develop Sumatra economically, the already existing fear of foreign intervention – all these Dutch circumstances helped to cause the war. They showed themselves in the Acheh policy of the ministers De Waal and Van Bosse. Fransen van de Putte, on the other hand, unmistakably aimed to preserve peace. Reid's view that Van de Putte lent powerful support to Loudon's aggression seems to be partly based on an incorrect interpretation of sources.[285] However, Van de Putte's attempts to curb Loudon's activities remained half-hearted and therefore unsuccessful. Indeed, his own effort to achieve a Siak-type settlement can also be regarded as imperialist, albeit in a much milder and more informal variant than Loudon's. Finally, it should be noted that the war did not really come unexpectedly for Parliament or public opinion. Some liberal circles had been demanding war from the very beginning.

Among these different factors, the threat of foreign intervention played a very important part in triggering off the Acheh War. Reid misjudges the 'realistic' elements of this fear, which was caused by the combined presence of foreign agents and warships, in the administrative centres of a small European power with large colonial possessions. When the United States and Italy declared their neutrality, this fear obviously subsided, though without disappearing altogether. After all, Acheh had clearly shown that it tried to obtain foreign support. Both The Hague and Batavia, however, attached great value to the 'undisturbed possession' of Sumatra, and it was therefore felt that the continuing independence of Acheh was

284. Fasseur, 'Koloniale paradox', pp. 162, 179–80.
285. Reid seems to have attributed Van Bosse's sharp criticism of the peaceful advice of the East Indian Council (24 April 1872) to Van de Putte, who did not take up office as a minister until 6 July. The confusion was further corroborated by Reid's source, De Klerck's *Atjeh-oorlog*, where Van Bosse's criticism is dated 26 August, with reference to a ministerial message of 1864. Cf. Reid, *Contest*, p. 89, fn. 3; De Klerck, *Atjeh-oorlog*, p. 359, fn. 3 and p. 361, fn. 1.

too much of a risk because of its proximity to the promising but vulnerable Deli.

If we follow Betts in understanding the striving for 'pre-emption', the exclusion of potential competitors and the geographical factor of 'contiguity' as typical features of modern imperialism, then the beginning of the Acheh War certainly fits into a more general pattern. After the Sumatra Treaty, Acheh did not passively accept Dutch restrictions to its independence but developed its own initiative, thus accelerating the transition to active imperialism on the part of the Netherlands.[286]

The Annexation of Acheh

This pattern was repeated with the second expedition to Acheh. Again, the outcome – this time formal annexation – was neither 'wish nor aim', though it had not been excluded in advance either. After the unfortunate development of the first expedition there was quite a general consensus in the Netherlands that another, stronger expedition should follow, which would force the sultan to accept Dutch authority. 'The company may have taken a few knocks, but the company keeps coming back – this is our *Nous maintiendrons*', Fransen van de Putte had reassured the Chamber, while pointing to the earlier wars with Bone and Bandjarmasin.[287]

Loudon, in the East Indies, had made it clear that the memory of the initial failure should be wiped out completely, with a view to maintaining law and order among the Muslim populations of Java and Sumatra.[288] In the Second Chamber some Liberal MPs were already urging for a complete annexation of Acheh.[289] This time Van de Putte seems to have been determined to ensure that things would not get out of hand again because of such sentiments. In consultation with the Privy Council the following political line was mapped out. From a military point of view, the expedition had to be equipped in such a way that there was no risk of another failure. Politically, however, Acheh first had to be given an opportunity to find a peaceful solution with the Netherlands, 'following in the

286. Cf. Betts, *False Dawn*, pp. 71–2.
287. *Handelingen Tweede Kamer* (Parliamentary Reports of the Second Chamber), 29 April 1873, p. 1398.
288. Cf. Loudon, 'Memoirs', p. 371, Loudon Collection.
289. Among others by De Roo van Alderwerelt and Oldenhuis Gratama, *Handelingen Tweede Kamer* (Parliamentary Reports of the Second Chamber), 28 April 1873, pp. 1380 and 1387. Cf. *Arnhemsche Courant*, 26 April 1873.

footsteps of the treaty concluded with Siak in 1858'. In order to pursue a policy that was both flexible and ready for battle, the civilian and military leadership of the expedition were to be combined.[290] The proposal for the new government commissioner and military commander given by Loudon to Van de Putte seems to have met these demands very generously. He was the retired general Van Swieten, Van de Putte's much valued fellow supporter of Liberal colonial politics. With an appeal to his country's interest and the prospect of a generous payment, he was soon found willing to serve.[291]

The king, who had his personal preferences and dislikes, especially in the military area, seems to have been against the 'provoked' appointment of an aged Liberal general from the very beginning.[292] In general, however, Van Swieten's appointment was received very favourably, even outside the Liberal camp. Van Swieten knew Acheh from first-hand experience, and – even more importantly – had he not been the East Indian supreme commander in 1860 after a similar fiasco in Bonie and succeeded in bringing the second expedition to a good conclusion? Experts spoke very highly of his role in upholding Dutch authority in Bonie, by his restrained military action and diplomatic behaviour, which had just been documented in a study. When Van Swieten left for Acheh, it was therefore a real triumph, as Van 't Veer has described graphically: it had all the trappings of official dinners, flower parades and music.[293] Van 't Veer also explained why Van Swieten's reception in the East Indies was considerably less cordial. The unsuccessful first expedition there had led to a series of conflicts, smear campaigns and intrigues, so that Loudon's authority seemed to be seriously undermined.

His choice of the civilian and military leadership for the new expedition gave rise to opposition among the advocates of a punitive expedition against Acheh, especially among the higher military,

290. Cf. Van Swieten, *Waarheid*, pp. 42–3.
291. Loudon, 'Memoirs', pp. 353–4. Cf. Van 't Veer, *Atjeh-oorlog*, p. 80.
292. For the complaints of *Het Loo* (the Dutch Royal Palace) see Loudon, 'Memoirs', pp. 378–9; cf. Van Swieten to Fransen van de Putte in January 1874, Fransen van de Putte Collection.
293. See the discussion of M. T. H. Perelaer, *De Bonische expeditien*, 2 volumes, Leiden 1872, by W. J. Knoop, *De Gids* (1873) ii, pp. 325–69; General A. W. P. Weitzel, *Militaire Spectator* (1873) pp. 113–27 and 164–77; G. H. van Soest, *TNI* (1873) I, pp. 47–68; *Het Algemeen Handelsblad*, 20 May 1873. Cf. Elout van Soeterwoude to Fransen van de Putte, 1 June 1873, on the 'wise and fortunate choice', Fransen van de Putte Collection.

where the appointment of a retired general was viewed with some resentment by those who felt they had been passed over.[294] Quite apart from personal antagonism, both the army and navy were in such deplorable material condition that the preparations for the expedition took much longer than had at first been anticipated. When enough ships had eventually been found to carry the 7,500 soldiers and 5,000 non-combatants, a cholera epidemic broke out among the densely packed men, just before they were due to leave.

Meanwhile, however, Van Swieten had had plenty of opportunity to develop a suitable strategy. In doing so, he co-operated closely with Loudon and Van de Putte, both of whom this time continued to maintain a direct communication link with the government commissioner. It was therefore mutually agreed first of all to instruct the government commissioner to aim at a treaty which followed the Siak model. However, he would also be empowered to depose the sultan if he refused to sign such a treaty, though Van Swieten did not expect that it would actually come to that.[295]

When he arrived in Acheh on 9 December, this plan was bitterly thwarted. In a carefully phrased letter Van Swieten promised the sultan that he could continue to govern the country and that the religion and customs of his people would be respected so long as he was willing to follow the example of his colleague in Siak. However, this letter was not even answered.[296] Shortly afterwards, when two of his personal envoys to the sultan had been killed and the cholera had spread further among the waiting soldiers, Van Swieten decided on 2 January 1874 to proceed with the attack. Finally, on 24 January and after fierce battles, the invasion force reached the *kraton*, the sultan's fortified palace, which they apparently found deserted. By now the cholera epidemic had also spread among the population of Acheh. On 26 January the sultan died of cholera without leaving a direct successor. Van Swieten, who had already remarked bitterly to Loudon that the sultan could hardly remain in power after a Dutch victory, officially declared the annexation of the sultanate on 31 January.

Reid and Van 't Veer have given the false impression that Van

294. Cf. Van 't Veer, *Atjeh-oorlog*, pp. 80–1.

295. Ibid., pp. 82–93. Cf. Van Swieten to Fransen van de Putte, 25 August 1873, Fransen van de Putte Collection.

296. Van Swieten to Fransen van de Putte, 7 November 1873, Fransen van de Putte Collection. Cf. items 2 and 3 of the instruction, Van Swieten, *Waarheid*, appendix I.

Swieten had acted completely without authority when he annexed Acheh and that Van de Putte reluctantly had to accept this *fait accompli*. However, Van Swieten had acted completely in accordance with his instructions. This was confirmed by Van de Putte on 2 February, when he gave his consent to the temporary abolition of the sultanate and the limited establishment of colonial administration around the former capital.[297] Van Swieten then tried to conclude sub-treaties with the sultan's former vasals, following the example of Siak. Although he was not very successful and skirmishes continued, he proclaimed the end of the second expedition on 20 April. The main force returned to Batavia, leaving behind a small occupation contingent and nearly 1,500 dead, most of whom had died of cholera.[298]

In the Netherlands, military operations were being followed with great interest. At first there was an atmosphere of anxiety. No glorious victory was happening, and the Dutch newspapers contained soldiers' letters about cholera and nocturnal attacks from the Achenese. There was growing concern that Van Swieten was being too cautious. 'There'll be unrest in our country,' W. H. Dullert, the speaker of the Second Chamber, warned Van de Putte.[299] When Van Swieten's telegram 'The kraton is ours!' arrived in the Netherlands on 27 January, there was great relief. 'We are in high spirits over the good tidings,' Van de Putte wrote enthusiastically to Loudon, 'and I was quite bowled over for a few days.'[300] The newspapers had clothed the report in bold headlines and words of euphoria. Spontaneous parades and demonstrations took place in the larger towns. In Rotterdam, a 'dense crowd of people' gathered together with banners and moved through the city in a procession, going to the town hall, where it sang 'patriotic songs'. In The Hague, the multitudes moved to the Department of Colonies, with fanfares, to congratulate the minister. The same evening, Van de Putte gave a 'magnificent soirée dansante', which was attended by the crown prince, ministers and ambassadors and was illuminated by 'brilliant gas lamps'. It seems that flags were put out everywhere in the Netherlands for a few days, including in the less expensive residen-

297. Van Swieten, *Waarheid*, appendix C.
298. Ibid., pp. 3434–5. Cf. Van Swieten to Loudon, 13 and 28 January 1874, Loudon Collection. Cf. Reid, *Contest*, pp. 157–8; Van 't Veer, *Atjeh-oorlog*, pp. 100–1.
299. Dullert to Fransen van de Putte, 9 January 1874, Fransen van de Putte Collection.
300. Fransen van de Putte to Loudon, 29 January 1874, Loudon Collection.

tial areas and in small towns. Amsterdam was the only place where nationalist excitement was clearly not on the agenda for the people, and festivities were limited to the decorations of a single shop.[301] The king, too, seems to have reacted in a rather surly way and was dissatisfied with Van Swieten's long delays. He even refused to give the general a suitable medal.[302] The Chamber, however, congratulated Van Swieten on his success with all their hearts.[303]

The Dutch annexation of Acheh, which was in effect far more important than the occupation of the deserted *kraton*, was at first not dwelt upon very much at all in this festive atmosphere. However, the merry-making soon disappeared when it became obvious that, after the conquest of the capital, the war was still far from over. 'After what has happened there is no longer any talk of making peace sooner or later', concluded Nierstrasz when Van der Putte had finally been interpellated about the annexation on 21 March. 'We have now entered into a phase where as many expeditions will follow as are necessary to subdue the local population.'[304] Even before the departure of the second expedition, in the aftermath of the first one, political opposition had already been aggravated. In June 1873, the *Standaard* had published eight articles by Keuchenius who, writing from the East Indies, condemned the Dutch declaration of war as a matter of principle as incompatible with international law and Christian civilisation.[305] *De Tijd*, too, distanced itself from the declaration of war, even though it continued to regard a second expedition as necessary on pragmatic grounds.[306] Even Liberal circles began to look for a scapegoat, and the Naval Defence Minister L. G. Brocx seemed to be the most suitable candidate. After years of being praised for his cutbacks in the naval budget, he was now held responsible for the Dutch navy in the East Indies being 'a load of wrecks' at the outbreak of the war. Brocx took offence: 'If, at the time, the government had demanded that I should see to it that the navy was in a condition to conduct a

301. For Rotterdam and The Hague, see *NRC* 27–31 January 1874; for Amsterdam, *Het Algemeen Handelsblad* of 30 January, which also mentions festivities in Utrecht, Den Bosch, Breda, Maastricht, Kampen, Assen and Schiedam. The extent of the rejoicing was confirmed by the Conservate *Dagblad* and the Roman Catholic paper *De Tijd*.
302. Loudon, 'Memoirs', pp. 378–9, Loudon Collection.
303. *Handelingen Tweede Kamer* (Parliamentary Reports of the Second Chamber), 23 February 1874, p. 827.
304. Ibid., 21 March 1874, p. 1136.
305. *De Standaard* of 14, 16, 17, 18, 20, 23, 24 and 25 June 1873.
306. Cf. *De Tijd* of 24 July 1873.

blockade of the empire of Acheen,' he answered, 'I would have resigned a day later.' Now he was forced to resign by the Chamber when, in December, his budget was rejected by 37 votes to 30.[307]

Van de Putte, too, came under increasing pressure. Although additional war funds were granted by the Chamber without a roll-call vote, the national euphoria about the initial success of the second expedition had died down. Finally, the Chamber inexorably enforced complete openness on all matters, starting from the first expedition. There had been demands for this for a long time. At the initiative of the Anti-Revolutionary MP J. Messchert van Vollenhoven, a definitive debate on the declaration of war against Acheh took place behind closed doors in April 1874.[308] In the end, however, the policy that had been pursued was only condemned completely by Conservative speakers. Nierstrasz and Fabius compared the Acheh War in this context with the 'policy of conquest' of Napoleon I and, more recently, Napoleon III and Bismarck.[309] The Roman Catholic spokesman C. van Nispen went less far: he felt that the declaration of war in itself was 'unwise' under the given circumstances.[310] According to the Anti-Revolutionary leader Kuyper, the policy from 1871 onwards could be justified quite well – until the moment when it became obvious that no interference from the United States or Italy was imminent. Kuyper felt that the subsequent declaration of war was 'indefensible', and he therefore put forward a motion in which his disapproval was expressed very clearly, although he withdrew it again when Fransen van de Putte announced that it would amount to a vote of no confidence.[311]

By now, even Liberal speakers had to admit that matters had been handled rather rashly from time to time, especially in Batavia. When defending their policies, they concentrated mainly on two areas: the implications of the Sumatra Treaty, which had been passed with the

307. *Handelingen Tweede Kamer* (Parliamentary Reports of the Second Chamber), 11 December 1873, pp. 671–86. The survey of available vessels which Brocx had submitted at the request of the enquiry committee, did indeed consist of a sad repetition of statements such as 'white ants', 'hull obsolete', 'weak boilers', etc.; cf. *Bijlagen Handelingen Tweede Kamer* (Parliamentary Reports of the Second Chamber, Appendices) 1874–5, nos 128, 119–27.
308. *Handelingen Tweede Kamer* (Parliamentary Reports of the Second Chamber), closed session, 16, 17, 18 and 20 April 1874, published in *Bijlagen Handelingen Tweede Kamer* (Parliamentary Reports of the Second Chamber, Appendices) 1881–2, no. 74.
309. Ibid., pp. 5 and 14.
310. Ibid., p. 19.
311. Ibid., pp. 20–3, 33 and 38.

votes of Nierstrasz and Fabius; and the real danger of foreign intervention, which Acheh had been seeking quite actively. The latter was particularly emphasised by Fransen van de Putte and Gericke. Commenting on the United States' supposed innocence, Van de Putte commented that 'the Americans won't directly found any state colonies, but the American residents will start colonies like in the Pacific Ocean, and these will then . . . be recognised by the American government.'[312] Thus, Van de Putte was able to defend himself against the attacks of 'Nierstrasz and Co' again. Shortly afterwards, however, when it became known that Van Swieten had concluded the second expedition with uncertain results, his position became considerably weaker again. Fabius's Conservative motion, whereby Van Swieten's conduct was implicitly disapproved, was only rejected by a small majority of 36 votes to 26. This time, a number of Liberals voted against their minister.[313]

The international context, mentioned so frequently in the secret parliamentary debate after the the first expedition, remained far more in the background when the second one was discussed. Earlier, in the spring of 1873, there had been mild panic when the Sultan of Turkey, who saw himself as the patron of all Islamic nations, offered his mediation in the Acheh War. With the help of the British government and the Russian ambassador in Constantinople, Turkish action could be limited to a 'démarche vague et platonique'. In the Turkish memorandum of 11 August there was no more than an appeal to the generosity and moderation of the Netherlands.[314]

The attitudes of the great European powers, particularly Britain, were far more important. Although, at the outbreak of the war, the current Liberal government had shown its loyalty and co-operation by prohibiting arms and ammunitions exports to Acheh, Granville began to show obvious signs of dissatisfaction when the Dutch blockade of Acheh took longer than anticipated and when there were increasing protests from the Straits.[315] Therefore, when the

312. Ibid., pp. 32–3. For the American penetration of Hawaii and Samoa, see Plesur, *Outward Thrust*, pp. 198–201. Sumatra, too, was occasionally visited by American traders and researchers; cf. Gould, *Americans*, pp. 4–7, 138–9.
313. Among others J. W. A. Rutgers van Rozenburg and T. J. Stieltjes, *Handelingen Tweede Kamer*, (Parliamentary Reports of the Second Chamber), 8 June 1874, pp. 1513–29. Cf. Van Bosse to Loudon, 5 May 1874, Loudon Collection.
314. For the Turkish note and the Dutch reply, see Woltring, *Bescheiden* I, nos 449, 453. Cf. the cabinet minutes of 13 May 1873, ibid., no. 390.
315. Cf. Reid, *Contest*, pp. 73–9, 97–104.

British Liberal Party lost the general election in January 1874 and was succeeded by a Conservative government, there was a good deal of anxiety in the Hague, because British Conservatives had always been against lifting Britain's guarantee of Acheh's independence. But, as Van Bylandt had already expected, the new Conservative government was also able to resist demands from the Straits and the British Parliament to intervene directly in the Acheh War.[316] The German government in Berlin had always been well-disposed towards Dutch action in Acheh. After the unsuccessful first expedition Bismarck had encouraged the Netherlands to persevere but to go about it rather more carefully.[317] President Thiers, in Paris, expressed himself in similar terms.[318] Finally, in Washington, Secretary of State Hamilton Fish made it quite clear again on 31 January 1874 that America had no interest in the area. 'C'est trop loin', he confided to the Dutch ambassador B. O. F. H. Westenberg during a party, pointing at Sumatra on a map of the world.[319]

Defensive and Aggressive Politics

The declaration of war and the annexation of Acheh were discussed in such detail in the previous section because they are of direct significance in the question of to what extent Dutch action towards Acheh can be called imperialist. The fact that, once the Acheh War had broken out, it did indeed begin to display features of imperialism seems to have been discussed considerably less.

According to Van 't Veer, the transition from the 'old' to the 'new times' was marked, in this respect, by the difference between the 'First' (1873) and the 'Second' Acheh War (1874–80).[320] Therefore we shall not go into any detail regarding the further development of the war as it has already been recounted in detail by Van 't Veer and Reid. The following paragraphs will be limited to an amplification of Van 't Veer's account of the 'paper war', conducted by the military and politicians in the Netherlands.[321] Broadly speaking, it was an argument between a 'defensive' and an 'aggressive' pacification scheme. Finally, in 1881, when neither approach seemed to warrant complete success and war expenses continued to rise, it was

316. Woltring, *Bescheiden* I, nos 488, 495, 532.
317. Ibid., no. 428C.
318. Ibid., nos 377 and 389.
319. Ibid., no. 487.
320. Van 't Veer, *Atjeh-oorlog*, p. 55.
321. Ibid., pp. 126–34.

unilaterally decided to declare an end to the war.

The advocates of a defensive policy favoured a limited military presence and aimed at a peaceful expansion of Dutch influence by means of partial treaties with the local rajahs. In the course of 1874 and 1875 they all had to abandon the field. After the termination of the second expedition, General Van Swieten went back into retirement. Fransen van de Putte resigned on 27 August 1874, and with him the other ministers of the Liberal Geertsema–De Vries cabinet, which had been seriously weakened as a result of the Acheh War. Finally, Loudon, who had become known as a loyal supporter of the defensive approach, handed in his resignation on 17 December, after a series of conflicts with the new Minister of the Colonies about Acheh and other administrational matters. Van de Putte's successor, the cool aristocrat and diplomat W. van Goltstein, was one of the few Dutch Conservatives who had spoken out in favour of the declaration of war to Acheh.[322] As a minister, he soon lost all confidence in a wait-and-see policy. 'It is as if the state of a sick man were judged according to the prescriptions of a physician who has neither seen nor examined him for months,' he remarked on Loudon's continuing references to Van Swieten and his instruction.[323]

From the beginning of 1875 until the end of 1880, the Netherlands pursued, in effect, a continuously aggressive policy towards Acheh, combining the blockade of the coastal areas with punitive expeditions inland, in order to enforce submission to Dutch authority. The new governor–general, the diplomat J. W. van Lansberge, and Van Golstein's Liberal successors F. Alting Mees, Van Bosse and Van Reese, continued to support this policy, though not always whole-heartedly.[324]

The real protagonists of the aggressive approach were the colonels – and, later, generals – J. L. Pel and K. van der Heijden, the dreaded 'King One-Eye'. Their actions, which may have resulted in the death of about 30,000 Achenese and the burning of some 500 kampongs, were at first widely supported in the Netherlands.[325] The Conservatives, who had so vehemently opposed the 'Liberal war' at the time, now supported their minister in the introduction of the

322. Cf. *Handelingen Eerste Kamer* (Parliamentary Reports of the First Chamber), 16 June 1873, pp. 344–5.
323. Van Goltstein to Loudon, 4 February 1875, Loudon Collection.
324. See the private correspondence between Van Lansberge and the secretaries of the colonies, included as appendices in Boon, *Van Lansberge*.
325. Van 't Veer, *Atjeh-oorlog*, p. 130.

aggressive approach.[326] Indeed, many Liberal MPs and journalists had by now become convinced that Fransen van de Putte and Van Swieten's wait-and-see policy had unnecessarily prolonged the war. And so the strategy òf 'unprecedented chastisement', which was adopted in Acheh by Van der Heijden after 1877, found a strong advocate in the Liberal Amsterdam MP J. W. H. Rutgers van Rozenburg. In a debate with Fransen van de Putte, he turned against the 'champions of a sickly humanitarian approach, with their whining about barbarity, the burning of kampongs, the devastation and scorching which is not of this century'. Such lamentations reminded him of 'faint-hearted animal protectionists, shedding tears when a wasps' nest was being burnt out'. The more forceful the action that was taken in Acheh, said Rutgers, the sooner the war would be over.[327] Despite such attacks from their own ranks, Van de Putte and Van Swieten consistently continued to pursue a more peaceful policy and to oppose a 'war of conquest' by the Netherlands.[328] However, in 1879 van de Putte had a mental break-down, described as 'brain fever' by his friend and fellow Young Liberal Pierson. Van de Putte left the Second Chamber and became a member of the more relaxed, but less important First Chamber in 1880.

Eventually, however, the majority of ministers, MPs and journalists no longer wanted to support the aggressive approach, either, though this was more a matter of finance than for humanitarian reasons. When, after 1876, the surplus in the East Indian budget gave way to a deficit, this was generally linked to the Acheh War, both by the Conservative spokesman Wintgens and the Liberal Minister Van Bosse. After all, war expenses that year exceeded about 18 million guilders, leaving a deficit of 16 million.[329] By now,

326. Cf. the general consultations, *Handelingen Tweede Kamer* (Parliamentary Reports of the Second Chamber), 11 November 1875, pp. 323–40.
327. Ibid., 27 November 1878, pp. 143–4. Cf. the increasing criticism in Quarles van Ufford, 'Koloniale kroniek', *De Economist* (1874) I, pp. 591–607; ibid. (1880) I, pp. 247–55. See also P. G. Booms, 'Atjeh', *De Gids* (1875) i, pp. 381–91; 'De afwachtende en de agressieve politiek in Atjeh', ibid. (1877) ii, pp. 327–63.
328. For Fransen van de Putte, see *Handelingen Tweede Kamer* (Parliamentary Reports of the Second Chamber), 26 September 1876, pp. 50–1, ibid., 27 November 1878, pp. 135–6; cf. 'Mijn advies aan den Minister van Koloniën nader toegelicht', *De Gids* (1876) iv, 507–19. See also Van Swieten, *Waarheid*. In *TNI*, too, the defensive approach was given complete support, cf. 'De vruchten der agressieve politiek', *TNI* (1878) II, pp. 74–82; 'Het Atjehse vraagstuk', ibid. (1880) II, pp. 367–80.
329. However, the main cause of the deficit, according to Wintgens, was the abolition of the system of forced cultivation, *Handelingen Tweede Kamer* (Parliamentary Reports of the Second Chamber), 25 November 1878, pp. 113–22. Cf. the

Van Bosse and Van Lansberge had already begun to suspect that, because of the military glory, promotion prospects and good payment, the commanding officers were aiming at an indefinite continuation of the war. They were whole-heartedly supported by suppliers of war material in the East Indies and the Netherlands.[330] Such notes were also sounded in the Netherlands. In 1878 another extension of the Acheh War budget was accepted by the Second Chamber with a good deal of grumbling by only 56 votes to 23. Until then, additional war expenses had always been accepted almost unanimously.[331] The insignificance of humanitarian objections to the war was reflected in the ratio of votes on Des Amorie van der Hoeven's proposal to conduct an official enquiry. The motion was presented in 1880, after a report that prisoners had been hanged during General Van der Heijden's latest military campaign. The motion, which was only supported by Keuchenius and a few other Christians in the Dutch Parliament, was rejected by 66 votes to 8.[332]

It was only when Van der Heijden's pacification was virtually completed that Van Goltstein, Minister of the Colonies since 1879, could be persuaded by Van Lansberge that the state of war should be brought to an end. Co-operating closely during 1880, they worked out plans for a regular civilian colonial administration in Acheh. The most important spokesmen in the Second Chamber accepted these in advance.[333] On 6 April 1881, despite continuing skirmishes, the end of the war was to be officially declared. Everybody in the Netherlands was more than willing to believe this. The Acheh War had been in the news almost continually since 1873. It had been a constant point on the cabinet's agenda and a permanent

---

letters of Van Bosse, Boon, *Van Lansberge*, nos 81, 88, 90, 98. See also Creutzberg, *Public Finance*, pp. 56–7.

330. Cf. Boon, *Van Lansberge*, nos 25, 55 and 94.

331. *Handelingen Tweede Kamer* (Parliamentary Reports of the Second Chamber), 14 May 1878, p. 750.

332. Ibid., 17 March 1880, pp. 785–96; cf. *Arnhemsche Courant* of 9 September 1879. Fransen van de Putte had also voted against this motion; an inquiry would have unnecessarily compromised the armed forces.

333. Boon, *Van Lansberge*, pp. 49–75. In the Second Chamber, the Liberals Van Rees and Van Gennep, the Calvinist Anti-Revolutionary Keuchenius and the Roman Catholic Des Amorie van der Hoeven spoke in favour of introducing civilian colonial administration, whereas the Conservative De Casembroot and the Liberal Rutgers van Rozenburg spoke against it; *Handelingen Tweede Kamer* (Parliamentary Reports of the Second Chamber), 29 September 1880, pp. 71–8; ibid., 28 March 1881, pp. 1115–25.

source of concern for the various secretaries of the colonies.[334] Every year the Second Chamber discussed the war thoroughly as part of its East Indian budget debate as well as on numerous other occasions. The official end of the war also meant a great relief for the Foreign Minister, because the inspection of contraband goods and other restrictions on trade and shipping around Acheh had become a constant source of tension with Britain. Foreign Minister Van Lynden van Sandenburg was now in a position to tell the British ambassador that such restrictions could be lifted together with the state of war.[335]

The blockade, which had been in force for large parts of Acheh almost uninterruptedly since 1873, constituted a problem of international law for the Netherlands, a small nation with great sensitivity in this respect. At the beginning, when the attitude of the great powers was still unclear, Gericke and Van de Putte had taken great care that international law was strictly respected and foreign vessels were spared as much as possible.[336] However, as most traders were non-Europeans, Achenese or Chinese from the Straits, Batavia soon began to try to find a justification for further control. For Achenese, argued the head of the Department of Justice in Batavia, international law was not really applicable, because it had been created for the relations between civilised, Western nations. It therefore ceased to be binding 'as soon as political and moral motives are absent'. Although Minister Van der Does did not object to a tightening of control as such, he felt that he would rather not go along with this argument.[337] Asser gave the same advice, pointing out that the indigenous Archipelago states must not be placed completely beyond the pale of international law:

> Such a theory could be dangerous, especially for a small state like the Netherlands. Towards the weaker states, too, we must uphold what we generally regard as law, so that we can demand of the stronger ones with even greater emphasis that they do not commit unlawful acts against us.

Nevertheless, because of its supremacy and responsibility in the Archipelago, the Netherlands was surely justified in taking special

---

334. Cf. Boon, *Van Lansberge*, nos 2, 12, 61, 109, 112, 169.
335. Woltring, *Bescheiden* II, nos 47 and 61; cf. Reid, *Contest*, pp. 190–8.
336. See Van de Putte's report to the King, 17 May 1873, Woltring, *Bescheiden* I, no. 397, cf. the instruction of the navy commander with Gericke's comment, ibid., nos 439–439A.
337. Ibid. II, nos 40–40A.

'police measures', according to Asser.[338] Traders from the Straits – British subjects, whether they were white or not – obviously did not see the logic of such reasoning. Here, a tightening of control could only be justified with reference to martial law, with all its unpleasant consequences for relations with Britain. The Ministry of Foreign Affairs therefore also welcomed an end to the war, especially now that problems with Britain had appeared in Borneo as well.

The Dilemma of the Outer Regions

Ever since 1815, Dutch claims of sovereignty over the vast Indonesian Archipelago had placed the Netherlands in a dilemma. These claims had to be maintained towards foreign powers as well as a large number of indigenous Archipelago states, even though only some parts, such as Java, could be effectively controlled and exploited. During the 1870s this dilemma was considerably aggravated, as the Acheh War continued to drag on, making demands on all the available power, while Dutch claims were also challenged in other parts of the Archipelago. The course of events forced the Netherlands to adopt an insecure, temporary solution of the dilemma: it would follow a strict policy of abstention outside Sumatra, unless direct conflict with a foreign power was imminent. The appearance of foreign adventurers or agents could no longer, for the time being, be regarded as sufficient cause for spreading Dutch rule. Both in The Hague and in Batavia there was a good deal of apprehension that there might be a 'second Acheh'.

Even before the Acheh War, however, it had been argued that concentration was desirable for Dutch expansion in the Archipelago. In the early 1870s, it was reported that quite a few foreigners were planning to establish themselves around the Archipelago, outside Dutch colonial rule, although the beginning of the Acheh War had of course shown that rumour and reality were very difficult to distinguish. After north Sumatra, Borneo and New Guinea particularly attracted attention, and it was said that Australians were planning to establish themselves in the western regions of New Guinea, which was officially a Dutch area, albeit without a permanent colonial post. Van Bosse was convinced that such a danger was, for the time being, rather theoretical, since the Australian colonies still had obtained neither the necessary degree of

338. Advice of 25 January 1877, ibid., no. 230.

independence nor the material means.[339] There was far greater concern in The Hague and Batavia when an Italian expedition was sent to the Archipelago with the objective of establishing a penal colony in Borneo. As we have seen, the presence of Italian warships near Singapore had already played its part in triggering the Acheh War. Not until the war had actually started did the Italian government withdraw its plans for Borneo, partly at Britain's request.[340]

Of all the Outer Regions, however, Sumatra had always been given the greatest amount of importance. For Dutch ministers of the colonies, the desirability of concentrating future expansion on that island had been the reason behind the Siak and Sumatra treaties. Fear of foreign intervention in this area had been significant enough for the Netherlands to risk a war in Acheh. When the war was about to break out, the thought even occurred in Batavia to send the Italians to New Guinea instead.[341] It is possible to see such pleas for concentration as an indication that the Netherlands did not have 'a "Grand Design" – a well-considered imperial policy'.[342] I have the impression, however, that it points to the limited, though purposeful expansionism of a small power. In any case, the Netherlands had the greatest interest in Sumatra. This interest was aimed at a number of different aspects: economic exploitation, scientific exploration and the spreading of Roman Catholic and Protestant missionary activities.

The most promising example of economic expansion in Sumatra was undoubtedly 'the miracle of Deli', that is its thriving cultivation of tobacco. During the first ten years of its existence, the Deli Company achieved a dividend of approximately 50 per cent. The fact that this success had already expressed itself in the form of direct dividends of 20 to 30 per cent must have contributed to the colonial administration's fast and powerful action when it quenched a revolt against the Sultan of Deli in 1872. Van Bosse could therefore whole-heartedly support Loudon's decision to send an expedition that was 'not too small'.[343]

339. Ibid. I, nos 191, 194, 226. Cf. Van Bosse to Loudon, 12 March 1872, Loudon Collection.

340. Woltring, *Bescheiden* I, nos 201–84, 293–4, 310, 314, 320, 371.

341. See the advice to the East Indian Council, 21 February 1873, ibid., no. 344. Cf. Loudon to Fransen van de Putte, 15 January 1873, quoted by Fasseur, 'Koloniale paradox', pp. 179–80.

342. Van Bosse to Loudon, 4 July 1872, Loudon Collection. Cf. P. J. Veth, 'Het landschap Deli op Sumatra', *TAG* (1877), pp. 160–5.

343. Boon, *Van Lansberge*, no. 19.

This intervention was followed, in 1873, by the establishment of a permanent colonial administration post. The treasured possession of a place like Deli also continued to be a source of latent fear that foreigners might intervene. In 1877, after a German application to establish a consulate in Deli had been turned down, Alting Mees remarked rather worriedly, 'They are probably going to turn to the sultan directly now.'[344] After all, many of the planters were Germans or from some other foreign country. The plantation workers were mainly Chinese who had at first been recruited from the Straits and later directly from China. The planters had their own ways to encourage production and maintain discipline among the labour force. When the local colonial administration tried to curb the worst excesses in the treatment of the workers, this was met with vehement protests. The young manager of the Deli Company and president of the Deli Planters Union, J. T. Cremer, argued the case for a more comprehensive, effective regulation of labour by the colonial administration eloquently in the Netherlands, by issuing a brochure and talking in person to the minister and several MPs. His arguments did not fail to have an effect. In 1880, a new 'Coolie Ordinance' was introduced, with a 'penal sanction' on any breach of contract on the part of the workers, enforced by the colonial administration. This ordinance, however, did not put an end to abuse by individual planters, and it created new abuse by individual administrators.[345]

The discovery of rich coalfields in Ombilin had initially caused even greater expectations than the cultivation of tobacco in Deli. During this period of 'steel and steam' this discovery had given rise to all kinds of large-scale plans for the exploitation of fields, the building of railway lines and the opening of coal depots which would provide coal and steamships in the entire Indian Ocean.[346] When the explorer and engineer W. H. de Greve requested a concession, he was supported by Prince Henry, though De Greve lost his life during some new research in Ombilin. To meet increasing demand, further opportunities for concessions were provided in

344. Ibid., p. 179.
345. Cremer, *Woord*. Cf. Boon, *Van Lansberge*, p. 128–9 and no. 17.
346. Cf. J. K. W. Quarles van Ufford, 'Steenkolen-ontginning en spoorwegaanleg op Sumatra', *De Economist* (1872) I, pp. 163–4, ibid. (1873) I, pp. 58–68; G. H. van Soest, 'Sumatra's toekomst', *TNI* (1872), pp. 120–41. For the coal depots, see the report of the consul in Jeddah, *Consulaire verslagen* (Consular Reports) 1874, I, pp. 519–20.

the mining regulations of 1873.[347] For the time being, however, these opportunities did not yield many results. Only on the small, easily accessible island of Billiton did tin-mining turn out to be a profitable business. Like Ombilin coal, however, most mineral riches could only be found in rather inaccessible and unknown parts of Sumatra. Thus, exploration became necessary, and this was the point where the Dutch Geographical Society offered its services.

The Dutch Geographical Society had originally suggested sending some of its research workers along with the second Acheh expedition. After all, its chairman Veth still had to make amends for his odd predictions at the beginning of the war. Van Swieten, though, objected because it was impossible for him to guarantee the safety of the geographers.[348] However, when the Society carried out a scientific expedition in the upper Djambi by itself, the authorities gave it all the necessary co-operation. Apart from geographical and ethnological research, the expedition was mainly meant to survey the opportunities for agriculture and mining. 'Perhaps the time isn't far off', warned De Casembroot, a leading member, MP and rear-admiral, 'when foreigners will make every effort to find sources of trade and welfare without us.'[349]

The response to this initiative – a 'real Dutch voyage of discovery' – was particularly enthusiastic. Prince Henry became its patron and assured the co-operation of the government. Of the necessary capital, the executive committee raised about 30,000 guilders from private sources, while the government contributed the remaining 20,000. The contributors included many important names from the Dutch world of trade and finance: apart from Prince Henry, there were, among others, Pierson, Wertheim, Boissevain, Van Eeghen, the Netherlands Trading Company and other Amsterdam businesses, and from Rotterdam there were, among others, Pincoffs and Muller.[350] The press, too, was full of praise, even though there was also some doubt, occasionally, as to whether such an ambitious undertaking was actually feasible.[351]

The expedition itself, which started at the beginning of 1877, was

347. Wellenstein, *Mijnbouwvraagstuk*, pp. 18–20, 42–8
348. See *TAG* (1876), pp. 11–12, 195–6.
349. Ibid., pp. 117–25. Cf. the information on the first plans by the board members and Prince Henry at the general meeting on 20 July 1874, ibid., pp. 70–1.
350. Ibid. supplementary sheet showing a survey of the first subscriptions; cf. ibid. 1877, pp. 77–8.
351. Cf. Quarles van Ufford's 'Colonial Chronicle' in *De Economist* (1876) II, pp. 977–8; ibid. (1878) I, pp. 253–8; ibid. (1880) I, pp. 338–40.

not an unqualified success. Its leader, Lieutenant J. Schouw Sant-voort, died shortly after its departure. Because of the hostile attitude on the part of the local population and insufficient co-operation from the local colonial administration, the remaining members had to omit part of their intended route. Together with the organising committee, D. D. Veth, a young engineer and son of the chairman, conducted the scientific examination of the soil and its minerals. Unfortunately, however, the results were not the ones that had been hoped for, though the final results of the entire research were extensive enough to be published in nine large volumes.[352] Never-theless, the expedition had enabled the Society to establish itself firmly, both nationally and internationally. In 1878, the number of members rose to nearly a thousand. And in 1880, when the partici-pants of the Sumatra expedition had only just returned to the Netherlands, Veth developed his first plans for a Dutch expedition to the interior of Africa, which was to be organised in co-operation with King Leopold of Belgium.[353]

In the area of Christian mission, Dutch organisations contributed considerably less to the development of Sumatra. Neither Roman Catholic nor Protestant missionaries from the Netherlands had, until then, succeeded in gaining a firm foothold. From 1862 on-wards, a German organisation, the Rhineland Missionary Society, had been working among the animist Batak tribes, who formed the largest mission field in the area. On the basis of state control over the Christian mission in the East Indies, the colonial administration preferred not to send other missionaries into such areas. Further-more, missionaries were given no access whatever to areas where other religions – such as Islam or Hinduism – had already estab-lished themselves.

Both rules, which were designed to prevent unrest among the local population, came under increasing criticism during the 1870s. In the Netherlands, Neurdenburg, in particular, argued from a 'political and ethical point of view' that the whole of the East Indies should be opened up to Protestant mission, in its fight against the 'deadly parasite' of Islam, which was advancing everywhere.[355]

---

352. See Veth, *Midden-Sumatra*.
353. 'Nederland en het onderzoek van Afrika', *TAG* (1881), pp. 41–2. Cf. ibid. (1879) p. 218.
354. Cf. Coolsma, *Zendingseeuw*, pp. 306f.
355. J. C. Neurdenburg, 'Hoe zal men de oogen van onze Regering en van ons gansche volk openen voor het feit dat de Islam in onze bezittingen meer en meer opdringt', *Mededeelingen* (1876), pp. 351–67; 'Het doordringen van den Islam in

Pointing out, in this context, that co-operation between Protestant mission and colonial rule had brought order, peace and civilisation to the Batak areas, he compared this with the devastating war of attrition in nearby Acheh against a 'population roused by religious and ethnic fanaticism'. Incidentally, though, the Dutch Missionary Society, which had its established mission fields elsewhere in the Archipelago, was very happy to leave the Batak areas to its German sister organisation.[356] On the other hand, the various Protestant Dutch missionary organisations protested vehemently against attempts of Roman Catholic missionaries to gain access to the Protestant mission fields of the Celebes and the Moluccas.[357]

In the Dutch Parliament, too, pressure from Protestant missionary organisations became more noticeable when Calvinist Anti-Revolutionaries gained an increasing number of seats in the Second Chamber. As Anti-Revolutionaries supported his policies in other respects, Van Bosse asked the colonial administration – though with his usual sarcasm – for a more flexible attitude towards missionaries: 'It seems to me that if they do want to go and preach among the Alfoor, Batak and Dayak, they should be given the full freedom to get themselves eaten up!'[358] In general, however, Van Bosse felt that Islam should be respected and that the Protestant and Roman Catholic missions should be kept well apart from each other: 'May the indigenous population be spared the strife between Geneva and Rome!'[359] In 1878, the colonial administration therefore denied Roman Catholic missionaries access to the Minahassa in the Celebes, to avoid turmoil caused by Protestant organisations in the Netherlands. This was done although the local Dutch administrator would in fact have welcomed the admission of Roman Catholics, 'to counterbalance Protestant missionaries'.[360]

During the 1870s, local government officials were generally more inclined towards experiments than the government in The Hague

---

Neêrlandsch-Indië', ibid., pp. 464–8; 'De Islam in Nederlandsch-Indië', *Handelingen Indisch Genootschap* (Reports of the East Indian Society), 5 March 1878, pp. 38–62.

356. Neurdenburg, 'De zegen van het Nederlandsch bestuur in de Battalanden op Sumatra', *Mededeelingen* (1876), pp. 124–8.

357. Cf. Report of the general meeting 1879, ibid. (1880), p. 92, Report on the Missionary Day of the Utrecht Missionary Association, *Berigten* (1880), p. 83.

358. Boon, *Van Lansberge*, no. 27; cf. *Handelingen Tweede Kamer* (Parliamentary Reports of the Second Chamber), 22 November 1877, pp. 70–3.

359. Boon, *Van Lansberge*, no. 36.

360. Ibid., nos 48, 56, 92.

and Batavia. In addition to the 7,500 troops fighting in Acheh, a military presence of only 450 was left for 'the extension of Dutch authority in the Outer Regions', compared with 1,600 a decade earlier. Under such circumstances, the 'frontier imperialism' of ambitious government officials was drastically curbed, as Fasseur has already shown.[361] In fact, The Hague wanted to go even further than Batavia. In co-operation with the local colonial administration, Van Lansberge had developed plans for the direct establishment of colonial rule on Halmahera and other islands in the Eastern parts of the Archipelago. However, these plans were finally blocked by ministers in The Hague.[362]

In the Second Chamber, there were repeated warnings of the financial consequences if expansion were pushed even further. Van Rees, in particular, urged that

> all those grand designs of conquest, annexation and the spreading of direct rule should be abandoned for good, and, if there are still civil servants in our Outer Regions who, out of ambition or a desire for war, want to pursue such a path, then such tendencies ought to be suppressed.

Des Amorie van der Hoeven gladly agreed, though he feared that the further spreading of colonial rule would be inevitable in the future, due to the continuing danger that other countries might establish colonial posts in the Archipelago.[363]

Indeed, when a mainly British concession in Northern Borneo seemed to put Dutch claims on the area in jeopardy, even The Hague was finally prepared to start spreading its colonial rule. In 1877 sovereignty rights were ceded by the Sultan of Brunei to the Austrian consul-general in Hong Kong, Baron Von Overbeck, and the British businessman Alfred Dent. At first, this was not regarded as sufficient cause for intervention. On 17 April 1878 Van Bylandt, in London, had informed the Dutch government about the concession.[364] On 9 May, during question time in the Second Chamber, the Conservative MP Wintgens and the Liberal MP Lenting reminded the government of the 'days of James Brooke'. But, as Van Bosse declared, with the support of most members, this

361. Fasseur, 'Koloniale paradox', p. 185; cf. [Colijn], *Politiek Beleid* I, p. 176; ibid. II-A, p. 211.
362. Ibid., pp. 133–49; cf. Boon, *Van Lansberge*, pp. 25–7.
363. *Handelingen Tweede Kamer* (Parliamentary Reports of the Second Chamber), 25 November 1878, pp. 100–1; 26 November 1878, pp. 123–4.
364. Woltring, *Bescheiden* II, no. 358.

was a matter of 'private individuals rather than powers'.[365]

It then became obvious, however, that the concession extended over a part of Eastern Borneo where the Netherlands claimed sovereignty rights, and this did indeed give rise to some anxiety. On 24 September Van Bylandt received an instruction from the Foreign Minister. With reference to the 1824 treaty which, after all, was aimed at preventing 'mixed possession' in the Archipelago, he was to request the British government not to lend any support to Dent and Von Overbeck's enterprise.[366]

However, the position of the Netherlands was not very strong in this respect. Only a year later, in November 1879, the British Foreign Secretary Salisbury was to announce the British point of view concerning the 1824 treaty, though it had already been well known in The Hague since the 1840s: according to the letter of the treaty, Britain only acknowledged Dutch sovereignty rights over Borneo for that part which lay south of Singapore.[367] Another problem emerged. Upon further investigation, it turned out that the treaty with the local rajah, which formed the basis of the Netherlands' specific claims in eastern Borneo, had never been made known to Britain. Since then Dutch maps had been published which showed faulty borders in this respect.[368] Minister Van Rees felt that, with regard to the very limited Dutch economic presence in Borneo, the possible advance of British economic influence should be prevented. To be on the safe side, the Batavian colonial administration sent a reconnaissance expedition to the disputed area in 1879. On 31 July it was decided in consultation with The Hague that 'to protect our borders at Batoo Tinagat, the Dutch flag shall be raised and guarded by an armed boat.'[369] The Foreign Affairs Department was also in agreement with this step. By now it had become rather suspicious of the evasive answers that were given by Salisbury and Pauncefote, the responsible under-secretary, with regard to British aims in the enterprise, which Von Overbeck had left by now. Thus, there was a good deal of speculation in the Dutch department of foreign affairs that the concession might receive the status of a British protectorate, even though Van Bylandt had been

---

365. Handelingen Tweede Kamer (Parliamentary Reports of the Second Chamber), 9 and 10 May 1878, pp. 689–704; cf. Boon, *Van Lansberge*, no. 56.
366. Woltring, *Bescheiden* II, no. 387; cf. no. 378.
367. Ibid., nos 458, 468.
368. Ibid., no. 387A; cf. the extensive departmental memoranda nos 446 A–B–C.
369. Ibid., no. 446; cf. nos 440, 446A; Boon, *Van Lansberge*, no. 111.

given the impression by Salisbury that it certainly would not come to that.[370]

On 24 June 1880, however, Van Bylandt was to learn from Granville, Salisbury's successor, that there had been plans for quite a while to give a Royal Charter to Dent's enterprise and that this had been suggested by Pauncefote. Granville gave the impression to Van Bylandt that the Dutch government would certainly be consulted before the Charter was actually awarded.[371] At the beginning of 1881, The Hague government learnt through personal contacts that on 16 December 1880 Pauncefote had promised Dent the Charter on behalf of the British government, even though no official British announcement had yet been made. 'By no means do I therefore wish to conceal the unpleasant impression', wrote Foreign Minister Van Lynden van Sandenburg to Van Bylandt, 'which the secretive and hardly confidential attitude of the British government made on me.'[372] He instructed Van Bylandt to submit a diplomatic note which explained very clearly on the basis of the 1824 treaty and Dutch sovereignty rights in north-east Borneo why the Dutch government objected to the Charter. It did this so clearly, in fact, that Granville told Van Bylandt informally that he could not possible accept it. He suggested withdrawing the note and replacing it with a milder version. Van Lynden agreed, convinced that Granville must have fully understood the seriousness of the Dutch objections. However, Granville's laconic reply to the new note – a vague promise that Dutch objections would be looked into again – did not meet Van Lynden's expectations at all.[373] When the Charter was officially granted on 1 November 1881, Van Bylandt found out through a report in The Times.[374]

In Parliament and the press in the Netherlands, the attitude of the government towards Britain on the Borneo question was branded as 'feeble' and even 'dangerous' by various sides. The unfolding of the Dutch flag over Batu Tinagat was welcomed by most MPs, 'even by those who did not generally advocate an extension of our colonial possessions'. However, when Von Overbeck's enterprise was able

370. Woltring, *Bescheiden* II, no. 468.
371. Ibid., nos 524, 530.
372. Ibid. III, no. 23; cf. Irwin, *Borneo*, pp. 204–5.
373. Woltring, *Bescheiden* III, nos 34, 42, 46, 51.
374. Ibid., no. 80. From the very beginning, there was very little sympathy in The Hague for Van Bylandt's approach to the Borneo question, partly 'because the 1824 treaty is Van Bylandt's hobby' (Van Goltstein); ibid., no. 92; cf. ibid. II, nos 387, 463, 526.

to proceed without being disturbed, De Casembroot commented: 'If only a warship had been sent at the time . . . and if the matter hadn't been settled with a good grace, then we'd have shown him the door with a bad grace, using our guns, and it would never have come to this.'[375] For many MPs it was obvious that the 1824 treaty made the Netherlands the legal owner of the whole of Borneo. The modification of this claim by Minister Van Goltstein gave rise to indignant reactions.[376]

British action in Borneo was seen by the Dutch press as related to Australian attempts to establish themselves in and around New Guinea. The British annexation of Ashmore Shoal in 1878, an insignificant reef where the Netherlands had originally claimed sovereignty, was regarded as significant in this context.[377] According to the Conservative paper *Dagblad*, Britain was pursuing a cunning 'policy of small bites' in the Archipelago.[378] 'If we don't do anything,' said Kuyper in the *Standaard*, 'then our innermost conviction tells us that it will only be a matter of time before the whole of Northern Borneo and New Guinea are under the British flag.'[379] In a much-quoted series of articles on Dutch rights in Borneo, published in *Themis*, L. van Woudrichem van Vliet, attorney at the highest court of justice in Batavia, warned of the sugary but ruthless power politics of British diplomats. If a small power such as the Netherlands gave in, then that would only stimulate Britain's gluttony even further: 'Our passivity would probably turn into painful suffering very quickly.'[380]

But there were also a number of less narrow-minded voices. The colonial expert Robidé van der Aa showed convincingly that the Netherlands could not possibly lay any claim to the whole of Borneo on the basis of earlier treaties. Several MPs, among them Keuchenius and Des Amorie van der Hoeven, also subscribed to

---

375. *Handelingen Tweede Kamer* (Parliamentary Reports of the Second Chamber), 22 October 1879; cf. ibid., *Bijlagen* (Appendices) 1879–80, no. 46.
376. Ibid., 22 October 1870, pp. 212–25.
377. For the British annexation of the Ashmore Reef, see Woltring, *Bescheiden* II, nos 435, 439, 449, 488. For Australian expansionism, see ibid., nos 93, 180, 423. Cf. Thompson, *Australian Imperialism*, pp. 38–40.
378. *Het Dagblad van Zuid-Holland en 's-Gravenhage*, 21 and 24 October 1879.
379. *De Standaard*, 17 December 1879.
380. L. van Woudrichem van Vliet, *Themis* (1879), pp. 37–95, 309–39, 370–455, 550–605.

this view.[381] Ex-minister De Waal, who had formerly called Britain the 'natural ally' of the Netherlands, even felt that Von Overbeck and Dent's enterprise should be welcomed. After all, the Netherlands was not capable of developing the whole island anyway.[382] However, a typical representative of mainline Liberalism such as Quarles van Ufford could not share De Waal's moderate view.[383]

Gradually, in 1881, the more moderate voices with regard to Britain were drowned even further, because, at the time, the Netherlands was intoxicated with its new discovery of kinship with the South African Boers. Was not Britain showing its true face in South Africa, where it was perfidiously trying to smother the Boers' struggle for freedom? And so it was with reference to Britain's action both in Borneo and in South Africa at the beginning of the 1880s that the term imperialism was first used.

381. P. J. B. C. Robidé van der Aa, 'De omvang van Neerlands rechten in den Indischen archipel', *Handelingen Indisch Genootschap* (Reports of the East Indian Society), 29 March 1881, pp. 1–28; cf. *Handelingen Tweede Kamer* (Parliamentary Reports of the Second Chamber), 22 October 1879, p. 216; 20 December 1879, pp. 690–1.
382. De Waal, *Indische Financiën* I; ibid. III, pp. 203–4, 212.
383. *De Economist* (1879) II, p. 1140.

2

The Scramble for Colonies
(1880–1890)

The rivalry between the European powers which had already become noticeable outside Europe during the 1870s led to a real scramble for colonies in the 1880s – a 'steeple chase' as some contemporaries called it.[1] Although the significance of the relationship between formal and informal imperialism as well as between European and non-European causes has tended to be qualified in recent historiography, there is no dispute about the phenomenon of this competitive struggle.

European colonial aspirations were above all directed at Africa, though the traditional colonial powers also continued to expand their spheres in Asia. However, unlike Asia, there was a direct clash between British and French interests in Africa. This rivalry had been triggered by the Egyptian crisis in 1882, which had also affected other parts of Africa such as the Congo estuary. Meanwhile, however, other European powers apart from Britain and France were also beginning to seek colonies, so that an element of frenzy was added to the whole race. Germany's new colonial aspirations were the most significant in this respect.[2]

But apart from leading to rivalry, colonial expansion also offered an opportunity to compensate for the deadlock in political and economic relations in Europe. Bismarck in particular was able to use both rivalry and co-operation to his own advantage. At the Berlin Conference in 1884–5, a solution to Anglo-French rivalry around the Congo was found under his guidance whereby the area was put under the rule of King Leopold's association. Furthermore, rules were fixed which were to give a more orderly character to the

1. H. Brunschwig, 'Imperialism, Scramble and Steeple-Chase', Louis, *Imperialism*, pp. 204–8.
2. Cf. Betts, *False Dawn*, pp. 93–8; Baumgart, *Imperialismus*, pp. 23–40; Eldridge, *Victorian Imperialism*, pp. 139f.; Fieldhouse, *Economics*, pp. 251f.

acquisition of colonies by European powers. Nevertheless, Bismarck could not – and would not – put an end to the scramble itself, a race that had been caused by the economic crisis in Europe, by European power politics and by various local crises outside Europe.[3] In the 1880s the interaction between an increasing number of competing European powers and an increasing number of non-European territories was giving this process a momentum of its own.

The Netherlands did not exactly play one of the leading parts in this new stage of European expansion. On the face of it, it seems as if the Netherlands pursued the exact opposite of imperialism in its foreign and colonial policies during the 1880s. After the cession of Elmina, Dutch diplomacy, as far as was possible, kept aloof from the partitioning of Africa. In Asia the Netherlands somehow or other adhered to the formal boundary claims of the Dutch East Indies. Within those boundaries it continued its policy of abstention, while at the same time concentrating its presence in Acheh. However, the Netherlands always had to deal with the imperialism of other countries, whether it wanted to or not. On closer inspection it turned out that the borders of the Dutch East Indies were not very clearly marked everywhere. At the Berlin Conference the Netherlands was therefore particularly concerned that the discussions on effective occupation should be limited to Africa.

But the conference also had some rather more direct implications for the Netherlands, in view of its extensive trade interests in the Congo area. And because of its trade route to the East Indies, it was also affected by developments in Egypt. Even in South America the Dutch position no longer seemed to be safe from the new assertiveness of the great European powers, and the century-old definition of Surinam's borders became a discussion point when France began to make territorial claims in the area. Despite all this, the Dutch government tried to maintain the status quo wherever possible. Nevertheless Dutch society in the 1880s did bring forth a new expansionist urge, though it was directed not so much at the extension of colonial possessions but the reinforcement of the Dutch presence in the South African republics with which a rather strong 'kinship' was felt.

---

3. Cf. Kennedy, *Rise*, chapter 10; Wehler, *Bismarck*, chapter 6; Gifford and Louis, *Britain*, chapters 1–2.

The Partition of the World

The Dutch Point of View

During the 1880s there was a good deal of discussion as to the attitude which the Netherlands should take towards the increasing colonial rivalry, and the phenomenon itself was discerned very clearly by contemporaries. 'A new partition of the world has started, and each nation is eager not to go empty-handed', wrote the Calvinist leader Kuyper in 1884. 'In history,' he added ominously, 'such a phenomenon has always signalled a turning point and the beginning of a new order of things.'[4]

From this point of view Kuyper himself zealously favoured a Dutch South Africa – Dutch not in a colonial sense but as a 'Dutch United States of Africa and continuing to be in close fellowship with the old Netherlands'.[5] Like many of his contemporaries, Kuyper knew how to distinguish clearly between the justified aspirations of a small nation like the Netherlands, which wanted to maintain its threatened position within and outside Europe, and 'the desire [of other European countries] to pursue large-scale colonial politics'. Seeing other European states as imperialist also meant that the Netherlands itself was regarded as non-imperialist and as a small European state which had already acquired extensive colonial possessions but might not be able to maintain these without damage.

As we have seen before, this dual perception concerned above all Dutch relations with Britain, the great colonial power which seemed to threaten Dutch interests both in Borneo and in South Africa. There had already been warnings of the 'perfidious Albion' at the cession of Elmina. But the fact that both colonial powers had to wage colonial wars as a result of their treaties – one on the Gold Coast and the other in Acheh – led to a feeling of solidarity rather than distrust. 'As far as colonies are concerned,' said Van Goltstein philosophically, 'it is our fate that expansion is necessary.'[6] 'Just like Great Britain,' Des Amorie van der Hoeven agreed, 'we will be forced to expand our sovereign authority.'[7] As for the Indonesian Archipelago, a far more pessimistic view was taken in the Nether-

---

4. *De Standaard*, 5 January 1884; cf. ibid., 4 January 1890.
5. *De Standaard*, 8 July 1884.
6. *Handelingen Eerste Kamer* (Parliamentary Reports of the First Chamber), 16 June 1873, p. 345.
7. *Handelingen Tweede Kamer* (Parliamentary Reports of the Second Chamber), 26 November 1878, p. 124.

lands with regard to the expansionist aspirations of new European powers such as Italy and also non-European countries such as the United States and even Australia, 'the future United States of the South', according to Van Bosse.[8]

This relatively mild view of Britain – as an old but familiar overseas rival – disappeared, however, when at the end of the 1870s Britain seemed to start a systematic policy of world-wide expansion under Disraeli. The powerful language with which this 'Imperial Policy' was inaugurated did not give rise to a lot of confidence in the future. When Disraeli declared that under his leadership Britain would never follow the fate of 'Genoa, and Venice, and Holland', this caused quite a lot of resentment in the Netherlands. The fact that, according to Wintgens, Britain had manoeuvred itself into the same perilous position in Afghanistan as the Netherlands in Acheh was poor consolation.[9] It was obvious, at any rate, that Britain was pressing forward in Borneo and South Africa – places which meant more to the Netherlands than the Gold Coast or Afghanistan. And so the pro-British *Handelsblad*, for example, on the Borneo question commented that it was 'more desirable to have colonial rivals as distant friends than close neighbours'. The *NRC* also warned of Britain's 'imperialist aspirations' in this context.[10]

Meanwhile the urge to expand or acquire colonies had also become apparent in other European countries: first in France, then in Germany, Belgium and Italy. 'In recent years, particularly in recent months, there seems to have been a reversal in ideas about colonial possessions', concluded Fransen van de Putte, a well-informed observer, at the beginning of 1885:

> We can see Britain and France fixing their eyes on an extension of their authority. We can see Germany, which apparently used to concentrate its powers on Europe, doing the same . . . and the iron hand of the German Chancellor stretching out for the South and the Far East.[11]

The increasing colonial rivalry between the European states was

8. Cf. Boon, *Van Lansberge*, no. 79.
9. *Handelingen Tweede Kamer* (Parliamentary Reports of the Second Chamber), 26 November 1878, pp. 121–2; ibid., 5 December 1878, pp. 271–2. Disraeli subsequently told the Dutch ambassador that he had not meant to denigrate the Netherlands with the offensive passage in his Guildhall Speech of 9 November 1878; Woltring, *Bescheiden* II, no. 398.
10. *Het Algemeen Handelsblad*, 28 May 1880; *NRC*, 5 January 1882.
11. *Handelingen Eerste Kamer* (Parliamentary Reports of the First Chamber), 18 April 1885, pp. 242–3.

regarded by most observers in the Netherlands with mixed feelings. The Liberal MP W. H. de Beaufort felt that it was 'a very serious situation for a great colonial state like the Netherlands';[12] whereas his colleague Van Houten saw it as a useful counterweight against 'British domination outside Europe'.[13]

Like Van Houten, many contemporaries were hoping that Britain would – under pressure from Germany or France – be a little more accommodating towards the Netherlands, for example in its attitude regarding Borneo and Acheh. When the Conservative Disraeli government was replaced by the Liberal Gladstone in 1880, this led at first to some hopeful optimism. In the Netherlands there was a good deal of trust in the person and policies of 'Aristides' Gladstone – in Christian circles even more than among Liberals. Kuyper, for example, considered Gladstone 'the true Christian statesman' of Europe.[14] In the case of South Africa this trust was indeed confirmed, whereas in other areas the Liberal government continued the expansionist policy of its predecessor, though more hesitantly and reluctantly. At times it seemed that the appearance of France and Germany as colonial powers made Britain adopt a harder rather than a more relaxed attitude towards the Netherlands, for example regarding the Suez Canal and New Guinea.

Even taken by itself, the emergence of new colonial powers was regarded by the Netherlands as not entirely without danger, particularly in the case of Germany. Bismarck's chosen role as an arbiter in international colonial disputes was undoubtedly appreciated by the Netherlands, though his own colonial initiatives were viewed with growing scepticism.[15] Christian spokesmen, in particular, felt rather apprehensive about the power politics of the Iron

12. *Handelingen Tweede Kamer* (Parliamentary Reports of the Second Chamber), 26 February 1885, p. 343.

13. S. van Houten, 'Onze internationale stelling', *Vragen des Tijds*, 1884, II, pp. 315–18. Cf. H. J. Bool, 'De koloniale wereld', *De Economist*, 1884, II, pp. 696–8; G. H. van Soest, 'Engeland en Rusland in Azië', *TNI*, 1884, I, pp. 198–9; *idem*, 'Duitschland als koloniseerende en koloniale mogendheid', ibid. II, pp. 220–1.

14. For Kuyper's great admiration for Gladstone as a 'Christian statesman' see Van Koppen, *Kuyper*, pp. 8–9 and 75–6. The appreciation of Gladstone in *De Tijd* was inspired by his attitude to the Irish question, 17 and 29 January 1881. In the *NRC*, however, Gladstone's 'hypocrisy' with regard to South Africa was at first criticised, 6 January and 7 February 1881.

15. Cf. T. M. C. Asser, 'De Congo-akte', *De Gids*, 1885, ii, pp. 318 and 339; G. H. van Soest, 'De Congo-conferentie', *TNI*, 1884, II, pp. 389–401; *Nederlandsche Industrieel*, 1 March 1885; *Amsterdammer* (weekly), 23 November 1884; *Het Handelsblad*, 27 June and 22 November 1884, 4 March 1885; *De Tijd*, 26 and 30 June 1884; *De Standaard*, 9 January, 20 September and 4 December 1884.

Chancellor. This, in fact, was to lead to a revaluation of the British role in colonial matters. 'It would be foolish to forget', the Catholic paper *De Tijd* warned at an early stage, 'that, as a colonial power, Britain would be our ally rather than our enemy if ever the answer to the question *Bedarf Deutschland der Colonien?* [Does Germany need colonies?] were to turn its sharp edge against us.'[16] A few years later, during the heated discussions of the Nisero question in the Dutch Parliament, Des Amorie van der Hoeven was to reject the suggestion sharply that support should be sought from Germany. 'It would be more dangerous for us', he said, 'to have Germany as a "friendly" neighbour than to be wronged by Britain.'[17] Also the experienced Conservative diplomat and politician Van Goltstein openly expressed the hope that Britain would find its self-confidence and initiative with regard to Germany again: 'Every Dutchman who sympathises with our powerful neighbour because of our common ground in morals, public institutions and colonial interests must wish this.'[18]

Apart from the potential political consequences of colonial rivalry, attention was also given to the economic implications in the Netherlands. The new imperialism itself was quite generally understood as a largely economic phenomenon, an attempt to find solutions outside Europe to the country's problems of increasing surplus production and over-population. This was the sense in which Disraeli's 'Imperial Policy' had already been interpreted at the end of the 1870s. The fact that British industry was increasingly threatened by German industry was seen very clearly.[19] French colonial expansion, too, was seen as a result of Germany's emergence, though primarily in a political sense, that is, as an attempt to restore its position as a great power outside Europe – a position which had been considerably weakened with its defeat by Germany.[20] Whether directly or not, Germany was seen as having a key role in the scramble for colonies in the 1880s. Bismarck's ulterior motives were also largely interpreted as economic, although

16. *De Tijd*, 7 March 1881.
17. *Handelingen Tweede Kamer* (Parliamentary Reports of the Second Chamber), closed session, 13 June 1884 (ARA), pp. 184f.
18. W. van Goltstein, 'Engelsch–Duitsche koloniale discussiën', *De Gids*, 1885, iv, p. 237.
19. *Nederlandsche Industrieel*, 9 February 1879. Cf. Woltring, *Bescheiden* II, no. 396.
20. Cf. *Standaard*, 5 and 8 January 1884; *De Tijd*, 5 and 7 July 1884; *Het Handelsblad*, 8 and 19 January 1884.

considerations of political strategies or tactics were not ignored, either. as Kuyper put it,

> now that nothing needs to be feared or done in Europe itself, the sharp-sighted Chancellor turns his eye towards overseas territories where he is hoping to find markets that enable him to bring welfare to the great German empire by means of a prospering trade and industry, where the surplus population can go without being lost to the fatherland.[21]

The economic crisis which generally dominated the mid-1880s strongly coloured any discussion of the new imperialism. According to De Beaufort, the scramble for colonies was 'a consequence of the economic reaction which seized the European governments, especially the revival of colonial policies . . . which is in fact nothing but one of the forms in which the revival of protectionism is currently manifesting itself.'[22]

Although the economic crisis had meanwhile become clearly noticeable in the Netherlands as well, the Dutch were generally less concerned about the economic consequences of the new imperialism than its political consequences. As a symptom of protectionism, which was gaining ground everywhere, it was of course deplored in free-trade circles. But the same people also pointed out that the newly acquired colonies could not possibly meet the high expectations. After all, according to seasoned observers in the Netherlands, one was dealing with territories 'where perhaps diplomatic laurels can be obtained but certainly not colonial fruits'. 'Amusing and even touching' was Robidé van der Aa's verdict on the 'euphoric shouts of joy' with which the German press greeted the occupation of the barren coast of South-West Africa.[23] Fransen van de Putte therefore felt that the Netherlands had very little to fear from the new imperialism in the future, 'because anyone who ventures out into that territory will realise that the assets are outbalanced by great liabilities'.[24] As long as Dutch trade was left unimpeded in the economically interesting areas, there was nothing to worry about.

21. *Standaard*, 4 December 1884. Cf. Van Soest, 'Duitschland als koloniseerende en koloniale mogendheid', pp. 218–19; Van Goltstein, 'Engelsch–Duitsche koloniale discussien', pp. 202–3.

22. *Handelingen Tweede Kamer* (Parliamentary Reports of the Second Chamber), 26 February 1885, p. 343.

23. P. J. B. C. Robidé van der Aa, 'Wat wil de Duitsche Regeering op de Westkust van Africa?', *TAG*, 1884, p. 592.

24. *Handelingen Eerste Kamer* (Parliamentary Reports of the First Chamber), 18 April 1885, p. 243.

The solemn proclamation of free trade for the whole of the Congo area at the Berlin Conference initially set everybody's mind at rest. In so far as anyone in the 1880s was still concerned about the economic consequences of increasing colonial expansion, these worries were still very much a continuation of the discussions of the 1870s and aimed at the backwardness of Dutch trade and shipping. The role of the government continued to be the central topic, both for the subsidising of new steamship lines and the extension of Dutch consular representation overseas. With reference to official proposals for a further extension and reform of the consular service at the end of the 1880s, the Chambers of Commerce urgently requested a larger number of professional Dutch consuls. What was new was their plea for a *consul missus*: in the future the state should 'send out consular civil servants as pioneers to show the way and prepare the field for private enterprise'.[25] The world of commerce, too, took steps in this direction. A special organisation called Het Buitenland (Foreign Countries) was founded. Its aim would be to send out 'Dutch youngsters' who would gather the necessary experience working for European trading companies.[26]

Meanwhile, the worries about adapting Dutch trade and shipping to the changing demands of the world economy remained. Rotterdam incidentally, found this much easier than Amsterdam, so that the Amsterdam-based merchant and journalist Muller felt prompted to warn of a 'dissipation' of efforts: 'Too many harbours and too many universities. Too many colonies, I almost added.'[27] And indeed trade figures during the 1880s showed a changing picture. Imports from the Dutch East Indies displayed a marked improvement, with an overall import share of 6.7 per cent in 1880 to 12.3 per cent in 1890. Exports to the East Indies, on the other hand, went back even further, from 7.4 per cent in 1880 to 4.9 per cent in 1890. Overseas trade, outside the East Indies, had increased somewhat to 5.7 per cent of imports and 2 per cent of exports. Nevertheless, a considerable amount of indirect exports to non-Western countries

---

25. *Verslag KvK Rotterdam* (Report of the Rotterdam Chamber of Commerce) 1888, Appendix XII. Cf. *Verslag KvK Amsterdam* (Report of the Amsterdam Chamber of Commerce) 1887, pp. 187–90; P. N. Muller, 'Onze Consuls', *De Gids*, 1888, i, pp. 279f.

26. G. M. Boissevain, 'Nederland's Buitenlandsche handel en de Vereeniging het Buitenland', *De Economist*, 1889, I, pp. 584–5. Cf. *Verslag KvK Amsterdam* (Report of the Amsterdam Chamber of Commerce) 1886, p. 16; ibid., Rotterdam, p. 12.

27. P. N. Muller, 'Een Handelsverslag', *De Economist*, 1886, II, p. 645.

remained. Despite a slight improvement, shipping continued to be the main sticking point in overseas trade.[28]

All in all, the new imperialism of the 1880s was viewed in the Netherlands in terms of interest, that is in terms of political and economic self-interest: 'The aims', said *De Tijd*, 'which provide the motivation for acquiring colonial possessions are selfish and hardly ever tempered with a small measure of idealism; the methods which are used are sometimes unfair and dishonourable.'[29] Most observers did not seem to gain the impression that there was much evidence of a civilising mission, as had been proclaimed for colonial expansion by the other European nations. There was only one exception, the Congo Free State of King Leopold II, the head of that other small state, neighbouring Belgium. But faith in his idealistic altruism was to be tested very severely in the Netherlands, though more because of interference with Dutch trade than because of the treatment of the black population by the administration of the Free State.

The Partition of Africa: Egypt and the Suez Canal

With increasing international rivalry about the partition of Africa, the Netherlands came to be affected by a borderland which it generally regarded as an important new link for traffic with the East Indies. This was Egypt and particularly the Suez Canal. The British occupation of Egypt meant that the Netherlands was faced with a choice: either to take sides with French and German opposition to British hegemony or to acquiesce to the situation for the sake of solidarity with – or dependence on – British colonial and commercial interests. Throughout the 1880s various foreign affairs secretaries were to tend more towards the one option or the other. The opinions of their advisers differed, too: whereas Asser insisted that the canal should be put under international control and that the Netherlands should participate actively in international talks, Privy Councillor Jansen preferred his country to stay aloof, feeling that Dutch interests were well protected under British hegemony. The political dilemma was related to differing views as to the scope that

---

28. See appendix 3.
29. *De Tijd*, 7 July 1884. Cf. *De Standaard*, 5 January 1884; *Het Handelsblad*, 10 January 1884. An exceptionally rosy view, on the other hand, was taken by Van Soest who regarded it as the 'glory of the nineteenth century' that 'Europe's colonial statesmanship has acquired a far more rational, humanitarian and noble character': 'Het kolonisatie-vraagstuk in den tegenwoordige tijd', *TNI*, 1885, II, p. 453.

the Netherlands might have in the face of international rivalry.

In 1882, the year of the Arabi Pasha Rebellion and the British occupation of Egypt, the Suez Canal became a topical subject. Because of the Netherlands' extensive colonial and maritime interests, the Foreign Minister, Rochussen, felt that it would be wrong to remain a passive onlooker.[30] Even before the outbreak of the rebellion he expressed his opposition to British attempts to exclude the Netherlands and other small nations from international jurisdiction in Egypt. The Netherlands might be a small nation, but it was the second colonial power in Asia and the third that used the Suez Canal. Furthermore, 'as far as good administration of justice is concerned', Dutch judges were far more knowledgeable than many of their colleagues from other European nations.[31] As soon as the rebellion broke out, the Dutch government decided to follow the suggestion of their consul-general and the example of 'other naval powers' and sent an intervention force to Alexandria to protect Dutch lives and goods.[32] Although the intervention was limited to sending out the *Marnix*, the smallest ship in the Dutch Mediterranean training squadron, the Netherlands nevertheless signalled that it was concerned.

After Britain's unilateral occupation of Egypt, Rochussen explicitly pointed out to Dutch representatives abroad that it was desirable for the Netherlands to take part in future talks on the status of the Suez Canal, if necessary without the co-operation of other small states. After the British occupation, he said, it was necessary to ensure the neutrality and the international character of the canal: 'Il est indispensable que le libre parcours soit assuré à tous les pavillons' (It is absolutely necessary that free passage should be guaranteed to all nations.)[33] Van Bylandt, the Dutch ambassador in London, did not find such an independent stance very constructive: 'It would be ... very careless of the Netherlands ... to try to frustrate British politics by associating or conspiring with other second-rate nations.'[34] Soon, however, it turned out that the Netherlands could also rely on support from the bigger nations, espe-

---

30. For developments in Egypt see Ramm, 'Great Britain and France'; Vatikiotis, *History*, pp. 134f.
31. Woltring, *Bescheiden* III, no. 141. Cf. H. J. Schmidt, 'De gemengde rechtspraak in Egypte', *Vragen des Tijds*, 1880, II, pp. 113–55.
32. Woltring, *Bescheiden* III, nos 159–60.
33. Ibid., nos 176 and 190.
34. Ibid., no. 143; cf. no. 191.

cially France.[35] Because of Britain, however, Rochussen preferred to do without French support, feeling that the increasing estrangement between Britain and France in itself made 'highly precarious' the position of the Netherlands in Europe: 'Breaking up the friendly disposition of France and Britain towards each other means total supremacy for Germany.' Therefore the Netherlands had a duty to be extremely careful, though without being totally neutral in Egypt.[36]

A number of MPs felt that Rochussen was being far too cautious. De Beaufort regretted that 'we should make ourselves smaller and less important in our own eyes than we really are.' Why send the smallest ship of the Mediterranean fleet and then replace it with the even more insignificant Bonaire which was looked upon as a small yacht by the British press?[37] Wintgens criticised the 'meekness' of Dutch diplomacy in even stronger terms: 'The Netherlands is a great power – not here in Europe but on the other side of the canal, and as such it has a major role to play in this matter.' He felt that the Netherlands should at least have formed a *'triple alliance'* with Spain and Portugal in order to safeguard its colonial and maritime interests towards 'that *concert Européen'*.[38]

However, when Granville eventually took the initiative for an international Suez Canal conference on 3 January 1883, he only invited the six great powers. Despite earlier promises to Van Bylandt, he now pointedly ignored the Dutch request to be admitted to the conference.[39] Nevertheless, the continuing differences between Britain and France gave Rochussen and his successor Van der Does de Willebois the opportunity to be invited after all, and in 1884 Van der Does succeeded in obtaining a place for the Netherlands on the supervisory board of the Canal Society. This position was given to Anslijn, the Dutch consul-general in Alexandria.[40] With its polite and patient insistence, the Netherlands subsequently managed to secure not only French support but also the support of Germany and Russia in order to be admitted to the international

---

35. For the French position see ibid., nos 178–9; for the German position nos 181 and 189.

36. Ibid., no. 144; cf. no. 190.

37. *Handelingen Tweede Kamer* (Parliamentary Reports of the Second Chamber), 6 December 1882, pp. 652–3.

38. Ibid., pp. 274–5.

39. Woltring, *Bescheiden* III, nos 282–282A, 287; cf. nos 180, 200, 248–50.

40. Ibid., nos 337, 341–4.

conference.[41] But Granville in London continued to react evasively, though without issuing a blunt refusal. In a typical reaction to the formal Dutch request, said Van Bylandt, Granville refused to 'give an aye or a nay'.[42] In 1885, when the conference finally met in Paris, both the Netherlands and Spain were admitted after all, as participants with a *voix délibérative*.[43]

Once admitted, the Netherlands was immediately confronted by the vehement conflict between France, which was aiming at international control over the canal, and Britain, which did not want to have its newly acquired sovereignty over Egypt limited. According to the Dutch delegate, Privy Councillor Jansen, it was not expedient in this climate to demand, as instructed, the internationalisation of the canal without being affected by the British–French controversy.[44] Therefore, according to Jansen, it was better for the Netherlands to stay outside the future control committee and to trust in its friendly relations with Britain: 'If we . . . obtain free passage through the Suez Canal without being forced by the great powers to put up with sacrifices on our part, then we . . . can be glad that we do not have to join the great powers in their Egyptian confusion.'[45] However, following the advice of Asser and others, Van der Does decided to press on. The Netherlands approached the preparatory committee and Asser was appointed representative. 'After mature consideration, also by the Council of Ministers,' Asser told Jansen, 'the decision has been made that if it is necessary to decide between the British and the French proposals . . . we cannot remain neutral but must take sides with France.'[46] In order to obtain admission to the future control committee, the Netherlands now also began actively to seek German support.[47]

This Dutch action, however, did not pass unnoticed in London. With the Borneo and Nisero conflicts still fresh in mind, Britain emphatically rejected Dutch requests to be admitted. 'Lord Gran-

41. Ibid., nos 428, 586, 591, 593.
42. Ibid., no. 585.
43. Ibid., nos 596–596A.
44. Ibid., nos 601–601A.
45. Ibid., no. 605.
46. Ibid., no. 610. Cf. Asser to Jansen, 3 and 14 April 1885; Van der Does to Asser, 29 May 1885, Asser Collection (ARA).
47. Van der Does was following a hint from the German delegate in Paris which he had received via Asser. On 16 May 1885 Jansen had also warned Asser: 'There is nobody here who does not see political attempts on the part of Germany, attempts which are aimed at making matters in Egypt as difficult for Britain as possible.' Asser Collection; cf. Woltring, *Bescheiden* III, no. 246.

ville said with definite resentment that the attitude of the Dutch delegates in Paris was not of the kind that would inspire much trust in future co-operation,' reported Van Bylandt.[48] The Netherlands clearly gave the impression that it was acting under the influence of France and Germany. Van der Does took great pains to remove this impression. Luckily for him, Granville had to make room for Salisbury who generally seemed less concerned about the attitude of the Dutch.[49]

The new Conservative government, however, did not want to ratify the convention which had finally, after great difficulties, gathered in Paris on 8 June 1885. Asser felt that the plan in itself gave 'every reason for satisfaction'. After all, except for a certain proviso with regard to Britain's vital interests in Egypt, it had agreed to guarantee free passage through the Suez Canal. Instead of an international committee, it was agreed that the countries represented at the Paris conference should see to it that this guarantee was observed. If the Netherlands was to join this committee, it would also acquire this right of supervision. A complicated plan, but 'in view of the different feelings in the Netherlands itself with regard to the desirability of our participation in the supervision, this form should perhaps . . . not be rejected', said Asser.[50] After all, not only diplomats like Jansen and Van Bylandt but also various MPs had expressed their concern about Dutch participation on a permanent committee. For 'in such cases . . . the small powers run the risk of being sacrificed at the expense of the great ones.'[51]

However, it took until the end of 1887 before Britain and France reached an agreement on a new draft for the convention. Concerning free passage it was analogous to the 1885 draft, though it contained more reservations with regard to British interests in Egypt. Privy Councillor Jansen felt that this was the least obstacle.[52] Asser regretted British reservations but strongly recommended under the given circumstances that the Netherlands should take part. 'Isn't it perhaps time for our diplomats to take a more *active* part in the whole matter?' he asked the Foreign Minister, Van Karnebeek, as soon as news of British–French agreement had be-

48. Ibid., no. 650.
49. Ibid., nos 651–651A.
50. Ibid., no. 672.
51. See the interim report on chapter III of the 1886 budget; *Bijlagen Handelingen Tweede Kamer* (Parliamentary Reports of the Second Chamber, Appendix) 1885–6, A, pp. 6–7.
52. Woltring, *Bescheiden*, IV, no. 151. Cf. Obieta, *International Status*, pp. 66ff.

come known.[53] This insistence was not excessive because quite a few obstacles still had to be tackled before Dutch participation could become a fact. Again, the British–French draft was aimed primarily at the great powers only. The British were by now less disinclined to accept Dutch participation than before, but they were unwilling to go to any great trouble about the Dutch cause, either.[54] Britain passed the matter on to France which was only too willing to put in a word for the participation of the Netherlands and Spain in the Suez Convention.

On 29 October 1888 the convention was finally concluded by the great powers, together with Turkey which still had suzerainty over Egypt. But under the ministry of the Conservative Amsterdam aristocrat C. Hartsen the Netherlands began to have its doubts again. Hartsen wanted the Netherlands merely to have the right to be consulted, without any obligation of being actively involved in international supervision. Indeed, he wanted assurance in this respect before ratification by the great powers. This paradoxical situation of an over-anxious France and an obstreperous Netherlands even made it possible to use Dutch participation in the Suez Convention as a means of pressuring France about the Surinam border issue.[55]

Eventually, however, on France's recommendation and after ratification at the Sublime Port, the Netherlands managed to get its participation in the convention arranged through an additional clause. It then took until 11 March 1890 before Hartsen finally accepted the umpteenth version of this one single article. Indeed, Asser had to remind the minister that the Netherlands as one of the most important users of the Canal should not 'allow itself to be pushed into the background because of prudence taken to extremes'.[56] Nevertheless, Dutch participation – 'sur la proposition du gouvernement de la République Française appuyée par le gouvernement de SM Britannique' (as proposed by the government of the French Republic at the instigation of the government of Her Britannic Majesty) – remained limited to a mere advisory role in international supervision. For constitutional reasons, no parliamentary approval

53. Asser to Van Karnebeek, 9 September 1887; Asser Collection. Cf. Woltring, *Bescheiden* IV, no. 241.
54. Ibid., no. 228; cf. nos 169 and 285.
55. Ibid., nos 264, 267 and 273; cf. 235–235A, 333.
56. Ibid., no. 415, note 3. For the subsequent Turkish and Dutch versions, see nos 338A, 376A and 409A.

of this symbolical participation was sought, so that it was hardly noticed when the Netherlands actually joined the Suez Convention. Van Hartsen's policies in connection with the Congo and Surinam, on the other hand, were to cause quite an uproar both in Parliament and among the general public.

The Partition of Africa: the Congo

Throughout the entire decade the Dutch showed more interest in the Congo than in the Suez question; more, in fact, than in several disputed islands in the Archipelago, such as New Guinea and even Borneo. As we have seen, this interest had arisen in the 1870s when the travel stories of Livingstone and Stanley were widely read in the Netherlands.[57] People's interest had the same objectives as in other European countries, that is trade, science and Christianity, although these were on a rather more modest scale than in Britain.[58]

In the Netherlands, trade was by far the most dominant aim, whereas missionaries were less directly involved in Africa. Dutch trade with the west coast of Africa was indeed quite considerable: between 1880 and 1890 imports rose from 6.4 to 8.1 million guilders and exports from 1.4 to 3.8 million. In 1890 about 60 per cent of all exports from the Congo still went to the Netherlands, in other words to Rotterdam. The New African Trade Company (NAHV) in Rotterdam paid fluctuating but nevertheless sometimes considerable dividends: 20 per cent, for instance, in 1880 and 13 per cent in 1889, though none in 1885 or 1886. The NAHV was regarded as one of the most important European commercial enterprises in the Congo, with about 50 out of 150 factories which were manned by about two hundred Europeans and roughly two thousand Congolese employees.[59]

The NAHV formed a little empire which organised its own expeditions and even waged their own little wars against the surrounding black tribes.[60] This went on until King Leopold's Free State took over around 1890 and excluded the NAHV from the

57. Spies, *Nederlander*, 12.
58. Cf. Anstey, *Britain*, chapters 5–6; Cairns, *Prelude*, chapter 9.
59. H. Blink, 'De Nederlanders aan Afrika's Zuid-Westkust', *Eigen Haard*, 1890, pp. 694–700, 713–18, 727–33; cf. *Verslag KvK Rotterdam* (Report of the Rotterdam Chamber of Commerce) 1891, p. 15.
60. For a punitive expedition of the NAHV, see the report of the Dutch consul in Luanda, *Consulaire verslagen* (Consular Reports) 1887, p. 549. Cf. Woltring, *Bescheiden* III, no. 245, fn. 2.

Congo, thanks to the sovereignty rights which had been given to it by the European states. The Dutch Georaphical Society had already felt the effect of King Leopold's imperialist ambitions at a much earlier stage. Profoundly disappointed, Veth decided in 1882 to withdraw Dutch membership of the association, 'as it became more and more obvious that the money which was sent from the Netherlands to Brussels was used not so much for the exploration and civilisation of Africa as for the exploitation of neighbouring Congo for the benefit of Belgian trade and industry'.[61]

However, the formation of King Leopold's independent Congo state in 1884–5 also met with positive responses in the Netherlands and was seen as the most suitable alternative to the colonial rule of either Portugal or one of the great powers. During the preceding years there had been increasing concern about the 'competition for Stanley Pool' between Britain, France, Portugal and the association. Minister Rochussen, too, felt that the Netherlands should not view the complications around the Congo with 'indifferent eyes'.[62] When it seemed that Britain was going to get rid of France by recognising Portuguese claims to the Congo estuary, the Dutch Foreign Affairs Department was at first rather pleased with the idea. Portugal, it was felt, should at least give the assurance that it would respect Dutch trade interests. 'If Portugal does not give it,' said a departmental memorandum, 'then we are entitled . . . to defend ourselves against Portugal's sovereignty and contest it, if necessary, by *force*. It is a different question whether we should do this *in spite of* Britain.'

In any case, the Netherlands should not become tempted to claim its own sovereignty rights in the Congo area; even the Dutch parties concerned did not demand that the government should employ such 'extreme and indeed rather daring methods'.[63] When, in February 1884, Portuguese claims were recognised by Britain without satisfactory guarantees for trade, the Dutch seemed at first to give up all thoughts of colonial rule in Central Africa. The Rotterdam MP J. van Gennep called the 'complete freedom of movement' under the current circumstances 'a better guarantee of order, peace and contentment than the strongest central authority'.[64] His colleague in

61. *TAG* (1883), pp. 38–9.
62. Woltring, *Bescheiden* III, no. 226.
63. Ibid., no. 257; cf. memoranda nos 235A–B.
64. *Handelingen Tweede Kamer* (Parliamentary Reports of the Second Chamber), 3 April 1884, pp. 1248–9.

the First Chamber, NAHV director H. Muller, expressed himself in a similar way. Minister Van der Does de Willebois realised that the interference of European powers was 'always detrimental to trade and often also peace' in Africa. But in view of the increasing extent of their interference he wondered whether the cancellation of the British–Portuguese treaty alone would really be sufficient: '*Gouverner c'est prévoir*' (To govern is to anticipate).[65]

Meanwhile not only the Chamber of Commerce in Rotterdam but also the ones in Amsterdam, Eschede, Hengelo, Oldenzaal and Tilburg had warned of the possible consequences of the British–Portuguese treaty for Dutch trade with the Congo.[66] In the *NRC* Britain's attitude in this matter was compared with that of an 'unwise judge who entrusted the interests of a rich ward to a compassionate but very miserly guardian'.[67] Van der Does therefore took steps to obtain more guarantees for Dutch trade interests from Britain and Portugal. Later, the British government withdrew the treaty under considerable internal and external pressure, although, as Van der Does had predicted, this did not solve the Congo question. When Bismarck took the initiative to settle the problems in Africa by means of an international conference, the Netherlands reacted quite positively. Only Van Bylandt expressed scepticism, because he did not trust Bismarck's new colonial policies.[68] But Van der Does felt that the Netherlands, which had been invited to the conference as one of seven interested nations, should definitely take part.[69]

Van der Does, however, felt that the conference still had far too many strings attached to it for the Netherlands. Of the three starting points which Bismarck had identified, Van der Does could only go along with the first two: freedom of trade in the Congo region and freedom of navigation on the rivers Congo and Niger. The third point seemed more difficult, though: 'définition des formalités à observer pour que des occupations nouvelles sur les côtes d'Afrique soient considérées comme effectives' (definition of formalities which must be observed so that new occupations on the

65. Ibid., *Eerste Kamer* (First Chamber), 26 April 1884, pp. 325–8.
66. Woltring, *Bescheiden* III, no. 422A; for the regular contacts between the parties involved and the department cf. nos 253, 262, 543. See also Verslag *KvK Rotterdam* (Report of the Rotterdam Chamber of Commerce) 1882, p. 46; ibid. 1884, pp. 16–27, appendix E; ibid., *Amsterdam* 1882, pp. 156–7; ibid. 1884, p. 156.
67. *NRC* 8 April 1884.
68. Woltring, *Bescheiden* III, no. 503; cf. nos 491 and 504.
69. Minutes of the Cabinet Council, 10 October 1884, ibid., no. 502, cf. no. 501.

coast of Africa can be considered effective). Van der Does was concerned that this might have implications for the Indonesian Archipelago, 'should later occupations be attempted under the pretext that Dutch rights of possession are not effective, and . . . the decisions of the Berlin Conference might be applied there as well.' He instructed the Dutch ambassador in Berlin, F. P. van der Hoeven, to adopt a wait-and-see policy in dealing with 'the third and most difficult point'. The Netherlands, he said, should not lose sight of the fact 'that on the continent we will always be the weaker neighbour of a powerful Germany and that we continuously rub shoulders with Great Britain in the Indian Archipelago where we might have permanent problems'.[70]

Wesseling rightly drew attention to this defensive 'East Indian' dimension of the Dutch policy in Africa.[71] When the conference convened in October 1884, the Dutch government had hardly recovered from the shock of its conflict with Britain over the Nisero question during the last few months. Throughout the conference, therefore, Van der Does would frequently and emphatically remind Van der Hoeven that he must always bear in mind the possible consequences for the East Indies, 'without mentioning them', of course. What had to be avoided was any attempt to extend the scope of the decisions to include areas outside Africa or even the east coast of Africa; in other words 'the coast of the Indian Ocean and thus the sea where our Indian Archipelago lies'.[72]

These considerations of 'higher politics' even tipped the balance whenever they conflicted with direct trade interests in the Congo. According to Van Does, the Netherlands was not to oppose the British proposal to restrict the import of firearms, gunpowder and stong liquor in the Congo, even though these goods were largely imported by the NAHV. After all, the Netherlands had obtained a similar embargo from Britain in the Archipelago: 'The Netherlands must not take a different position towards Britain – at the Congo Conference – than the one it would like Britain to have in connection with Acheh!'[73] During the conference, Dutch diplomacy therefore kept the necessary distance from Dutch interest groups. Van der Does deliberately made sure that the expert who joined the

---

70. Ibid., nos 505, 508 and 511.
71. Wesseling, 'Nederland', p. 571. Cf. Louis, 'Berlin Congo Conference'; Fisch, *Expansion*, pp. 87–91.
72. Woltring, *Bescheiden* III, nos 524, 529, 530, 534.
73. Ibid., no. 521.

Dutch delegation was not the NAHV director and member of the First Chamber, Muller, but a less prominent representative – much to the displeasure of Muller who subsequently went to Berlin independently.[74]

When the conference was over in February 1885, however, all Dutch interest groups had reason to be satisfied. Complete freedom for trade and shipping was declared for the Congo area, and the British proposal to curb the trading of weapons and alcohol had to give way. The guidelines for occupation remained restricted to the west coast of Africa. Neutrality and the international character of the new legal situation seemed to be given special assurance when King Leopold's Association was accorded sovereignty rights. Muller, who had meanwhile understood that some form of colonial rule was inevitable for the Congo, strongly recommended in Berlin that the Dutch should recognise the association's sovereignty for the sake of friendly relations with Belgium and because of Leopold's efforts to further trade and civilisation in Africa.[75] However, the Netherlands did not recognise the association until Britain had done so.[76] This recognition was also unanimously welcomed outside Rotterdam. The liberal journalist Van Soest saw the association itself as 'the most idealistic colonial enterprise that had ever been attempted and accomplished'.[77]

The other results of the conference also met with a positive response. Asser, who had attended the conference as a legal adviser, felt that the 'legal status brought about by the Congo agreement . . . is completely new in international law', and he anticipated a 'great effect on future legal development'. At the same time, however, he warned against excessive expectations, because 'experience teaches that such clauses written in times of peace mean very little when passions are aroused and start clamouring for war.'[78] Nobody seemed to regret that the Netherlands itself had definitively renounced the option of acquiring further colonies in Africa. Only Muller from Amsterdam reminded everyone of the 'political shortsightedness' ten years ago, 'when our government withdrew from African soil, turning a blind eye on the promising future of that land

---

74. Ibid., no. 512. Cf. Muller, *Muller*, pp. 371f.
75. Woltring, *Bescheiden* III, no. 543.
76. Ibid., no. 555.
77. Van Soest, 'Het Kolonisatie-vraagstuk', p. 437. Cf. *Standaard*, 9 January, *Het Handelsblad*, 23 January, and *Nederlandsche Industrieel*, 1 March 1885.
78. Asser, 'Congo-Acte', p. 339.

which even non-colonising nations saw as the economic Jerusalem'.[79]

The passionate enthusiasm about the Congo Free State only lasted as long as it was no more than 'an embryo of a state'.[80] When it seriously started to exercise its sovereignty rights and began to look for new sources of income, it inevitably came into conflict with Dutch trade interests. At first the Foreign Affairs Department asked the general agent of the NAHV, who was also acting as the Dutch consul at the time, to be obliging towards the Free State.[81] But it soon became obvious that the Free State was indeed systematically obstructing Dutch trade in order to promote its own commercial ventures. In this light there was a certain amount of scepticism in 1889 when King Leopold, supported by Britain, took the initiative in organising an anti-slavery conference in Brussels. The king wanted to restrict the import of weapons and alcohol, which were seen as an important reason for the slave trade, though such a step would also help the Free State to obtain new revenues. At the time the Dutch government consisted of what was the first clerical coalition cabinet and so was in an awkward position when it was invited to this conference. The aims of the conference were fully endorsed by the clerical rank and file, especially the supporters of missionaries who deeply regretted Dutch involvement in the alcohol and arms trades.[82] The NAHV, on the other hand, denied any connection with the slave trade and started a vehement campaign against the abolition of import rights, as this would go against the Berlin Congo Act of 1885.[83]

But even before the conference it became obvious that the Netherlands might be isolated if it continued to oppose a possible change in the agreement. The Dutch government was therefore divided on the issue of participation. The orthodox Calvinist and Minister of the Colonies Keuchenius would himself gladly have taken the initiative in the fight against the international slave trade which, he said, was perpetrated everywhere by fanatical Muslims, mainly Arabs, both in

79. P. N. Muller, 'Een nieuw koloniaal tijdschrift', *De Gids*, 1885, iii, p. 493.

80. Woltring, *Bescheiden* IV, no. 55. For the development of the Free State, see Gann and Duignan, *Rulers*, chapters 2–4.

81. Woltring, *Bescheiden* IV, no. 180.

82. Cf. W. F. K. Klinkenberg, 'Overzicht van het Zendingswerk naar Buitenlandsche Berichten', *Mededeelingen van het Nederlandsch Zendelinggenootschap*, 1886, pp. 381–2. The conference was supported by the Dutch Association for the Abolition of Strong Liquor: see their letter to Hartsen of 28 August 1889, *De Standard*, 12 July 1890.

83. Cf. Woltring, *Bescheiden* IV, nos 292, 294A, 383.

the Congo and the Indonesian Archipelago.[84] Hartsen, on the other hand, 'would . . . prefer HM's government not to get involved in the issue at hand'. Considering, however, that Britain was so strongly in favour of the convention and that negotiations over Borneo had just opened with Britain, the Netherlands could hardly decline the invitation.[85]

The course of the conference, which took place in 1890, was indeed not exactly favourable for the Netherlands.[86] The Dutch delegate, Gericke van Herwijnen – ambassador to Brussels and ex-minister – tried to achieve as much as possible for the Netherlands by making dependent on the level of the suggested alcohol tariff how the changes in the Berlin Congo Agreement would be handled. In this he was supported by his expert, the general NAHV agent in the Congo, who soon realised in Brussels that a categorical 'no' would not do any good in the long term.[87] A charge of 10 per cent *ad valorem* could certainly be countenanced. 'If we resist, we might bring the entire proposal down,' Gericke wrote to Hartsen, 'but I would not dare to advise such resistance against the whole of Europe.'[88] At first Hartsen agreed completely. But his colleague, the Minister of Shipping, Commerce and Industry, J. P. Havelaar vehemently opposed any levying of import duties. In his view, it was a 'misapprehension' that the NAHV would put up with this tariff. The management of the NAHV and the Rotterdam Chamber of Commerce were indeed against it, because it would have given the Congo Free State the power to make life impossible for Dutch trade and shipping by means of customs inspections and other methods of control.[89] Hartsen accepted Havelaar's view and instructed Gericke not to sign the agreement which was to be concluded in Brussels on 2 July 1890. The unhappy Gericke, who had already hinted that the Netherlands would eventually agree, had to publicise this Dutch refusal on the eve of the festive banquet that

84. Ibid., no. 370.
85. Ibid., no. 411. For the invitation see 28 August 1889, *Bijlagen Handelingen Tweede Kamer* (Parliamentary Reports of the Second Chamber, Appendix) 1890–1, no. 136, p. 2.
86. For the background of the Brussels conference as well as the conference itself, see Miers, *Britain*, pp. 229f.
87. Woltring, *Bescheiden* IV, no. 420; cf. 417.
88. Ibid., no. 448.
89. Ibid., no. 449. For protests from the world of commerce, see *Verslag KvK Rotterdam* (Report of the Rotterdam Chamber of Commerce) 1890, pp. 18–21; cf. *NRC*, 25 May 1890.

concluded the conference.[90]

Once Hartsen had taken this categorical point of view, he stubbornly clung to it. At the follow-up conference, which was to work out the practical implementation of the new Congo Agreement, Gericke was instructed to submit alternatives for the alcohol duty. However, as the Netherlands had totally rejected the convention, he was not allowed to take part in the discussions.[91] As the ratification deadline of six months was approaching, Hartsen found it more and more difficult to continue his refusal. Not just Gericke but all the Dutch ambassadors in the other European capitals reported increasing irritation over the Dutch attitude. Van der Hoeven, for example, reported from Berlin that

> the German government deeply regretted that on the issue of import duties the Dutch government allowed itself to be guided by the less important interests of several commercial companies. Thus it seemed to ignore the cultivation of friendly relations with most European states and particularly its good relationship with Germany.[92]

Faced with increasing international pressure, Hartsen finally changed his mind and suggested to the Cabinet Council that the Netherlands should ratify the Congo Convention under protest. Havelaar and the Minister of Finance voted against this.[93] The new Queen Emma personally intervened to delete the note of protest from the official Dutch entry to the convention. On 30 December 1890, several days before the deadline, a greatly relieved Gericke signed the convention for the Netherlands.

However, now that foreign pressure had been lifted, Hartsen came under a different kind of pressure from within the Netherlands. The Liberal opposition, which had already succeeded in forcing Keuchenius to resign, saw the Congo question as a new opportunity to make life difficult for the coalition. On 15 December 1890, long after it had emerged that the Netherlands would have to

90. Miers, *Britain*, pp. 289–90.
91. Woltring, *Bescheiden* IV, no. 476.
92. Ibid., no. 484. According to Van der Hoeven, the 'extreme position' of Berlin was mainly motivated by the anti-slavery stance of the Centre Party and concern to keep the Congo Free State as a buffer against French colonial expansion; cf. no. 492. The British response was milder; cf. 489, 491 and 494. When minister Hartsen refused to ratify the Brussels Convention Lord Salisbury declared at first that Britain would not sign, a move that may have increased German wrath against the Netherlands even more. See Miers, *Britain*, 290.
93. Minutes of the Cabinet Council, 24 December 1890; ibid., no. 521; cf. no. 516.

yield to international pressure and sign the agreement after all, Van Houten declared on behalf of the Liberals that 'the government was making its decisions but the Chamber reserved the right to judge afterwards whether the government had acted well.'[94]

When the agreement was signed, it became obvious to many Liberals that the government could not have done much good anyway. As Rutgers van Rozenburg pointed out, the government had to choose between 'refusing to ratify and ratifying quickly', and had no other options; the Netherlands was now 'the laughing stock of Europe'. Just as in the Surinam border issue, Hartsen was criticised so sharply that the Anti-Revolutionary, F. W. C. P. van Bylandt, commented: 'It is true that we are powerless against the other countries, especially when the person in charge of policy making is condemned over every international issue that we deal with.'[95] Eventually, however, Dutch participation in the Congo Convention was accepted by the Second Chamber with an over-whelming majority of 82 to 3.[96]

Miers has raised the question of which domestic issue had the greatest influence on the Dutch opposition during the Brussels conference: was it trade interests or the insecure position of the clerical cabinet? Of these two, it seems that the cabinet's insecurity did indeed play the most important part.[97] After all, Hartsen was already under considerable pressure in connection with the Lawa issue in Surinam, where he had been criticised for too much complacency towards France by the Liberals. Minister Mackay felt that 'opposition to those two issues [Lawa and Congo] was largely due to their desire to be unpleasant to Hartsen and to finish him off (*afmaken*) as far as possible'.[98]

Apart from domestic party politics and trade interests in the Congo itself, the East Indies also began to play a role again during the final phase of the Congo issue, though rather more indirectly

94. *Handelingen Tweede Kamer* (Parliamentary Reports of the Second Chamber), 15 December 1890, p. 296.

95. For the petition of J. P. R. Tak van Poortvliet on the occasion of the Dutch ratification, see ibid., 21 January 1891, pp. 603–20.

96. *Bijlagen Handelingen Tweede Kamer* (Parliamentary Reports of the Second Chamber, Appendix), no. 163. Cf. *Handelingen Tweede Kamer* (Parliamentary Reports of the Second Chamber), 28 May 1891, pp. 1475–81; ibid., *Eerste Kamer* (First Chamber), 18 June 1891, p. 141.

97. Cf. Miers, *Britain*, p. 289, note 335.

98. Mackay based this impression on confidential comments by Fransen van de Putte; Ae. Mackay to C. Pijnacker Hordijk, 5 April 1892; Pijnacker Hordijk Collection (ARA).

this time. Beside Keuchenius's initial preoccupation with Islam as the source of the slave trade and other evils in Africa and Asia, the East Indies was also touched by the decision making in connection with Italy's claims to Ethiopia, which it put forward during the Brussels conference. The Dutch ambassador in Rome advised that these claims should be recognised, because 'it is desirable to have more than just one single power – Britain – to deal with in the Red Sea', and above all because Italian expansion in Africa might prevent the 'further development of ideas' from 1873 – particularly expansion in the Indonesian Archipelago.[99] For the time being, however, these considerations disappeared into the background again as soon as the Italian claims were abandoned.

Meanwhile, of course, Dutch trade interests had also been established on the east coast of Africa, particularly in Mozambique. The son of the NAHV director, H. P. N. Muller had launched the Mozambique Trading Company there, later to be renamed the East African Company.[100] This sister enterprise of the NAHV met with a good deal of obstruction from the Portuguese colonial authorities. Like before, in the case of the Congo, the Dutch government had little trouble in subsequently putting pressure on Portugal. In 1887, when diplomatic efforts no longer seemed effective, the Netherlands sent a warship to Mozambique to show the Dutch flag. The commander was instructed to make every effort to avoid 'anything that might seem like a threat, even though this provides an opportunity to show quite emphatically to all colonial administrators that the Dutch government is concerned about the rightful interests of its subjects in remote parts of the world'.[101]

Commercially, the East African Company was not an unqualified success. However, young Muller felt far more attracted to South Africa than East or West Africa and was more interested in academic pursuits than in trade. In connection with his travels around the Boer republics he was to have given lectures to the Dutch Geographical Society as well as leading international conferences. Finally, at the instigation of Veth, he took his doctorate at the University of Leipzig in 1894.[102] The Dutch Geographical Society continued to show

---

99. Woltring, *Bescheiden* IV, nos 447 and 454.
100. Spies, *Nederlander*, p. 12ff.; cf. Muller, *Muller*, pp. 341ff.
101. Woltring, *Bescheiden* IV, nos 74 and 136; cf. note 63 above.
102. Spies, *Nederlander*, pp. 48ff. See H. P. N. Muller, *Land und Volk*; cf. *idem*, 'Herinneringen uit de Transvaal', *De Gids* 1888, ii, pp. 223–75.

interest in the colonisation of Africa,[103] though attention had meanwhile shifted from exotic Central Africa to the Dutch 'kinsmen' in
South Africa.

On the Periphery of the Partition: South America

Apart from the Surinam border issue, Dutch interest in South America
was rather limited during the 1880s. However, because of its commercial connections, the Netherlands continued to be in touch with the
most important developments on that continent. The Pacific War at
the end of the 1870s between Peru, Chile and Bolivia had already
attracted attention to the unexpected significance of guano and nitrate
for Dutch imports. These rose from approximately 4 million guilders
during the war in 1880 to 13 million in 1890.

The war had been caused by the nationalisation of the nitrate mines
by the Peruvian government. The foreign owners were given certifi-
cates as compensation, but these turned out to be inadequately secured. In 1880, together with other alarmed investors, the Dutch
owners followed the example of their British fellow sufferers and
founded a committee for the promotion of their interests. However,
the Dutch government decided to be cautious and follow Britain in its
policies.[104] Chile's final victory over Peru in 1882 was therefore
regarded very positively. A number of observers felt that the victory
clearly showed the superiority of liberalism over the 'artificial meddle-
someness' of the state: economically, because Chile handed the conquered mines back to private enterprises; and militarily, because the
Chilean civilian army, though smaller, had shown far greater flexi-
bility and efficiency than the cumbersome Peruvian and Bolivian
forces. Also, there was a considerable amount of interference from
Britain and the United States in the bloodshed, and the war was
therefore seen as evidence that 'arbitration' was 'desirable' in international disputes.[105]

With regard to Dutch exports to South America, there was
considerably more interest in the east coast, Argentina and Brazil.
The Dutch consuls in those countries therefore continually pointed
out the great opportunities for Dutch exports, observing with
jealousy the increasing interest in Africa, 'which was still in the first

103. Wesseling, 'Nederland', p. 575.
104. Woltring, *Bescheiden* III, nos 37 and 43; ibid. IV, nos 42 and 42A–B–C.
105. F. H. Boogard, 'Zuid-Amerikaansche toestanden', *Vragen des Tijds*, 1882, I,
pp. 179–99. Cf. Burr, *Reason* pp. 124ff.

stages of its development', whereas the south of Latin America was relatively well developed and could therefore offer far more to the Netherlands.[106]

However, there were strong competitors, not just from Britain but increasingly also from North America and Germany, and these certainly asked for a greater effort. According to the enthusiastic Dutch consul in Rio Grande de Sul and Buenos Aires, L. van Riet, Dutch manufacturers ought to pay more attention to brand names, packaging, and so on, because 'most consumers are more interested in a glamorous outer appearance than the inner value of things.' Together with other colleagues in South America, he therefore recommended that market research should be conducted as well as sales promotion by a travelling sales representative in the country itself.[107] But the most important element, according to Van Riet, was a direct steamship connection with the Netherlands, which would boost not only trade and investment but also the emigration of Dutch settlers to Argentina. Van Riet's enthusiastic reports did not fail to make an impression in the Netherlands, where the Holland–America Line (HAL) opened a direct service to La Plata in 1888. Between 1888 and 1891 hundreds of Dutch settlers moved to Argentina, tempted by the 'immediate advantages for immigrants', as Van Riet had summed them up; these included government loans for the crossing, advance payments based on the expected high incomes, and 'an abundance of open land'.[108]

However, the whole project failed miserably. Having suffered heavy losses, the HAL stopped the steamship connection again in 1890. Of the Dutch settlers, so many had been reduced to beggars that the Liberal MP H. Pyttersen raised the point in the Second Chamber and insisted on a discussion of Van Riet's information.[109] Van Riet believed that the disappointing results were merely caused by a temporary slump in the Argentinian economy and the low quality of Dutch settlers, who were 'farmers, rag-pickers, organ-grinders, oyster-scrapers, artisans, people who seem to have spent less time on their trade than on socialist theories as well as many who had failed on all counts in their profession in the Netherlands

106. Cf. *Consulaire verslagen* (Consular Reports) 1884, pp. 242–3; ibid. 1886, pp. 216–18.
107. Ibid. 1884, pp. 244–6; cf. ibid. 1880, pp. 470–5.
108. Ibid. 1888, pp. 1248–56. 3,742 Dutch emigrants arrived in Argentina between 1888 and 1891; ibid. 1893, no. 196. Cf. De Boer, *Honderd jaar*, p. 146.
109. *Handelingen Tweede Kamer* (Parliamentary Reports of the Second Chamber), 3 December 1891, pp. 294–6.

and who are weak in body and spirit'.[110] Subsequently, however, he was to express himself less boastfully about the enormous future prospects of Argentina.

During the 1880s the most important South American trading partners were the Dutch colonies Surinam and the Antilles. Indeed interest in Surinam had increased quite considerably, spurred on by Eldorado tales that gold had been discovered in the basins of the big Surinam rivers. The first gold concession had been given by the colonial administration in 1875, in the hope that this would provide a welcome source of income beside the gradually declining plantation economy. By 1882 about 6,000 square kilometres worth of concessions had been granted, yielding about 500 kilograms of gold altogether.[111] One of the most promising places in this respect seemed to be the Lawa region, in the border area between Surinam and French Guyana. Since 1861 there had been a difference of opinions with regard to the exact location of the border: according to the Netherlands, it was the Lawa river, whereas France insisted on the Tapanahoni, further west. A provisional investigation showed that according to existing contracts the Netherlands had the best documents, and France dropped the matter for the time being. But when news of the gold discoveries in the border area became known and mining licencees approached the French government about a concession, France decided to approach the Netherlands about the border issue again.[112] The French government suggested dividing the disputed territory for the time being, while the French colonial administration actually started granting concessions west of Lawa. According to the Dutch ambassador in Paris, A. L. F. de Stuers, 'we cannot and must not put up with the conceited, unjustified and offensive behaviour of France without abandoning our national pride.' But as France was a great power and the Netherlands a small one, De Stuers suggested to minister Hartsen that the border dispute should be submitted to international arbitration.[113]

In the Netherlands, where the idea of arbitration had increasingly gained ground since 1870, the suggestion was certainly welcomed by Hartsen.[114] However, it was impossible to persuade France to accept a solution based on international law which might frustrate

110. *Consulaire verslagen* (Consular Reports) 1891, pp. 30–5.
111. Cf. the entry s.v. 'goudindustrie' (gold industry) in the *Encyclopaedie van Nederlandsch West-Indië.*
112. Woltring, *Bescheiden* IV, nos 144–144A.
113. Ibid., no. 210.

its *de facto* control over the disputed area as well as the mining it had already started. A deadlock followed which was only broken at the end of 1888. De Stuers found that French obligations towards the Netherlands in connection with the Suez Convention provided an opportunity 'de . . . établir une connexité entre les deux questions en faveur de Suriname' (to link up the two issues in favour of Surinam). Although De Stuers thus found an opportunity to put 'the screws' on his French counterpart so that he accepted arbitration in principle, the general agreement of 29 November 1889 made it possible for the future arbiter to divide the disputed territory exactly as France had envisaged.[115] And so the Dutch Parliament reluctantly accepted the agreement, while looking forward to the application of arbitration as such. Hartsen was urged, however, to discuss with France the possibility of further limiting the authority of the arbiter to a simple choice between the rivers Lawa and the Tapanahoni as the border.[116] But it turned out to be impossible to agree retrospectively on the scope of the arbitration rulings.

The Netherlands and France had no difficulty in agreeing on the choice of an arbiter: the tsar of Russia.[117] However, after long hesitation, in January 1890 he refused to act in this capacity, because the Dutch and French requests showed such a clear difference of views. For France the refusal was very convenient, but the Dutch were devastated. Hartsen feared that there would be French annexation of the Lawa territory if the arbitration finally failed. In his letter to the king, Hartsen pointed out that giving in to French demands and dividing the disputed territory would be an 'extremely dangerous precedent' for the Netherlands' extensive colonial possessions. But as France was apparently not willing to agree to any different terms of arbitration, he felt that there was no choice but to give in. On 28 April 1890 France and the Netherlands concluded a new, broad arbitration agreement, which was also acceptable to the tsar.[118]

Meanwhile, strong opposition to this course of events had arisen in the Netherlands, especially in Liberal circles. During the dis-

114. Ibid., no. 219; cf. Kamphuis, *Vredebond*, pp. 105f.
115. Woltring, *Bescheiden* IV, nos 269A–B. See also note 55 above.
116. *Bijlagen Handelingen Tweede Kamer* (Parliamentary Reports of the Second Chamber, Appendix) 1888–9, no. 72. Cf. *Handelingen Tweede Kamer* (Parliamentary Reports of the Second Chamber), 22 December 1888, p. 807; ibid., *Eerste Kamer* (First Chamber), 24 January 1889, p. 141.
117. Woltring, *Bescheiden* IV, nos 368–368A.
118. Ibid., no. 433; cf. nos 401 and 403.

cussion of the appropriate bill, criticism was above all directed at France: 'We would not have expected', said ex-minister Cremers, 'that the government of such a nation, carried away by the currently prevailing desire to acquire or extend colonies or perhaps blinded by the discovery of gold, would attempt to seize territory which has belonged to us for centuries.' Cremers and other Liberal spokesmen felt that Hartsen should therefore never have agreed that the arbiter, whose impartiality had by now become doubtful, should be given such far-reaching authority. De Beaufort pointed out the danger that the principle of international arbitration, designed 'specially for the benefit of small powers', should be undermined in this way. Finally, however, the agreement was accepted by the Second Chamber after all, with 57 votes to 21. The First Chamber also endorsed it, with 36 votes to 3.[119] The Liberal press criticised Hartsen particularly sharply, though according to the Anti-Revolutionary *Standaard*, the government had acted wisely in 'loyally venturing to involve the decision of an arbiter and not exposing itself to a situation whereby ... first gold-diggers and then the French colonial army would put to us a *fait accompli*'.[120]

The outcome of the tsar's arbitration, which he finally announced in 27 May 1891, did indeed bear out Hartsen and not his Liberal critics. The tsar unambiguously decided that the river Lawa should form the border between the two territories – though to satisfy France the Netherlands was put under obligation to honour the concessions which had already been granted by the French colonial administration in the disputed territory.[121] The latter decision aroused a lot of opposition among the white settlers of Surinam. Governor-general T. A. J. van Asch van Wijck had great difficulty in getting the appropriate bill through the Council of Surinam.[122] In the Netherlands, on the other hand, there was general relief that another colonial border issue had been got rid of. For Hartsen such a 'very satisfactory solution' of the Lawa issue meant that his policy in this 'thorny issue' was now fully justified.[123]

119. *Bijlagen Handelingen Tweede Kamer* (Parliamentary Reports of the Second Chamber, Appendix) 1889–90, no. 155. Cf. *Handelingen Tweede Kamer* (Parliamentary Reports of the Second Chamber) 1890, pp. 1614–32; ibid., *Eerste Kamer* (First Chamber), 14 July 1889, pp. 452–6.

120. *De Standaard*, 15 May 1890; cf. *NRC*, 21 May; *Het Vaderland*, 14 May.

121. Woltring, *Bescheiden* V, nos 71 and 77.

122. Van Asch van Wijck to Mackay, 31 October 1891, Mackay Collection (ARA).

123. Hartsen to Asser, 30 May 1891, Asser Collection.

On the Periphery of the Partition: Asia

Apart from the Dutch East Indies, Asia rarely provided front-page news items for the Dutch press. However, the significance of this colony continually attracted a good deal of attention to developments in other parts of Asia. The colonial administration in Batavia, for example, was greatly concerned about the development of militant reform movements in Islam, particularly from northern Africa and the Middle East. 'Now that the Muslims have been defeated not only in Egypt but also on the north coast of Africa, both by Britain and France, they are going to turn their eyes towards the Dutch East Indies', predicted the Governor-general F.'s Jacob in 1882 after he had read reports from Djeddah.[124]

The Colonial Affairs Department therefore subsidised a secret study journey to Mecca in 1884–5 of the young orientalist C. Snouck Hurgronje, commissioned by the Royal Dutch Institute. The Dutch consul in Djeddah, J. A. Kruyt, was also closely involved in the journey and its preparations. Later, in 1889, Snouck Hurgronje was to act as governmental adviser on Islamic affairs in Batavia, where he advocated an extension of the consulate in Djeddah so that the annual stream of pilgrims from Batavia could be supervised better.[125] This was because only half of the about 10,000 annual pilgrims had until then registered with the Dutch consulate. Many decided to stay in Mecca longer, and were exposed to the influence of Islamic revival movements.[126]

In other parts of Asia there was the same concern with the East Indies, and in the Netherlands there was increasing interest in consular and diplomatic relations. Dutch representatives generally felt that the stagnation or recession of Dutch trade was due to the lack of a good steamship connection with the Netherlands. Furthermore, there were no local trade posts or credit facilities to help the individual trader hold out against the increasing number of foreign competitors. 'Without Dutch houses or agents of trading companies in the Netherlands trade with Dutch goods cannot develop satis-

---

124. 's Jacob to De Brauw, 26 December 1882, loose leaves 76 B 57 (KB).

125. C. Snouck Hurgronje, 'Het consulaat te Djeddah', Gobée and Adriaanse, *Adviezen* II, pp. 1466–9. For the journey, see Gobée's introduction, ibid. I; Van Koningsveld, 'Snouck Hurgronje', pp. 770–4. For the results of Snouck's enquiries, see *Mekka*.

126. Noer, *Movement*, pp. 25–9; cf. *Consulaire verslagen* (Consular Report) 1891, no. 192, pp. 7–8.

factorily in China', said the Consul-general Ferguson in Peking.[127] 'It is a great disadvantage for our trade and industry . . . that there are no Dutch trading houses whatever', reported the Dutch consul in Calcutta.[128] A large part of Dutch sales therefore continued to reach their destination via London, Antwerp and Hamburg, as the consul-general in Singapore, G. Lavino, noted: 'Large quantities of goods of Netherlands manufacture are now imported via England, Germany, Belgium and Egypt.'[129]

Trade and shipping between the Dutch East Indies and the rest of Asia also developed rather sluggishly during the 1880s. The steamship service between Surabaya and Amoy via Macassar, Manila, Macao and Hong Kong was continually in the red, despite an increase in the government subsidy from 40,000 to 120,000 guilders in 1882. When the contract with the Dutch East Indian Steamship Company expired, it was not extended by the government. The company subsequently tried to continue the China link in its own strength, though without much success, and in 1891 the ailing enterprise was given up.[130] Ferguson felt that just then new opportunities were beginning to open up for a steamship service: 'What should undoubtedly be an important boost for Dutch shipping traffic with China is the conveyance of Chinese field-workers (coolies) from Chinese ports to Surinam and the agricultural enterprises of the east coast of Sumatra.[131] At the end of the 1880s, after a difficult initial period, more and more Chinese contract workers finally began to emigrate to Deli and Surinam – with the help of German consuls and foreign shipping companies. As Van Dongen has shown very clearly, the so-called 'coolie trade' for the Dutch colonies formed the most important topic in Dutch–Chinese relations at the time.[132] His description shows that there was a certain amount of tension between the Dutch government and its representatives on the one hand and the pressure group of Deli planters, whose interests were well represented in the Dutch Parliament on the other.

As soon as Dutch representation was established in China, the Deli Company began to urge the government to promote the direct

127. Ibid. 1881, pp. 846–7; cf. ibid. 1888, pp. 329–30.
128. Ibid. 1891, no. 241, p. 44; cf. ibid., 1885; pp. 1106–7.
129. Ibid. 1885, pp. 218–19.
130. Cf. Brugmans, *Chinavaart*, p. 27.
131. *Consulaire verslagen* (Consular Reports) 1891, no. 221, pp. 10–11.
132. Cf. Van Dongen, *Neutraliteit*, chapters 4–5.

emigration of Chinese contract workers to Deli. Emigration had been proceeding via Singapore, without any guarantee of continuity or quantity. The spokesman of the Deli Company and the Deli Planters Union, Cremer, travelled through southern China himself in 1875 to examine the possibilities for direct emigration. The Chinese government, however, objected greatly to this coolie trade and Consul-general Ferguson could understand this very well indeed, in view of the treatment which the Chinese contract workers received in Deli, and he appreciated the attempts of the Chinese government to establish consulates in the Dutch East Indies. Ferguson's carefully balanced view of the coolie issue earned him several reprimands from The Hague. However, there was at first a good deal of reluctance to demanding direct emigration from China, to avoid having to concede to Chinese requests for Chinese consuls in the East Indies.[133] During the 1880s the Deli Company stepped up its pressure on the minister, as did the Second Chamber, where Cremer was elected as a Liberal MP for Amsterdam in 1884.

In 1888 Hartsen was finally persuaded to send Ferguson to Swatow in southern China where he would temporarily promote emigration.[134] With the help of the professional German consul in Swatow, a relaxation of local emigration policies was indeed achieved, and the direct recruitment of contract workers to Deli rose from 1,658 in 1888 to 7,151 in 1890. In 1890 a new Dutch consulate-general was opened in Amoy, southern China so that a relieved Ferguson was able to return to Peking. Meanwhile the central Chinese government continued in vain to demand the admission of Chinese consuls to the East Indies. The Dutch colonial administration was vehemently against this, afraid that the Chinese consuls might break through the isolated and subordinate position of the Chinese in the East Indies and thus endanger Dutch authority. 'History teaches', it was reasoned in Batavia, 'that the Chinese do not have the slightest scruples when it comes to hitting a score whenever they feel that the circumstances are favourable . . . There is no need to demonstrate that the danger becomes greater to the extent that their number increases and the political importance of China assumes larger proportions.'[135]

133. Woltring, *Bescheiden* II, nos 100, 119, 328, 346. Cf. Van Dongen, *Neutraliteit*, pp. 99–107.
134. Ibid., pp. 106–28. Cf. Woltring, *Bescheiden* IV, nos 211 and 262, *Handelingen Tweede Kamer* (Parliamentary Reports of the Second Chamber), 6 December 1889, pp. 378–82, 384–5.
135. See the advice of the director of Education, Religion and Industry of 3

The separate status of the 'strange Orientals' in the East Indies also played a part in Dutch relations with Japan. At first the Netherlands tried to resist Japanese demands for their own consulates in the East Indies. But Japan's case was different from China's. Not only were there fewer Japanese immigrants in the East Indies, but the Japanese government was a far stronger opponent than the Chinese one.[136] This had already become obvious in the course of a conference, held – with interruptions – in Tokyo since 1882, which was to revise the unequal treaties between Japan and the Western powers. The Japanese government wanted to deal with the greater powers only, preferably one by one, and quite unceremoniously ignored the Netherlands. The Japanese government already felt offended that after the enforced removal of Wttewaal in 1881 he had not been replaced by a fully fledged diplomat but by the commercial agent J. J. van der Pot as ambassador to Tokyo. When the latter self-confidently went ahead as the representative of the 'first power of secondary rank' at the conference, the Japanese government found a reason to declare Van der Pot *persona non grata*.[137]

This was unjustified, according to a departmental memo, although the Dutch government was not entirely blameless either. When Van der Pot was appointed, it was decided that 'our representative in Japan should act as a friend of that country', but 'the enquiries of later ministers showed that Mr Van der Pot had turned out to be the most embarrassing of negotiators, which led to a request for his withdrawal.' 'We can no longer make up for it by means of a *tour de force*,' read the memo, 'though we can act wisely by calmly letting the matter take its course and sending an envoy . . . to Japan as quickly as possible so that we can pursue further negotiations for a treaty.'[138] And this did indeed happen. In 1890 Van der Pot was replaced at his own request by the young Count D. L. van Bylandt, who subsequently sat on the fence until Britain and Japan concluded a separate revision agreement in 1894.

October 1891, taken over by the governor-general of the East Indian Council, Woltring, *Bescheiden* V, nos 184A–B.

136. Ibid., cf. ibid. IV, no. 503.

137. Ibid. no. 201A, note 3; cf. no. 94. For the negotiations in Tokyo see also Araki, *Geschichte*, pp. 119ff.

138. Woltring, *Bescheiden* IV, no. 312B; cf. nos 201, 263, 305.

Uncertainties over the Dutch East Indies

Possession and Control

Just as colonial interests were an important factor in Dutch foreign politics, so international developments continued to have a great influence on Dutch colonial affairs during the 1880s. At a time of economic and financial crisis, the increasing interest in colonial possessions among the other European powers aggravated a dilemma which we have already seen in the 1870s. On the one hand the Netherlands was claiming rather extensive territory, but on the other hand it only had very limited means with which to enforce its claims.

It may be regarded as symptomatic that many contemporaries – not just lawyers – tried to define and solve the problem in legal terms. In 1881, for example, J. E. de Sturler of Leiden University suggested in a doctoral thesis that the threat of foreign violations of Dutch sovereignty was mainly caused by the failure of Dutch legislation to give a detailed definition of the Dutch East Indian territories – 'because we might easily forget to include something' had been the minister's unsuspecting comment at the time. De Sturler felt that this omission should be remedied as quickly as possible, now that there was such an increasing interest in the Archipelago: 'Would foreigners then still dare to violate our legally defined territories?'[139] De Sturler was convinced that they would not, though the Utrecht professor J. de Louter and other experts could not share his optimism. According to De Louter, De Sturler had ignored the fact 'that a legal definition, that is a unilateral constitutional act can never automatically become instituted in international law. To achieve this, one would need either a treaty or a *de facto* occupation of an unoccupied territory'.[140] Neither of these conditions had been sufficiently met in the Archipelago, as could be seen in numerous misunderstandings during the 1880s between the Dutch colonial administration in the East Indies and foreign governments or private persons.[141]

However, the argument over Dutch colonial possessions went much further than problems of legal legitimacy. For the right-wing Liberal politicians and civil servants who were in charge in The

---

139. De Sturler, *Grondgebied*, chapter 1.
140. De Louter, *Handleiding*, chapter 1.
141. Cf. Fievez de Malines, *Overzicht*, pp. 29ff., 112ff., 137ff.

Hague and Batavia until the end of the 1880s, the whole issue was above all a matter of power. Their concern for the financial and military position of the Netherlands was in fact closely linked to anxiety about their own positions.

Their policies in this respect hardly ever formed a very uplifting spectacle. Take, for example, the rather hasty and generous way in which Governor-general 's Jacob (1881–4) – himself a former entrepreneur – extended the extremely advantageous contract of the Billiton Company until 1927. This was in sharp contrast to his usual pleas for 'great cautiousness and calm consideration' with regard to Borneo, Acheh and the growing unrest in Java.[142] The Minister of the Colonies, W. M. de Brauw, who was honest but politically inexperienced, had to defend this extension against an indignant public and a vengeful Parliament. He did this loyally, while making it perfectly clear to 's Jacob that he regarded his action as 'imprudent' because it would inevitably give the 'impression of favouritism'. But De Brauw soon learnt that he was not only dealing with the open opposition of Keuchenius and his followers but also with the ambitions of different Liberal leaders who tried to take advantage of the Billiton affair so that they could take 's Jacob's place as governor-general. According to Van Brauw, the worst intrigues – 'You may have guessed' – came from Van Rees, who had served as vice-president of the East Indian Council and Minister of the Colonies and who was now chairman of the Second Chamber: 'King Otto'.[143] After the policy had been officially denounced by a parliamentary inquiry committee, De Brauw had to resign immediately. Every effort was made by 's Jacob to delay his own resignation, but when he finally had to take his leave, Van Rees could score a hit. At his instigation, his former right hand in the East Indies and financial expert P. J. Sprenger van Eyck was appointed Minister of the Colonies (1883–8), and he himself was made governor-general (1884–8).

However, Van Rees's term of office in the East Indies turned out to be just as unsuccessful. Having initially raised great expectations in the Netherlands, he, too, eventually had to resign under the general criticism. 'As a former celebrated Liberal, he probably only had financial advantages from his time as governor-general, the post

142. 's Jacob to De Brauw, October 1882 (KB).
143. De Brauw to 's Jacob, 25 November 1883; cf. 8 December 1882 and 6 January 1883 (KB). See also De Brauw to A. Schimmelpenninck van der Oye, 28 November 1882, Schimmelpenninck van der Oye Collection (ARA).

for which he had intrigued so tremendously,' Minister of the Colonies Mackay commented in retrospect; 'I have never known a greater cynic.'[144] Van Rees's authoritarian behaviour towards the European inhabitants eventually led to his downfall, though in the meantime he was held responsible for the harsh colonial policy of tax increases and budget cuts imposed by Sprenger van Eyck in The Hague. According to an anonymous article in the *Indische Gids*, the influential colonial magazine which had been published in the Netherlands since 1879, this short-sighted policy of exploitation not only provoked 'possible dangers within the East Indies' but also 'the likelihood of foreign dangers'.

> One has to be as blind as a bat if one wants to close one's eyes deliberately to the signs of the times and refuse to see that, so far as colonies are concerned, there is a general movement in world politics which bodes no good for the peace of the colonising nations and where the backlash will also be noticeable in our far-away East Indies.[145]

The editor-in-chief of the *Indische Gids*, C. E. van Kesteren, was a protagonist of the colonial reform movement launched from Java by the politically committed journalist P. Brooshooft. This forerunner and name giver of what was later known as the 'ethical policy' strongly advocated both socio-economic reforms in Java and a more forceful stance for the Netherlands in the Outer Regions. Whenever the fight against opium abuse or Islamic 'fanaticism' or the promotion of education and welfare was under discussion, then this radically liberal, extra-parliamentary opposition in the East Indies was very much in agreement with the parliamentary opposition led by Anti-Revolutionaries and Catholics in the Netherlands.[146]

For the Christian parties the management of colonial possessions was not so much a matter of legal order or power politics but of ethics – at least while they were in the opposition. In *Ons Program* (Our Programme), the party manifesto for the newly formed Calvinist Anti-Revolutionary Party, Kuyper emphatically argued in 1879 against the existing colonial system, the system of exploitation as implemented directly by the Conservatives and indirectly by the

144. Mackay to C. Pijnacker Hordijk, 5 April 1892, Pijnacker Hordijk Collection (ARA). For the expectations of a 'second Daendels' as a result of Van Rees's policies, see De Brauw's sceptical remarks in his letter to Schimmelpenninck, 17 April 1884, Schimmelpenninck van der Oye Collection.
145. 'De heer Otto van Rees', *IG*, 1885, II, pp. 338–9.
146. Cf. Locher-Scholten, *Ethiek*, pp. 309ff.

Liberals. Kuyper contrasted this with a system of guardianship, that is, the material and moral development of the local population. At the same time, however, Kuyper was not averse to an extension of Dutch authority in the Archipelago, as long as it was motivated by a policy of guardianship. Kuyper said:

> The Archipelago does indeed form a single group of islands that belong closely together. And once the Netherlands has *de facto* sovereignty over about two-thirds of the inhabited area there, then it will go without saying that these scattered islands will be reunited and form one community of peoples under our own flag.[147]

Arguing for a statue to commemorate the seventeenth-century Governor-general Jan Pieterzoon Coen, the Catholic leader and priest H. J. A. M. Schaepman expressed himself in similar terms. 'You must consider that it is not right to take whatever you can get from the East Indies,' he told the East Indian Society in 1887; 'rather, your first and foremost objective should be to make the East Indies great and to develop it.'[148] However, when Keuchenius and Des Amorie van der Hoeven attacked the Liberal and Conservative policy in the Second Chamber, they questioned Dutch possession of the East Indies as such. 'It may well be feared', said the Anti-Revolutionary Keuchenius, 'that if the Netherlands proves itself to be no longer worthy of its East Indian possessions . . . we might lose our colonies altogether, either through the recalcitrance of their people or an attack by foreign enemies.' The Catholic Van der Hoeven expressed himself even more pessimistically on the Nisero issue.[149] As was typical in this context, the Calvinists also took it as a sign of doom when Mount Krakatau erupted in 1883.[150]

When the Christian parties gained a narrow majority in the 1888 elections for the Second Chamber and formed their first coalition cabinet, this alarmist perspective was somewhat toned down, though without disappearing altogether. At the formation of the cabinet there were already problems with finding a suitable minister for the Colonial Affairs Department. Schaepman wanted to have

147. A. Kuyper, *Ons Program*, chapter 2.
148. *Handelingen Indisch Genootschap* (Reports of the East Indian Society), 22 November 1887, p. 127.
149. Cf. note 214 below. For the quotation of Keuchenius, see *Handelingen Tweede Kamer* (Parliamentary Reports of the Second Chamber), 15 November 1881, p. 167; cf. ibid., 11 November 1885, p. 421.
150. Cf. *De Standaard*, 1 January 1884.

Des Amorie van der Hoeven for this post, but a Catholic in charge of colonies was regarded as 'pernicious' among Anti-Revolutionaries.[151] 'The rank-and-file Anti-Revolutionaries will indeed find it indeed hard to swallow if the "Kôch", as you are known by the "people", would be missing', wrote the leader of the Anti-Revolutionaries in the Second Chamber, A. F. De Savornin Lohman, to Keuchenius. 'Also, to keep an eye on church politics, I regard your participation as necessary.[152] Thus, Keuchenius became Minister of the Colonies after all. When shortly afterwards Van Rees resigned as governor-general, this gave the Anti-Revolutionaries an opportunity to appoint their own man for the post. The discussion of the pros and cons of different candidates gives quite a good picture of the dilemmas in defining a Christian policy of guardianship.

The Anti-Revolutionary MP and mayor of Amersfoort Van Asch van Wijck discreetly offered his services but was regarded as too inexperienced for the East Indies. He had to make do with Surinam, instead.[153] Under the Conservative–Liberal government W. K. van Dedem had proved to be a progressive and humanitarian expert, both as an MP and as chairman of the East Indian Society. However, as Keuchenius put it, 'he is unmarried and therefore exposed to dangerous temptations which might damage the honour and dignity of Dutch authority.'[154] Then there was the Liberal Amsterdam banker and prominent economist Pierson – not really a colonial expert but a practising Protestant. As such he was certainly not a friend of 'fundamentalism'. Kuyper therefore strongly advised against such a choice, pointing out that 'the whole town is in the hands of the Pierson–Gunning family clique – it's unbearable.'[155] Following Kuyper's advice, Keuchenius finally appointed C. Pijnacker Hordijk as governor-general. Hordijk, a professor a law, was a former Liberal Minister of the Interior, and was the provincial governor in Drenthe. Certainly not a colonial expert and not exactly

151. De Savornin Lohman to Keuchenius, 3 April 1888, Keuchenius Collection (KB), Cf. Van Wely, *Schaepman*, pp. 386–7; Suttorp, *De Savornin Lohman*, pp. 50 and 216; Kasteel, *Kuyper*, p. 145.
152. Lohman to Keuchenius, 3 April 1888, Keuchenius Collection.
153. Van Asch van Wijck to Keucheniusj, 31 May 1888; cf. Kuyper to Keuchenius, 10 May and 1 June 1888; Keuchenius Collection.
154. For the same reason Keuchenius also found Van Dedem unsuitable for other higher posts in the East Indies; Keuchenius to Pijnacker Hordijk, 28 January 1889, Pijnacker Hordijk Collection.
155. Kuyper to Keuchenius, 23 April 1888, Keuchenius Collection, 24 June 1888. Cf. Kuitenbrouwer, 'Pierson', pp. 2–3; Kuiper, *Voormannen*, pp. 176–7.

a Christian, 'but with his sense of righteousness and his warmth of heart he is probably better among you than some cold-blooded Anti-Revolutionaries', Lohman admitted.[156]

Obviously, however, a Christian policy of guardianship had to include more than responsible appointments. Kuyper felt that it was 'still too early for really great measures'. Opposition from the 'civil service clique' in The Hague and Batavia was still too strong. But he passionately entreated Keuchenius to implement at least one policy that was motivated by Christian principles – preferably the abolition of opium farming by the state, the 'main cause of injustice'.[157]

In his legislation Keuchenius subsequently shrank away from such drastic measures, though in his daily policy making he hardly needed Kuypers's encouragement. For example, he instructed Pijnacker Hordijk to raise the moral standards of the European civil servants, to supervise the Javanese aristocracy more strictly and above all to curb the growing influence of Islam wherever possible. He therefore suggested to the inexperienced governor-general that he should seek advice from Protestant missionaries in this respect and not merely from Snouck Hurgronje and other governmental advisers.[158] In an official circular he especially encouraged Dutch missionaries to make an even greater effort and to co-operate with one another to prevent foreign – or Catholic – missionaries from replacing them in their fight against Islam.[159]

The Liberal colonial experts, who were already viewing Keuchenius's policies with scepticism, followed the Christian zeal of the new minister with increasing irritation. Van Rees saw Keuchenius as a 'fanatic without common sense, political wisdom or knowledge of the specific conditions in the East Indies'. Van Dedem felt he was a 'dangerous religious zealot'. With malicious glee, he noted that the Catholics, too, were turning away from Keuchenius: 'the torrent of

---

156. Lohman would have preferred Pierson; Lohman to Keuchenius; 24 June 1888; cf. Kuyper to Keuchenius, 10 May 1888; Keuchenius Collection.

157. Kuyper to Keuchenius, 6 and 14 November 1888, Keuchenius Collection.

158. Keuchenius to Pijnacker Hordijk, 28 January 1889, Pijnacker Hordijk. See also copies of the letters to the governor-general of 16 August 1889 and 6 June 1890, Keuchenius Collection.

159. For Keuchenius's circular letter of 8 May 1888 and Neurdenburg's response of 21 May 1888, see *Mededeelingen*, 1889, pp. 336–49. For critical notes on Islam and Roman Catholic missions, see the file 'Persoonlijke aanteekeningen over zending', Keuchenius Collection. For the continuous frictions between Protestant and Roman Catholic missions as well as the difficulties of both during the 1880s, see Mulders, *Missie*, pp. 83–4; Coolsma, *Zendingseeuw*, pp. 441–5, 519–21, 592–6.

opposition against K. is growing!'[160] On 31 January 1890 the First Chamber, where Liberals were still in the majority, rejected the colonial budget and forced Keuchenius to resign. The most important complaint of Fransen van de Putte, the main Liberal spokesman, who called Keuchenius a 'Christian Hadji' during the debate, was that the minister's policy threatened to stir up unrest among the Islamic population of the East Indies. This was not merely a convenient argument, as Islam had indeed played an important part in causing the rebellion in Banten, Java, in 1888.[161]

After Keuchenius's resignation, the Christian coalition government continued in office at the instigation of Lohnman and Schaeper and very much against Kuyper's wishes.[162] To the satisfaction of Liberal experts, the person who was to take charge of the Colonial Department was the Anti-Revolutionary head of government and Minister of the Interior, Mackay. Though totally inexperienced in colonial matters, he was a 'gentleman' in the eyes of the Liberals. Mackay, in turn, was far more worried about Kuyper than the Liberal opposition.[163] And so Kuyper felt from time to time that he had to include Mackay's status quo policy in his usual attacks on Liberal colonial policies. Commenting on British and German expansion in the Archipelago, for instance, he obliquely criticised Mackay for continuing a 'policy without honour or pride, so that we might eventually lose everything'.

Kuyper felt that the Netherlands would do much better to cede Borneo to Britain and New Guinea to Germany as quickly as possible, before it was forced to do so. After all, the Netherlands was unable to make full use of these 'immeasurably vast islands' and there was still a lot of work to do in Java, Sumatra and the other islands. Furthermore, such a solution would mean that the Netherlands would 'find a basis for our European policies and also a friend and neighbour . . . in our colonies'.[164]

160. Van Dedem to Pijnacker Hordijk, 8 January 1890; cf. Van Rees to Pijnacker Hordijk, 10 April 1890; J. Röell to Pijnacker Hordijk, 12 February 1890, Pijnacker Hordijk Collection.

161. *Handelingen Eerste Kamer* (Parliamentary Reports of the First Chamber), 31 January 1890, pp. 315–30. Cf. Kartodirdjo, *Revolt*, chapter 5. For the defensive elements in Islamic renewal, see Noer, *Movement*, pp. 20–4.

162. 'The cabinet must stand or fall with you', wrote Kuyper to Keuchenius, 1 February 1890, Keuchenius Collection. Cf. Van Wely, *Schaepman*, pp. 437–8; Suttorp, *De Savornin Lohman*, pp. 57–60.

163. Mackay to Pijnacker Hordijk, 10 July 1890; cf. Van Rees to Pijnacker Hordijk, 10 April 1890, Pijnacker Hordijk Collection.

164. *De Standaard*, 19 June 1890 (leading article).

The Liberal press indignantly rejected such a suggestion out of hand, though the counter-arguments did not exactly show a great deal of confidence in the Netherlands as a colonial power, either. According to the *Indische Gids*, for example, it was rather unlikely that Britain or Germany would be contented with just Borneo or New Guinea in exchange for protecting the Netherlands in Europe: 'Don't be surprised if tomorrow they try to purloin Java, Sumatra and the other islands.' Furthermore, in view of the tense relations between Britain and Germany in colonial matters, it would never be possible to find a satisfactory solution for both powers. 'If the situation of the Netherlands is so desperate that it needs support from abroad . . . then it may as well affiliate itself to Germany', reasoned the commentator of the *Indische Gids* and, with him, some other Liberal colonial affairs spokesman.[165]

Concentration of Forces in Acheh

Dutch mistrust towards Britain, caused by the events in Borneo and South Africa, had taken extreme forms in the Nisero issue. But before dealing with the diplomatic conflict with Britain, we must pick up the thread of the Acheh War, which formed part of the background for it. In 1881 the Dutch government had unilaterally declared peace and introduced civil rule in Acheh, at the insistence of the colonial administration in Batavia as well as the majority of Dutch parliamentary and public opinion. 'The Acheh War is finished,' the colonial affairs correspondent of *De Economist*, Quarles van Ufford, said with relief; 'Thank God.'

However, this relief did not last. The pacification which was supposed to form the basis of peace turned out to be rather ineffective, and in the course of 1881 resistance flared up again. 'The chronicler, alas, made a mistake and many others with him at the same time', Quarles van Ufford was to realise within a year.[166] Governor-general 's Jacob confirmed that the war parties had apparently not surrendered after the peace, neither on the Achenese nor on the Dutch East Indian side. He also noted that there was increasing pressure from the military apparatus and the East Indian press to abolish civilian rule again, though he added that 'only under the most extreme conditions would I be prepared to give a free hand

165. *IG*, 1890, II, pp. 1757–8; cf. *Het Handelsblad*, 18 June 1890.
166. Cf. *De Economist*, 1880, I, p. 241; ibid. 1881, I, p. 83.

to the military again.' Furthermore, the governor-general felt that the personality of the new governor of Acheh, A. Pruys van der Hoeven, did not exactly contribute to a flexible handling of civil rule. Although he was a 'man with character', he was also 'stubborn and dogmatic' in his devotion to civilian rule and peace.[167] In 1883, at the instigation of The Hague, he was replaced by P. F. Laging Tobias, a less outspoken opponent of the military. As a result, occasional acts of war increased in Acheh, though officially the country was at peace. According to minister De Brauw, there was now a 'state of uncertainty, which is called peace but is in fact war'.[168]

De Brauw could therefore report to 's Jacob that Acheh was threatening to become 'the most dominant issue, not just in the East Indies but also here'. The opponents of civil rule had gathered around the aggrieved General van der Heijden, sending a torrent of petitions to the king, 'in which His Majesty is asked to make some provision in this "desperate" situation'. William III was surrounded by such a large number of former East Indian officers that De Brauw was quite alarmed: 'Even the cabinet council is haunted by the intrigues of the military party.'[169] Rutgers van Rozenburg and De Casembroot opened an offensive in the Dutch Parliament that was aimed at forcing the government to replace civilian rule by military rule again, preferably under the leadership of Van der Heijden. But at the end of 1882 these attempts failed one after another, because most Liberal and clerical MPs refused to resume such a costly war. After the King's Speech, Rutgers submitted an amendment to the parliamentary reply, requesting that military rule should be reinstated. However, this was rejected by 65 votes to 10.[170] When General Van der Heijden was accused of atrocities under his leadership, he indignantly requested that a committee of inquiry be set up. However, this did not lead to the full exoneration of the general as demanded by De Casembroot and Rutgers.[171] At the end of the year De Brauw could state with relief that the war partly had lost their cause in the Netherlands.[172]

167. 's Jacob to De Brauw, 10 September 1882; cf. 's Jacob to Van Goltstein, 22 August 1882 (KB).
168. De Brauw to 's Jacob, 22 October 1882 (KB).
169. Ibid., cf. 4 November 1882.
170. *Handelingen Tweede Kamer* (Parliamentary Reports of the Second Chamber), 27 September 1882, p. 73.
171. Ibid., 7 December 1882, pp. 581–2; cf. 2 December, pp. 488–512.
172. De Brauw to 's Jacob, 25 November 1882 (KB).

So for the time being, there was to be no resumption of the war. But what was the alternative? Everyone agreed that the current twilight situation could not continue for long. According to 's Jacob, Acheh would thus continue to cost far too much in terms of finance and manpower. To protect the borders of the Outer Regions and to maintain 'law and order' only a few hundred troops were available, while there was literally no personnel left for a possible extension of colonial rule.[173] The governor-general found the situation most alarming. Firstly, there was the possibility of threats from outside, both from European powers and from the pan-Islamic movement; and secondly there was increasing general unrest among the East Indian population, not just in the Outer Regions but also in Java.[174] In the Netherlands, too, there were warnings about the East Indies' vulnerable military situation, for example from E. B. Kielstra, a former officer, influential journalist and Liberal member of the Second Chamber from 1884 onwards.[175] The military problems were aggravated by a tightening of the financial situation, now that the economic crisis was becoming more and more noticeable both in the Netherlands and the East Indies. And so, in the course of 1883, there was an intensive discussion of alternative policies for Acheh in The Hague, Batavia and Kota Radja (the colonial capital of Acheh). Opinions were divided in all three places, though eventually the majority tended towards a concentrated reduction of the Dutch presence in the immediate surroundings of Kota Radja, in order to save expenses and make the troops available for the rest of the East Indies. The final parliamentary proposals for this move were submitted by the government in 1884, in connection with the Nisero crisis.

Later, colonial civil servants and historians were to blame the introduction of this system of concentration entirely on the Dutch government and Parliament. 'The Acheh drama', Somer commented at the time, 'took a different turn in the secret session of the Dutch Parliament of 16/17 July '84, when the most crippling and demoralising of all systems was invented, that is, the "system of concentration".'[176] However, such a conclusion gives an unbalanced idea in a number of respects. Firstly, the closed parliamentary

173. [Colijn], *Politiek beleid* I, p. 177.
174. 's Jacob to De Brauw, October (undated) and 26 December 1882 (KB).
175. E. B. Kielstra, 'De toestand van het Indisch leger', *De Gids*, 1884, ii, pp. 154–87. Kierstra also wrote influential articles for *Het Algemeen Handelsblad*.
176. Somer, *Korte Verklaring*, p. 218. Reid also speaks of 'Sprenger van Eyk's false solution', *Contest*, pp. 245ff.

session in which the government presented the concentrated system was largely about the Nisero question and took place on 13 June 1884. It was then approved by the Second Chamber in an open session on 16 June. Secondly, the first initiatives for such a system had actually come from Batavia rather than The Hague. At the end of 1882 Governor-general 's Jacob had already advocated a 'reduction of military occupation', following the example of 'General Van Swieten's scheme to occupy the kraton with a number of outstations and access to the sea'.[177] The governor's ideas seem to have been supported by the East Indian Council. In the Netherlands Rutgers van Rozenburg, alarmed by the current state of affairs, therefore interpellated De Brauw's successor F. G. van Bloemen Waanders about the imminent 'decision to reduce forces' which, he felt, would eventually lead to the 'ruin of the Netherlands as a colonial power' and to its becoming a 'third-rate power'.[178] Like his predecessor, however, Van Bloemen Waanders was not very much in favour of a reduction of forces and 's Jacob subsequently abandoned his idea again. To achieve a lasting political solution, Waanders put more hope in the restoration of the sultanate. However, an examination of this option by Laging Tobias in Kota Radja was opposed by 's Jacob and the East Indian Council in Batavia. At the end of 1883, the Acheh policy had come to a hopeless deadlock.[179]

Using General A. W. P. Weitzel's diaries, Van 't Veer has shown conclusively that Weitzel successfully managed to impose the system of concentration as Minister of War and interim Minister of the Colonies. In view of the simultaneous resignation of 's Jacob and Van Bloemen Waanders, Weitzel first of all ensured the support of their successors, Van Rees and Springer van Eyk.[180] Convincing the new cabinet members of the necessity of reducing the Dutch presence did not require much effort. So far Acheh had already cost nearly 150 million guilders – about 10 per cent of the East Indian

177. 'S Jacob to De Brauw, 28 October and 8 December 1882 (KB). 'S Jacob, however, warned against a 'rushed' implementation of the reduction, because this would be taken as 'proof of impotence' in the rest of the Archipelago. This is why he subsequently urged Weitzel to teach the enemy in Acheh 'a proper lesson' first; cf. Van 't Veer, *Majesteit*, p. 157.

178. *Handelingen Tweede Kamer* (Parliamentary Reports of the Second Chamber), 21 June 1883, p. 1116.

179. Ibid., cf. *Bijlagen* (Appendix) 1882–3, nos 46 and 13. Cf. Reid, *Contest*, pp. 211–16; Alfian, 'Sultanate', pp. 150ff.

180. Van 't Veer, *Majesteit*, pp. 154–62; cf. *Atjeh-oorlog*, pp. 145–7.

budget. For a military solution, it would have been necessary to use at least 10,000 permanent troops out of a total military capacity of 30,000. The current number of 7,000 was apparently totally unable to control the whole of Acheh. 'Furthermore,' concluded Van Rees, 'I cannot see how continuous fighting can bring about a solution.'[181] Once he had arrived in the East Indies, he expressed the idea of reducing the Dutch presence in such a way that it seemed like the latest plan, developed in the East Indies itself and after intensive discussions in Kota Radja and Batavia. Military power was to be concentrated in the area around Kota Radja, supplemented by a naval blockade around enemy ports in the rest of Acheh. Minister Sprenger van Eyk could thus present the new system to the Dutch Parliament on the authority of the Governor-general Van Rees.[182]

The minister made use of this approach at the closed session of the Second Chamber on 13 June 1884, which had been requested by the Anti-Revolutionary MP W. G. Brantsen van de Zijp to discuss the Nisero issue. The Chamber had asked for further information on the imminent conflict with Britain, but was first of all given an up-to-date summary of the Acheh policies, culminating in a passionately delivered plea for reducing forces: 'The situation in Acheh is miserable, and it has had extremely unfavourable repercussions on other matters.'[183] Des Amorie van der Hoeven vehemently protested against such a confusion of issues: 'The Acheh question is at this moment the Nisero question . . . this is the *question brûlante* which makes all other matters vanish into nothing, and it is not just our position in Acheh which depends on it, but our sovereignty as a colonial power.'[184] Even MPs who were less pessimistic, such as Keuchenius and Van Houten, pointed out that the planned blockade would be more likely to aggravate the conflict with Britain than defuse it, because of the obstruction of trade and shipping from the Straits. Indeed, both speakers already felt that the government plans as such were unsatisfactory: Keuchenius, because the concentrated system would not put an end to the 'lengthy barbarian and unjust war';[185] Van Houten, because he did not have much hope in the

181. See the comments of General A. R. W. Gey van Pittius of talks with Weitzel and Van Rees, 11 and 21 February 1884, Gey van Pittius Collection (ARA). Cf. [Colijn], *Politiek beleid* I, pp. 112ff.
182. Cf. Reid, *Contest*, pp. 216–17.
183. *Handelingen Tweede Kamer* (Parliamentary Reports of the Second Chamber) in closed session, 13 June 1884 (ARA), pp. 17–27.
184. Ibid., p. 82.
185. Ibid., pp. 64–7.

envisaged strategy of forcing the Achehnese to submit individually by means of the blockade, as if Acheh could be 'eaten up leaf by leaf like an artichoke'.

Without a certain amount of political unity this little game could continue indefinitely. Therefore he strongly advocated the restoration of the sultanate in Acheh.[186] Rutgers van Rozenburg, finally, found the government plans 'cowardly and half-hearted'. Under prevailing circumstances, one had to choose between total pacification and complete withdrawal; Rutgers obviously preferred the first solution, though he took the opportunity to suggest sarcastically that Acheh might as well be ceded to Britain.[187]

The majority of Liberal speakers, however, hesitantly supported the ideas of the government. For instance, J. Röell advised that all doubts should be set aside and the suggestions of the governor-general should be followed, as 'the man who has great influence and authority in this Chamber'.[188] 'I believe', he said, 'that we must be very careful right now, not just in the Outer Regions but also in Java. Our prestige has suffered a lot under the Acheh War.'[189] After this debate the government felt rather insecure about its parliamentary majority; and this insecurity was reflected in the speed with which they subsequently rushed the necessary credit application through the Chamber. Rather unexpectedly and in the absence of their most prominent critic, Keuchenius, the government suddenly called for a ballot on 16 June. After Rutgers's motion to postpone the ballot was rejected by 30 votes to 25, the Chamber finally approved the credit application with 45 votes to 10, on condition that the reduction of forces and the blockade would be implemented in close co-operation with the governor-general.[190] Even an expert like Van Dedem did not find out until years later that the reduction of forces bill had been forced by Weitzel in the Netherlands, rather than Van Rees in the East Indies, even though the first initiative had indeed originally come from Batavia.[191]

The new system, however, did not bring about the unqualified success which its protagonists had led everyone to expert. It is true

186. Ibid., pp. 49–55.
187. Ibid., pp. 92–3.
188. Ibid., pp. 92–3.
189. Ibid., p. 107; cf. note 185 above.
190. *Handelingen Tweede Kamer* (Parliamentary Reports of the Second Chamber), 16 June 1884, pp. 1597–9.
191. Van Dedem to Pijnacker Hordijk, 8 January 1890, Pijnacker Hordijk Collection.

that the military expenditure for Acheh could be cut back considerably, especially when the naval blockade was lifted again in 1885. But in order to occupy several dozen square miles within the concentrated territory, it was still necessary to maintain some 5,000 troops, who were exposed to epidemics and constant attacks from the Achehnese. Rather than being reduced, the number of dead, injured and sick was in fact on the increase under the concentrated system.[192] As a result, there was considerable criticism in the Netherlands. Rutgers van Rozenburg continued his attacks on the new system in the Second Chamber, which he claimed had ruined all prospects of subjecting Acheh to Dutch rule.[193] Outside the Dutch Parliament ex-governor Laging Tobias, who had resigned when the system of concentration was introduced, actively fought against it, for example in lectures at the Amsterdam Liberal association Burgerpligt (Civic Duty) and the East Indian Society.[194]

However, finding alternatives to the unpopular system was far from simple. The military and financial objections to a resumption of the war were still valid, particularly when it became obvious after the Banten Rebellion in Java that there were real dangers in other parts of the Archipelago. Nor was it possible, unfortunately, to withdraw from Acheh altogether, 'in view of our international position', as Van Houten said bitterly.[195] While Van Houten, Laging Tobias and other spokesmen continued to advocate the restoration of the sultanate, it was thought that the young Mohammed Daud, who was designated sultan by the Achehnese leaders, was too much of a figurehead set up by the war party.[196]

The Arab affairs specialist and former governmental adviser L. W. C. van den Berg finally suggested a new and far-reaching solution to the Acheh issue. Acheh, he said, should be colonised by Amboinese settlers, preferably ex-soldiers, in fortified kampongs. These could then gradually oust the 'anarchistic' and 'degenerate' Achehnese: 'in the same way that savages withdraw from the spreading of civilisa-

192. [Colijn], *Politiek beleid* I, pp. 120–1.
193. *Handelingen Tweede Kamer* (Parliamentary Reports of the Second Chamber), 27 November 1889, p. 228; cf. ibid., 11 November 1885, p. 401.
194. P. F. Laging Tobias, 'Onze tegenwoordige politiek in Atjeh en hare gevolgen', *De Gids*, 1886, ii, pp. 274–308; cf. *Handelingen Indisch Genootschap* (Reports of the East Indian Society), 3 January 1888, pp. 1–35.
195. *Handelingen Tweede Kamer* (Parliamentary Reports of the Second Chamber), 28 November 1889, p. 254, Cf. Kartodirdjo, *Revolt*, p. 276–80.
196. P. F. Laging Tobias, 'Het herstel van het protectoraat in Atjeh', *IG*, 1886, II, pp. 1722–67; 'Enkele opmerkingen over het Sultanaat in Atjeh', ibid. 1887, II, pp. 1109–12. Cf. Reid, *Contest*, pp. 254–5; Alfian, 'Sultanate', pp. 158ff.

tion, I expect that the present inhabitants . . . will make way for the new military colonies, and unless they change completely, they will die out anyway.'[197]

Not everyone rejected such a social Darwinist strategy out of hand. The leader of the right-wing Liberals in the Second Chamber, Röell, observing that 'as long as our authority in Acheh is not secured our authority in the whole Archipelago will remain insecure', wrote to Governor-general Pijnacker Hordijk: 'It immediately seemed to me that this idea was not as foolish as it might appear on the surface.' According to Röell, quite a few higher civil servants at the Colonial Affairs Department took rather a positive view of it.[198] However, in Christian circles, it was felt that Van den Berg's ideas were going too far with regard to Acheh, even though they had unanimously welcomed his plea for the strengthening of Christianity over Islam in the East Indies.[199] The Anti-Revolutionary colonial affairs ministers therefore continued to maintain the system of concentration – Keuchenius, because he feared a resumption of the war 'which would cost millions and many lives'; and Mackay, because he generally tried to maintain the status quo as much as possible.[200]

The Nisero Issue

International relations had played a major role in the introduction of the system of concentration in Acheh – indirectly because there was a widespread atmosphere of uncertainty and apprehension towards other countries, and directly because of the Nisero issue which strongly determined the implementation of the system and made it easier to accept. The Nisero issue temporarily also influenced other overseas questions, as we have already seen in the case of the Congo and the Suez Canal. On the one hand, it reinforced the necessity of taking Britain into account, though on the other hand it also opened up the possibility of seeking support from Germany in overseas matters. Generally the first tendency

197. L. W. C. van den Berg, 'De toekomst van Atjeh', *TNI*, 1890, I, pp. 209–19; an extended version of his article in the *NRC* of 4 March 1890.
198. Röell to Pijnacker Hordijk, 3 June 1890, Pijnacker Hordijk Collection.
199. *De Standaard*, 1 August 1890; cf. L. W. C. van den Berg, 'Het kruis tegenover de halve maan', *De Gids*, 1890, iv, pp. 67–102.
200. Cf. *Handelingen Tweede Kamer* (Parliamentary Reports of the Second Chamber), 28 November 1889, pp. 248–50; *Bijlagen* (Appendix), 1890–1 B nos 4 and 37.

prevailed over the second one, especially in governmental policies and also in the Dutch Parliament and in public opinion. In this section we shall concentrate particularly on the international aspects of the Nisero issue which have received less attention in the relevant literature than colonial aspects.

The origins of the entire issue did indeed lie in the area of the colonies – at least inasmuch as Acheh can be regarded as a colony. During the night of 8–9 November 1883 the British steamship Nisero had run aground off the coast of Teunom, nominally a 'dependency' but in reality an independent coastal state in western Acheh. The rajah of Teunom, who had once recognised Dutch 'sovereignty', took the crew hostage at first in order to give more emphasis to his demands for debt repayments from a Chinese trader in the Straits settlements and subsequently to put pressure on the Dutch East Indian colonial administration. The ransom which he demanded for the 28 shipwrecked men therefore varied between $10,000 and $400,000, depending on his current power position. This had increased considerably at the beginning of 1884 when the colonial administration of the Straits had first got involved with the matter and when a military rescue operation by the Dutch East Indian administration had failed completely. Eventually the British government became more and more alarmed over the continuing hostage situation.

On the suggestion of the British government and with the approval of the Dutch government, an official mission was sent to Teunom from the Straits in order to negotiate the release of the hostages. For the rajah this was a good enough reason to raise his demands to $400,000 and a formal British guarantee to maintain his position as well as free trade for Teunom – demands that were regarded as unacceptable by The Hague and Batavia.[201] The Dutch now began to prepare a naval blockade, mainly to pressurise Teunom but also to reinforce their concentrated system which had already been planned.[202] However, the announcement of the blockade caused an outcry in Britain. Under the increasing pressure of public opinion, led by the sailors' organisations and Straits rep-

201. Reid, *Contest*, pp. 218–34; cf. Van 't Veer, *Atjeh-oorlog*, pp. 148–51; Coolhaas, 'Nisero-kwetsie', pp. 271–84.

202. The Nisero documents are partly included in the Appendix of the Parliamentary Report (*Bijlagen*) of 1883–4, and partly in *Bescheiden*. For the introduction of the blockade, see Woltring, *Bescheiden* III, no. 418; *Bijlagen Handelingen Tweede Kamer* (Parliamentary Reports of the Second Chamber, Appendix) 1883–4, nos 231 and 20.

resentatives, Granville officially offered British mediation in the Teunom conflict on 29 April 1884: 'In view of British interests concerned and the fact that the treaty engagements of 1824 and 1871 . . . were intended to secure the freedom and the development of trade, and the maintenance of peace in these regions'.[203]

The British offer was particularly embarrassing for the Dutch government. In international law, mediation always presupposed a conflict between two independent parties, so that British recognition of Dutch sovereignty, at any rate, seemed to have been partly lifted. Furthermore, the offer obviously thwarted the Dutch plans for a blockade and would only reinforce the rajah in his obstinacy. And finally Granville's interpretation of the 1824 and 1871 treaties, which he put forward in this context, did not augur well for the future, in view of the problems with Britain in Borneo and other parts of the Archipelago. On 1 May the Cabinet Council therefore unanimously decided to reject the British offer of mediation as unacceptable interference in the internal affairs of the Netherlands.[204] Van Bylandt was given the thankless task of communicating this decision to a dissatisfied Granville who repeated his offer, this time even for the whole of Acheh, also suggesting – much to Van Bylandt's alarm – that the sultan should be included in the mediation.[205]

It was now minister Van der Does de Willebois who reacted with particular indignation to the 'striking, if not to say arrogant way in which the British Foreign Office was putting pressure on us from all sides, at least to intimidate us'.[206] Van der Does therefore thoroughly investigated the mood in Berlin. When it turned out that the German government found the Dutch attitude in the Nisero issue *correct* and indeed *unanfechtbar* (indisputable), Van der Does de Willebois decided to reject the British offer for a second time.[207] The introduction of the blockade also continued, though – following Asser's advice – it was now referred to as 'police action', because in terms of international law the word 'blockade' would have implied a measure of independence for Teunom as well as the rest of

---

203. Ibid., no. 21.
204. Woltring, *Bescheiden* III, no. 432.
205. *Bijlagen Handelingen Tweede Kamer* (Parliamentary Reports of the Second Chamber, Appendix), nos 231, 23; cf. 22, 25, 26.
206. Woltring, *Bescheiden* III, no. 440.
207. The German government also expressed their view quite unambiguously to the British government, who did take it into account, according to Van Bylandt; ibid., no. 441; cf. no. 436 note 3.

Acheh, and this was precisely what the Dutch government wanted to deny in dealing with Britain.[208] Behind the scenes, however, there were continuous attempts to solve the diplomatic deadlock. Informal attempts were made, among others, by the managing director of the Java Railway Company, H. D. van Daalen, and by Lord Reay a former Liberal member of the Dutch Second Chamber, who had an influential position in British governmental circles.[209] But when the Dutch government was interpellated on the Nisero issue by Brantsen van de Zijp on 9 June, discussions with Britain still seemed to be at a complete deadlock.

Brantsen van de Zijp asked the government to make the secret documents on the conflict with Britain available.[210] Van der Does agreed to this request, provided that the Second Chamber would discuss them behind closed doors. During the closed session on 13 June Sprenger van Eyck then proposed the introduction of the reduction of forces and a blockade as a police measure, where appropriate; the blockade in particular was intended to gain the 'release of the crew imprisoned in Teunom'.[211] We have already seen that Des Amorie van der Hoeven did not want to discuss these measures because of the seriousness of the conflict with Britain, and also that even Keuchenius and Van Houten advised against the introduction of the blockade as a police measure, even though, for different reasons, they were less concerned about the conflict. Keuchenius' optimism with regard to Britain showed itself in his unshakeable confidence in Gladstone and his devotion to the 'cause of righteousness, on any occasion'.[212] His Liberal colleague Van Houten was unable to share this confidence, though he felt that his country should not 'give an inch' to British attempts to turn the Netherlands into a 'semi-vassal state'. 'In our resistance to Britain's arrogant tone we will certainly not be on our own', he stated pointedly.[213]

Van der Hoeven did not particularly trust either Gladstone's sense of justice or Bismarck's apparently disinterested offer of support. However, he felt that British intervention would still be

208. Ibid., no. 447; cf. no. 450.
209. Ibid., no. 443. Cf. Lord Reay to D. A. W. Tets van Goudriaan, 31 May 1884, Tets van Goudriaan Collection (ARA).
210. *Handelingen Tweede Kamer* (Parliamentary Reports of the Second Chamber), 9 June 1884, pp. 1530–4.
211. Ibid. in closed session, 13 June 1884, p. 26.
212. Ibid., pp. 70 and 80.
213. Ibid., pp. 58–9.

preferable to active support from Germany: 'that, I fear, would give us *far more* of a disadvantage than if Britain takes away part of our territories.' The latter was not unlikely, according to Van der Hoeven; if not now, then probably later:

> I think we all have to realise that the colonial territories of the Netherlands are indeed not in proportion with our power, so that we shall continually have to make the greatest effort to maintain them. In the long term, we may not always be successful, though through no fault of our own.[214]

In this context we must bear in mind, of course, that Van der Hoeven was 'tortured by pessimism', and that he had a 'view of history which tended towards apathy'.[215] But even Rutgers van Rozenburg warned that 'history will tell how the sixteenth- and seventeenth-century Dutch struggled and persevered to gain and conquer colonies and how the Dutch of the nineteenth century only had enough energy to inherit these colonies and were too inert to defend and maintain them.'[216] But even less dramatically inclined speakers, such as J. G. Gleichman and Van Dedem, expressed special concern about the conflict with Britain, and these worries certainly did not disappear when Van der Does soothingly pointed out that Britain had a lot of problems both at home and abroad.[217]

Finally, it was Heemskerk's turn, as the Conservative head of the government, to point out to the Second Chamber that relations with Britain had been good during the last few decades, 'though, on the other hand, the lessons of history have not been written for us in vain, and we know how much our fathers suffered in wars with Britain'. There was no acute danger, he felt, but it would be just as wrong to ignore British steps.[218]

This 'definition of the situation' was indeed confirmed by the further events in the Nisero issue. When the British government made its final decision on 5 July 1884 there were indeed some who advocated unilateral action in Acheh. The Home Secretary, Harcourt, in particular 'upbraided us for our degeneration from the days of Palmerston, insisting on our throwing over the Dutch, and

214. Ibid., p. 181; cf. pp. 45–7.
215. Cf. Van Wely, *Schaepman*, pp. 326–7.
216. *Handelingen Tweede Kamer* (Parliamentary Reports of the Second Chamber) in closed session, 13 June 1884, p. 178.
217. Ibid., pp. 1445–5; cf. pp. 150–3, 219–20.
218. Ibid., pp. 217–18.

that orders should be sent to our men of war to seize the prisoners *coûte que coûte*,' Granville later wrote to Gladstone.[219]

A majority, however, supported the proposals of Granville and Under-secretary Pauncefote to send a joint Anglo-Dutch mission to Teunom in order to make the rajah release the hostages. In exchange, they would offer a moderate ransom and the lifting of the blockade, threatening joint military action should he refuse to co-operate. The idea of joint Anglo-Dutch action had originally been put forward to the Dutch government by the aged General Van Swieten.[220] The government then sent ex-governor Pruys van der Hoeven and secretary-general of the Colonies H. van der Wijck to London in order to bring this plan discreetly to the attention of the British government. Together with the sorely tried Van Bylandt, they eventually succeeded in winning Pauncefote for the plan, who subsequently convinced the majority of the British cabinet that such joint action was desirable. 'It has been a hard struggle,' Van Bylandt reported on 6 July, 'but I think the result can be seen as highly satisfactory.'[221] The Dutch government was of course only too willing to accept its own suggestions. When the definitive Anglo-Dutch agreement was formulated, there were still a number of difficulties, but the joint venture itself went entirely as planned. The rajah accepted the conditions and released the remaining crew on 10 September 1884.[222]

The conclusion of the Nisero issue was welcomed with mixed feelings in the Netherlands. Keuchenius and Kuyper saw their confidence in Gladstone confirmed by the event,[223] and Des Amorie van der Hoeven stated with relief that the British reaction could have been far worse.[224] Brantsen van de Zijp, however, commented: 'it is interference that we should take joint action against our recalcitrant vassal together with a *foreign* power on *our* territory.'[225]

In Liberal circles reactions were even stronger. Rutgers van Rozenburg expressed his 'shame and annoyance' at the 'humiliating

219. Quoted in Reid, *Contest*, pp. 241–2.
220. Woltring, *Bescheiden* III, no. 451A.
221. *Bijlagen Handelingen Tweede Kamer* (Parliamentary Reports of the Second Chamber, Appendix) 1883–4, nos 232, 24; cf. Coolhaas, 'Nisero-kwestie', no. XI.
222. Cf. Reid, *Contest*, pp. 242–5; Van 't Veer, *Atjeh-oorlog*, pp. 154–7.
223. Cf. *De Standaard*, 4 and 7 August 1884.
224. *Handelingen Tweede Kamer* (Parliamentary Reports of the Second Chamber), 31 July 1884, p. 1846.
225. Ibid., p. 1841.

development of the Nisero issue'.[226] In the Liberal press there was already an almost general mistrust towards Britain, the 'jealous neighbour' of the Netherlands in the East Indies: 'Everything in the entire Teunom affair forces us to be suspicious and makes a lack of suspicion synonymous with a lack of caution.'[227] Several commentators saw Britain's action as a last-minute attempt to gain a foothold in Sumatra.[228] Professor Harting felt that this was Britain's way of taking revenge for Dutch support for the South African Boers.[229] According to Van Houten and other observers, the Nisero issue had shown clearly that it was necessary to look to Germany in overseas matters. Owing to Britain's fear of Germany, a worse development had been prevented, and if this had happened earlier, then 'the Nisero issue would have given Britain ample excuse to take Sumatra away from us.'[230]

Such views persisted for a while, though they were no more than the typical talk of the opposition. The Nisero issue did not bring about any great change in Dutch policies towards Britain. 'Nisero scandal still unrevenged', an anonymous Dutchman wrote resentfully to minister De Beaufort in 1900, on the occasion of his cautious policy at the time of the Boer War.[231]

Borneo and New Guinea

While the Nisero issue was keeping people's minds occupied in 1884, the Borneo question was still not solved. In addition, problems with Britain were now threatening to emerge in connection with New Guinea as well. Minister Van der Does's head of cabinet, D. A. W. Tets van Goudriaan, even thought it likely that the Nisero issue was being used by Britain in order to 'break our intractability in the Borneo border issue'.[232] When the Nisero issue was over,

226. Ibid., pp. 1845–6.
227. 'De Nisero-questie en de Gouverneur-generaal London', *IG*, 1884, II, pp. 285–6. A lot of suspicion was also expressed in *NRC* of 15–18 June, 25 July 1884 and the *Vaderland* of 24 July 1884; a more moderate note was sounded in the *Het Handelsblad* of 28–29 May and 12 July 1884, and *De Amsterdammer* (weekly) of 8, 15 and 22 June 1884.
228. Cf. 'Nisero-kwestie', *IG*, 1884, II, p. 115; *NRC*, 16 August, 1884.
229. Cf. Coolhaas, 'Nisero-kwestie', pp. 298–9.
230. Van Houten, 'Onze internationale stelling', *Vragen des Tijds*, 1884, II, 318. Cf. note 13 above.
231. See the jacket of 'Curiosa' under no. 33 in the De Beaufort Collection (ARA).
232. Woltring, *Bescheiden* III, no. 400.

colonial circles continued to be concerned that 'tomorrow there will be another, possibly even more serious issue'.[233]

However, the problems with Borneo and New Guinea's borders were subsequently solved peacefully by British and Dutch diplomats, though perhaps partly under the influence of the Nisero issue. Nevertheless, the Netherlands did not come out unscathed in Borneo, and the Dutch flag, which had been hoisted so proudly above Batu Tinagat in 1881, had to be taken down again ten years later.

Anxieties about a serious conflict with Britain over Borneo had not been entirely unfounded. When a Royal Charter was given to the British North Borneo Company in 1881, the British government became directly involved in the frontier clash between the company and the Netherlands. The attempts of the company to hoist their own flag south of Batu Tinagat had nearly led to skirmishes with the occupying Dutch forces.[234] In 1884 the incident prompted Granville to propose a joint Anglo-Dutch inquiry into the conflicting claims so that worse things could be prevented. 'The continued existence of the conflicting claims as to boundary cannot fail to lead to misunderstanding, possibly even to collision,' he warned Van Bijlandt.[235] Earlier, minister Rochussen had rejected a similar proposal on the grounds that it would put the 'incontestable rights' of the Netherlands on the same level as the 'dubious claims' of a British company.[236]

The pose of the British government as an impartial arbiter in the Borneo affair had made Ruchussen extremely suspicious. When it became known that Consul-general Read (Singapore) had acted as the commissioning agent of the North Borneo Company, Rochussen personally saw to it that he was replaced: 'Do we require stronger evidence that we cannot have Dutch interests represented by an Englishman in Singapore?'[237] In view of the Nisero issue, however, minister Van der Does did not want to reject the renewed British proposal for a joint border inquiry out of hand, even though he regarded it as a *'véritable déception'*.[238] However, now that new

233. 'Nisero-quaestie', *IG*, 1884, II, p. 451; cf. 'Het "Nisero" vraagstuk', *TNI*, 1884, II, pp. 319–20.
234. Woltring, *Bescheiden* III, no. 36, cf. Irwin, *Borneo*, p. 208.
235. Woltring, *Bescheiden* III, no. 403.
236. Ibid., nos 268, 284, 298, 300.
237. Ibid., nos 304; cf. nos 269, 288.
238. Ibid., nos 415, 587.

and more urgent problems had arisen, including the Nisero issue, Granville decided to drop the Borneo affair.

The border issue became topical again when the Conservative British government of Lord Salisbury set up an official protectorate over north Borneo in 1888. The Dutch had already expected such a move for some time, but Minister Hartsen did not think it wise to protest against this inevitable development. He felt it was more sensible to try to 'make use of the situation in order to obtain compensation from Britain in the form of an advantageous settlement of the border issue, with recognition of our rights in Borneo'.[239] But once the protectorate had been announced, it began to seem doubtful whether the Netherlands could even maintain Batu Tinagat. Hartsen, however, did not press his British counterpart too hard. When Van Bylandt made preparations again to raise the question of Dutch rights in accordance with the 1824 treaty, Hartsen urged that 'it is no longer fitting to argue about the meaning of the treaty'.[240]

When it became obvious that the British government would not be contented with less than Batu Tinagat, Van Bylandt advocated international arbitration, so that 'the other governments should not be left unaware of the disdain for all principles of international law displayed by the British government; for public opinion can be very influential in this matter, just as it was in the Nisero issue.'[241] Nevertheless, in view of mutual power relations and the nature of the historical evidence, Hartsen preferred the original British proposal of a joint inquiry to arbitration, even if such an inquiry was likely to lead to the cession of Batu Tinagat.[242]

Eventually, even Van Bylandt was to give in to this course of events. Now that Britain had managed to establish itself in Borneo after all, and Germany was extending its influence in New Guinea, he felt that the Netherlands should take great care to maintain 'a good relationship with its most powerful neighbour, which is so much to be desired, even if it can only be obtained at the price of a small territorial concession'.[243] Finally, on 20 June 1890, the Anglo-

---

239. Ibid. IV, no. 226.
240. Ibid., no. 282.
241. Ibid., no. 311. Cf. the note in which Salisbury explained the British claims and rejected the Dutch ones, no. 301.
242. Unlike in the border dispute with France in Surinam, Hartsen did not think it was justified to have third parties interfering in Borneo; ibid., nos 288, 317 and 331.
243. Ibid., no. 455.

Dutch border convention was concluded. Following the results of the joint inquiry, Batu Tinagat was indeed assigned to Britain.[244]

Throughout the negotiations Hartsen was frequently concerned about a possible negative reaction from the Dutch Parliament, which had already caused him so much trouble in the Congo and Lawa issues.[245] When he presented the appropriate bill, he therefore emphasised that it was important to achieve a definitive settlement of the lingering border conflict in Borneo. He played down the cession of Batu Tinagat by pointing out that 'before there were any differences over the border issue, the Dutch government had never . . . taken much interest in this out-of-the-way corner of its territories, an area which was unknown to it and indeed totally uninhabited.'[246]

This time the Second Chamber found it conspicuously easy to accept Hartsen's ideas, although the lengthy course of diplomatic negotiations with Britain came under a good deal of criticism.[247] Considering that a colonial post had been established in Batu Tinagat in 1883 and indeed at the instigation of the Second Chamber, the cession was of course generally regretted, but nobody saw it as an insurmountable difficulty. De Beaufort thought that the cession of territories as such was far more difficult for a small power than a great one, because it easily gave the impression that it was an 'act of weakness, caused by the pressure of more powerful states'. But he felt that in this case it was far more important that the cession should concern Britain, 'a power with whom we . . . have gradually achieved a *modus vivendi* with regard to our East Indian territories. Better Britain than some other country'.[248] The 1824 treaty, which had been quoted by the Second Chamber so frequently in connection with Borneo, met with very little support this time. After all, as H. J. Bool pointed out, north Borneo – including Batu Tinagat – was above the line of Singapore and not below it. Eventually the border convention was endorsed without a division by both Chambers of the Dutch Parliament.[249]

The Borneo convention was also accepted by colonial experts

244. Ibid. V, no. 53A–B, 89.

245. Ibid. IV, no. 348.

246. *Bijlagen Handelingen Tweede Kamer* (Parliamentary Reports of the Second Chamber, Appendix) 1890–1, no. 187, 3.

247. Cf. the temporary report, ibid., 1891–2, no. 43.

248. *Handelingen Tweede Kamer* (Parliamentary Reports of the Second Chamber), 8 March 1892, pp. 708–9.

249. Ibid., p. 717; cf. ibid. *Eerste Kamer* (First Chamber), 1 April 1892, p. 198.

outside the Dutch Parliament, though with even less enthusiasm. In the East Indian Society and the Dutch Geagraphical Society there was at first some talk of 'national honour' and 'inalienable rights', but such voices fell silent once the convention had become a fact.[250] After all, as Professor P. A. van der Lith explained in *De Gids*, Batu Tinagat had only been occupied by the Netherlands after the beginning of the border conflict: 'Measured against the only document of international law – the Congo Act – our claims would not be regarded as very strong.'[251] The Borneo issue in the Netherlands gradually fizzled out. This calm complaisance ten years later was in fact quite noticeable compared with the excitement when the issue first arose. Relations with Britain had clearly calmed down, as they had in other parts of the East Indies and in South Africa. However, this new accommodating spirit towards Britain seems to have been caused not so much by greater trust in Britain as by greater mistrust towards Germany. Since the emergence of the Nisero issue and the Berlin conference Germany itself had become an expanding colonial power and was now establishing itself in New Guinea, in the direct vicinity of the Dutch East Indies.

In the Netherlands New Guinea had always aroused far less interest than Borneo, and the western parts of the island, which were regarded as Dutch East Indian territory, did not even have a Dutch colonial post. This situation was hardly regarded as a problem in The Hague while no foreign powers were trying to establish themselves in New Guinea. However, for quite a while there had been such attempts by Australia. When Queensland annexed part of eastern New Guinea in 1883, there was a certain amount of concern in The Hague, though it subsided for a while when the British government refused to sanction the unilateral annexation. Moreover, the British government emphasised its recognition of Dutch rights in the western parts.[252] Subsequently, however, the Gladstone government was very quick to reverse its decision when, in 1884, Germany prepared to occupy part of eastern New Guinea. Having formally accepted that with the Australian annexation no *de facto* occupation had taken place, in the British press doubt was

250. *Handelingen Indisch Genootschap*, 12 February 1889, p. 24. The Dutch Geographical Society continued to argue in vain with its British sister organisation about the edition of a map on which the borders had been drawn according to British claims: *TAG*, 1888, pp. 248–55; ibid. 1889, pp. 47–55.

251. P. A. van der Lith, 'Het Noord-Borneo-tractaat', *De Gids*, 1891, iv, p. 476.

252. Woltring, *Bescheiden* III, no. 318, 347, 364. See also Thompson, *Australian Imperialism*, chapters 4 and 5.

expressed whether Dutch claims could be maintained in the absence of a *de facto* occupation.

Now that the imperialist fever had taken hold of Britain, Van Bylandt felt that the German presence in New Guinea was not entirely unfavourable for the Netherlands: 'it seems likely to me that each of the two great powers will want to protect us against the greed of the other.'[253] Not everybody, however saw British–German rivalry as a satisfactory guarantee of Dutch rights. After all, the increasing display of German and British power in eastern New Guinea meant that the absence of a Dutch post created a dangerous power vacuum in the western part. 'We shall either have to abandon New Guinea completely or show at least that we value its possession', warned De Beaufort in 1885.[254]

However, only the Utrecht Missionary Society favoured a permanent outpost, which would certainly have been of value to Dutch missionaries in New Guinea in dealing with the 'heathen Papuans'. These 'bloodthirsty savages' seemed particularly to want to take revenge on their converted fellow countrymen. However, the colonial administration refused to interfere in the 'domestic affairs' of the Papuans and only sent a warship to 'chastise' the troublesome tribes on very rare occasions.[255] Not until the 1890s did the Dutch government decide to provide permanent outposts and a more definite demarcation of borders, and this only happened after there had been British complaints about Papuans attacking from the 'Dutch' half.

The Financial and Economic Crisis

The sparse occupation of the Outer Regions reflected in the first place a power-political dilemma for the Netherlands. In the course of the 1880s there also emerged a financial and economic dilemma, caused by the international crisis which paralysed both commerce and industry as well as leading to a decline in government revenue. As Java still had the most important position in commerce and industry and formed the most important source of income for the

253. Woltring, *Bescheiden* III, no. 530; cf. nos 528, 563; Thompson, *Australian Imperialism*, chapter 6.
254. *Handelingen Tweede Kamer* (Parliamentary Reports of the Second Chamber), 17 November 1885, p. 468.
255. *Berigten van de Utrechtsche Zendelingsvereeniging*, 1887, pp. 58–65; ibid. 1888, pp. 161–6; ibid. 1890, pp. 49–50, 74–7.

government, there was automatically more interest in new opportunities for exploitation in the Outer Regions, both among private individuals and government agents. Entrepreneurs were particularly thinking in terms of agricultural enterprises, following the example of Deli, whereas the colonial administration was aiming more at mining, as it offered opportunities for government exploitation.

However, as private and public funds were so scarce, not many of these initiatives were particularly successful at first. With a view to the future exploitation of the Archipelago, the most important new development was probably the formation of the Royal Dutch Packet Company, which was supported by the Dutch government.

The crisis affected above all sugar cultivation in Java, which had to suffer increasingly under competition from European sugar beet. The market crash in 1884 led to a series of bankruptcies, not only in Java but also in the Netherlands. In Amsterdam, where more than half of all cultivation companies were based with about 70 per cent of the invested capital, the chain reaction could be broken – though with difficulty – through the intervention of several large-scale capitalists, in particular by the Netherlands Trading Company, that became even more a banking institution in the process; by an *ad hoc* committee formed by the Deli men P. W. Janssen and Cremer, both already millionaires; the owners of shipping companies J. Boissevain and W. H. van Leeuwen; and the leading banker A. C. Wertheim.[256] Under these critical circumstances there was now an increasing demand for the abolition of export duties for sugar and other agricultural products.

In 1885, however, Sprenger van Eyk did not wish to go any further in his bill on the new East Indian tariff law than a lowering of export duties, as he had already been confronted with decreasing revenues as state cultivation was being abolished. Export duties on sugar were to be halved, and coffee went down by two-thirds. Import duties, on the other hand, went up from 6 to 10 per cent, except for textile products, to spare Twente manufacturers and consumers in Java.[257]

In the Second Chamber the bill was criticised by two different camps. Firstly, there was the Catholic MP B. M. Bahlmann, who was inclined towards protectionism and spoke in the name of

256. *Verslag KvK Amsterdam* (Report of the Amsterdam Chamber of Commerce) 1884, pp. 7–8. Cf. Rijxman, *Wertheim*, pp. 114–15.
257. *Bijlagen Handelingen Tweede Kamer* (Parliamentary Reports of the Second Chamber, Appendix) 1885–6, no. 79.

'Dutch manufacturers and their work force'. He protested against the indiscriminate raising of import duties for most of the Dutch export products. Secondly, a complete abolition of export duties was proposed by Cremer for a number of agricultural products, in order to alleviate the situation for colonial trade and industry. Bahlmann did not succeed in his attempt to re-establish differential rights.[258] And Cremer's proposal to abolish export duties was eventually rejected by 39 votes to 37.[259] In 1886, the situation of the Javanese sugar industry had deteriorated so much that Sprenger van Eyk proposed a suspension of export duties on sugar for two years. On the insistence of the Amsterdam business world, the Second Chamber then decided on five years.[260]

Although trade primarily continued to be directed at Java, the crisis meant that the share of the Outer Regions increased quite considerably. The export figures for typical Javanese products such as sugar and coffee sank, whereas non-Javanese products such as tobacco and tin increased. In 1880 the government raised 15 per cent of its tariffs in the Outer Regions and in 1890 as much as 25 per cent.[261]

In the course of the 1880s it was therefore repeatedly argued that trade and industry in the Outer Regions should expand. In 1880, for example, the young M. E. F. Elout started a new East Indian Company which was to help develop the Archipelago by means of *colons explorateurs* (colonising explorers). But despite a large and enthusiastic response in the Netherlands, this ambitious project never took off.[262] Similar plans in connection with the 1883 World Fair in Amsterdam never went further than an extension of the Colonial Museum in Haarlem to include a collection from the Outer Regions.[263] Although private initiatives from the Netherlands yielded very few concrete results, there still remained a lot of

258. His most important budget amendment was rejected with 51 votes to 22. *Handelingen Tweede Kamer* (Parliamentary Reports of the Second Chamber), 22 March 1886, p. 1277.
259. Ibid., 25 March 1886, p. 1314.
260. Ibid., 16 December 1886, p. 551; cf. *Verslag KvK Amsterdam* (Report of the Amsterdam Chamber of Commerce) 1885, pp. 132 and 180–2, ibid. 1886, pp. 9–10.
261. See the entry 'Scheepvaart en handel' (Shipping and trade) in the *ENI*; cf. Burger, *Geschiedenis* II, pp. 78–9.
262. M. E. F. Elout, 'De oprichting eener nieuwe Oost-Indische Compagnie', *Handelingen Indisch Genootschap* (Reports of the East Indian Society), 20 January 1880, pp. 1–32. Cf. *De Economist*, 1880, I, pp. 115–20; ibid. 1881, I, pp. 71–2, 276–80.
263. Ibid. 1883, I, pp. 593–6; II, pp. 1142–8.

opposition to state-owned mines even with regard to minerals that were difficult to mine. The mining of the well-known Ombilin coal in Sumatra was delayed for years.

After the Second Chamber had agreed to the building of a state-owned railway line in 1887, state-owned mining of coal was finally approved by the Dutch Parliament in 1891. Despite a large number of pleas for private mining, no viable applications for concessions actually materialised.[264] In Celebes and Borneo Dutch entrepreneurs did indeed engage in gold- and coal-mining, but, just like coal-mining in Ombilin, this did not begin to bear fruit until the 1890s. For the time being, the developed parts of the Archipelago continued to be 'scattered oases . . . in the midst of an immense territory that is still wasteland', as Pruys van der Hoeven graphically wrote.[265]

Economic growth in the Outer Regions during the 1880s was therefore mainly due to the large, established enterprises, such as the Deli and Billiton companies. These enterprises made a lot of profit and regularly paid dividends of over 100 per cent in the 1880s. It is against the background of these amazing investment profits as well as the decreasing state revenue that we must see the excitement when Governor-general 's Jacob temporarily extended the advantageous contract of the Billiton Company to 75 years. 'The extension has become known at a time when shareholders received dividends of over 100 per cent, and it has therefore given rise to the greatest resentment', explained minister De Brauw to the surprised governor-general, who replied, 'I am not a friend of state-owned mines'.[266]

The most important critics in the Second chamber, Keuchenius and Van Houten, did not advocate state-owned mines either but felt that a greater state share than the current 3 per cent of the gross proceeds was a very reasonable one indeed. At their instigation, a parliamentary inquiry committee was set up which strongly condemned the extension, recommending that 'the supreme government should retain its full freedom so that at the termination of the

264. Wellenstein, *Mijnbouwvraagstuk*, pp. 21–3. See the many arguments between advocates and opponents of state exploitation in *De Economist* and *De Indische Gids* during the second half of the 1880s; cf. *Handelingen Indisch Genootschap* (Reports of the East Indian Society), 21 October 1890, pp. 168–230.
265. A. Pruys van der Hoeven, 'Versterking der Indische middelen', *De Economist*, 1885, II, p. 862.
266. 's Jacob to De Brauw, 17 January 1883; cf. De Brauw to 's Jacob, 25 November 1882 (KB).

original ... concession ... it could observe the country's best interests.' On 15 February 1883 this conclusion was accepted by the Second Chamber, with 52 votes to 26, resulting in the resignation of De Brauw and 's Jacob.[267]

In the course of the 1880s, however, the combined effect of the crisis and the gradual abolition of state cultivation led to a further decrease in state revenue, which sunk from 142 million guilders in 1883 to 120 million in 1888.[268] The government in The Hague and Batavia therefore began to show more interest in the development of new resources in the Outer Regions. Minerals, in particular, were considered to be a very suitable resource for the state to mine. Because of the possible presence of minerals, Sprenger van Eyk, who was usually rather careful with money, was prepared to subsidise the 1885 expedition of the Dutch Geographical Society to New Guinea. But the Second Chamber felt it was better to promote the further development of existing resources than to explore new ones in remote, uncultivated areas such as New Guinea. 'The resources *may* well be there, but we know *for certain* that we have them in other parts of our Archipelago', explained Cremer, with the common-sense logic of a director of the established Deli Company and a rising Liberal MP from Amsterdam. He proposed that the subsidy should be cancelled, and his motion was carried with 49 votes to 21 – much to the disappointment of the Dutch Geographical Society who, because of the 'narrow-mindedness' of the Dutch Parliament, had to make to do with a less ambitious destination.[269]

On the suggestion of Governor-general Van Rees, the Society subsequently investigated the small Sunda islands in 1888–9, including Flores which was said to be particularly rich in tin.[270] At the time, the colonial administration was considering a concession application from a German merchant in Flores, which was later turned down so that state-owned mines could remain an option. The colonial administration then sent expeditions to Flores itself, first a scientific and then a military expedition. Because of these tin expeditions, the government had its knuckles rapped by the Second Chamber again – though not until afterwards this time. Inciden-

267. Wellenstein, *Mijnbauwvraagstuk*, pp. 11–12.
268. Cf. Creutzberg, *Public Finance*, pp. 57–8.
269. *Handelingen Tweede Kamer* (Parliamentary Reports of the Second Chamber), 17 November 1885, pp. 469–70. Cf. *TAG*, 1886, 287 and 330; for the expedition plans see W. F. Versteeg, 'Nieuw Guinea, in 't bijzonder Onin en Kowiai', ibid. 1885, pp. 114–72.
270. Ibid. 1888, pp. 5–6 and 194; ibid. 1889, pp. 414 and 442–8.

tally, had the administration waited for the geological report of the Dutch Geographical Society, there would have been no need to plunge into this adventure, as it turned out that there was no tin in Flores that could be mined easily.[271]

The notorious Flores tin expeditions themselves of 1889–90, as well as their background and consequences, have been described very clearly in Jobse's study. This first mining expedition had been prompted mainly by financial and economic motives. But when the resistance of the local population made it impossible to reach the interior of Flores, considerations of prestige began to prevail.[272] Shortly afterwards a military expedition was sent by the colonial administration, which was, however, equally unsuccessful in penetrating to the interior of the island. Governor-general Pijnacker Hordijk hesitated to take any decisive action, so that the troops were left in their bivouacs in Flores without achieving anything, until minister Mackay, under pressure from the Second Chamber, ordered them to leave the island as quickly as possible.[273]

On 14 and 15 October 1890 Cremer had interpellated the minister in the Second Chamber on the Flores affair. Cremer, Van Houten and other Liberal speakers had already found it rather difficult to show much appreciation for the first expedition which, after all, had been equipped to explore opportunities for state-owned tin mines in Flores, after a private concession application had been turned down. The subsequent military expedition to the independent interior of the island even reminded Cremer of Pizarro's behaviour in Peru. However, his strongly worded motion, which urged the immediate cancellation of the expedition, was rejected by 59 votes to 26.

Keuchenius had asked Cremer sarcastically before the vote how he had managed to acquire his 'tobacco palace' in Amsterdam. And although several Liberals could understand the colonial administration's endeavour to keep foreign applicants – such as this German one – out of Flores, no one wanted to face a 'second Acheh'. The Second Chamber therefore unanimously accepted Röell's motion, in which the minister was requested not to continue the expedition any longer than was strictly necessary.[274] After the parliamentary

271. A. Wichmann, 'Bericht über eine im Jahre 1888–89 im Auftrage der Niederländischen Geographischen Gesellschaft ausgeführte Reise nach dem Indischen Archipel: III, Flores', ibid. 1891, pp. 188–293.
272. Jobse, 'Tin-expedities, pp. 59–60.
273. Ibid., pp. 42–4.
274. Ibid., pp. 45–9.

debate, an aggrieved Hordijk first offered his resignation, but then carefully avoided new intervention in the Outer Regions during his remaining term of office.[275]

In many of these government or private initiatives to further develop the Archipelago there was also the underlying fear – directly or indirectly – that foreign entrepreneurs might tackle the job first, with all the risks that were involved. 'Other nations', P. N. Muller warned in the Netherlands, 'are coveting our colonies. In fact, not only is Acheh threatened, but so are all our economic interests in our East and West Indian colonies.'[276] It was symptomatic that when the colonial administration searched for and eventually expelled a group of foreign gold-diggers in northern Celebes in 1890, there was a general atmosphere of panic.[277] Fear of foreign influence played a decisive role when the Royal Dutch Packet Company was granted the steamshipping concession for the Archipelago in 1888. This was a case where political and economic considerations weighed far more heavily than financial ones.

Ever since 1863 steamship links had been in the hands of the Dutch East Indian Steamship Company, an enterprise which was Dutch in name but really British. A long time before the contract was to expire both governmental circles and the world of commerce were making plans to give the concession to a Dutch company. The joint concession application of the Amsterdam shipowners Boissevain and P. E. Tegelberg as well as their Rotterdam colleague W. Ruys underlined the 'national character' of the company that was to establish itself.[278] When Sprenger van Eyk presented the government contract with the new Royal Packet Company, which carried a first subsidy of 680,000 guilders, to the Second Chamber, he therefore used similar words: 'It is of paramount importance . . . that steamship traffic should be made a national matter'; and he pointed out the strategic significance of the steamship connections in the Archipelago, both to maintain and extend Dutch authority

---

275. Ibid., pp. 49–53. To supplement the sources used by Jobse, see also the private correspondence between Pijnacker Hordijk and Mackay in the Pijnacker Hordijk Collection (ARA).

276. P. N. Muller, 'Koloniaal gevaar', *De Gids*, 1886, iii, p. 354.

277. For the so-called 'Glanggis Affair', see Arts and Van Beurden, *Goud*, pp. 15–19.

278. See the historical survey of M. G. de Boer in the annals of the KPM, *Halve Eeuw*, pp. 28–38. Cf. *Handelingen Indisch Genootschap* (Reports of the East Indian Society), 14 February 1888, pp. 75–110.

and also to ensure economic development.[279]

These considerations were contended by Keuchenius, who criticised the 'oppressive' monopoly of preferential government treatment and maintained that the loyalty of the discarded concession holder was beyond all suspicion.[280] A number of Liberals were also rather doubtful about this national but nevertheless 'prohibitively expensive' preferential treatment. The Rotterdam MP Van Gennep thought, for instance, that there were 'positive and negative sides to a subsidised shipping service throughout the entire Archipelago, a service that is sure to obtain all state cargoes in the East Indies and that is loaded with Dutch sympathies and devoted to Dutch interests'.[281] Finally, however, this belief in national interests won decisively over financial and economic objections, and the agreement was accepted by 51 votes to 3.[282] Later, when Keuchenius himself was in office, he loyally helped to carry out the decision.

A New Holland in South Africa?

The Discovery of 'Kinship'

If national sentiments about the East Indies often sounded defensive and low-key, they became considerably more strident with regard to South Africa in the 1880s. The Transvaal, of course, was not a beleaguered Dutch colony but a former British one in which the white 'kinsmen' of the Dutch had gained freedom from British imperialist rule. The 'struggle of the Transvaalers', as Lion Cachet characterised the liberation efforts of the Boers, created quite a stir in the 'old motherland'.[283]

After the restrained reaction to the British annexation in 1877, there were massive and fiery protestations of support in the winter of 1880–1 when the Boers successfully rebelled against British rule. This great contrast has been referred to by a number of historians,[284] and can partly be explained by the changed attitude of

---

279. *Bijlagen Handelingen Tweede Kamer* (Parliamentary Reports of the Second Chamber, Appendix) 1887–8, nos 85, 3.

280. *Handelingen Tweede Kamer* (Parliamentary Reports of the Second Chamber), 23 February 1888, pp. 741ff.; ibid., 24 February 1888, pp. 765 and 779.

281. Ibid., p. 776.

282. Ibid., p. 780.

283. See Lion Cachet, *Worstelstrijd.*

284. Cf. Van Winter, *Hollanders* I, p. 31; Kossmann, *Lage landen*, p. 283; Schutte, 'Nederland', p. 575; Van Koppen, *Kuyper*, p. 79.

the Boers themselves, developing from initial apathy to passive and finally active resistance to British annexation.[285] However, the Dutch reaction was undoubtedly also symptomatic of a rising Dutch nationalism, which, according to Schutte, was to assume imperialist traits towards the Transvaal. Schutte sees the roots of this nationalism in the 'modernisation and revitalisation of Dutch society'.[286] Such influences were particularly noticeable in the behaviour of the Anti-Revolutionaries and Radicals who emphatically referred to the 'people behind the voter' in the Transvaal issue. In addition, nationalist feelings were subsequently connected with the excitement which had arisen over the British expansion in Borneo between 1877 and 1880, particularly among Liberals and Conservatives. I shall merely point out the presence of such influences. The interaction between Dutch, South African and East Indian developments will be dealt with at the end of this chapter.

The support movement for the Boers, which emerged in the Netherlands during the 'First Transvaal War of Independence' (i.e. the First Boer War), was noticeable for its extent and its broad base, with nearly all political and ideological currents represented in it. The initiative for the pro-Boer movement had first been taken by the Utrecht science professor Pieter Harting, who published a petition entitled 'To the British Nation' in the local press on 23 December 1880. Harting was a Liberal, and unlike his Conservative colleague Vreede in 1877, he made a positive and direct appeal to the 'sense of justice of the British nation'.[287] The petition was taken over by a variety of national dailies and within a few weeks about 6,000 Dutch readers had signed it, including prominent professors, politicians and other leading citizens. Interestingly, a large number of Protestant ministers (374) and officers (335) were among those who signed. But the petition movement was far more comprehensive and included more than the established middle classes, with only 20 per cent of the signatories from an academic background.[288] The response was so wide that Harting set up a 'General Committee for the Promotion of the Interests of Transvaal Boers', to co-ordinate active support for the Boers. Apart from Harting and his

---

285. Cf. Van Zijl, *Protesbeweging*; Van Jaarsveld, *Vrijheidsoorlog*; Lehmann, *Boer War*.

286. Schutte, 'Nederland', p. 589.

287. *Het Utrechtsch Provinciaal en Stedelijk Dagblad*, 23 December 1880. Cf. Van Cittert-Eymers and Kipp, *Herinneringen*, pp. 134ff.

288. Cf. Schutte, 'Nederland', p. 576.

liberal colleagues De Louter, C. H. D. Buys Ballot and J. A. Fruin, the committee was also joined by the Anti-Revolutionary aristocrat G. J. T. Beelaerts van Blokland.

After this Utrecht initiative, other Transvaal support committees were set up throughout the Netherlands. The most important one was in Amsterdam, where it was based even more broadly than in Utrecht. Prominent members included the Liberal professor and philosopher C. Bellaer Spruyt; the editor-in-chief of the *Handels-blad*, A. G. C. van Duyl; the Anti-Revolutionary leaders Kuyper and Lion Cachet; the Conservative aristocrat and later foreign affairs minister Hartsen; and Radicals such as J. de Koo and W. Heineken.

Another example of a Transvaal committee with a radical orientation was the one in Purmerend which managed to collect 11,000 signatures for a petition to Queen Victoria. Among the Protestant contingent of the population, the Patrimonium Workers' Association was particularly active with protest meetings, petitions and collections.[289] Even Dutch Roman Catholics spoke out for the Transvaal Boers, albeit with some reservation and without giving any active support. The *De Tijd* said:

> If the 'Afrikaners' were suddenly brought over to the Netherlands they would certain be among our fiercest opponents, both politically and religiously. And yet it is mainly Dutch blood which flows through their veins, just as it flows through ours. Indeed there burns a wound, cut into our sense of justice by Britain's perfidy, more painful than many other wounds because this is a matter of Dutch kinship.[290]

Dutch opposition to Britain in the Transvaal issue was therefore not so much religious or party political; rather, it showed foreign implications of domestic nationalism such as the anti-British tenor in 'kinship' claims and its possible consequences for relations with Britain. In itself the resistance of the Boers against British dominion already brought to mind the struggle of their 'glorious forefathers' of earlier centuries who had also fought against the British. The idea of the Boers as the '*Geuzen* of the nineteenth century' (comparing

289. Ibid., pp. 577–9; cf. Van Koppen, *Kuyper*, pp. 80–2.
290. *De Tijd*, 3 February 1881. The Roman Catholic spokesman in the Second Chamber P. J. F. Vermeulen spoke out in favour of the Boers, but there were also anti-Boer sentiments among Roman Catholics. *Handelingen Tweede Kamer* (Parliamentary Reports of the Second Chamber), 7 March 1881; cf. Schutte, 'Nederland', p. 577.

them with the militant anti-Spanish Calvinists of the sixteenth century, the Sea-beggars), was proclaimed not only by Kuyper and Lion Cachet, but also by the prominent Liberal historian R. Fruin from Leiden university. This image was then popularised by journalists and teachers.[291]

The military victory of the Boers against the British served to stimulate this nationalism even further. 'The glory of Ingogo and Langnek', said H. P. N. Muller, 'partly also reflects on us, the Dutch.'[292] Obviously, Britain's initial attempt to use violence in suppressing the Boers' struggle for independence had a devastating effect on its image. In particular, the arrogant behaviour of the local colonial administrators and the 'fanatical antagonism' of British missionaries towards the Boers were generally condemned. When Neurdenburg and other missionary friends tentatively suggested that there might well be a grain of truth in allegations that the black population was being suppressed by the Boers, this idea was indignantly rejected out of hand. The British High Commissioner Sir Bartle Frere also came under a good deal of criticism.[293] And even Gladstone, who had criticised the annexation in 1877, was now accused of 'complicity' and 'hypocrisy', because of his apparent capitulation to the demands of the 'jingoists'.[294]

The cease-fire in May and the Pretoria convention of August 1881, in which the British government recognised the independence of the Transvaal with reservations, only partly served to take away the unfavourable impression. 'Whatever may happen,' concluded Veth in *De Gids*, 'it seems to me that nothing can save Britain's honour any more!' He then went on to describe in detail his disappointment with Britain, 'that proud nation' which he had always cherished since his early childhood like his own native

291. For the analogy with sixteenth-century *Geuzen*, see Kuyper's leading articles and Lion Cachet's series of articles in *De Standaard* of December 1880 and January 1881; cf. Fruin, 'Hollandsch Woord', p. 411. See also the appeal 'Aan de Onderwijzers in Nederland' (To Teachers in the Netherlands) to pick up the thread from the 'deeds of the glorious forefathers' and to teach children about the struggle of the Boers, *NRC*, 18 February 1881.

292. Schutte, 'Nederland', p. 588; cf. Spies, *Nederlander*, p. 28.

293. Cf. W. H. de Beaufort, 'Sir Bartle Frere over de Transvaal', *De Gids*, 1881, i, pp. 524–55; P. J. Veth, 'Onze Transvaalsche Broeders', ibid., pp. 355–66; Fruin, 'Hollandsch Woord', *passim*, *NRC*, 15–16 February and 2 March 1881 and *Het Utrechtsch Dagblad*, 14 February 1881.

294. Cf. *NRC*, 6 and 27 February 1881; *De Tijd*, 7 March 1881. Kuyper continued to judge Gladstone far more leniently, Van Koppen, *Kuyper*, p. 6. For Gladstone's dilemmas, see Schreuder, *Gladstone*, chapter 3.

country: 'How thou hast fallen, O Lucifer!'[295]

Such massive protest put the Dutch government in a difficult position. Even after Harting had sent his moderate, conciliatory petition, the Foreign Minister Van Lynden van Sandenburg expressed concern when he asked Van Bylandt about reactions in Britain. There the Dutch petition had generally been received with understanding, but Granville had asked on behalf of Queen Victoria what the official attitude of the Dutch government was.[296] The government had come under increasing pressure from public opinion to take active steps in favour of the Boers and against Britain. Schutte felt that the pro-Boer demonstrations, particularly by Anti-Revolutionaries and Radicals protested against 'an attitude of the Dutch Parliament and government that was too moderate and displayed too little national self-confidence.'[297] The pro-Boer movement seemed to be mainly concerned with humanitarian causes, as can be seen in the general call for Red Cross ambulance units to be sent to the Transvaal. However, other considerations in favour of active Dutch involvement were also proposed. 'Silence is more dangerous here than speaking out', wrote the Radical activist H. H. Timmer to the *Handelsblad*: 'It started with Borneo, then there was the Transvaal, and later they will use the same law of the strongest to get into our colonies, thinking that the Netherlands is no longer a nation.'[298]

Some even felt that not just the maintenance of the colonies was at stake but indeed the continued existence of the Netherlands itself. Based on the right to exist as a small nation, the General Dutch Peace Alliance petitioned the British government to grant independence to the Transvaal. Its chairman Van Eck later used the same argument when he approached the Dutch government, requesting that it should officially offer to mediate between Britain and the Boers. 'The victim is a small nation again', he reminded the Second Chamber; 'Let us be forewarned: you today, me tomorrow!'[299] Van Lynden was interpellated on the Transvaal issue in the First and in the Second Chamber. Apart from Van Eck, Keuchenius and

295. Veth, 'Broeders', p. 366.
296. Woltring, *Bescheiden* III, no. 4; cf. ibid. II, no. 553.
297. Schutte, 'Nederland', p. 583. Cf. *De Standaard*, 19 and 21 February 1881; *De Amsterdammer* (weekly), 23 January and 16 February 1881.
298. Quoted by Schutte, 'Nederland', p. 583. See also the conservative *Het Dagblad van Zuid-Holland en 's-Gravenhage*, 17 February 1881.
299. *Handelingen Tweede Kamer* (Parliamentary Reports of the Second Chamber), 7 March 1881, p. 950. Cf. Kamphuis, *Vredebond*, pp. 123–24.

Lenting also urged the government to approach Britain and to take steps in favour of the Boers. Van Lynden, however, continued to prefer a position of formal aloofness: 'The position of the Netherlands, like that of any other state, is the position of a third party, in other words a state that is outside the warring parties.'[300]

Meanwhile it had become quite clear to him that the British government did not at all welcome official Dutch steps. Following the advice of Beelaerts van Blokland, who had the necessary international connections, Van Lynden unofficially asked Van Bylandt to gauge the mood in London, and Van Bylandt observed that a Dutch offer of mediation would only meet with 'resentment' in Britain.[301] Van Lynden and Van Bylandt also showed very little sympathy for the representatives of the Transvaal movement who approached them. 'Vive le Transvaal, périssent les Pays-Bas!' (Long Live the Transvaal, and may the Netherlands perish!), Van Lynden warned a Patrimonium delegation: the working-class delegates may not have understood the minister's words, but they certainly understood what he meant.[302]

Not only the government but also the 'respectable' leadership of the Transvaal committees began to be concerned about the crude anti-British mood that had developed among their rank and file. The Utrecht committee initially refused to take part in the big Transvaal meeting organised by the Amsterdam committee, 'with a view to the impression this may well create in Britain'. Van Duyl felt that the Utrecht professors were 'fish-blooded wise men who are afraid of getting burnt in cold water'. But other organisers were also frightened of this outspokenly anti-British mood which prevailed among about 2,000 gathered in Artis on 5 March 1881.[303] In the Purmerend committee plans even circulated to form a voluntary corps together with Irish nationalists who would then actively fight the British in South Africa.[304] Apart from a desire to continue assistance for the Boers after the cease-fire, it was this increasing anti-British agitation which prompted the leaders of the Utrecht and Amsterdam committees to join forces so that they could be more firmly in control of the Transvaal movement. Despite con-

300. *Handelingen Eerste Kamer* (Parliamentary Reports of the First Chamber), 1 March 1881, p. 279.
301. Woltring, *Bescheiden* III, no. 16; cf. nos 11, 13, 15.
302. *NRC*, 27 February 1881. Cf. Woltring, *Bescheiden* III, nos 17 and 19B.
303. Van Koppen, *Kuyper*, p. 84; cf. *NRC*, 7 March 1881.
304. Schutte, 'Nederland', p. 578.

tinuing arguments between the Utrecht and Amsterdam committees as well as the Liberal and Anti-Revolutionary members among them, the Dutch South African Association (NZAV) was finally founded on 12 May 1881.

The NZAV set itself the aim of 'continually promoting the interests of our kinsmen, not just in the Transvaal but in the whole of South Africa . . . and to keep the public constantly informed, both at home and abroad, of the situation in South Africa'. At the suggestion of Kuyper, Harting was elected honorary chairman. Kuyper himself joined the committee, together with Liberal politicians such as De Beaufort, Van Naamen van Eemnes and W. J. van Welderen Rengers, as well as Liberal entrepreneurs, including the chairman of the Amsterdam Chamber of Commerce D. Cordes, Heineken, J. Wertheim, the young H. P. N. Muller and the Liberal university professors De Louter, Buys Ballot and J. T. Buys. The day-to-day management was handled by an 'office' under the chairmanship of Cordes. About 300 members joined the new association. Co-operation between Liberals and Anti-Revolutionaries within the NZAV was surprising, as they were sharply divided at the time on the issue of the Dutch educational system, the so-called 'school struggle'. Both camps criticised the scrupulous neutrality of the NZAV. At the first opportunity, however, after a year, this 'artificial unity' broke up again when the NZAV became really involved in the Transvaal situation.[305]

The Visit of the Transvaal Deputation

None of the committee members of the newly founded NZAV knew South Africa from their own experience. The management committee therefore started a closer investigation into the object of their association by talking to experts such as Lion Cachet and Burgers's former secretary, T. M. Tromp. Although members of the NZAV were also interested in the Orange Free State and the British Cape Colony, it was decided to concentrate their activities on the Transvaal for the time being.

In October 1881 the NZAV therefore contacted the Transvaal government, though they did not receive an official reply until June 1882. Earlier letters were said to have gone astray, possibly as a result of the rivalry between the Dutch Attorney-general E. J. P.

305. Cf. Van Koppen, *Kuyper*, pp. 85–7; *Nederland–Zuid–Afrika*, pp. 100–1.

Jorissen and the Education Secretary from the Cape, S. J. Du Toit, who was rather reluctant to be influenced by the Netherlands. According to President Kruger, the young republic required above all capital – capital for a national bank and a railway link with the sea. As such, these wishes of the Transvaalers tied up very well with the aims of the NZAV who wanted to 'open up and develop resources of agriculture, industry, trade and other material interests in consultation with them and for them'.[306] The management committee therefore decided to send a 'commissioner' to the Transvaal to find out about local conditions and to further discuss the requirements of the Transvaal government. De Louter suggested the young Liberal H. F. Jonkman for this mission, the former secretary of the Utrecht committee; this choice subsequently led Kuyper to break away from the NZAV.

Although the emphasis varied, 'kinship' always had a double meaning for Kuyper: it implied both a common origin and language and also religious and political convictions. As regards religion and politics, he felt that he had found a congenial spirit in Du Toit, with whom he started some intensive correspondence. In his letters he presented himself as the assigned contact person within the NZAV. 'In the South African Association', he assured Du Toit, 'I am the only one who is not modern. All the others are of the same kind as Burgers. Until now they have been doing exactly as I have told them, as they presume that the Transvaalers will not do anything against my advice or without consulting me.'[307]

It is not entirely unlikely that when, in the absence of their Anti-Revolutionary colleagues on 4 September 1882, the Liberal members of the NZAV committee made their decision to send Jonkman they did so in order to put an end to Kuyper's monopoly on contacts with Pretoria. Kuyper, in turn, wanted to reverse the decision, arguing that sending a progressive Liberal would not tally with the political and religious character of the Transvaalers. When the members' meeting of the NZAV nevertheless approved the

306. Ibid., pp. 101–2; cf. *Verslag NZAV* (NZAV Report) 1881–2, pp. 5–6. For relations inside the South African Republic see Van Winter, *Hollanders* I, chapter 3; cf. Davenport, *South Africa*, pp. 71–5.

307. Quoted by Van Koppen, *Kuyper*, p. 88; cf. ibid., pp. 56–7. Du Toit did indeed feel inspired by Kuyper at first; the programme of the Afrikaner Bond which he had set up in the Cape Colony in 1879 closely reflected *Ons Program* (Our Programme). But Du Toit was, first and foremost an Afrikaner nationalist and he therefore found Kuyper's view of kinship rather too much geared towards the Netherlands; cf. Davenport, *Afrikaner Bond*, pp. 51–2.

choice of Jonkman by a large majority, Kuyper, Lion Cachet and other Anti-Revolutionaries resigned their membership.[308]

Although Jonkman's visit to the Transvaal eventually took place in a good atmosphere, the activities of the NZAV initially yielded very few concrete results. Of the many thousands of Dutch people who had supported the Transvaal movement during the Boer War, only a few hundred became members of the association. The Dutch government turned out to be in no hurry to appoint a consul to promote economic relations from Pretoria. Even the sending of textbooks in co-operation with the Dutch Literature and Bible Societies did not work particularly well. This may have been due to the composition of the shipping organisations where Fruin had made sure that the work of the Liberal leader Thorbecke would be particularly prominent.[309]

But even Kuyper's contact with Du Toit received its first setback when it emerged that his friend had welcomed Jonkman with goodwill. In the Netherlands, after resignation from the NZAV, Kuyper tried in vain to take charge of the Emigration Committee. This committee, the most important Transvaal organisation after the NZAV, had been set up in 1882 by Van Duyl, J. W. Gunning and other representatives of the 'home mission', as well as by the 'red radicals' Timmer and D. H. Schmüll, an Amsterdam dye merchant who was acting as the consul of Hawaii at the time. Kuyper did not really manage to come to grips with this colourful group of people. Instead, his endeavours led to conflicts between the committee and the NZAV. Meanwhile there was virtually no emigration at all. Generally, divisions among the Transvaal friends had increased, while concrete results were still lacking.[310]

The arrival of the Transvaal deputation, which visited Europe during 1883–4, meant that Dutch interest in South Africa again increased quite considerably. The deputation originally consisted of Kruger, Jorissen and General N. J. Smit, who had been empowered by the Transvaal Parliament to negotiate a revision of the Pretoria Convention with the British government, to approach the Portuguese government about a possible railway link with Delagoa Bay, and to borrow Dutch capital for the financing of their railway

308. See the minutes of the committee meetings of 4 September, 16 October, 6 and 20 November 1882, NZAV Archives.

309. *Verslag NZAV* (NZAV Report) 1882–3, pp. 1–5. Cf. Smit and Wieringa, *Correspondentie Fruin*, no. 272.

310. Van Koppen, *Kuyper*, pp. 95–101.

system and a national bank. Jorissen had travelled ahead a year earlier, in 1882, to prepare the negotiations. In his absence, however, Du Toit succeeded in persuading the Transvaal Parliament to remove him as attorney-general, whereupon Du Toit himself took his place in the deputation. The dismissal of the liberal Dutchman Jorissen threatened to cast a shadow over the visit of the deputation. Among Liberals especially there was a great deal of indignation. De Louter felt that Jorissen's discharge could not be 'justified' and refused to act as legal adviser to the deputation.[311] His place was taken by Beelaerts van Blokland, who had been elected to represent the Anti-Revolutionaries in the Second Chamber, but who had remained a member of the NZAV and was also familiar with South Africa and the Afrikaners. Partly due to his advice, the deputation succeeded in obtaining a favourable revision of the Pretoria Convention in London, although the Gladstone government continued to insist on some control over the foreign policies and the borders of the Transvaal.[312]

Even Kuyper hesitated to endorse Du Toit's schemes, and he felt that Jorissen's dismissal was 'awkward', to say the least.[313] But for the Dutch Transvaal enthusiasts higher interests were at stake. After his arrival in the Netherlands, Jorissen himself had already pointed out the great mutual importance of Dutch finances for plans to build a railway system and set up a bank in the Transvaal. 'There is room and there is a need for Dutch capital and Dutch industry', he had told the NZAV leadership. When the president and the managing director of the Dutch National Bank, W.C. Mees and Pierson, expressed their approval of the Transvaal plans, the Liberal Transvaal enthusiasts overcame their indignation about Jorissen's dismissal and prepared a cordial welcome for the deputation.[314]

The enthusiasm with which the Transvaal triumvirate was received in the Netherlands in the spring of 1884 exceeded all expectations. As soon as they arrived in Rotterdam on 29 February, Kruger, Du Toit and Smit were welcomed by the cheers of an 'incredibly large mass of people'. Once they were in The Hague, they continually had to appear on the balcony of the hotel Des

311. Minutes of the committee meeting 3 November 1883, NZAV Archives, Cf. Van Koppen, *Kuyper*, pp. 101–4.
312. Cf. Schreuder, *Gladstone*, chapter 7.
313. Van Koppen, *Kuyper*, pp. 102–3.
314. Minutes of the committee meetings of 26 May 1883, 3 November 1883 and 14 January 1884, NZAV Archives. Cf. Pierson's diary, 10 February 1884, Pierson Collection (Amsterdam University Library).

Indes to receive ovations from the masses who had gathered in the centre of the city.[315].

In the hotel itself, the gentlemen from the NZAV and the Emigration Committee paid their respects. And during the following few days there was a series of receptions, banquets and soirées which were attended by ministers, members of the Dutch Parliament and diplomats. The absence of the British ambassador at the 'splendid soirée' organised by Cremers, the speaker of the Second Chamber, gave the Foreign Minister, Van der Does de Willebois, cause for concern. He advised greater caution, 'to avoid what might possibly give the impression of ovations which would probably be less than pleasing to the British government'. The audience with King William III was therefore rather more 'cool', according to Du Toit.[316] However, the reception of the deputation by the politicians in The Hague was a demonstration of national unity again, and at the large-scale dinner at the Oude Doelen, speeches were made not only by Liberal politicians and men of letters but also by Keuchenius, Schaepman and Wintgens.[317]

During their visit to Amsterdam, however, the Transvaalers were to come face to face with the opposing views in Dutch society. Their reception in the capital on 6 March still proceeded reasonably harmoniously. While Gunning, Kuyper, Van Duyl and Schmüll were welcoming the three men at the central station, their four little daughters were scattering flowers in the four Transvaal colours and the expectant masses were singing patriotic songs. This was followed by a long tour through the city, where 'incredibly large masses of people' were cheering the three men again. During the days that followed they had a number of meetings with Liberal bankers and university professors about the Dutch contribution to the development of the republic. '*The bank* and *the railway* – those are the means by which the Transvaal can be helped', emphasised Du Toit in a speech to Burgerpligt.[318] On 11 March, however, when they were received by Patrimonium in Plancius, Kuyper was to raise completely different matters.

315. See the report in *De Standaard* and the *NRC* of 1 March 1884.
316. Van Koppen, *Kuyper*, p. 107. Cf. Woltring, *Bescheiden* III, no. 411.
317. Cf. *De Standaard* and *NRC* of 3 March 1884.
318. *Het Handelsblad*, 17 March 1884. For the reception of the deputation in Amsterdam, see *Het Handelsblad* and *De Standaard* of 6 and 7 March. The deputation was also given a cordial welcome by *De Tijd* of 7 March, though the exaggerated homage that was paid to them by the reception committee was seen rather more critically.

Kuyper opened his speech by declaring that the reception of the deputation should be dominated 'not by faith, but by the bonds of blood'. During the preceding days, however, he had been challenged by the belligerent Liberal I. A. Levy who had warned the 'preachers of no matter what orthodoxy' about a 'strong constitutional protest . . . in words, if possible . . . in deeds, if necessary' if ever they should try to impose their will on the Dutch state.[319] Levy's remarks prompted Kuyper in Plancius to state that 'should they make life unbearable for us Christians in this country, then the core of those Christians will cross the sea to the Transvaal!' The same, he said, would also happen if there were a German annexation of the Netherlands: 'then there would always be a core, and certainly not the least national core, who would prefer to leave for the Transvaal rather than remain under the German yoke.' Kuyper also repeatedly mentioned the British threat. 'Give me your hand,' he said when the Transvaal flag was handed to General Smit, 'and promise: *never will this flag be in the hands of the British.*' 'The spirit of the meeting was beyond description,' said the report in *De Standaard*, 'and there were thunders of applause from the vast crowds.'[320]

Kuyper's speech met with sharp criticism. In Liberal circles it caused 'general surprise and disapproval'. Harting, who was already getting worried about the course of the Nisero issue, particularly condemned Kuyper's anti-British remarks.[321] The argument with Levy took an even more unsavoury turn when his Jewishness was explicitly mentioned in *De Tijd*; Keuchenius, too, was to attack Levy in similar terms.[322] Kuyper, in turn, reacted with indignation at the negative interpretations of his 'improvised' speech which he had made 'with ardour', and therefore, when his 'Plancius speech' was published as a brochure, he toned down a number of remarks. He felt especially offended when he read that Du Toit had called his speech 'discordant' – a remark which, despite Kuyper's insistence, Du Toit only took back after some time.[323]

Apart from Amsterdam, Rotterdam and The Hague, the Transvaalers also visited Arnhem, Amersfoort, Leiden, Utrecht, Kampen,

319. *De Amsterdammer* (daily), 28 February 1884.
320. *De Standaard*, 13 March 1884.
321. Cf. the correspondence between Harting and Kuyper as well as the review of Liberal press reactions in *De Standaard*, 22 March, 3, 9 and 14 April 1884.
322. *De Tijd*, 11 April 1884; cf. Taal, *Liberalen*, pp. 105–6.
323. Van Koppen, *Kuyper*, pp. 112–13.

Groningen and – on 1 April – Den Briel. Their trip round the Netherlands permanently confirmed the image of the Boers as the *Geuzen* of the nineteenth century, an image which had been formed during the Boer War. The simple, 'calm' behaviour of 'Uncle Paul' Kruger and the martial demeanour of 'combative General Smit' corresponded completely to the ideas which the Dutch public had already formed in their minds. Despite Jorissen's dismissal, even the fundamentalist but well-educated Du Toit had succeeded in gaining the confidence of the Liberal elite in the Netherlands. After meeting the deputation in person, De Louter emphatically denied that 'the orthodoxy of the Transvaalers should be an obstacle to their spiritual and material development . . . Furthermore, there is not a more tolerant nation in the world.'[324] Apparently, when Kruger and Du Toit had promised De Louter to appoint Dutch experts to government posts in the Transvaal, this had helped everyone to forget Jorissen's dismissal. However, when Liberal professors such as De Louter, Fruin, Pierson, and J. P. Moltzer suggested that Dutch graduates should be appointed in the Transvaal and that places at Dutch state universities should be given to Transvaal students, Du Toit's agreement totally alienated Kuyper. His complete disregard for Kuyper's Calvinist Free University furthermore formed the final breaking point in a relationship that had already begun to show cracks before the visit of the deputation. Partly as a result of this breach, Kuyper completely turned away from South Africa in later years.[325]

At first it seemed as if the deputation had also done good business with Liberal capitalists. A railway concession had been granted to the experienced engineers C. Groll and D. Maarschalk, and through the mediation of Pierson and Moltzer a tender for a big loan had been advertised that would finance both the concession and a national bank. It was not a matter of giving charity to a backward Transvaal, Pierson had said, but it was business which would be of interest to the Netherlands itself. However, the Amsterdam capitalists, who had already been hit by the Javanese sugar crisis, had little enthusiasm for such risky investment in South Africa, and at the end of 1884 only 2 million out of the 15 million guilders had been subscribed to.[326] The Liberal Transvaal enthusiasts were, of course,

324. J. de Louter, 'De Transvaalsche Deputatie', *De Gids*, 1884, ii, pp. 530–1.
325. Cf. Van Koppen, *Kuyper*, pp. 116–17.
326. Van Winter, *Hollanders* I, pp. 75–80. Cf. Pierson's letter to the editor in *Het Handelsblad* of 24 June 1884 and his diary of 21–8 September and 11 November 1884, Pierson Collection.

disappointed about this financial fiasco. But Kuyper felt that it was 'not the Transvaal loan which has been a fiasco, but the Dutch nation'. He thought it was 'sad, extremely sad, that the arrival of the deputation in this country should have shown clearly to the whole world what a pleasure-loving, frivolous and reckless nation we have become.'[327] The government, on the other hand, was hardly sorry that the Netherlands could, for the time being, remain outside the South African imbroglio, half-way between the Nisero issue and the Berlin Congo Conference. After all, as Van Bylandt reported from London, it was felt in Britain that 'the utterances of the Dutch element in the south of Africa' could be ascribed to the 'direct influence of the German government – a view which, however untrue it may be, can only be harmful.'[328]

Towards a New Holland in the Transvaal

Eventually, however, the Delagoa railway was indeed built and run by a Dutch company, even though it was mainly financed by German capital. Together with the public services, the educational system, economic relations and famous 'public figures', Schutte has described the Dutch South African Railway Company as one of the most important ways in which Dutch influence penetrated the Transvaal after 1884.[329] Whether we call this influence imperialist or not, the Dutch idea of 'kinship' began to display rather a presumptuous and expansionist tendency during the 1880s. During the First Boer War it was mainly the moral and humanitarian element that dominated. In the following years, however, the idea began to gain ground that there were mutual Dutch–South African interests in the development of South Africa.

During and immediately after the visit of the deputation, this common interest was emphasised in the Dutch press in particular. Both Liberals and Anti-Revolutionaries – though from different philosophical points of view – saw the birth of a 'New Holland' in South Africa, which could serve as a source of inspiration, as a place for settlements and indeed a refuge for the old, tired Holland in Europe. Commenting on the Transvaal, Kuyper remarked in his

---

327. *De Standaard*, 21 July 1884 (leading article).
328. Woltring, *Bescheiden* III, no. 507; cf. no. 504. See also Schreuder, *Scramble*, pp. 113ff.
329. Cf. Schutte, *Hollanders*, pp. 47ff.; the most detailed and extensive study of the Dutch presence in South Africa is still Van Winters, *Hollanders*.

Plancius speech that 'a New Holland has come into being, with the old language and the old blood, but with new fire and new power.'[330] The same future opportunities which, according to Kuyper, were open to the Protestant Christians among the population, were envisaged by Liberals such as Fruin, De Louter and Bellaer Spruyt for the entire Dutch nation. Spruyt, who was the driving force in the NZAV after 1884, saw the 'victory of the Dutch element in South Africa' as the 'last chance for our people to exert its influence in world history'.[331] The appeal of such a viewpoint can be gathered from the rising membership of the NZAV, which was below 300 in 1884 but rose to over 1,400 in 1888.

The necessary preparations and reconnaissance for building a New Holland in the Transvaal in the mid-1880s had, in a way, taken place already. At the same time, there was also a good deal of interest in other parts of Southern Africa, though, according to H. P. N. Muller who had visited Natal, the Orange Free State and the Cape Colony at the beginning of the 1880s, these territories had already reached an advanced stage of 'Anglicisation'.[332] After the breach with King Leopold's Association, the Dutch Geographical Society had sent an expedition to Umptata in south-western Africa. Led by Veth junior, it was aimed at exploring the opportunities for development in a large area where, until then, only 'Trek Boers' had settled. However, these opportunities turned out to be rather disappointing. Veth felt that the population was 'idle, greedy, insolent and unbearable', and that the land was 'barren', 'infertile' and 'infested with flies'. He himself soon became seriously ill and died in 1885. According to his father, Veth had taken part in voyages of discovery to central Sumatra and Southern Africa, because 'the sluggish triteness and insipid frugality of our Dutch society were an abomination to him.'[333] Insofar as South Africa could offer any alternative for the Netherlands, this obviously had to be sought in the Transvaal, where the pro-Dutch element dominated among the Boers, the climate was bearable and the soil was fertile and rich in gold.

Traditionally, the Dutch had always held important government

330. *De Standaard*, 13 March 1884.
331. Quoted in *Nederland–Zuid–Afrika*, p. 104. Cf. Fruin, 'Hollandsch Woord', p. 417; De Louter, 'Deputatie', p. 538.
332. Cf. Spies, *Nederlander*, pp. 26ff.
333. *TAG*, 1886, p. 339; cf. the letters of D. D. Veth, ibid., pp. 22–38, 191–209, 327–38.

positions in the South African Republic, and these turned out to be of great – sometimes crucial – importance for the spread of Dutch influence. Although the proportion of Dutch-born civil servants never exceeded 20 per cent, their share grew steadily with the civil servant apparatus itself after the discovery of gold in 1886, and rose from 51 in that same year to 160 in 1892. Moreover, they always occupied the highest positions.[334] With a view to a 'New Holland', it was particularly important that, after Jorissen's resignation, he was replaced by another Dutchman, the energetic young lawyer W. J. Leyds.

Leyds's appointment had been suggested to the Transvaal delegation by his Amsterdam teachers Moltzer and Pierson. As attorney-general and – after 1888 – state secretary, he was to play a key role in the foreign and domestic politics of the South African Republic (SAR), acting as the right hand of Kruger. When a power struggle arose between them, he gained the upper hand over Du Toit. He maintained close contact with the Transvaal lobby in the Netherlands, and whenever important domestic matters were under discussion – such as the construction of the railway line and South Africa's educational policy – he succeeded in using his influence to further Dutch interests. 'Apart from the interests of this republic,' he reassured Moltzer, 'I have also borne the Netherlands in mind. Obviously, I would not have considered the latter in cases where there was a conflict between the two . . . But now that there have been so many areas where they could co-operate, I am very pleased.'[335]

He conducted foreign policies in close consultation with Beelaerts van Blokland, who had acted as the official South African representative in Europe since 1884. Both in foreign and domestic affairs Leyds felt he was continually struggling against 'British encroachments'.[336] Even so, he felt generally unable to have much sympathy for the Boers, whom he found backward and unreliable: 'It would be terrible for me . . . if one of my daughters wanted to marry one of them.' When half of his original contract period was over, he and his wife celebrated with a bottle of champagne. Nevertheless, they remained among the Transvaal Boers until 1898.

334. Schutte, *Hollanders*, pp. 48–49.

335. Leyds to Moltzer, 1 August 1886, Leyds Collection (ARA). Cf. Van Winter, *Leyds*, pp. 1–10; Schutte, *Hollanders*, pp. 68–71.

336. Leyds to Moltzer, 22 February 1885; cf. his extensive correspondence with Beelaerts van Blokland, Leyds Collection.

'Now my job is to co-operate in improving their civilisation, and I find this idea quite attractive', he wrote to Moltzer. 'Not everyone is given such an opportunity to experience part of history.'[337] The details which Leyds reported about the character of the Boers obviously rather disappointed the Transvaal enthusiasts in the Netherlands. 'I used to think', said Moltzer in his reply, 'that the Boers in the Transvaal saw us more or less as their elder brothers . . . Now, however, they are giving me the impression of being suspicious children who do not trust us.' However, he urged Leyds not to resign, 'in the interest of our country and our people'.[338] Leyds, in turn, urged the home front to make a greater effort to support the Dutch cause in the Transvaal. Immediately upon his arrival he had experienced resentment among the Transvaalers, caused by the failure to obtain a loan from the Netherlands. Kruger eventually gave the concession for a national bank to a German consortium. Leyds felt that the railway concession, too, would be lost unless the Netherlands showed some active interest in it.

In order to restore trust in the Netherlands and to strengthen his own position within the SAR, he tried to obtain another small loan at the beginning of 1886. Thanks to Pierson's nephew, the Amsterdam banker A. D. de Marez Oyens, and the influential Liberal politician Van Naamen van Eemnes, the required 500,000 guilders were soon raised. Moltzer was particularly hopeful that the Amsterdam aristrocrats who had contributed money would do a lot for the 'development of the Transvaal movement in this country'. After all, he said, these were 'people of great wealth . . . religious people, but fierce anti-Kuyperians, who could still be made enthusiastic for something other than material gain.' And so they did indeed finance part of the risky railway concession.[339]

Leyds felt that the Delagoa railway was a 'political railway' and as such extremely important for both South Africa and the Netherlands: 'I for one cannot see any future for this country unless it has a railway system. And once the railway system is there, it will have a

337. Leyds to Moltzer, 1 August 1886; cf. 22 February 1885, 25 March 1886, Leyds Collection. See also Schutte, *Hollanders*, pp. 70–1.
338. Moltzer to Leyds, 24 July 1886, Leyds Collection.
339. In this context Moltzer also described the Amsterdam capitalists as being different from 'all that dirty Jewish money from Britain', as well as from 'the Germans and Jews' (his letters to Leyds of 7 September 1886 and 7 March 1888). Cf. Leyds to Moltzer, 1 January 1886 and Moltzer to Leyds, 21 April 1886, Leyds Collection.

great future.' With Kruger's support, he was able to manoeuvre the Dutch concession through the South African Parliament in 1886, despite opposition from Du Toit who was supporting a request from the British Cape Colony. In 1887 the Dutch South-African Railway Company (NZASM) was founded, with a starting capital of which half was financed by Amsterdam capitalists and the SAR and the other half by German banks.[340] Leyds also urgently requested Dutch investment in other sectors of the South African economy. 'Is the Netherlands now going to leave our gold-fields as they are?' he wondered with concern after spectacular quantities of gold had been found. Dutch interest was indeed rather limited at first. Leyds had to observe with great regret that most of the mining industry had ended up in British hands.[341]

British influence in the Transvaal had originally come from the Cape Colony and then spread through the entire country via Witwatersrand. To counteract it, Leyds thought it was extremely important for Dutch influence to assert itself in education. 'The original Dutch language must be preserved here', he repeatedly wrote to the Netherlands; 'a good education alone can help the Republic to maintain its language and thus also its independence.' Under Du Toit, education was mainly in the hands of Cape Afrikaners, whereas Leyds felt that 'Capifying' meant 'Anglicising'.[342] In the Netherlands it was above all the NZAV which developed activities aimed at strengthening Dutch influence in intellectual matters. In 1885 it created a scholarship scheme for South African students in the Netherlands and in 1890 a school fund for sending Dutch teachers to South Africa. In the Republic itself Leyds succeeded in obstructing Du Toit's 'Afrikaner' education policy until Du Toit resigned as Education Secretary in 1889 and was succeeded in 1891 by N. Mansvelt, a Dutch teacher and convinced advocate of the Dutch language with years of teaching experience in the Cape Colony.[343]

340. For the further financing of the railway line, the NZASM mainly had to rely on German capital, however. Cf. Van Winter, *Hollanders* I, chapter 9; Van Helten, 'German Capital', pp. 373–5. For Leyds' vision of the 'political railway', see his letter to the founder and first director of the NZASM, R. W. C. C. van der Wall Bake, 8 June 1888, Leyds Collection.
341. Leyds to Schmüll, 2 November 1885, Leyds Collection. Cf. Schutte, *Hollanders*, pp. 55–60; Van Winter, *Hollanders* II, pp. 14–20.
342. Leyds to G. A. van Hamel, 13 June 1885; cf. Ledys to Moltzer, 22 February 1885; Leyds to Bellaer Spruyt, 16 April 1886, Leyds Collection.
343. Ploeger, *Onderwys*, chapters 3 and 7, cf. *Nederland–Zuid–Afrika*, pp. 103–7.

Although, in the second half the 1880s, strategic posts began to be occupied by Dutchmen in government as well as in the economic and cultural life of South Africa, the expected stream of Dutch colonists never materialised. Year after year, no more than a few dozen or, at the most, several hundred Dutch people emigrated to the Transvaal. These also included some Calvinist 'common people', fundamentalists who followed Kuyper's advice and wanted to settle in South Africa as farmers and craftsmen.

However, they were often bitterly disappointed by their new life in South Africa. Apart from the relatively expensive sea crossing and the small amount of co-operation on the part of the Transvaal government, Schutte quotes the disappointing economic circumstances in the Transvaal as the most important reason for the limited extent of the emigration.[344] Leyds, too, advised against emigration without sufficient financial backing and firm future prospects in the Transvaal. Nevertheless, in the Netherlands there continued to be a great deal of enthusiasm for promoting emigration to South Africa. 'For our own country, where thousands are trying in vain to find work, it is important that . . . South Africa should remain a country where Dutch people can find a second home', said Spruyt. After all, unlike in other emigration countries, the Dutch could preserve their language and maintain their 'national heritage' in the Transvaal. But since no mass emigration was forthcoming, the NZAV limited itself to selectively helping individual emigrants by setting up a Bureau for Emigrants to South Africa in 1888.[345] Even the NZASM had difficulties at first in recruiting suitable personnel from the Netherlands. Middelberg, one of the NZASM managers, therefore rather wondered 'whether we, the Dutch, are suitable as colonisers at all'.[346]

The Dutch government did even less to promote emigration to the Transvaal than the SAR government. In the course of the 1880s it became quite clear that if there should ever be a 'New Holland' in South Africa, it would certainly not be due to the efforts of the Dutch government. The slow process whereby the first Dutch representative in Pretoria was appointed – despite urgent requests

344. Schutte, *Hollanders*, pp. 43ff. Out of 3,131 Dutch emigrants in 1890 only 294 went to South Africa; the majority went to the United States; Schotanus, *Betrekkingen*, pp. 24–5.
345. *Nederland–Zuid–Afrika*, p. 106. For Spruyt's plea, see the NZAV prospectus, June 1886, Leyds Collection.
346. *TAG*, 1891, p. 303. Cf. Van Winter, *Hollanders* II, pp. 78–9.

from the SAR and the NZAV – was characteristic in this context. When H. C. Bergsma, a former associate of Burgers, was finally appointed consul-general in 1888, he was given detailed secret instructions by minister Van Karnebeek. 'The consul-general should take particular care in his dealings with the Transvaal government . . . and in his effort to support the Dutch element in the Transvaal not to offend the British government', warned the minister.[347] Leyds and Beelaerts van Blokland noted with regret that not much support could be expected from the Dutch government for their endeavours to develop the Transvaal and thus to break through the British 'policy of encirclement'. 'If our Dutch government were different', said Beelaerts, commenting on St Lucia Bay, the last free access to the sea, 'I would have the bay occupied immediately . . . for trade with the Transvaal.'[348]

The Anti-Revolutionary election victory in 1888 obviously raised hopes that there would be a change in the Dutch Transvaal policy. 'My advice will weigh more heavily with the new ministry', Beelaerts reassured Leyds. And it seemed indeed that minister Hartsen, who had been one of the active members of the Amsterdam Transvaal Committee, would show more interest and sympathy than his predecessor for the NZASM and its attempts to obtain the vital railway concession to Delagoa Bay.[349] But when a Portuguese request for mediation in its territorial controversy with Britain offered the Netherlands an opportunity to become more closely involved in the development of Southern Africa, Hartsen followed Van Bylandt's advice and carefully kept his distance.[350] If there was any Dutch imperialism at all in South Africa in the 1880s, this was in spite of and not because of the Dutch government.

The Netherlands, the East Indies and South Africa

According to Schutte, there was indeed imperialism behind all the 'fine talk about kinship': a form of imperialism with a strong

347. Woltring, *Bescheiden* IV, no. 188. For the new trade and friendship treaty with South Africa, which was rather identical with the annulled one of 1876, see ibid., no. 191. Cf. Leyds's urgent request to send a 'consul missus' as quickly as possible via Beelaerts, 18 November 1886, Leyds Collection.
348. Beelaerts to Leyds, 8 June 1887 and 28 December 1884; cf. Leyds to Moltzer, 6 August 1886, Leyds Collection.
349. Woltring, *Bescheiden* IV, nos 175, 185, 203, 389. Cf. Beelaerts to Leyds, 25 April 1888, Leyds Collection.
350. Woltring, *Bescheiden* IV, nos 411–14, 471–2.

cultural bias. And as the Dutch government kept completely aloof, Schutte prefers to talk about 'cultural imperialism' than about 'imperialism *tout court*'. This cultural imperialism, however, was a symptom of a broader nationalism, resulting from the general modernisation and revitalisation of Dutch society after the national identity crisis in the 1840s.[351]

Kossmann points out that this nationalism was potentially dynamic but effectively powerless. The Dutch economy in the 1880s was still far from capable of imperialist initiatives. Moreover, Dutch influence in the Transvaal continued to be dependent on the interests of the Transvaal government. It was very conspicuous where Kruger desired it, but insignificant and fortuitous in other areas.[352]

Apparently, whenever the two historians mention imperialism, Schutte mainly emphasises imperialist *efforts* and Kossmann the *conditions* and *results* of imperialism. In my view, there was a degree of informal Dutch imperialism during the 1880s, as far as the policies of the SAR were shaped by Dutch lobbies in promotion of Dutch interests. Kruger may have wanted Dutch influence in administration, the Education Department and the railway system, but he did not have much choice at first. Even so, Leyds had to overcome a certain amount of resistance before this influence was properly established. 'I have considerably improved the position of the Dutch,' he himself said in 1887, 'but things are still not as they should be.'[353]

Seen like this, the idea of a 'New Holland' in South Africa had a defensive side to it. South Africa was seen, first and foremost, as a colonisation ground for the Netherlands, but at the same time a refuge, in the event that the Netherlands should lose its independence in Europe. 'We are often overcome by fear that we are doomed to disappear from among the nations', declared Kuyper in his Plancius speech. Like Kuyper, Spruyt was hoping that

if in due course Old Holland has to yield to the forces of history whereby the small nations are absorbed by the large ones, then the most vigorous and active elements of our people will find a new home in South Africa where we can continue our historical language and the Dutch race.[354]

351 Cf. Schutte, *Hollanders*, pp. 24–6; 'Nederland', pp. 587ff.
352. Kossmann, *Lage landen*, p. 321.
353. Leyds to Moltzer, 24 June 1887, Leyds Collection.
354. Quoted in *Nederland–Zuid–Afrika*, p. 194; cf. note 320 above.

Government circles, too, were concerned about the continued existence of the Netherlands, but such doubts were never expressed in public and never had any real consequences. Dutch foreign affairs ministers and diplomats experienced the period following the Eastern Question of 1876–8 as a 'period of ferment'. They were less afraid of a sudden annexation by Germany than of a war between France and Germany, which might well lead to such an annexation. 'Where two nations are, as it were, armed to the teeth, with their hands clutching the hilts of their swords, very little is needed to spark off a war', the Dutch ambassador Van der Hoeven warned from Berlin in 1887.[355]

While it was felt that a possible annexation of the Netherlands could really only come from Germany, a future loss of the East Indies was ascribed above all to Britain. For a historically minded Dutchman there was a direct connection between Anglo–Dutch rivalry in the Indonesian Archipelago and in South Africa. Blaas has pointed out recently that during the period of modern imperialism the 'touchiness of a small nation with a great past' expressed itself mainly in overseas issues; sometimes it would take the form of pride about the past and sometimes anxiety about the future.[356] And for the present, South Africa was at first able to offer something that was missing in the East Indies: the opportunity for a large number of Dutch colonists to settle down.

The Anti-Revolutionaries, in particular, saw South Africa as a 'counterweight against that precarious imbalance with which we have been seeking safety in nothing but the exploitation of the tropical territories for such a long time', as Kuyper observed.[357] A number of Liberals agreed. 'We still possess the East Indies,' said the writer J. H. Hooijer in De Gids, 'but nobody has given us a guarantee that we shall continue to own our colonies for ever.' He felt that the growing Dutch influence in South Africa proved that 'the role of our nation on the great stage of the world has not yet come to an end.' In particular, Hooijer was thinking of 'Young Holland' and the future prospects of the Transvaal, now that it was

355. Woltring, Bescheiden IV, no. 73; cf. ibid. III, nos 166, 170, 224, 277–8. Minister Van Karnebeek therefore made it quite clear to the German ambassador in 1888, that 'in my opinion the neutrality of the Netherlands, if loyally respected, would turn out to be the most advantageous attitude for Germany, should there be a large-scale European war.' Ibid. IV, no. 176.
356. In the words of the historian G. W. Kernkamp; cf. Blaas, 'Prikkelbaarheid', p. 292.
357. De Standaard, 8 July 1884; cf. 30 May 1890.

often so difficult to find suitable employment in either the Netherlands or the East Indies.[358]

Clearly not everyone saw South Africa as an alternative to the East Indies. The Liberal colonial magazine *Tijdschrift voor Nederlandsch-Indië* (Dutch East Indian Magazine) described the foundation of the Dutch South African Association (NZAV) as 'foolishness'. It was regarded with great disapproval that 'people in the Netherlands allow themselves to be led astray, seeking fanciful colonial deviations, so that the small amount of interest in colonial affairs which still exists and on which we are to a great extent directly dependent is now wasted on the Cape settlers'.[359]

The government did not see South Africa as a real alternative for the East Indies, either. As it was necessary to maintain friendly relations with Britain in the Archipelago, it tried as much as possible to avoid involvement in South Africa. Kuyper, too, felt that it was appropriate for the Netherlands to show moderation in its disapproval of British imperialism in South Africa, in view of the similarities with Dutch behaviour in Acheh.[360] The Socialists went one step further: 'Sea-beggars against the Spanish, the Irish and Transvaalers against the British, the Achehnese against the Dutch – these express the same concepts for us', declared a 'proletarian' in *Recht voor Allen* (Justice for Everyone) in the name of '*mankind*'. Obviously, the middle classes had very little sympathy with this point of view. At a Transvaal meeting in Haarlem in 1881 a working-class man had been thrown out of the hall, because he 'was unable to understand why there was so much zeal for the Transvaal if the Dutch themselves had annexed Acheh'. In the Second Chamber the lonely Socialist MP F. Domela Nieuwenhuis also met with disapproval when he mentioned the Transvaalers' fight for freedom in his plea for a Dutch withdrawal from Acheh.[361]

This suspicious reaction sometimes resembled a phenomenon that was called 'social imperialism' in other countries. Occasioned by comparisons between Acheh and the Transvaal and observing the growing social unrest in the Netherlands, the former governer of Acheh Laging Tobias in 1886 advocated

358. J. H. Hooijer, 'De toekomst van onzen stam', *De Gids*, 1890, i, p. 359.
359. 'De NZAV', *TNI*, 1881, I, pp. 468–71.
360. *De Standaard*, 9 February 1881 and 10 November 1884.
361. *Handelingen Tweede Kamer* (Parliamentary Reports of the Second Chamber), 27 November 1889, pp. 235ff. Cf. *NRC*, 11 February 1881; *Recht voor Allen*, 12 May 1886.

the possession of a large colonial empire which will offer welfare and even wealth to its sons . . . including those who have reached the edge of despair in our mother country because of hunger and want, and who gladly listen to the most inane theories of demagogues, theories that are dangerous for society.[362]

It was undoubtedly due to ethnocentric prejudice that the comparison between Acheh and the Transvaal met with resistance: after all, the Achehnese were considered vicious, 'coloured' enemies and the Boers heroic, white kinsmen. Nevertheless the comparison seemed wrong even from a more pragmatic point of view. Compared with British expansion in Africa, Dutch behaviour in the Archipelago during the 1880s hardly seemed like imperialism at all. From the political, military and economic points of view there appeared a tendency towards a concentration of the Dutch presence rather than expansion. Paradoxically, inasmuch as there was any expansionist urge in the Netherlands, it was directed precisely at South Africa. However, even Dutch expansion in the Transvaal remained dependent on the Netherlands' established colonial interests in the East Indies. The Transvaal railway loan in 1884 had failed partly because of the Javanese sugar crisis. 'If the military and economic situation in the East Indies had not been so profoundly alarming', wrote Moltzer, 'there might well have been some chance that our government would have been willing to do something for the railway.'[363] However, the situation in the East Indies continued to be anything but rosy.

The 1880s were uncertain times for the Netherlands, both at home and abroad. In its foreign relations, the Dutch position seemed threatened by a possible war in Europe and the emergence of modern imperialism. At home, Dutch society was affected by a socio-economic crisis and split by conflicts over the educational system, the issue of universal suffrage and the so-called social question, the growing socio-economic tensions. According to Schöffer, the critical years in Dutch politics were between the polarising Liberal Education Act of 1878 and the difficult revision of the Dutch constitution in 1887.[364]

362. Laging Tobias, 'Tegenwoordige politiek', pp. 291 and 306; cf. note 294 above. Bahlmann's pleas for protectionism in the East Indies and Bellaer Spruyt's appeal for emigration to South Africa can also be understood as social imperialism; cf. notes 258 and 345 above.
363. Moltzer to Leyds, 7 September 1886, Leyds Collection.
364. Schöffer, 'Politiek bestel', p. 635, Cf. Kossmann, *Lage landen*, pp. 230–1; Tamse, 'Politieke ontwikkeling', pp. 208ff.

Among the elites, particularly the Liberal elite, there was often a mood of despondency in view of all these problems. The gloomy reactions to Prince Alexander's death in 1884 – the 'year of the crisis' – were particularly characteristic in this respect. 'There will be hard times for the Netherlands', warned the *NRC*. 'The last son and heir of the House of Orange has been buried, there are divisions which sometimes even stifle the idea of national unity, and factions which shrink at nothing; what will the future bring?'[365] The political and economic crisis also affected the colonies. The enforced resignation of most ministers and governor-generals in the 1880s was a clear symptom.

A number of Liberals and Anti-Revolutionaries, however, felt that South Africa could offer an alternative option for the restoration of unity, self-confidence and welfare. During the 1890s such a plan would eventually succeed. Only temporarily in South Africa, which would cease to be an area for Dutch expansion, but with unexpected success in the Indonesian Archipelago. Success originated from new, active strategies of the colonial administration and colonial army. The following Dutch expansion in the Archipelago showed, however, a great deal of interaction with the decline of supposed foreign threats and the increase in political and social stability in the Netherlands.

365. *NRC*, 22 June 1884; cf. *De Standaard* and *De Tijd* of 24 June 1884.

3

Power and Justice (1890–1902)

The scramble for colonies which had started in the 1880s continued undiminished throughout the 1890s. Although most problems could be solved relatively peacefully, rivalries still kept flaring up. In Africa, Anglo–French rivalry reached a new climax, while in Asia Anglo–Russian rivalry continued. Anglo–German antagonism was also increasing, although a number of colonial agreements were reached. The only stabilising factor in this world-wide rivalry seemed to be the co-operation between powers that were not directly affected by one another's expansion, such as France and Russia or Britain and Japan.

At the turn of the century it seemed to some contemporaries as if the general rivalry was going to degenerate into a war of everyone against everybody else. Apart from the old colonial powers Britain and France, as well as European newcomers such as Germany and Italy, the colonial arena had now been entered by the United States of America and – in Asia – by Japan. The rivalry was no longer about the last white spots on the map of Africa, but the partition of large non-European empires such as China and even Turkey now seemed imminent. Spain, which had once been the first colonial power, lost its colonies in Asia and South America to the new world power of the United States in 1898. The South African Boer War (1899–1902) ended with the British subjugation of the Boers and the annexation of their republics. This world-wide expansion, which was generally known as imperialism by 1900, had interacting economic, strategic and nationalist causes.[1]

According to the social Darwinist doctrines of those years, this was an inevitable and indeed wholesome struggle towards human progress, between the newly emerging powers and the declining

1. Koebner and Schmidt, *Imperialism*, chapters 9 and 10. Cf. Langer, *Diplomacy*, *passim*; Kennedy, *Rise*, chapters 12 and 13; Eldridge, *Victorian Imperialism*, pp. 190ff.; Gillard, *Struggle*, chapter 8; Iriye, *Estrangement*, chapter 3.

ones. However, part of the public generally saw the new imperialism as 'power over justice' – certainly an objectionable situation where this concerned the behaviour of other countries. The term was therefore used mainly by opponents of the phenomenon.

The conviction that world politics was increasingly dominated by a power struggle gave rise to a counter-movement aimed at a strengthening of international law. Indeed, because of their growing arms budgets, even the governments of the bigger countries were looking for peaceful ways of solving conflicts. Initiated by the tsar, the first Peace Conference in The Hague was a good example of these efforts.[2] Especially in the Netherlands, the host nation of the conference, a lot of importance was attached to international law as a warranty for world peace and the continued existence of the small nations. British aggression towards the Boer republics so shortly after the Peace Conference was therefore seen as a particularly cynical expression of 'power over justice' – a view which was shared by the entire European continent. In the Netherlands, however, indignation was even stronger, as the development in South Africa was not merely a matter of legal principles and humanitarian considerations but also affected feelings of kinship and material interests.[3]

Some contemporaries, however – especially socialists – felt that there was no substantial difference between the British subjugation of the Boer republics and the Dutch conquest of Acheh which took place at about the same time. After the hesitant policies of the 1880s, which were aimed at concentration, the Netherlands' colonial expansion in the 1890s did indeed correspond more and more with that of other colonial powers. There was still the fear that the East Indies might be lost, but it now gave rise to intervention rather than abstention. The Lombok expedition of 1894 marked the turning point and the beginning of Dutch expansion, not only on the levels of government and colonial administration, but also that of public opinion. From 1896 onwards Acheh was systematically pacified, and the surrender of the sultan in 1903 was seen as the end of the war. At the same time there was a considerable increase in economic expansion in the Archipelago. In the public debate on overseas relations at the turn of the century Acheh and the Transvaal formed two poles of imperialism and anti-imperialism. Outside the East Indies, however, the Dutch government remained as aloof as poss-

2. Dülffer, *Regeln*, pp. 19ff.; cf. Gollwitzer, *Geschichte*, pp. 24–7 and 253ff.
3. Cf. Kröll, *Buren-Agitation*, pp. 139ff.

ible, not only concerning the Boer War but also the international complications surrounding China and Venezuela.

The Netherlands and World Politics

Modernisation, Nationalism and Pillarisation

The imperialism debate in the Netherlands was only partly a reaction against overseas developments in the East Indies or South Africa. During the 1890s a number of domestic tendencies had begun to influence foreign and colonial policies to a greater extent than before. Throughout this book we have frequently noted the roles of modernisation, nationalism and pillarisation (i.e. formation of religious and ideological subcultures with corresponding organisations). But if, for example, we compare the situation around 1900 with that of 1870, it seems that there had been considerable changes in these areas. With this in mind, I shall therefore elaborate on the meaning of these terms and their significance with regard to overseas relations of the Netherlands in 1900.

Of these terms, 'modernisation' describes the most general but also the most diffuse panorama of changes in Dutch society between 1870 and 1900. In fact, one may well wonder whether modernisation is a useful concept for historians at all. Many of Brands's objections to the modernisation theory in social sciences seem to be particularly cogent when applied to the Netherlands.[4] First of all, there is the usual identification of modernisation as industrialisation: this definition, as we have seen, cannot be applied to the Dutch economy around 1870. Although it was modern at the time, it was only partly industrialised. There is also the tendency to assume that economic and political developments ran simultaneously in the modernisation process. But at first the political modernisation that was implicit in the constitutional revision of 1848 met with very little support in the socio-economic sphere of the Netherlands. Then, until the constitutional revision of 1887, there was an increasing estrangement between government policies and the development of society at large. Finally, the modernisation theory assumes – implicitly or explicitly – that there is a dichotomy between 'traditional' and 'modern', whereas phenomena such as nationalism and pillarisation were precisely characterised by the

---

4. Brands, 'Modernisering'; cf. Wehler, *Modernisierungstheorie*.

continuation or even invention of traditions within a modern framework.

Nevertheless, despite these reservations, the development of Dutch society during the 1890s did indeed conform to the theory of modernisation; or rather, it did not contradict it. De Jonge, for example, has shown conclusively that after the international economic recovery of 1895 industrialisation in the Netherlands clearly proceeded much faster; and this development, in turn, stimulated other sectors.[5] Overseas markets fulfilled an important role in this industrialisation. The East Indies became an incubation area for many new branches of industry. For a new large-scale enterprise such as Werkspoor the supply of railway material to the Dutch South African Railway Company (NZASM) was extremely important. Also the spectacular growth of the Dutch shipping and naval engineering industry, in particular, turned out to be very significant for overseas relations. These sectors had been the main sticking points in 1870 and the following years. As we shall see, the Dutch East Indian Royal Packet Company (KPM) functioned as a driving force in attracting business for the Dutch shipping and naval engineering industry. Industrialisation was pushed forward and directed by capital interests to a considerable extent – in Amsterdam by colonial and commercial capital, in particular.[6]

However, the modernisation of the Dutch economy cannot simply be reduced to such interests. Kossmann, for example, has rightly pointed out that the economic development in the 1890s had been prepared in both direct and indirect ways by the educational reforms of the 1860s and 1870s. Such an interaction between economic and non-economic factors was noticeable in a variety of spheres in the 1890s. The constitutional revision of 1887 had finally made it possible to bridge the gap between the 'realm of the law' and the 'realm of reality'. Although the new constitution did not offer a satisfactory solution to the education dispute and the question of universal suffrage, it nevertheless prepared the ground to resolve these problems in a peaceful way. The need to reduce socio-economic inequality, too, was now more generally accepted, so that both the Liberal government under Pierson and Goeman Borgesius (1897–1901), and the Christian one under Kuyper (1901–5), gave priority to social legislation[7] – although Kuyper's social image

5. De Jonge, *Industrialisatie*, especially chapter 12.
6. Ibid., pp. 355–6; cf. Kossmann, *Lage landen*, pp. 310–15.
7. Ibid., pp. 259–61 and 376–7. Cf. Tamse and Minderaa, 'Politieke ontwikkeling',

became somewhat tarnished by his repression of the great railway strike in 1903. The colonial version of the social question was that of the 'welfare deficit' in Java, an issue which had been raised so emphatically by the left-wing Liberal journalist and colonial expert C. Th. van Deventer in his famous *Gids* article of 1899, 'the debt of honour', referring to the 830 million guilders of East Indian budget surpluses, which had been transferred to the Dutch treasury between 1830 and 1876. From the First Chamber Fransen van de Putte welcomed Van Deventer's ideas, but his old friend, Prime Minister and Minister of Finance Pierson, showed little enthusiasm. The Kuyper government, however, clearly felt that it had a 'moral calling' towards the East Indian population and made funds available for colonial welfare projects. This 'Ethical Policy', however, had already been prepared by the gradual growth and reform of the colonial administration in the East Indies from 1870 onwards.[8]

In the Netherlands there was a growing symbiosis of socio-economic and political developments around 1900, a process that has been phrased the 'mutual penetration of state and society' by Romein.[9] The content and direction of this process was partly also determined by cultural values. In other countries, whenever supposedly traditional values were pursued by means of modern politics, this often led to nationalism. In the Netherlands, such pursuit increasingly took the form of pillarisation (the formation of subcultures). Indeed, this pillarisation process displayed the same characteristics which Gellner generally noted for nationalism; that is, it was part of the country's culture, education and political power structure.[10]

Dutch authors, however, often tend to regard nationalism and pillarisation as direct opposites of one another and feel that the latter was stronger in the Netherlands. According to Stuurman, there was 'no soil for a conservative nationalist mass movement whatsoever', so that there was even more ground for pillarisation. Furthermore, Stuurman felt that the vulnerable international and colonial position of the Netherlands as a small power prevented the formation of a 'strong officers' caste' or an 'autonomous colonial party' which might have stood in the forefront of such a nationalist

---

pp. 223–5 and 462–74.

8. Kossmann, *Lage landen*, pp. 304–5; Van Doorn, *Engineers*, p. 21. Cf. C. Th. van Deventer, 'Een eereschuld', *De Gids*, 1899, iii, pp. 205–58.

9. Cf. Romein, *Breukvlak* I, chapters 18 and 19.

10. Gellner, *Nations*, p. 97; cf. Blom, *Verzuiling*, pp. 23–4.

movement.[11] Earlier, Schöffer and Daalder had already pointed out the relatively gradual and moderate character of political and social developments in the Netherlands.[12]

Nevertheless, nationalism was undoubtedly an important factor in Dutch society at the turn of the century. It expressed itself particularly strongly in overseas issues, the South African Boer War and the colonial wars in the Indonesian Archipelago. It also played a role in the army reforms and the education dispute and was even reflected in the arts. However, in those areas nationalism was mainly restricted to small groups of officers, intellectuals and artists. The reactions of these nationalist groups to the Boer War and Dutch expansion in the East Indies will be discussed in more detail below. To illustrate the conditions in which nationalism could develop around 1900, I shall merely point to the 'Pro Patria' article in *De Gids* by the Leiden scholar G. Kalff, which was well known at the time.[13] In it Kalff stated with great pleasure that in the course of the nineteenth century there had been an increase in patriotism and national unity. 'Our nation felt united when the king called us "to arms" in 1830, as well as during events like the arrival of the Transvaalers in our country, the defeat of Lombok and the raid of Jameson', he wrote in 1898, at a time when the Boer War and the pacification of Acheh were yet to take place. Developments at home, such as the emancipation of the Calvinists and Roman Catholics, the extension of suffrage and the new willingness to tackle the social question, were regarded positively by Kalff, as they cleared the ground of a new unfolding of national forces overseas. 'Again,' he wrote, 'though on a smaller scale than in the seventeenth century, the Dutch are leaving their nests to swarm out over the world.' And he concluded his article with the words:

> There should be no chauvinism, but – more importantly – there should be none of that narrow-minded scornfulness towards one's own country and people: that spineless way in which some dwell on our own weakness; the repulsive gratefulness for the tiniest little scrap when a good word is said about us in foreign parts.

With regard to South Africa and the East Indies, however, the national self-confidence to which Kalff appealed so emphatically was

---

11. Stuurman, *Verzuiling*, pp. 310–11.
12. Daalder, 'Netherlands'; Schöffer, 'Politiek bestel'.
13. G. Kalff, 'Pro Patria', *De Gids*, 1898, ii, pp. 397–440.

to turn frequently into chauvinism at the turn of the century, though in subsequent years this extreme nationalism gradually subsided again. This was because South Africa was no longer a suitable area for expansion, and in the East Indies it had soon reached its limits. Furthermore, domestic problems, such as the social question, the suffrage issue and the education dispute, remained dominant until their 'pacification' by the constitutional revision of 1917. As Stuurman himself has correctly pointed out, by the year 1900 pillarisation had not yet become dominant, but during the following twenty years the whole country gradually organised in four main pillars: the Protestants, the Catholics, the Liberals and the Socialists.[14] Pillarisation, however, did not put an end to nationalism, and in colonial matters there continued to be an element of aggressiveness in Dutch nationalism until after the Second World War.

General tendencies such as modernisation, nationalism and pillarisation also had repercussions on the attitudes and relations described at the beginning of chapter one – the Dutch government and Parliament, pressure groups and public opinion. From a formal, constitutional point of view, not much had changed in overseas relations since 1870. The constitutional revision of 1887 had in fact increased the influence of the Dutch Houses of Parliament on foreign affairs, and treaties which entailed financial commitments, in particular, were now subject to parliamentary approval.

In practice, however, the influence of the crown, particularly of the king himself, had become greater rather than smaller. After the death of William III in 1890 the popularity of the House of Orange had grown again, and this was shown particularly clearly at the inauguration of Queen Wilhelmina in 1898. Unlike King William III, Queen Emma and Queen Wilhelmina took an active and well-informed interest in foreign and colonial affairs. Their views and the views of their advisers in the Privy Council were therefore taken very seriously by the ministers involved.[15] In colonial affairs, as we shall see in the case of Lombok and Acheh, Emma and Wilhelmina insisted especially on an extension of Dutch authority

---

14. Stuurman, *Verzuiling*, pp. 167–8.
15. In 1900, apart from the queen of the Netherlands, Asser, ex-minister Rochussen and the former Minister of the Colonies H. van der Wijck were members of the foreign affairs committee in the Dutch Privy Council. The colonial affairs committee included Van der Wijck, former MP Van Gennep and the financial and economic expert J. E. Henny; *Staats-Almanak*, 1901, pp. 38–40. Cf. Van Raalte, *Staatshoofd*, pp. 160ff.

in the Archipelago. During the Boer War Wilhelmina pleaded with Queen Victoria and Kaiser Wilhelm II on behalf of the Boers, though without for one moment losing sight of Dutch neutrality. Later, Kuyper was to discover this to his cost when he was seeking a *rapprochement* with Belgium and Germany.

Of the departments of the colonies and foreign affairs, the former had continued to be more important in its extent and significance than the latter. Compared with 1870 the Foreign Affairs Department had not undergone any obvious changes, and in 1900 there were no more than 18 civil servants at the rank of deputy clerk or higher, compared with 11 thirty years earlier. Its second, trading division had become more important and the consular service had gradually been extended. However, the key positions within the department and the most important diplomatic posts were still in the hands of the same patrician families. The orientation and style of the young Van Bylandts, Gericke van Herwijnens, Van der Does de Willebois' and Rochussens were hardly different from those of their fathers. Also, the right-wing Liberal aristocrats who filled minister-ial posts during the 1890s – G. van Tienhoven, followed by Röell and then De Beaufort – continued the political traditions of their predecessors. This is also true for their Anti-Revolutionary succes-sor R. Melvil van Lynden, although this weak politician turned out to be a poor match for the dominating figure of Kuyper.[16]

In the Dutch Parliament, around the turn of the century, there continued to be rather little interest in foreign affairs, with the exception of relations with the South African kinsmen, the Boers. Even then, however, colonial affairs were given far more attention. At the Colonial Affairs Department there were now 68 civil servants at the rank of deputy clerk or higher, as compared with 35 in 1870. Of the colonial affairs ministers, the Liberals Van Dedem and Cremer were well-known, politically experienced figures, as were the Anti-Revolutionaries Van Asch van Wijck and Idenburg; whereas the unknown East Indian civil servant J. H. Bergsma, who served as minister under the right-wing Liberal government of Röell–Van Houten, was regarded as rather weak politician. The current governor-general of the East Indies, the experienced admin-istrator C. H. A. van der Wijck, therefore resolutely took his own initiatives during the Lombok and Acheh crises. Both the Dutch Parliament and the general public repeatedly complained during

16. *Staats-Almanak*, 1901, pp. 45–6. Cf. Jurriaanse, *Nederlandse ministers*, pp. 356–401; Wels, *Aloofness*, pp. 127–8.

Bergsma's term of office that too much of the decision making was taking place in Batavia rather than The Hague. Under minister Cremer's government the balance was redressed in favour of The Hague again, especially when Van der Wijck was succeeded by W. Rooseboom in 1899, a former general and Liberal MP without any experience in the East Indies who showed little initiative and independence in Batavia.[17]

In the Dutch Parliament the relevant colonial issues were not just discussed by the East Indian colonial experts but also by the above-mentioned politicians. It is noticeable that there was an increase in former officers among the colonial experts: Kielstra and J. B. Verhey among the Liberals, and the tough old veteran and Roman Catholic B. R. F. van Vlijmen as well as the ethical Anti-Revolutionary A. W. F. Idenburg among the Christians.

In 1897 H. van Kol was elected as one of the representatives of the Social Democratic Workers' Party. For several years this fiery but generally moderate Social Democrat had worked in Java as an irrigation engineer. He came to be regarded as one of the most authoritative colonial experts in the Second Chamber, even though initially he was rather isolated with his fierce attacks on 'the rapaciousness of imperialist politics'. Minister Cremer was therefore more concerned about the pragmatic criticism of his Acheh policies by the elderly Fransen van de Putte in the First Chamber. Broadly speaking, however, Liberals and clericals in the 1890s had increasingly come to an agreement over the most important aspects of colonial politics, including the pacification of Acheh. This Liberal–Christian consensus was particularly apparent under Kuyper. Compared to the fierce opposition with which the Liberals had reacted to Keuchenius's policies, their response to the ethical reform programme of Van Asch van Wijck and his successor Idenburg must be seen as rather positive. The area of foreign politics, too, was at first regarded as part of the 'neutral zone' by the Liberal spokesman Van Karnebeek.[18] However, this certainly changed as soon as Kuyper began to take a personal interest in foreign affairs.

The most important change which had taken place both inside and outside the Dutch Parliament since 1870 was perhaps the emergence of modern mass parties: the Calvinist Anti-Revolutionary Party (ARP)

17. For the ministers and governor-generals, see the biographical entries in the *ENI*; for the department cf. *Staats-Almanak*, 1901, pp. 588–93.
18. *Handelingen Tweede Kamer* (Parliamentary Reports of the Second Chamber), 7 December 1901, pp. 393–4. Cf. Idema, *Geschiedenis*, pp. 144ff.

in 1879, followed by the mainstream Liberal Union (LU) in 1885; the Social Democratic Alliance (SDB) in 1886; the Radical Alliance (RB) in 1892; the Social Democratic Workers' Party (SDAP) in 1894; the loosely organised, right-wing Free Liberals (VL) in 1897; the left-wing Liberal Democratic Alliance (VDB) in 1901; the politically conservative and religiously moderate Protestant Christian Historical Union (CHU) in 1908; and the Roman Catholic State Party (RKSP) as late as 1926. While pillarisation had almost certainly shown itself in this formation of parties, nationalism played a role in the emergence of pressure groups on certain overseas issues.

One group that was particularly nationalist was the Algemeen Nederlandsch Verbond (ANV, General Dutch Alliance), an offshoot of the Dutch Language and Literature conferences. Initially, under the chairmanship of the gentle Indologist and Leiden professor J. H. C. Kern, the ANV confined itself to the cultivation of linguistic unity between the Netherlands, Flanders and South Africa. In 1899, the divisions of the society in these 'core countries' had 1,400, 700 and 800 members respectively. Pierson, Kuyper and the Catholic leader Schaepman were prominent members of the Dutch division. During the Boer War the society gave a wider and more aggressive meaning to their idea of the 'Greater Netherlands'. Under the leadership of their energetic secretary H. J. Kiewiet de Jonge the press office of the ANV became the most important centre of pro-Boer propaganda in Europe. When South Africa was no longer one of the 'core countries' of the association, the ANV concentrated more and more on the Dutch colonies. In 1904 the Dutch division had 2,800 and the East Indian division 600 members.[19]

During the Boer War dozens of pro-Boer committees and organisations were set up in the Netherlands, many of which were very nationalist in orientation. The most important society was the NZAV with an increase in membership from 1,700 in 1898 to 6,600 in 1901. Shortly before the war there was a change in management, and the older, more academically oriented generation of Spruyt was succeeded by a younger leadership that was more inclined towards politics and economics. The director of the NZASM, Middelberg, became chairman, the Amsterdam banker J. B. Loman treasurer and the Amsterdam shipping-line director P. den Tex secretary of the NZAV. Although Middelberg was fervently religious and a prominent ARP member, nationalism in the NZAV – at least at the top ·

19. *Neerlandia*, June 1899; ibid., May 1904. Cf. Kröll, *Buren-Agitation*, pp. 176ff.

level – retained its rather liberal and moderate character.

A positively Christian and outspokenly nationalist organisation was the Christian National Boer Committee, under the leadership of the Calvinist principal of a teacher training college, H. Bijleveld. In 1902 this organisation had 5,500 members. Both the NZAV and this Christian society seemed to recruit their membership mainly from the middle classes. In 1898 26 per cent of the NZAV members had any academic background and in 1901 only 14 per cent. The percentage was probably even lower for the Christian Committee. The different pro-Boer organisations worked together under the umbrella of the Dutch Committee for the Transvaal where all political parties were represented, except for the Social Democratic Workers' Party. After the war the pro-Boer movement was to lose a large portion of its members again. In 1910 the NZAV only had 2,200 members and the Christian National Boer Committee had all but spent itself.[20]

Most colonial associations in the Netherlands had rather nationalist tendencies, too, although they never achieved such a large membership as the pro-Boer movement around 1900. Pillarisation in this area was of course particularly noticeable in the Christian missions. Although control of Roman Catholic missionary activities remained firmly in the hands of Rome, the missionaries of the Sacred Heart, who had established themselves in Tilburg in 1882, received increasing support from the Dutch province of their church.[21] The Calvinist churches in the Netherlands only set up a temporary 'missionary order' in 1892, which did not become permanent until 1902. Meanwhile the Utrecht Missionary Association was given support by fundamentalists, so that it had about 600 members in 1898 and was supported by 480 congregations in the whole of the Netherlands.[22] The Dutch Missionary Society – after Neurdenburg's death in 1896 under the leadership of the Protestant minister J. W. Gunning – continued to be the largest missionary organisation in the Netherlands, working closely together with the Dutch Reformed Church. However, like the Utrecht Association, it was unable to finance its growing activities in the Archipelago from its own resources. The success of Protestant missions was to a large extent due to the increasing support and co-operation of the Dutch government.

20. Ibid., chapter 9. Cf. the membership list in the *Verslagen* (Reports) of the NZAV.
21. Mulders, *Missie*, pp. 84–5.
22. See the annual report for 1898, *Berigten*, 1899.

During the 1890s both the Dutch government and the East Indian colonial administration developed a more positive attitude towards Protestant missions in the Archipelago. In turn, missionaries such as A. C. Kruyt and N. Adriani played an important role as mediators and advisers in the extension of colonial administration in Celebes and Sumatra.[23] These missionaries also became very active in the areas of science and ethnology, whereas the Dutch Geographical Society had lost much of its old energy after its disappointing experiences of the 1880s. Between 1883 and 1893 its membership was reduced from nearly 900 to about 600. After Veth's death in 1893 the membership of the society remained at the same level for a number of years, according to his successor, the Amsterdam professor in geography C. M. Kan.[24] Around 1900, there was an increase in membership again and the Society took an active part in the scientific exploration of the Archipelago.

The most important Dutch organisation in colonial matters continued to be the East Indian Society, even though its membership had only risen from 200 in 1870 to less than 300 in 1900. This distinguished and authoritative society was national rather than nationalist in character. Apart from the established Liberal and Christian colonial experts, the Society was joined around 1900 by Van Deventer and Van Kol. The chairman at the time was the former Governor-general Pijnacker Hordijk. The membership of other colonial organisations also remained limited, with societies ranging from the militant association Moed, Beleid en Trouw (Courage, Statesmanship and Loyalty) of the Acheh General G. M. Verspeyck to the ethically oriented Oost-Indische Kiesvereeniging (East Indian Constituency Association).[25] As for publications, the *Indische Gids* (East Indian Guide) was still the most influential colonial magazine, though the Dutch *Gids* also devoted a good deal of attention to the East Indies. In 1900 Van Deventer joined the editorial team. Economically and commercially, the Chambers of Commerce were still the most important interest groups in the Netherlands. It was typical of the closer relationship between the government and industry that a Trade Politics Committee was set up in 1891, an advisory body which included both senior civil servants and major entrepreneurs.

23. Cf. Coolsma, *Zendingseeuw*, pp. 449ff. and 613ff.
24. *TAG*, 1896, pp. 196–7.
25. See the entries under 'genootschappen' (societies) and 'vereenigingen' (associations) in the *ENI*.

Parallel with the formation of political parties, the development of the Dutch daily press from 1870 onwards was also characterised by modernisation, pillarisation and – to some extend – nationalism. Of the Christian newspapers, *De Standaard* almost doubled its circulation and reached 4,500 during the 1890s. Apart from the conservative *De Tijd* and *De Maasbode*, there was also the progressive Catholic *Centrum*, first published in 1885 with Schaepman as its editor-in-chief. Socialist papers were newcomers on the scene, and by the year 1901 the SDAP party newspaper *Het Volk* had acquired 5,000 subscribers, with the Social Democratic leader P. J. Troelstra as editor-in-chief. The theoretical magazine of the SDAP, *De Nieuwe Tijd*, rather Marxist in orientation, had only a few hundred subscribers. Independent of the SDAP was the influential political and cultural magazine *De Kroniek*, with the former radical and moderate Social Democrat P. L. Tak as chief editor. With the disappearance of the Conservative Party, on the other hand, the Conservative press also ceased to exist, and the *Dagblad voor Zuid-Holland en 's-Gravenhage* finally closed down in 1904. The great Liberal papers – the *NRC*, the *Handelsblad* and the *Vaderland* – hardly recorded any growth at all after 1880. Nevertheless, their influence continued to be considerable, especially in foreign and colonial affairs. The editor-in-chief of the *Handelsblad*, Charles Boissevain, once characterised as a 'fearless gentleman with a poetic vein', displayed an outspoken nationalism in his commentaries. The foreign affairs summaries in *De Gids* by the historian W. G. C. Bijvanck, showed a more moderate form of national concern.

The most impressive growth figures since 1870 were achieved by the popular press: their sales were greater than those of the Liberal, Christian and socialist press put together. During the 1880s the *Nieuws van den Dag*, and the *Rotterdamsch Nieuwsblad* achieved circulations of nearly 40,000 each, and *De Telegraaf* had a circulation of about 10,000. This is by no means insignificant when we consider that the number of people eligible to vote had increased equally noticeably, reaching about 50 per cent of all male adults in 1897. As for party politics, most of these 'popular papers' were either 'neutral' or indeed 'national' in orientation; when it came to subjects like Acheh and the Transvaal, they were always outspokenly nationalist.[26]

26. Cf. Schneider and Hemels, *Nederlandse krant*, pp. 216ff.; Scheffer, *Tindal*, pp. 302ff.

Neutrality, Defence and International Law

Around the turn of the century domestic developments such as modernisation, nationalism and pillarisation began to influence Dutch foreign relations, while conversely foreign developments also influenced the situation in the Netherlands itself. The reaction to the Boer War is the most obvious example of such interaction. At the same time, however, it is important not to lose sight of the autonomy of the policy level. Dutch policies were still subject to the 'primacy of foreign politics': that is, the idea of maintaining aloofness in Europe together with the protection of colonial interests overseas. In addition to these objectives, however, the Netherlands also endeavoured to promote international law, so that its traditional policy of neutrality and aloofness – intentionally or unintentionally – acquired a more active meaning. In this context the term 'policy of self-reliance (*zelfstandigheidspolitiek*)' was already used occasionally.[27] Compared with the 1880s there was now more confidence in the sphere of world politics.

The first impulse came from outside. Around the 1890s there had been a certain *détente* in international relations, both in and outside Europe.[28] This breathing space gave Liberal and Christian spokesmen an opportunity to take a closer look at the options of Dutch foreign politics, with a view to future crises. Some advocated disarmament and international arbitration; others a strengthening of the country's defences and co-operation with other states; whereas the majority of observers were trying to find a combination of power politics and international law. As early as 1889 Kuyper had recommended looking into various options for an alliance. Liberal historians have in fact seen this recommendation as an attempt to achieve a 'defensive Dutch–Belgian link with the Triple Alliance', though Van Koppen has shown very clearly that Kuyper certainly had no such concrete and far-reaching plans at the time.[29] And indeed, even Liberal circles began to discuss less timidly the possibility of participating in alliances. According to ex-Minister of War H. J. Enderlein, 'neutrality' should no longer be understood as 'complete aloofness', as the Netherlands would then become a

27. Cf. Smit, *Nederland*, pp. 1–9; De Leeuw, *Nederland*, pp. 13–19; Wels, *Aloofness*, pp. 15–23.
28. See the annual survey in the *NRC*, 3 January 1891. Cf. Langer, *Diplomacy*, pp. 6–7; Kennedy, *Rise*, pp. 205ff.
29. *De Standaard*, 7 October 1889. Cf. Van Koppen, *Kuyper*, pp. 4–7; Van Hamel, *Nederland*, p. 410.

puppet of power politics in Europe. He therefore suggested speaking of a 'policy of self-reliance' instead, which would not exclude co-operation with other states.[30]

Even when the international situation deteriorated again at the end of the 1890s, this new self-confidence did not disappear. Expecting virtually nothing positive from the new century and convinced of 'impending disaster', Kuyper repeatedly advocated a strengthening of Dutch defences as well as more openness to possible alliances, to which he also added the promotion of international law.[31] The *Handelsblad* argued that the Netherlands should stop 'playing hide-and-seek' behind a 'negative view of neutrality'.[32] Even minister De Beaufort wanted to have his hands free and emphatically rejected the idea that his country should follow the Belgian example and make a formal declaration of neutrality: 'because', he argued, 'history teaches me that a declaration of neutrality is a liability rather than an asset to small states, as it takes away their freedom to enter into alliances without providing any guarantee that they will never be dragged into a war'. And he added that 'for the Netherlands, with its large colonial possessions, such a declaration of neutrality would be especially problematic.'[33]

In practice, De Beaufort's 'free hands policy' amounted to extreme caution and restraint, whereas Kuyper, with his notion of self-reliance, took active steps in the direction of Germany and Belgium. Although he was probably not envisaging simply a link with Germany or the Triple Alliance, his foreign travels did indeed give that impression both in the Netherlands and abroad.[34] The consensus between Liberals and Christians then quickly disappeared. Pierson and De Beaufort even felt that Kuyper's endeavours in foreign affairs were becoming 'increasingly *staatsgefährlich*' (dangerous to the state).[35]

Eventually, in 1905, Queen Wilhelmina herself was to point out to Kuyper the dangers of any alliance in peacetime. The most important obstacle, according to the queen and her advisers, lay in the fact that 'the Netherlands and its colonies have such strongly

---

30. H. J. Enderlein, 'Neutraliteit', *Vragen des Tijds*, 1891, I, pp. 1–15.
31. Cf. *De Standaard*, 16 June 1899, 23 February, 18 April and 6 June 1900.
32. *Het Handelsblad*, 20 June 1900.
33. *Handelingen Tweede Kamer* (Parliamentary Reports of the Second Chamber), 6 December 1898, p. 347.
34. Cf. Smit, *Nederland*, pp. 3 and 15–18.
35. Pierson to De Beaufort, 15 December 1902, De Beaufort Collection (ARA). Cf. De Beaufort, *Vijftig jaren* II, pp. 3–4.

conflicting interests: for the motherland itself it would be desirable to seek an alliance with a great power on the continent, whereas for the colonies it would be preferable if we allied ourselves with a great sea power.'[36] The special position of the Netherlands as a small European but great colonial power thus seemed to exclude both a formal declaration of neutrality and a formal alliance.

Because of this insecure and potentially contradictory position, the 'world politics' of the old and new powers were watched very attentively in the Netherlands. 'The centre of the world is moving outside Europe', concluded Bijvanck on the occasion of the turn-of-the century celebration of New Year's Eve 1899.[37] At first, however, the emergence of America and Japan made a greater impression in colonial than in diplomatic circles. Dutch diplomacy continued to be strongly oriented towards European relations. Britain and Germany were generally regarded as the most important powers for the Netherlands. Britain had a particularly negative press around 1900, mainly – though not only – because of the Boer War. After all, everywhere in the world and in all kinds of spheres there were signs of British imperialism, capitalism, jingoism and social Darwinism – depending on the preoccupations of the Liberal, Christian and Socialist observers in the Netherlands. The chief culprit was of course Chamberlain, the 'manager of imperialism'.[38] Only very few wondered whether perhaps British world politics was really so much more 'perfidious' than that of the other great powers.[39]

Many observers, however, felt that Britain's world-wide imperialism made it dangerously blind and imposed too much of a burden. Both the Dutch ambassador in London, Van Goltstein, and several commentators in the Netherlands spoke of a 'giant with clay feet' in this context.[40] When Britain entered into an 'unholy alliance' with 'heathen Japan' in 1902, Kuyper felt that it had alienated all 'Christian nations', and that its pact might herald the ruin of the British Empire.

After Gladstone's death in 1898, Kuyper seems to have increas-

---

36. Smit, *Bescheiden* II, no. 412.
37. *De Gids*, 1900, i, p. 193.
38. *De Standaard*, 17, 22 and 24 August 1900. Cf. *Het Handelsblad* of 1, 13 and 22 October and *NRC* of 5 November 1899; *De Tijd* of 19 August and *Het Centrum* of 23 October 1899; *De Sociaal-Demokraat* of 18 November and 30 December 1899.
39. L. Simon, 'Perfide Albion?', *De Gids*, 1896, iv, pp. 3–37.
40. Woltring, *Bescheiden* VI, no. 322. Cf. *NRC*, 5 November, *De Standaard*, 6 November and *Het Handelsblad*, 22 December 1899.

ingly lost his trust in Britain.[41] Most Liberals, however, were convinced that the British people would eventually find their common sense again. Meanwhile, good relations with Britain continued to be a corner-stone of Dutch foreign policy – most certainly under Pierson, but with certain reservations under Kuyper as well. 'In view of our overseas possessions, there is too much at stake for us', Van Goltstein had warned at the outbreak of the Boer War. After all, in order to maintain the East Indies, the Netherlands was still dependent on British support.[42]

This is why closer relations with Germany could not go too far, as Queen Wilhelmina explained to Kuyper. During the 1890s there had been a considerable increase in trade with Germany, whereas trade with Britain had reduced. The modernisation of the Dutch economy was to a large extent based on German markets, investment and technology.[43] Wilhelmina's marriage with Henry of Mecklenburg-Schwerin also resulted in closer dynastic links with Germany.[44] Around the turn of the century Germany repeatedly advocated a common customs union as well as closer political and military co-operation in Europe and overseas. Tets van Goudriaan, the Dutch ambassador to Berlin, reported that both Admiral Von Tirpitz and other 'high-ranking naval and army commanders' as well as 'industrialists, merchants and academics' were strongly recommending such co-operation, especially with a view to Britain: 'Great hopes are being placed in the irresistible logic of future developments, but it is regretted that there is no *Verständnis* [understanding] at all for this view in our country.'[45]

These German ideas, however, were welcomed in virulent anti-British circles in the Netherlands. According to the *Utrechtsch Dagblad*, an 'offensive and defensive union' with Germany would enable the Netherlands to take an active stand against 'Anglo-Saxon imperialist greed for conquests' in South Africa. In Amsterdam the

41. Van Koppen, *Kuyper*, p. 9; cf. *De Standaard*, 1 August 1900 and 26 March 1902.
42. Smit, *Bescheiden* I, no. 18. Cf. Pierson's diary, 29 April, 25 September and 2 October 1900, Pierson Collection. See Kuyper's declaration of policy, *Handelingen Tweede Kamer* (Parliamentary Reports of the Second Chamber), 24 September 1901, pp. 58–9.
43. Von der Dunk, *Niederlande*, pp. 12ff. Cf. Bos, *Brits-Nederlandse handel*, pp. 316ff.
44. Smit, *Nederland*, pp. 73–7.
45. Von Bülow, according to Tets, expressed himself far more moderately about British–German and German–Dutch relations; Tets to De Beaufort, 25 April, 19 July and 8 December 1899, De Beaufort Collection.

pro-German faction in the Chamber of Commerce was led by Van der Wall Bake, the founder and chairman of the NZASM.[46] In general, however, the idea of closer economic and political ties with Germany was rejected. The general and privy councillor J. C. C. den Beer Portugael, felt particularly strongly about it and explained in the *NRC* that such co-operation would eventually lead to the annexation of the Netherlands by Germany and the loss of the East Indies to Britain. Kuyper, too, rejected the plans for a customs union and warned against the ' "Germanisation" of our nation in all kinds of areas'.[47] It seems therefore that when Kuyper tried to approach Germany during this term of office, this was more a misfiring tactical move in his policy of 'self-reliance' than a manifestation of ideological solidarity. According to Von der Dunk, national self-confidence with regard to Germany was generally growing with the modernisation that was taking place in Dutch society – a process which, paradoxically, had been caused precisely by German influences and developments.[48]

Around the turn of the century this increase in national self-confidence in relation to other countries went hand it hand with efforts to strengthen Dutch defences. The initial success of the Boers prompted some progressive Liberals to demand the formation of a real 'people's army'. It was hoped that the defensive strength of the entire Dutch nation could be increased by fostering military virtues and skills in education, particularly physical education. The resulting discipline would then 'also be of benefit to the work force in times of peace', wrote one journalist. 'No issue is as national as this one', declared another.[49] Indeed in 1900, at the initiative of the former minister of war, Colonel A. L. W. Seyffardt, and the above-mentioned literary scholar Kalff, an association called Volksweerbaarheid (Popular Defence) was set up, supported by Kuyper, Schaepman and the radical leader M. W. F. Treub. However, most Liberals and Christians preferred a strengthening of the regular

46. Smit, *Bescheiden* VI, nos. 3 and 15. Cf. *Utrechtsch Dagblad*, 29 October 1899.

47. *De Standaard*, 27 September 1899, 11 and 15 October 1900. Cf. *NRC*, 3 March 1900; *De Tijd*, 19 July 1899; *Het Vaderland*, 8–9 October 1899.

48. Von der Dunk, *Niederlande*, p. 31. Cf. Smit, *Nederland*, pp. 18–19; Van Koppen, *Kuyper*, p. 7.

49. H. Verploegh, 'Een volksbelang', *Vragen des Tijds*, 1902, I, p. 299; cf. G. Polvliet, 'Sociale en militaire vaardigheid', ibid. II, p. 69. See also S. van Aken, 'Volksweerbaarheid', *De Gids*, 1900, iv, pp. 294–322. For the 'national' character and the broad political support for *Volksweerbaarheid*, see the sceptical commentary by P. L. Tak, *De Kroniek*, 29 January 1900.

forces, a step which seemed to be facing enough opposition already. With great difficulty the Pierson government managed to get a number of bills through the Dutch Parliament to pave the way for some modest modernisation of the Dutch forces – particularly the introduction of conscription in 1898 and the Army Act of 1901, whereby more men were drafted into the army and navy but the time of service was shortened. The Socialists fought against the manifestation of 'militarism' in such laws mainly as a matter of principle. Many Liberals had objected on more practical, financial grounds. The Catholics were, as they always had been, concerned about the demoralising influence of life in the barracks.[50]

However, apart from these demands for a strengthening of national defences, there were also advocates of international disarmament and arbitration. Of course, the two objectives were not necessarily mutually exclusive, as could be seen in the policies of the Dutch government at the turn of the century. Nevertheless, consistent followers of the two camps often fought each other quite passionately. The discussions among educationalists about the content of history as a school subject was typical in this context. It seems that during the 1890s – at least in state education – pacifist views were more influential than militarist ones.[51]

However, only very few impulses still came from the long-existing General Dutch Peace Alliance, that had only 600 members in 1900. By then, its most important aim – international arbitration – had already become a very common one in Dutch policies, and at first the Peace Alliance had great difficulties with the new, radical demands for international and, if necessary, unilateral Dutch disarmament, as well as with the formal declaration of neutrality. These demands had been put forward mainly by Social Democrats and advocates of women's emancipation. The latter, in particular, were actively involved in the Dutch Women's Union for International Disarmament, under the leadership of the vociferous Mrs J. M. C. B. Waszklewicz-Van Schilfgaarde. Despite their mutual differences of opinion, the ladies and gentlemen of the middle-class peace movement merged in 1901 to form the General Dutch Peace Alliance 'Peace through Justice'.[52] In the Dutch Parliament Van Kol

---

50. Pierson's diary, 22–31 May 1898, 12 March, 1 and 27 April 1901, Pierson Collection; De Beaufort, *Vijftig jaren* I, pp. 274–7. See also Smit, *Nederland*, pp. 139–44; Kossmann, *Lage landen*, pp. 264–5.
51. Kamerbeek, 'Geschiedenis', p. 35.
52. Cf. Kamphuis, *Vredebond*, chapter 5.

spoke regularly in favour of unilateral disarmament and a formal declaration of neutrality on the part of the Netherlands. Social Democrats, were on the whole rather sceptical towards the middle-class peace movement, as it failed to recognise the capitalist causes of war: '"Get rid of all weapons!" may be a very nice slogan, but unfortunately it is no more than that.'[53]

The less ambitious effort to promote international law had by now been almost generally accepted in the Netherlands. Dutch MPs played an active role in interparliamentary conferences which, since 1889, had been meeting with this purpose in various European capitals. In 1894 the conference took place in The Hague.[54] At the Department of Foreign Affairs the question was being discussed: 'what would be more expedient for a small power: a state of legal security, with arbitration, and thus the limitation of its sovereignty, or a state of so-called absolute sovereignty, without arbitration, but without legal security? At the beginning of the 1890s this question was definitively decided in favour of arbitration.[55]

An important test case for the Netherlands' firmness of principle in this respect was the issue of the *Costa Rica Packet* – an Australian whaling vessel which had seized an unmanned proa from Macassar in 1888. Although this had quite probably happened at high sea, the Dutch East Indian authorities took the opportunity to have the captain arrested and imprisoned in 1891. When he was released again, the British government submitted a considerable claim for damages to the Netherlands, on behalf of the captain, the crew and the shipping agent of the *Packet*, because of the resultant loss of income. Although the legal procedure in the East Indies had not been impeccable, the Dutch government nevertheless agreed to the British proposal for extensive arbitration, which would also include the amount of the damage claims. Van Goltstein, who had succeeded Van Bylandt as ambassador to London, was completely against this. The issue was committed to the tsar of Russia again, whose predecessor had already mediated between the Netherlands and France in the Lawa issue. After lengthy investigations his councillor, F. de Martens, decided that the Australian claimants were entirely in the right, so that the Dutch government was now obliged to pay slightly reduced damages. This pronouncement gave

53. *De Sociaal-demokraat*, 20 May 1899. Cf. *Handelingen Tweede Kamer* (Parliamentary Reports of the Second Chamber), 6 December 1898, pp. 341–2.
54. Kamphuis, *Vredebond*, pp. 128–9.
55. Woltring, *Bescheiden* V, no. 300.

rise to indignation in legal and colonial circles, as there had been no final proof that the proa had been picked up outside Dutch territorial waters in 1888.[56]

Nonetheless, although the result of this arbitration was disappointing, the Dutch government and Parliament responded very positively to the tsar's famous call for an international peace conference in 1898. Thanks to the efforts of Mrs Waszklewicz, the Dutch peace movement subsequently collected over 200,000 signatures in support of the tsar's peace initiative. However, when the tsar then chose the Netherlands for the honourable role of host nation as well, De Beaufort wrote to Tets van Goudriaan: 'The prospect of a peace conference here rather fills me with mixed feelings.'[57]

De Beaufort was right in expecting difficulties with the organisation of the conference, as the Netherlands now had to bear the responsibility for the wishes of the great powers. Problems did indeed arise, particularly when De Beaufort decided not to invite the Boer republics and the pope, because of Britain and Italy respectively. The exclusion of the Boer republics, which caused vehement indignation in all political parties in the Netherlands, will be discussed more fully below. But it should perhaps be pointed out at this juncture that the Peace Conference gave cause not only for internationalism, but also for nationalism and even pillarisation. After all, Catholics seemed to be the only ones in the Netherlands to protest against the exclusion of the pope, and although Schaepman spoke on behalf of 'two-fifths of the Dutch population', the Netherlands as a whole formed – according to De Savornin Lohman – a 'Protestant nation' who were unable to see the pope as the 'prince of peace', let alone the 'head of Christianity'.[58]

When the Peace Conference convened in The Hague is spring 1899, the 'best' was already over for Kuyper and many other Dutchmen, because – quite apart from the exclusion of the Boer republics – it now seemed that the tsar's ideas for disarmament had been watered down quite considerably. The most important result of the conference, the setting up of a Permanent Court of Arbitration with its seat in The Hague, was only a very poor consolation as

56. Ibid., nos 342, 361, 431, 437, 43A*; ibid. VI, nos 4–5*. For the judicial decision and press reactions, see *IG*, 1897, I, pp. 515ff.

57. Smit, *Bescheiden* I, no. 10; cf. no. 3. Cf. Kamphuis, *Vredebond*, nos 164–7; Smit, *Nederland*, pp. 30ff.; Dülffer, *Regeln*, pp. 19ff.

58. *Handelingen Tweede Kamer* (Parliamentary Reports of the Second Chamber), 5 December 1899, pp. 595ff.

it had failed to become a real 'Aeropagus'.[59] Nevertheless, De Beaufort and the Dutch delegate Van Karnebeek felt that by helping with the organisation of the conference the Netherlands had at least succeeded in giving the introduction of international arbitration a 'little push'.[60] But many spokesmen did not find such a limited contribution satisfactory – especially when, shortly after the Peace Conference, the Boer War broke out. For the Liberal professor De Louter, the 'task of a small state' implied the active defence of international law whenever it was violated by any of the great powers, such as Britain. According to *De Standaard*, 'the smaller states can not spend their money better than by preaching international law', provided they did not fail to strengthen their defence at the same time. Apart from the defence and promotion of national unity, Boissevain especially emphasised the pacification and development of the colonies as the condition for a fruitful contribution to international law: 'We can fulfil our international obligations extremely well if we carry out our duty in the East Indies unselfishly and courageously.'[61]

This mixture of nationalism and internationalism, of power politics and ethical arguments, seemed to be typical of the Dutch *zeitgeist* at the turn of the century.[62] However, not all tendencies of public opinion were typical in this way, and articles in the *Vaderland* and *NRC*, for example, displayed far more modesty about the international significance of 'our little country'.[63] Socialist journalists such as Henriëtte Roland Holst and P. L. Tak criticised both the 'anachronism' of Dutch diplomacy and the 'megalomania' of nationalist intellectuals.[64] Among some Catholic intellectuals there was complete indifference towards 'the transitory clamour of world history'. 'It's only movement at the surface', commented *De Katho-*

---

59. See the sceptical commentaries in *De Standaard*, 17 April and 16 June, *De Amsterdammer* (weekly), 8 August, *De Sociaal-Demokraat*, 20 May, and *De Tijd*, 2 July 1899.
60. De Beaufort, *Vijftig jaren* I, pp. 216–18; *Handelingen Tweede Kamer* (Parliamentary Reports of the Second Chamber), 5 December 1899, pp. 604–7. For the Royal House and the Dutch contribution to the conference see also the papers and notes in the Asser Collection (ARA).
61. *Het Handelsblad*, 12 August 1900. Cf. *De Standaard*, 18 April 1900; De Louter, *Taak*, pp. 18–19.
62. Boogman, 'Netherlands', pp. 494–5; cf. Kossmann, *Lage landen*, p. 318.
63. *Het Vaderland*, 3 January 1898 and 24 November 1899; *NRC*, 25 and 26 November 1899.
64. H. Roland Holst, 'De balans van den Zuid-Afrikaanschen oorlog', *De Nieuwe Tijd*, 1900, pp. 261–2; P. L. Tak, 'Onze diplomatie', *De Kroniek*, 26 November 1899.

liek, 'a movement in which the waves keep overwhelming one another and being overwhelmed by one another; a movement where it makes very little difference which wave happens to be the highest for a little while.'[65]

A New Partition of Asia?

Western overseas expansion, however, continued to cause a lot of 'transitory clamour' in world history. Kuyper, who regularly reported on the 'partition of the world', stated in 1898 that the independent, still uncolonised areas were getting smaller each year. The expansionist urge of the competing great powers therefore shifted from Africa to Asia, that is, either to the remaining Asian States such as the Ottoman or Chinese empires, or the colonies of the weaker powers.[66] The powerful expansion of the United States and Japan was regarded by many observers as a new and potentially dangerous development. After all, whether directly or indirectly, the East Indies remained the focal point of Dutch interest in Asia.

The changes in the Asian context of the East Indies were clearly reflected in the relations between the Netherlands and Japan. By 1896, when the two countries finally agreed on a revision of the 'unfair treaties' of 1858 and 1864, their mutual power relations seem to have changed drastically. Japan had now become a strong modern power, both economically and with regard to its military forces, and since its victory over China it even had its own colonies and spheres of influence – a development which was observed with a mixture of admiration and concern in the Netherlands.[67] The trade agreement which Japan had concluded on an equal footing with Britain in 1894 was the beginning of growing co-operation between the two island empires and broke the deadlock which Dutch–Japanese negotiations had reached in the 1880s.[68] The initiative for a resumption of negotiations came from Japan, with the Anglo–Japanese treaty as the starting point. The Netherlands was to learn to its cost that Japan really meant business when it insisted on the

---

65. A. M. C. van Cooth, 'De toewijding van de twintigste eeuw, *De Katholiek*, 1901, p. 38.
66. *De Standaard*, 7 January 1898.
67. Ibid., 18 April 1895. Cf. Bijvanck's comment in *De Gids*, 1895, i, pp. 573–4.
68. Cf. Storry, *Japan*, pp. 21ff.; Araki, *Geschichte*, pp. 123ff.; Van Kleffens, *Betrekkingen*, pp. 151ff.

principle of reciprocity. With a view to the special position of the 'Foreign Orientials' in the East Indies and the revenue from customs tariffs, the Dutch Colonial Affairs Minister Bergsma tried as hard as possible to keep the East Indies outside the new contractual definitions. However, he was finally persuaded by his Foreign Affairs colleague, Röell, and also by the Committee for Trade Politics that Japanese subjects and products in the East Indies were not to be discriminated against.[69] This was explained very clearly in the explanatory memorandum of the relevant bill: 'However important . . . concessions to Japan may be, they generally only contain something which, in all fairness, would have been impossible to deny the empire in the long term, especially after the latest war in China and the far-reaching changes which have taken place as a result.'[70] The treaty was accepted by both Chambers without a division or public debate.

As soon as the treaty came into force in 1899, mutual trade was to increase quite considerably, both between the Netherlands and Japan and between Japan and the East Indies. As for the East Indies, however, there was relatively little concern about Japan's economic expansion. Although, under the new system of preferential treatment, there had been some spectacular growth in Japanese industry and shipping, the Dutch consul in Yokohama stated reassuringly that 'the majority of Japanese merchants were still far from being on the same level as the European ones.'[71] There was far more concern about Japan's territorial expansionism, after Russia seemed to have blocked off any opportunities for Japan's northern expansion. The Dutch representative in China, F. M. Knobel therefore warned that Japan might be taking 'an offensive attitude towards the South'.[72] In Batavia it was reasoned that 'if there is any danger for our East Indian empire, then it must come from Japan, which wants to and has to expand.' In 1897 Batavia almost gave way to panic when a number of Japanese colonists tried to establish themselves in New Guinea.[73] Meanwhile, the emergence of Japan had also given rise to

69. Woltring, *Bescheiden* VI, nos 48, 56, 82, 142; cf. the summary by Hannema, nos 183A–C.

70. *Bijlagen Handelingen Tweede Kamer* (Parliamentary Reports of the Second Chamber, Appendix) 1896–7, nos 150, 3.

71. *Consulaire Verslagen* (Consular Reports) 1899, pp. 608ff.; cf. H. S. M. van Wickevoort Crommelin, 'De opkomst der Japansche nijverheid', *De Economist*, 1896, I, pp. 476–84.

72. Woltring, *Bescheiden* VI, no. 104.

73. Ibid., no. 313A–B.

some concern in The Hague.[74] But all the excitement about a single private colonisation attempt was regarded as grossly exaggerated by the colonial and foreign affairs departments. 'A few planners who know nothing about the Dutch East Indies – *voilà tout*', was the laconic comment from foreign affairs.[75] The Anglo–Japanese entente of 1902, however, made a much greater impression on the Netherlands, and there were now doubts in government circles that the traditional British guarantee of Dutch colonial possessions could still be relied upon. But according to Knobel's successor in Peking, J. Loudon, the entente meant that there was now less of a chance that Japan would expand southwards.[76]

Meanwhile, after America had defeated Spain and occupied the Philippines in 1898, Knobel felt a little more at ease. With a view to Japan, he felt that the occupation was 'not unwelcome' because the weak and despised Spanish administration had been an unstable buffer. Tets van Goudriaan, on the other hand, would have preferred the Spanish in the Philippines to be replaced by some other European power, preferably Germany.[77] The fast emergence of the United States as a great imperial power was a controversial issue in the Netherlands, attracting more attention at first than the emergence of Japan at the same time. Those who were most resentful of the 'Yankees', 'the sharks of large-scale capitalism', were the Roman Catholics who unreservedly took sides with their European fellow Catholics. The 'brutal plundering' of the Spanish colonies was also seen as a dangerous precedent for the Dutch colonies. 'Me today, you tomorrow', warned *De Tijd*.[78] The same paper started a fierce controversy with the champions of the 'great republic', the *Handelsblad* and *De Standaard*.

Kuyper felt at first that the American intervention was 'perfectly justified' in view of the Spanish 'reign of terror' in Cuba and the Philippines. After the American annexations, however, he was to express himself rather less enthusiastically: 'It is a great pity that the glory of America's intervention should have been darkened by the

74. Ibid., no. 338; cf. Smit, *Bescheiden* VI, no. 129.

75. Woltring, *Bescheiden* VI, no. 313A; cf. no. 172. For the discussion in Japan on whether to expand northwards or southwards, see Iriye, *Estrangement*, pp. 57–60.

76. Smit, *Bescheiden* I, no. 595; ibid. II, nos 157–9; ibid. VI, no. 129. For Kuyper's reaction in *De Standaard*, see note 41 above.

77. Woltring, *Bescheiden* IV, nos 465 and 512, note 1. Cf. Dobson, *Ascent*, pp. 97ff.; Miller, *Assimilation*, pp. 13ff.

78. *De Tijd*, 23 April, 12–13 and 23–5 May 1898. Cf. *De Maasbode*, 6, 9 and 26 April 1898; *Het Centrum*, 21 and 23 April 1898.

blood-stained glow of an objectionable *expansion* policy!'[79] Boisse-vain, too, believed that the intervention had been the outcome of 'the wrath of the American people', rather than 'at the instigation of Wall Street'.[80] Socialists, on the other hand, were convinced of the opposite from the very beginning. 'You can feel capital interests and yet more capital interests sneering at you everywhere', commented the *Sociaal-Demokraat*. But, as such, Tak felt it was 'no reason for distress' that the cruel Spanish regime had been driven out.[81]

In government circles reactions to the American–Spanish war were equally ambivalent: 'One cannot really wish victory on either of them', the Liberal Prime Minister Pierson wrote in his diary.[82] Both in The Hague and Batavia there were many who wondered what consequences the American occupation of the Philippines might have for the East Indies. The recent attempt of Standard Oil to take over a small Dutch oil company seemed to bode ill. For Governor-general Van der Wijck it was quite obvious 'in which direction those Yankee gentlemen are beginning to dream'.[83]

Partly because of fast and decisive action by Van der Wijck and minister Cremer, it was possible to frustrate Standard Oil's move, as we shall see later in this chapter. Compared with the largely passive attitude of the 1880s, this active defence was typical of Dutch reaction patterns in the 1890s. The magazine *De Tijd* even advo-cated closer co-operation with other European powers, based on common interests in Asia, 'interests which must be defended both against younger rivals such as North America, who have no sense of belonging to the old world or any historical past, and against Islam and a possible flood of Asian barbarity'.[84]

The spread of the pan-Islamic movement from the Turkish Em-pire was regarded as a threat by the Dutch government. As more and more East Indian pilgrims to Mecca decided not to return, it was made clear to the Sublime Porte that the Netherlands would not recognise the one-sided naturalisation of 'Dutch–East Indian sub-jects'.[85] When the new Turkish consul-general in Batavia in 1898 was clearly seen to be spending his time on pan-Islamic propaganda,

79. *De Standaard*, 6 January 1899; cf. 1, 2 and 6 June 1898.
80. *Het Handelsblad*, 13 and 17 April 1898. *NRC* and *Het Vaderland* were far more sceptical towards the American action. Cf. note 106.
81. *De Kroniek*, 8 May 1898; cf. *De Sociaal-Demokraat*, 27 April 1989.
82. Pierson's diary of 24 April 1898, Pierson Collection.
83. Van der Wijck to Cremer, 26 July 1898, Van der Wijck Collection (ARA).
84. *De Tijd*, 23 April 1989; cf. 14 October.
85. Woltring, *Bescheiden* VI, nos 107–8, 154–5, 168–9.

he was replaced immediately.[86] Traditional mistrust towards Turkey was further corroborated in connection with the East Indies by the persecution of Armenians and other Christian groups within the Turkish Empire. The Turkish participation in The Hague Peace Conference therefore caused a good deal of indignation among Anti-Revolutionaries and Catholics. Meanwhile the Dutch government had already sent a warship to the coast of Asia Minor several times, whenever political unrest seemed to be threatening the lives and property of Dutch nationals.[87]

Dutch interest in China also had a defensive, colonial background. During the 1890s the traditional East Indian 'fear of the Chinese' became linked to the more recent international fear of the 'yellow danger'.[88] At the same time there were increasing demands to provide sufficient security for Dutch and East Indian interests in China, both in trade and particularly in the recruitment of contract labour – if necessary by acquiring territorial military bases. Although such aspirations were forcefully promoted by Dutch representatives in China and met with support among parts of the general public in the Netherlands and the East Indies, they were hardly shared by the government in The Hague. The development of Dutch relations with China 'between neutrality and imperialism' have already been sufficiently described and analysed by the Dutch scholar Van Dongen.[89] In the following paragraphs we shall therefore only deal with the most important options and most relevant protagonists.

Knobel, the Dutch representative in China from 1895 to 1901, came from a simple background and had made a career in foreign affairs via the consular service. In his previous post in Tehran he had proved to be particularly ambitious in promoting Dutch trade interests.[90] He continued his activities in China, and indeed not unsuccessfully, as there was a noticeable increase in Dutch trade relations with China in the 1890s.[91] However, even more important

---

86. Ibid., nos 384A–B, 476, 479.

87. Ibid., nos 101, 109A, 219 and 221A. Cf. *De Standaard*, 17 June and 6 July. *De Tijd*, 9 July 1899.

88. G. A. Römer, 'Chineezenvrees in Indië', *Vragen des Tijds*, 1897, II, pp. 193–224, 289–327. Cf. *De Standaard*, 13 January 1896, 22 July 1900; *De Tijd*, 10 August 1899. For views outside the Netherlands see Gollwitzer, *Gelbe Gefahr*.

89. Van Dongen, *Neutraliteit*, pp. 193ff.

90. Ibid., pp. 195–6. Cf. *Consulaire verslagen* (Consular Reports) 1891, no. 54; ibid. 1893, no. 125.

91. Ibid., 1899, pp. 487–9; ibid. 1900, pp. 311–13.

than the modest amount of trade was the recruitment of contract labour in southern China on behalf of the export plantations and of mining in the East Indies. Around 1890 the Netherlands had, though with difficulty, been able to consolidate these colonial interests. When China was gradually divided in spheres of influence between the great powers after its defeat by Japan, Knobel felt that the colonial and commercial interests of the Netherlands were greatly jeopardised. As Van Dongen has shown, there were now three political options for the Netherlands: to promote an 'open door' policy in China; to associate with one of the great powers in whose sphere of influence Dutch interests could then be secured; or to acquire its own sphere of influence.[92]

In The Hague preference was of course given to the first option, though it turned out to be difficult to put into practice. After all, British and American endeavours to keep an 'open door' in China were resisted by the other great powers, and if the Netherlands had supported this option, it might have endangered its neutral position. Close co-operation with one of the great powers, for instance Germany, was therefore equally impossible for The Hague. Against this background Knobel suggested that the Netherlands should act independently in China. 'As the Netherlands has now become genuinely active in the East Indies', he declared in 1898, 'the time seems to have come, more than ever before . . . to acquire a voice for ourselves in the Far East.' Minister De Beaufort, however, did not want to know about an active Dutch role and placed the envoy in Peking under an obligation to observe 'the most scrupulous impartiality and neutrality'.[93] Nor did the idea find favour that the Netherlands should acquire a concession for the 'coolie warehouse' of Swatow, although plans had already been worked out by the Dutch consul in Hong Kong. 'The Netherlands already has very large colonial possessions,' said De Beaufort, 'and it has to make every effort in order to maintain and secure these.'[94]

Knobel's ideas, however, were welcomed in several colonial, commercial and academic circles in the Netherlands – partly as a result of a very outspoken *Gids* article he had written.[95] In government circles Cremer seemed less disinclined towards Knobel's proposals than his colleague, the Foreign Minister. Indeed, Cremer

92. Van Dongen, *Neutraliteit*, pp. 199ff.
93. Woltring, *Bescheiden* VI, no. 393.
94. Ibid., no. 395; cf. no. 381A.
95. K(nobel), 'Ook met het oog op Indië', *De Gids*, 1899, iii, pp. 467–73.

was the one who offered the least 'opposition on principle' against active participation in the military intervention of the great powers during the Boxer Rebellion of 1900.[96] The government decided to send a squadron of warships from the East Indies to China, though for the time being without taking military action. Even De Beaufort felt that 'some display of power' was desirable, 'in view of our position as a great colonial power in Asia.'[97] But it soon turned out that Knobel had survived the siege of Peking, so that the Dutch forces did not need to take action, to the great relief of the ministers in The Hague. Knobel was subsequently authorised to sign the collective memorandum of the great powers whereby China was made to pay damages. This, however, was subject to the proviso that the Netherlands would not take part in punitive military measures, should these become necessary. Eventually, neutrality got the better of imperialism, even though this neutrality was more a matter of pragmatism than principle.[98]

This does not alter the fact that there were a number of voices in the Netherlands that demanded tough military action during the Boxer Rebellion, if necessary by occupying territorial bases in China. 'Now or never', declared Kuyper during the rebellion. He had already suggested that the Dutch government should find out 'if there were still some old documents in the archives which can be used successfully . . . in order to revive our old rights.'[99] The *Handelsblad* repeatedly published articles demanding a Dutch extra-territorial concession in China, particularly by the sinologist and former vice-president of the East Indian Council, W. P. Groeneveldt, the director of a large shipping company E. Heldring and the officer O. van Beresteijn.[100] Similar views could be heard in the Dutch Geographical Society, where Groeneveldt had been chairman since 1897.[101] In Catholic circles, too, decisive action was at first advocated, because of the large number of Roman Catholic

96. Cremer was particularly concerned about the lack of winter clothing for the soldiers from the East Indies; Pierson to De Beaufort, 3 August 1900, De Beaufort Collection, Cf. Woltring, *Bescheiden* VI, no. 512.

97. Smit, *Bescheiden* I, no. 231; cf. 233 and 251.

98. Ibid., no. 367. Cf. Van Dongen, *Neutraliteit*, p. 353.

99. *Handelingen Tweede Kamer* (Parliamentary Reports of the Second Chamber), 22 November 1899, p. 415. Cf. *De Standaard*, 30 June 1900.

100. *Het Handelsblad*, 13 and 20 June, 22 August, 5, 7 and 18 September 1900.

101. J. J. le Roy, 'De staatkundige verhouding van het hedendaagsche China tot de buitenwereld', *TAG*, 1900, p. 141; C. Kraay, 'Reisindrukken uit Oost Azie', ibid., pp. 149–50; G. Schlegel, 'De oorsprong van den vremdenhaat der Chineezen', ibid., pp. 803–4.

missionaries in China, some of whom were indeed killed during the rebellion. However, *De Tijd* soon joined the *NRC* in distancing itself from pleas for imperialism in China. According to *Net Volk*, the limited participation of the Netherlands in international interventionism had already gone too far.[102] And in the Dutch Parliament the cautious policies of the government were accepted by a large majority. 'There is a lot of talk about kinship with the Boers,' commented the *Indische Gids* with a note of sadness, 'but if the national honour is violated anywhere, as is happening in Peking at the moment, then the public remains completely calm and the press praises the government measures.'[103] After 1900 there was also less danger that China would be divided up, and Dutch interest further diminished.

Intervention and Non-Intervention in South America

Shortly after the 'Chinese riots' the Netherlands was confronted with another choice between neutrality and imperialism, this time in connection with the Venezuelan crisis of 1902–3. Although the Dutch government finally decided not to take part in the intervention by the great powers, it did not pursue a strict policy of neutrality either. Dutch relations with Venezuela and other countries in the Caribbean were to a large extent determined by the emerging activities of the United States. As in Asia, this new international situation had caused apprehension about the vulnerability of Dutch colonial possessions, although in South America, of course, considerably less was at stake.

Long before the outbreak of the Spanish–American War the United States had already demanded a special position for itself in South America, based on the Monroe Doctrine. This almost certainly met with understanding and even sympathy in the Netherlands. 'This is the declaration of the emancipation of a new part of the world, the declaration of the greatness of the United States', Bijvanck commented on the Monroe Doctrine, after America had taken a successful stand against Britain in the Venezuelan crisis of 1895.[104]

102. *Het Volk*, 3 July, 31 August, 8 October 1900. Cf. *NRC*, 22 August and 14 November 1900. *De Tijd*, 10 and 12 September 1900.

103. *Indische Gids*, 1900, II, p. 1246. Cf. Van Dongen, *Neutraliteit*, pp. 291–2, 317–18.

104. 'Monroe-doctrine', *De Gids*, 1896, i, p. 205; cf. Tak, 'De Monroe-leer', *De Kroniek*, 26 January 1896. See also Wehler, *Aufstieg*, pp. 157ff.; Dobson, *Ascent*, pp. 77ff.

For many observers, however, the slogan *America for the Americans* acquired dubious overtones when, after the American victory over Spain in 1898, the United States annexed Puerto Rico, made Cuba a *de facto* protectorate and started looking for new military bases in the Caribbean. As we saw above, American intervention was mainly condemned by Dutch Catholics and defended by Anti-Revolutionaries and some Liberals. The Catholic press saw the Monroe Doctrine as no more than a front for American imperialism which formed a direct threat to the Dutch colonies – both in the West and in the East.[105] But there were a number of Liberals who became equally sceptical and concerned. The expert in international law and chairman of the Peace Alliance, J. B. Breukelman, sharply criticised the 'expansive interpretation of the Monroe Doctrine' and felt that a joint protest by the European nations was appropriate.[106] The government was above all apprehensive that the Dutch Antilles might get involved in the Spanish–American War, because of the lively trade in weapons and contraband goods going on in those parts. The Netherlands had immediately and emphatically declared its neutrality and an extra warship was sent to the West to ensure that this declaration was respected.[107]

After the Spanish–American War, concern about the position of the Dutch Antilles persisted, as the United States was now trying to establish more and more military bases in the Caribbean, and taking a particular interest in the colonies of the small European powers. In 1901, prompted by the American–Danish negotiations over the sale of the Danish Virgin Islands, the American ambassador in Caracas approached his Dutch colleague about a similar transaction that would involve the Dutch Antilles.[108] From a Dutch point of view, this was out of the question, though American interests could not be ignored completely. This became obvious in the international crisis about Venezuela. The supposed American threat further reinforced the dilemma between intervention and non-intervention for the Dutch policy makers.

The most prominent advocate of tough Dutch action against Venezuela, the head of the first foreign affairs division J. J. Rochussen, felt that intervention was necessary in view of Dutch pos-

---

105. *De Tijd*, 15 April and 3 September 1898; cf. *Maasbode*, 29 May, and *Het Centrum*, 1 September 1898.
106. *Vaderland*, 19, 27 and 30 April; cf. *NRC*, 25 April, 1 May and 20 September 1898.
107. Woltring, *Bescheiden* VI, nos 423, 438, 444.
108. Smit, *Bescheiden* I, no. 453.

sessions in the West Indies, and he warned against giving an impression of 'indolence and a feeling of powerlessness' if the Netherlands didn't intervene. His opponent S. Hannema, head of the foreign trade division and – soon afterwards – secretary-general of the Department of Foreign Affairs, felt that American interest in a military base was precisely a reason for remaining aloof: 'As soon as we do anything at all or they let us do anything, we will be asked for such a military base as compensation.' Despite Rochussen's objections to such a submissive attitude towards the United States, Hannema's point of view finally prevailed. The Dutch government did, however, decide to send a couple of warships to the West Indies, though not without notifying the American government in advance. This was simply meant to show Washington 'that we value our colonies'.[109]

Otherwise, it was the same old song with Venezuela. Dutch–Venezuelan relations, severed in the crisis of 1875, had only just been resumed again in 1894 when yet another crisis announced itself. Due to the familiar controversy between the Dutch government and Parliament as to whether a representative in Venezuela should have diplomatic or consular status, A. F. van Leyden had just been appointed consul-general and chargé d'affaires to Caracas. He subsequently reported that there was growing internal unrest in Venezuela, an increasing number of shipping incidents, refusals to pay debts and finally a unilateral declaration of Venezuelan jurisdiction over all international debts.

At the end of 1902 Germany, Britain and Italy decided, after consultation with the United States, to make a military blockade of all Venezuelan ports. Germany acted particularly aggressively.[110] As the shipping incidents had also involved Curaçao and Dutch vessels, there was enough reason, according to Rochussen, for the Netherlands to take part in the international blockade. Hannema, however, pointed out that such a hard line had yielded very few financial and economic results in the past, and – partly for the sake of foreign trade – the Dutch government decided not to intervene.[111] But when foreign debts were finally dealt with after the blockade, the Netherlands still got the worst of it.[112] Although

---

109. Ibid., no. 612; cf. the exchange of notes between Rochussen and Hannema, nos 605–10.

110. Cf. Corporaal, *Betrekkingen*, pp. 238ff.; Hood, *Gunboat Diplomacy*, pp. 163ff.

111. Smit, *Bescheiden* I, nos 645–6, 653.

112. Corporaal, *Betrekkingen*, pp. 403ff.

it had not actively participated in the blockade, it had co-operated quite considerably in the practicalities of it, which the Venezuelan government had not failed to notice. The customary Dutch declaration of neutrality had even been set aside so that Germany could use Curaçao as a refuelling station for its squadron. According to Smit, this had been done at Kuyper's instigation.[113] Inasmuch as Dutch MPs and the general public showed any interest in the Venezuelan issue at all, the international blockade was received rather critically. Only in Catholic circles was there any understanding for the armed action of the great powers. Nobody, however, advocated Dutch participation.[114]

Africa after the Partition

With the exception of the Boer War, not many Dutch people still showed much interest in Africa around the year 1900. In 1893, the aged Veth wrote in his survey of three centuries that the Netherlands had 'actually played a very important role in Africa and had a significant part in the unveiling of this part of the world'.[115] And indeed he gave 'many glorious reminiscences' from earlier centuries, though without mentioning the slave trade even once. Involuntarily, however, the last decades of his account were mainly about territorial cessions, failed expeditions and trade conflicts.

The well-known statement that trade always follows the flag had acquired some unpleasant overtones for the Netherlands in Africa. First, after the cession of Elmina, Dutch trade with the Gold Coast had largely disappeared altogether. And now the consolidation of the Congo Free State was leading to the demise of the Dutch trading empire in Central Africa, too. Dutch trade in Africa could only survive the partition of Africa by concentrating on less lucrative areas such as Liberia and the Portuguese colonies instead. Between 1890 and 1900 the overall value of Dutch imports from the entire West Coast of Africa dropped from 8.1 to 4.4 million guilders, and exports from 3.8 to 3.1 million guilders.[116]

---

113. Smit, *Nederland*, pp. 18, 210. Cf. *Bescheiden* I, nos 668–9, 673.

114. Corporaal, *Betrekkingen*, pp. 371, 404. Cf. *De Tijd*, 11–14 December; *De Standaard*, 15 and 17 December, *NRC*, 18 and 28 December; *Het Volk*, 7, 12 and 24 December 1902.

115. P. J. Veth, 'De Nederlanders in Afrika', *TAG*, 1893, pp. 240–95.

116. *Jaarcijfers*, 1900, pp. 168–9, *Verslag KvK Rotterdam* (Report of the Rotterdam Chamber of Commerce) 1900, pp. 190–1.

As expected, the Congo Free State authorities did indeed use the decisions of the 1890 anti-slavery conference in order to keep Dutch traders out of the Congo basin. In 1891 the Dutch consul and general NAHV agent J. Gresshoff was in fact expelled from the Free State and the main factory of the company in Kinshassa remained closed for a while. At first the protests of the NAHV met with sympathy in the Dutch press and Parliament. But the Minister for Foreign Affairs did not go any further than requesting an explanation from Brussels.[117] Although nobody was particularly pleased with the protectionist trade policies of the Free State, the Department of Foreign Affairs appears to have given up Dutch trading interests rather quickly.[118]

When a new conference was set up in Brussels in 1898, in order to readjust the 1890 agreements, it seemed at first as if the Netherlands was going to be passed over, since it no longer had any sovereignty rights in Africa. De Beaufort reacted rather laconically to the possible exclusion of the Netherlands, despite the trading interests in the Congo that were still pending. 'Our interest is hardly of a highly moral nature,' he commented on the gin exports from Schiedam, 'and I am therefore rather reluctant to fight this issue with any great vehemence.' Owing to the mediation of the German government, the Netherlands was eventually invited after all, though during the conference in 1899 the Dutch representative only objected to the new increase in alcohol import duties as a matter of form.[119]

Apart from the declining Congo trade, direct trouble with Africa was only caused by a number of shipping incidents in the 1890s. When Moroccan Riff Kabyles held up and plundered a Dutch schooner, the Dutch government immediately sent out a warship. The instructions stipulated that 'the chastisement in the given case shall consist in shooting at the villages and hamlets which were involved ... in the hold-up and which are to be specified more closely, but there will be no question of landing and occupying one or more points along the coast.' In order to spare innocent women and children, the shooting was to be announced clearly and well in

117. *Handelingen Tweede Kamer* (Parliamentary Reports of the Second Chamber), 2 and 3 December 1891, pp. 280–3, 304. Cf. F. de Bas, 'Een Nederlandsch reiziger aan den Congo', *TAG*, 1895, pp. 538–72, 657–727; Woltring, *Bescheiden* V, nos 13, 34, 37, 79, 106, 171, 173.

118. Ibid. VI, nos 8 and 18.

119. Ibid., no. 425; cf. nos 375, 436, 455, 460, 510. See also Miers, *Britain*, pp. 308–9.

advance. However, according to the German ambassador who mediated for the Netherlands in this matter, one could not do business in Morocco in such a humanitarian way. The Dutch government was already wondering whether to send a real punitive expedition instead, when the Sultan of Morocco himself suggested paying damages. Having arrived at the Moroccan coast, the Dutch warship could confine itself to a peaceful showing of the flag.[120] Shortly afterwards, a Dutch freight ship called the Poelwijk was captured by the Italian navy in the Red Sea on the grounds that it was carrying contraband goods to Ethiopia. But after the Italian defeat at Adowa in 1896 the Dutch government had little trouble in achieving the release of the ship.[121]

In general, the operations of the great powers and the partitioning of the remaining independent parts of Africa were followed simply with dismay in the Netherlands. The British advances in Sudan and the confrontation with France at Fashoda in 1898 mainly attracted attention because of the implications of British expansionist endeavours 'from the Cape to Cairo' for the Boer republics in the south.[122] In the meantime the Dutch government wanted to be as little involved as possible in the dénouement of the partition. In 1896 Röell categorically rejected the possibility of Dutch participation in police action in Egypt, even though the Netherlands had fourth place as users of the Suez Canal. 'Quite frankly,' he said to Tets van Goudriaan, 'it is my conviction that we must concentrate on *keeping* and further developing the East Indies and that we must not take on any other task. This is why I have always been an *interested* and *sympathetic* observer in the Transvaal and no more.'[123]

Trade and the Colonies around 1900

The year 1900 saw the publication of a book by D. Wanjon on the history of Dutch trade since 1795. It showed a picture of continuous progress, especially since the introduction of free trade in the 1850s and 1860s. Between 1871 and 1898 Dutch imports (of consumer

---

120. Woltring, *Bescheiden* VI, nos 51, 54, 59, 64, 66.

121. Ibid., nos 190, 192–8, 201–2, 208, 242.

122. F. Beelaerts van Blokland, 'Egypte en de expeditie naar Khartoem', *De Gids*, 1897, ii, pp. 342–5; Bijvanck, 'De opening van de deur', ibid. 1899, i, pp. 386–90; *De Standaard*, 3 November 1898 and 16 January 1899.

123. Woltring, *Bescheiden* VI, no. 146.

Table 1 Comparative Values of Imports and Exports of Major
Trading Partners

	position in 1898	position in 1871	value in 1898 (in million guilders)	value in 1871 (in million guilders)
Imports (consumer goods)				
Prussia	1	2	313	104
United States	2	6	279	26
Britain	3	1	269	195
Dutch East Indies	4	3	261	80
Belgium	5	4	209	79
British India	7	8	261	80
Brazil	12	—	21	—
Peru and Bolivia	13	9	21	6
Turkey	16	16	8	2
West Africa	17	17	4	2
Exports (from free traffic)				
Prussia	1	1	788	183
Britain	2	2	338	112
Belgium	3	3	161	65
Dutch East Indies	4	4	64	31
United States	5	10	44	4
Turkey	10	9	6	5
West Africa	15	19	3	1
British India	16	20	2	0.5

Source: D. Wanjon, *Geschiedenis van den Nederlandschen handel Sedert 1795*, Haarlem 1900, pp. 78, 194.

goods) had risen from 587 million to 1,796 million guilders, and exports (from free trade) from 587 million to 1,516 million guilders. In a survey which can only be reproduced here in part, Wanjon had established a comparative order of the twenty most important trading partners (see table 1).

The results were especially reassuring for all those who had expected far-reaching changes for Dutch commerce from the opening of the Suez Canal, the increase in steamships, the extension of European colonial possessions, the introduction of free trade and other developments around 1870. The most important shifts had occurred within Europe itself, particularly between Britain and

Germany. The emergence of the United States as a major power was equally striking, but on the whole trade outside Europe displayed a very stable pattern. In the area of foreign trade the Netherlands had apparently survived modern imperialism very well indeed – both in its own colonies and in those of other countries. It is worth noting in this context that the Dutch East Indies and British India had a very stable position in the list.[124]

Obviously, this dichotomy between 1871 and 1898 in Wanjon's survey did not show the fluctuations and shifts which had occurred in the intervening period, particularly with regard to global newcomers such as West Africa or Peru and Bolivia. Trade with tropical Africa had generally been more significant during the 1880s, while trade with Latin America did not begin to grow until the 1890s. Furthermore, actual trade with the overseas world in 1898 was far more extensive than shown by the trade statistics. Trade with Argentina, Egypt and China, for example, mainly proceeded via ports outside the Netherlands.[125]

This situation, however, had already improved when Dutch shipping began to recover from its malaise of the 1870s and 1880s. Between 1872 and 1897 the proportion of steamships in the tonnage of the Dutch merchant navy rose from 15 to 80 per cent, while the total number of actual steamships had risen from 52 in 1870 to 176 in 1898.[126] With 30 steamships in 1897 the Royal Packet Company played an important role in the restoration of Dutch shipping and naval engineering, mainly with their packet ships in the Archipelago, but soon also through its foreign lines, particularly the Java–China–Japan line which was opened in 1902. The KPM now increasingly handled the East Indian trade, as Singapore-based companies were soon to find out to their cost.[127]

In 1900 the share of the overseas world outside the East Indies was 8.8 per cent of imports and 1.4 per cent of exports, compared with 4.4 and 2.3 in 1870. Although the number of consuls had reached about 500 and had thus more than doubled since 1870, the reform of the consular service continued to be a constant concern in the Netherlands. As well as the Chambers of Commerce and the

124. Wanjon, *Geschiedenis*, pp. 78 and 194. For trade with British India, see *Consulaire verslagen* (Consular Reports) 1898, pp. 79–111, 395–405.
125. Ibid., pp. 683–7, 822–6, 883–5.
126. Wanjon, *Geschiedenis*, pp. 116–120. Cf. De Jonge, *Industrialisatie*, pp. 148ff.; De Boer, *Honderd jaar*, pp. 147ff.; De Vries, *Herinneringen* I, pp. 107ff.
127. *Halve eeuw*, pp. 66. Cf. *Consulaire verslagen* (Consular Reports) 1902, pp. 34 and 41.

Liberal MPs J. A. van Gilse and E. E. van Raalte, the Social
Democrat MP J. H. A. S. Schaper strongly advocated such a
reform.[128] Meanwhile the share of the Dutch East Indies in imports
to the Netherlands had gone down from 15.9 per cent in 1870 to
13.8 per cent, and exports from the Netherlands to the East Indies
from 7.9 per cent to 3.8 per cent. The share of the Netherlands in
East Indian trade had gone down from 77 per cent in 1870 to 38 per
cent for exports and from 41 to 36 per cent for imports.[129]

Nevertheless, the Dutch East Indies continued to be far more
important for the Netherlands than all the other overseas markets
put together. Whenever colonial interests clashed with other overseas interests, the former were chosen without hesitation. This was
true not only for the cautious foreign affairs ministers, but also for
energetic ministers of colonial affairs such as Cremer, who had no
objections at all 'that we should continue to play a powerful role in
other countries'. However, the pacification of Acheh and the development of the Archipelago were considered even more important.
'Both in industry and commerce', said Cremer in 1898, 'it is still felt
that the Netherlands is a small nation whose resources are naturally
to a large extent used by its extensive colonies.[130] For foreign trade
this concentration on the East Indies meant that there were two
permanent areas of concern: keeping foreign markets open for East
Indian export products; and staving off foreign competitors from
strategic sectors in the colonial economy.

At a time of growing protectionism and increasing competition it
was not always easy to sell East Indian sugar, coffee and tobacco.
Sugar plantations, in particular, went through a very hard time
during the 1890s. In view of the difficult international position of
Javanese sugar, the Second Chamber agreed unanimously in 1898
that minister Cremer's idea should be accepted and that export
duties should definitely be abolished. In the Netherlands a lot of
value was therefore attached to the international conference on
sugar subsidies which convened in Brussels in 1898. It was only
after the 1903 Sugar Convention, when the worst forms of preferential treatment were abolished, that the Dutch sugar trade began to

128. *Handelingen Tweede Kamer* (Parliamentary Reports of the Second Chamber), 6 December 1900, pp. 377–8; cf. ibid., 14, 15 and 19 February 1901, pp. 966ff.
See also *Verslag KvK Amsterdam* (Report of the Amsterdam Chamber of Commerce) 1893, pp. 340–5; ibid. 1900, pp. 42–426; ibid., *Rotterdam*, 1901, pp. 22–4.
129. See appendix 3; cf. Burger, *Geschiedenis* II, pp. 82 and 84.
130.Woltring, *Bescheiden* VI, no. 512.

recover again. There was even a new heyday for Javanese sugar.[131] The United States was a particularly awkward customer and indeed not even represented at the Brussels conference. Since the introduction of the McKinley tariff in 1890 the Dutch ambassador in Washington had constantly had to contend with 'the powerful "sugar trust"' which was trying to get Congress to impose ever-increasing supplementary taxes on East Indian sugar'.[132] In order to maintain a certain measure of reciprocity the Dutch government itself threatened to raise import duties on American petroleum in the East Indies.[133] Javanese sugar continued to be heavily taxed in the United States, although no truly prohibitive measures were taken.

In turn, the Dutch authorities and parties concerned increasingly saw the Americans as dangerous competitors in the Dutch colonies. The Dutch government and Parliament were generally able to resist the temptation of reintroducing protection in the East Indies. The most prominent pressure group, the Association of and for Dutch Industrialists had broken up at the beginning of the 1890s. Protectionism, however, continued, particularly in Christian circles. Partly with a view to the colonies, Kuyper advocated a tariff reform, 'not in the sense of extreme protection but quite certainly in the form of countervailing duties'.[134] In practice, however, the policies of Liberal and Christian ministers were largely a matter of protecting individual key sectors against foreign domination. This is why the KPM was entrusted with packet shipping in 1889 and why its contract was extended in 1899.

It was for the same reason that minister Cremer and Governor-general Van der Wijck temporarily interfered when Standard Oil were trying to get into the promising oil production in Sumatra. At the beginning of 1898 Van der Wijck warned from Batavia that Standard Oil had made an agreement with the small Dutch company Moeara Enim. In The Hague Cremer then took the necessary steps to 'stop the St.O.C., from doing to its Dutch East Indian competitors what it has done in America'.[135] Under considerable pressure from Cremer and several 'national thinking' entrepreneurs such as

131. Idema, *Geschiedenis*, pp. 109–10; Burger, *Geschiedenis* II, pp. 78–81. Cf. N. P. van den Berg, 'Over suikerpremiën en suikerrechten', *De Economist*, 1900, I, pp. 18–39; Woltring, *Bescheiden* VI, no. 463.
132. Ibid., nos 346ff.; cf. nos 29 and 375.
133. Ibid., nos 291–3, 302, 307 and 335.
134. *De Standaard*, 19 and 21 December 1900. Cf. De Jonge, *Industrialisatie*, p. 332.
135. Cremer to Van der Wijck, 4 March 1898; cf. Van der Wijck to Cremer,

the banker B. Heldring and the KPM manager L. P. D. op ten Noort, the Moeara Enim management finally yielded and the agreement with Standard Oil was cancelled. It was the American ambassador's turn to protest to the Dutch government about discrimination against American interests.[136] In this matter, however, the Dutch government had the full support of the general public – and even the Socialists. 'The invasion of American monopolists is certainly a danger to . . . the permanence of our colonial power', said Tak, who also felt that the local population was worse off under 'Yankee exploitation' than under the Dutch colonial system. However, he was also convinced that after preventing the Standard Oil coup the danger was by no means over. 'Petroleum in our colonial possessions could be the same as gold in the Transvaal: the end of peace.'[137]

Expansion in the Archipelago

Keeping and Developing the East Indies

During the Boer War Tak's ominous comparison was also made by other observers in the Netherlands. However, it did not come to anything like that in the East Indies. In fact, like other small oil companies Moeara Enim soon merged with the larger Royal Dutch Oil Company that had been founded in 1890 by pioneering oil contractors from the East Indies, colonial and commercial bankers from Amsterdam, and some Liberal MPs and former colonial officials from The Hague. The production of oil became one of the most important sources of development in the Archipelago and in many people's eyes a corner-stone of Dutch rule.

After all, Cremer believed that a prosperous and contented population was the most important guarantee for keeping the East Indies. Indeed, he stated that he no longer feared 'clashes' with other countries, because the borders between Borneo and New Guinea had finally been marked out.[138] In private he added a number of

---

4 February 1898, Van der Wijck Collection.

136. Cremer to Van der Wijck, 15 April 1898, Van der Wijck Collection. See also Gerretson, *Geschiedenis* II, pp. 60ff.; Woltring, *Bescheiden* VI, nos 401, 409, 420, 437.

137. 'Moeara Enim', *De Kroniek*, 28 February 1898.

138. *Handelingen Tweede Kamer* (Parliamentary Reports of the Second Chamber), 21 November 1900, pp. 399–401.

other reasons, such as the rivalry between the different great powers, who would never want to allow each other to possess the East Indies, and the successful pacification of Acheh, which resulted in increased prestige for the Netherlands, both within and outside the Archipelago.[139] Foreign Minister Röell's advice to 'concentrate on keeping and further developing the East Indies' was successfully carried out in the 1890s.[140] In the Netherlands it formed the basis of colonial co-operation between Liberals and clericals and one of the most important starting points for its 'Ethical Policy'.

Although not everyone shared Cremer's publicly announced confidence in the security of the formal borders of the Dutch East Indies, there can be no doubt that these borders were now more secure than in the 1880s. However, as soon as the borders in Borneo had been settled with Britain in 1891, there was the problem of the openness of New Guinea's borders. These had given rise to British complaints about attacks from the Papuan population who lived in the officially Dutch but in fact unoccupied part of the island. In 1892 the Dutch government started negotiations with Britain in order to achieve a satisfactory definition of the Borneo borders and the Dutch East Indian colonial administration established a temporary colonial post in New Guinea, after it had sent the usual warship for the 'chastisement' of the Papuans.

In 1895 the British and Dutch governments came to an agreement, which was subsequently approved by the Dutch Parliament without a discussion or vote.[141] However, at the end of 1897 there was some controversy over government plans to turn the temporary colonial post into a permanent one. Such a permanent post had been repeatedly requested by the missionaries of the Utrecht Missionary Association, and minister Cremer therefore defended it 'on humanitarian grounds'.[142]

External power-political reasons, however, seem to have played a greater role than simply the promotion of 'civilisation' among the Papuans. In 1897 a Japanese colonisation plan had already given rise to the fear that 'a stream of Japanese' would flood into New Guinea. Although this fear was not shared by the Dutch government, it was

139. Cremer to Van der Wijck, 28 June 1898, Van der Wijck Collection. Cf. Woltring, *Bescheiden* VI, no. 512; Smit, ibid. VI, no. 49.
140. These were Röell's words, see note 123 above.
141. Van der Veur, *Documents*, pp. 86ff.; cf. Woltring, *Bescheiden* V, nos 282, 291, 403, 408–9.
142. *Handelingen Tweede Kamer* (Parliamentary Reports of the Second Chamber), 19 November 1897, p. 175.

nevertheless concerned about possible Japanese outposts near New Guinea. Not surprisingly therefore, there was a sudden surge of interest in the insignificant Mapia Islands north of New Guinea, for which the international status seemed to be in doubt. Even De Beaufort strongly recommended that the Netherlands should show the flag regularly, to 'prevent Japan, for example, from declaring itself master of these islands'.[143] In the Second Chamber, the establishment of a permanent colonial administration was contested by left-wing Liberals and socialists who argued that, with so much international interest in the area, one would risk turning it into a 'second Acheh' or a 'new hornets' nest'. However, the bill was passed by 49 votes to 23.[144] Meanwhile, the border with the German section of New Guinea had been more or less determined as a result of the existing Anglo–Dutch and Anglo–German treaties, and in 1902 talks with Germany began which would redefine these borders.[145]

As a large number of great powers were directly or indirectly affected, the Dutch government was extremely cautious in dealing with the various border issues, but at first it showed considerably less consideration towards Portugal, in the case of Timor. Based on an agreement of 1859, Dutch–Portuguese relations on this small island had long seemed unsatisfactory. After 1890, with Portugal's impending national bankruptcy, it became increasingly likely that it would eventually have to sell its colonial possessions. The Dutch government therefore began to insist on a closer definition of territorial and economic relations, with explicit recognition of preferential treatment for the Netherlands in the event that Portugal should want to sell Timor. Such preferential treatment was demanded in colonial circles, in particular where the danger of a British, German or American take-over of the Portuguese part was frequently pointed out. The Dutch ambassador to Lisbon had already confirmed at an earlier stage that 'all the governments are like hungry ravens, with their eyes fixed on everything that poor Portugal will or might have to cede.'[146] As a concession for such preferential treatment, the Dutch government was prepared to waive long-standing demand for compensation, which had long

143. Woltring, *Bescheiden* VI, nos 338, 447. Cf. notes 72–5 above.
144. *Handelingen Tweede Kamer* (Parliamentary Reports of the Second Chamber), 19 November 1897, p. 179.
145. Woltring, *Bescheiden* VI, no. 73; cf. Van der Veur, *Documents*, pp. 140ff.
146. Woltring, *Bescheiden* V, no. 133; cf. nos 129, 210, 213, 244, 286.

been regarded as 'lost' anyway. To avoid causing unnecessary offence to Portuguese feelings, the two ministers Van Tienhoven and Van Dedem agreed to the Portuguese request that preferential treatment should be mutual, and an appropriate clause was therefore included in the treaty.[147] The new Timor Treaty was signed and ratified in the course of 1893, and mutual preferential treatment was 'generally and unanimously welcomed' in the Second Chamber.[148]

At the turn of the century, however, many observers warned that such paper guarantees might cause a false feeling of security. 'You never know what may be in store for us in the Far East', said Fransen van de Putte on the occasion of the Spanish–American War; 'Power is more important than justice there, and self-interest and greed are very much in the foreground.' Van de Putte therefore repeatedly advocated a strengthening of East Indian defences, particularly by the Dutch navy.[149] *De Standaard, De Tijd* and the *NRC* agreed whole-heartedly.[150] Government circles, too, were convinced that the defences of the East Indies were grossly inadequate. Quite apart from financial problems, recent developments in Asia only served to aggravate the dilemmas which had always confronted military plans in the East Indies. The question was whether priority should be given to external defence or the internal pacification of the Archipelago; to Java or to the Outer Regions; to the army or to the navy. The different state committees which had discussed these military problems around 1890 had only considered the theoretical possibility of a British attack on the East Indies. Their advice therefore tended in the direction of a double strategy – internally and externally – that was aimed at keeping the balance between army and navy, concentrating on Java. Many experts, however, felt that these points of departure should now be revised, as the United States and Japan had turned into potential aggressors.[151]

147. Ibid., nos 230, 233, 249, 258, 263, 268, 273, 278–9.
148. *Bijlagen Handelingen Tweede Kamer* (Parliamentary Reports of the Second Chamber, Appendix) 1893–4, no. 206; ibid. 1893–4, no. 47.
149. *Handelingen Eerste Kamer* (Parliamentary Reports of the First Chamber), 8 June 1898, p. 287; ibid., 12 July 1898, pp. 378–9; cf. ibid., *Bijlagen* (Appendix) 1897–8, pp. nos 193–7.
150. *De Standaard*, 6 May, *De Tijd*, 17 June and *NRC*, 15 May 1898.
151. Cf. Nijpels, *Japan–Nederland*, pp. 142–7, 187–91; Anonymous, 'Indische militaire belangen', *IG*, 1899, I, pp. 671–90; II, pp. 1058–78 and 1228–55; ibid. 1900, I, pp. 202–35, 624–43. See also Teitler, *Militia Debate*, pp. 10ff.

During the 1890s the government did indeed begin to emphasise the external defences of the East Indies, particularly its naval defences. Fransen van de Putte played a prominent role in the relevant state committee. Like the army, the navy acquired a double function in 1896, that is, 'to do its utmost to protect Dutch rights and interests and to maintain the sovereign authority of the Netherlands, if necessary against the local population'. The strength of the 'auxiliary squadron', the section of the Dutch navy permanently stationed in the East Indies, was boosted to six medium-sized cruisers in 1898, while between 1898 and 1903 four heavy cruisers or ironclads were launched.[152]

Apart from naval defences, communication links were also extended, not only between the Netherlands and the East Indies but also within the Archipelago. In 1895 on the small island of Pulu Weh, strategically situated with regard to Acheh and the Straits of Malacca, a refuelling station and a military base were set up. As there had been disruptions in the telegraph system during the Boer War, the Dutch government started negotiations with Germany in 1900 with a view to breaking its own dependence on Britain for telegraph links with the East Indies. Having concluded a cable agreement with Germany in 1901, the Netherlands also achieved one with France in 1904 and a common telegraph link with the Asian colonies was established.[153]

Despite border treaties and the strengthening of colonial defences there was still a vague feeling of discomfort around 1900 about the security of the Dutch administration in the East Indies. This discomfort could be seen in the continuation of radical and clerical warnings from the 1880s that the Netherlands could easily endanger its possession of the East Indies if it neglected the material and spiritual development of the native population. Partly as a result of the international situation, these views were revived again around 1900. In government circles, too, there was concern that foreign developments might have repercussions on internal relations within the East Indies.

The formal distinction between 'Europeans, natives and foreign Orientals' had already been undermined by the fact that the Japanese had been given full equality with the Europeans in the so-called

---

152. Bosscher, 'Oorlogsvaart', pp. 330–1; cf. G. Jungslager, *Halve eeuw*, pp. 12–34; Beunders, *Vlootwet*, pp. 24–30.
153. Smit, *Nederland*, pp. 219–22.

'Japanese Law' of 1898, which was a direct result of the new trade agreement between the Netherlands and Japan.[154] Especially following the Boxer Rebellion, it was expected that this new equality would necessarily lead to unrest among the Chinese population. When a strong squadron was sent to China around 1900, this was probably also intended to intimidate the Chinese in the East Indies.[155] Cremer and Van der Wijck were at first also concerned that the struggle for independence in the Philippines would spread to the Indo-Europeans in the East Indies. Cremer, however, felt that the harsh repression of the freedom fighters by the Americans would calm down the 'hot-headed' among the 'Indo's.[156] And of course, there was also the threat of the pan-Islamic movement which was spread above all by the Turkish consul in the East Indies.[157]

For the representatives of the new 'Ethical Policy' in the colonies such vague, external dangers formed equally valid arguments for internal reforms in the Indonesian Archipelago. '*Les idées marchent*', Van Deventer warned in 1899, 'even in the East Indies and among the native population.' Pointing to the recent fate of Spain, he suggested that 'there is no better way of ensuring that we keep the East Indies than a policy of righteousness and honesty.'[158] Virtually all Liberal, Christian and Socialist spokesmen in the Netherlands were in agreement that a contented population was the most important condition for maintaining the East Indies, whether they accepted the idea of a 'debt of honour' or not. According to Locher–Scholten, the 'Ethical Policy' therefore became part of 'a system of peaceful defence' for the East Indies.[159] Conversely, Cremer was already expecting in 1898 that 'the more favourable position we have reached with regard to our power and prestige will enable us to embark upon a journey of spiritual and economic development for the peoples of our Archipelago.'[160]

After 1901 the 'Ethical Policy' also seemed to command a broad consensus as a developmental policy. Only very few shared Pier-

---

154. Lijnkamp, *Japannerwet*, pp. 74ff.

155. Cf. Van Dongen, *Neutraliteit*, pp. 260, 271.

156. Van der Wijck to Cremer, 12 December 1898; Cremer to Van der Wijck, 23 February 1899, Van der Wijck Collection. For American action, see Miller, *Assimilation*, pp. 57ff.

157. L. W. C. van den Berg's alarmist vision was typical: 'Het Panislamisme', *De Gids*, 1900, iv, pp. 228–70, 392–432. Cf. Noer, *Movement*, pp. 28–30.

158. Van Deventer, 'Een eereschuld', *De Gids*, 1899, iii, pp. 251–2.

159. Locher-Scholten, *Ethiek*, p. 197.

160. Cremer to Van der Wijck, 28 June 1898, Van der Wijck Collection.

son's view that a fight against Java's welfare deficit would be at the expense of social legislation in the Netherlands. At a time of economic growth it was easy enough to avoid such an unpleasant choice. Furthermore, nearly every single group had their ideals or interests which could be promoted as part of the 'Ethical Policy'. Many civil servants saw it as a continuation of activities which had started during the 1880s in the areas of irrigation, education and the government monopoly on opium. In the Netherlands, less ethical Liberals than Van Deventer appreciated above all the favourable side-effects of the development measures for trade and industry. The 'Ethical Policy' also enabled the Christian parties to give a boost to Roman Catholic and Protestant missionary activities. And a moderate Social Democrat such as Van Kol really only differed from the others with regard to the speed of colonial reforms.[161] However, this fundamental agreement disappeared as soon as Dutch authority – or, as Van Kol put it, 'the imperialism of the Netherlands' – was to be established in the Outer Regions.

The Lombok Expedition

Even before Van Kol was elected by the Second Chamber in 1897, the spokesmen of the other parties had become increasingly convinced that the traditional policy of abstention had become outdated. This consensus was less broad than on the 'Ethical Policy' and there were dissidents both among Liberals and Christians, but it was still broad enough to withstand the later attacks of the Socialists. Although the policy of abstention was still under discussion and not abandoned for good until 1898, the Lombok Expedition of 1894 nevertheless formed an important turning point in favour of expansion – both for the government and colonial administration and also for the Dutch parliament and the general public. The importance of the Lombok expedition and its effect on the Acheh policy has been dealt with by Van Goor, in particular, whose work is taken as the starting point for this section.[162]

In the last chapter we saw that the policy of abstention was very

---

161. Cf. Locher-Scholten, *Ethiek*, pp. 200–3; Kuitenbrouwer, 'Pierson', pp. 18–22; Tichelman, *Sdap*, pp. 11–12; Van Doorn, *Engineers*, pp. 21–2; Brouwer, *Houding*, pp. 17–20.
162. Van Goor, *Episode; Kooplieden*, chapter 2. Cf. Van der Kraan, *Lombok*, chapters 1–5.

strictly adhered to during the 1880s – by the government and the colonial administration because they had no choice, and by the Dutch Parliament and the general public more as a matter of principle. In 1890, in fact, the Flores expedition had to be stopped due to considerable pressure from the Second Chamber. Governor-general Pijnacker Hordijk then tried to avoid further new interventions in the Outer Regions. This soon became obvious with regard to Lombok, where the Islamic Sasaks rebelled against their Balinese lords in 1891 and asked the Dutch government for help. The East Indian Council advised taking action, and minister Van Dedem in The Hague felt that the governor-general should be given 'a completely free hand' in those parts. Indeed, he was already anticipating that Pijnacker Hordijk would feel that the time had come when, 'despite our limited means, action will become inevitable, to be promoted by good political conduct.'[163] Pijnacker Hordijk, however, did not feel that this moment had come. Quite apart from the military risk, he thought that such interference would contradict the limited nature of Dutch 'supreme authority' over Lombok.[164]

On this point, however, views differed widely, both in Batavia and in The Hague. When asked in 1890 whether the independent Batak lands in Sumatra were part of Dutch East Indian territory, minister Mackay had already decided that this was indeed the case. There may not have been any effective Dutch occupation, but it was in 'the nature of things' that this would follow 'as soon as the time came'.[165] These words were also considered applicable to other, similar cases, so that the policy of abstention had, in principle, been abandoned. However, not only Pijnacker Hordijk but indeed the entire Second Chamber continued, in practice, to adhere to it. In 1893 strong opposition in the Chamber urged Van Dedem himself to withdraw his ideas about strengthening the colonial administration in Ceram, an idea which he had prepared in consultation with the new Governor-general Van der Wijck.[166]

Van der Wijck's appointment was more or less due to the political controversies over Tak van Poortvliet's ballot act. Pijnacker Hor-

163. Van Dedem to Pijnacker Hordijk, 11 December 1891 and 30 June 1892, Pijnacker Hordijk Collection.
164. Van Goor, *Episode*, pp. 10–11; van der Kraan, *Lombok*, pp. 40–6.
165. [Colijn], *Politiek beleid* I, pp. 167–8.
166. *Handelingen Tweede Kamer* (Parliamentary Reports of the Second Chamber), 23 November 1893, pp. 220–2. Cf. Groen, 'Soldaat', pp. 205–9.

dijk preferred the conservative Röell, but Van Dedem was against the appointment of a Liberal 'who is known to be against our proposals for an electoral reform'. Van Houten, too, was regarded as unacceptable 'for more than one reason'. The experienced and relatively progressive Cremer showed little enthusiasm – not only would he be obliged to give up temporarily his functions in the Deli Company and other enterprises, Cremer was also suffering from strong headaches, following sunstroke in Deli. Finally, after his brother Herman, secretary-general of the colonies, had also declined the offer, Carel van der Wijck was appointed governor-general in 1893.[167] Van der Wijck was a man with a good deal of experience in the East Indian civil service. As vice-chairman of the East Indian Council, he had proved to be an outspoken advocate of decisive action in the Outer Regions, such as the Flores and Lombok expeditions. The terms 'authority' and 'prestige' were constantly on his lips. When Van Dedem appointed Van Wijck, he made him promise to respect the existing policy of concentration in Acheh. But, like his predecessor, he was given a free hand in Lombok. And so he immediately set to work, wanting to 'wipe out the blemish which sticks to us with regard to Lombok'. 'What a scandal!' was his comment on the policy of abstention which had been followed until then.[168] There were no longer any legal obstacles now that the Balinese were cruelly suppressing the rebellious Sasaks and the local dynasty was trying to obtain foreign support via Singapore. In May 1894 Van der Wijck laconically announced 'an expedition to Lombok which has become inevitable, unless we want to cross out Lombok as no longer part of the Dutch East Indies'.[169]

When the Dutch forces arrived in Lombok, they met with very little resistance at first. Negotiations about a new treaty were opened with the local prince, and these were to include his replacement. While – from a Dutch point of view – negotiations were still in progress, the Balinese suddenly attacked on the night of 25–6 August, causing a veritable bloodbath among the unsuspecting Dutch troops. Of 2,400 officers and soldiers over 100 were killed,

167. Van Dedem to Pijnacker Hordijk, 9 June 1893; Röell to Pijnacker Hordijk, 2 April 1893, Pijnacker Hordijk Collection.
168. Van der Wijck to Van Dedem, 14 December 1893, Van der Wijck Collection.
169. Van der Wijck to Bergsma, 10 May 1894; Van der Wijck Collection. Cf. Van Goor, *Episode*, pp. 11–13. Van der Kraan observed that Balinese rule was only repressive in the recently conquered eastern part of Lombok; Van der Kraan, *Lombok*, 6.

and a total of 560 men were put out of action. The main body of the forces was driven back to sea, and the commander, General J. A. Vetter, recommended that the expedition be called off.[170]

The 'treachery of Lombok' made a profound impression both in Batavia and The Hague. The predominant reaction was not that the Netherlands should 'withdraw' but that 'Dutch prestige should be restored', and some even demanded 'revenge'. Van der Wijck immediately sent two reservist battalions to Lombok and urged Bergsma to make additional troops available. With this reinforcement General Vetter succeeded in taking the initiative again. On 18 November the prince's palace was captured – a decisive blow which cost the lives of 76 Dutch troops and about 2,000 Balinese men, women and children. As a result, the prince and most of the Balinese leaders surrendered. The prince was removed and exiled, and the Balinese aristocracy remained subject to a direct form of Dutch administration.[171]

In the Netherlands, the Lombok expedition had been almost totally uncontroversial from the very beginning – or at least considerably less controversial than Van der Wijck and Bergsma had expected after previous expeditions. In the First Chamber Pijnacker Hordijk, the former governor-general, questioned the new minister about the intended expedition, but his formal complaints met with little sympathy. Apart from Bergsma's prestige argument, it seems that the humanitarian argument – the protection of the suppressed Sasaks – made a particularly strong impression on the Dutch Parliament and the general public.[172] When the defeat of Lombok became known, there was at first great alarm in government circles. 'I need not tell you', wrote Bergsma to Van der Wijck, 'what difficult days I have had since the first negative reports from Lombok.' Bergsma had first learnt about the outcome of the expedition through the *Nieuws van den Dag*, the first paper to report on the 'treachery'. 'Luckily,' Bergsma wrote later, 'I was able to keep my calm despite all this, despite the turmoil around me and the unrest in the country.' 'To calm down the public', the Cabinet Council immedi-

170. Ibid., pp. 78–83.
171. Ibid., pp. 95–100. The large number of victims on the Balinese side was partly the result of ritual suicide or *puputan*; cf. Ricklefs, *History*, p. 128; Geertz, *Negara*, pp. 11–12.
172. *Handelingen Eerste Kamer* (Parliamentary Reports of the First Chamber), 8 June 1894, pp. 12–19; Bergsma to Van der Wijck, 10 June 1894, Van der Wijck Collection. Cf. *Het Handelsblad*, 26 May, 17 and 22 June, *NRC*, 27 May and 12 June; *Standaard*, 31 May and 12 June 1894.

ately decided to make a naval detachment available to the colonial
administration and subsequently to draft more men into the Dutch
East Indian army.[173] In The Hague there were, above all, fears that
this 'unexpected and horrible disaster' might lead to repercussions in
Bali and Acheh. Fransen van de Putte was involuntarily reminded of
'the years 1873–4', and he expressed the fervent hope 'that no political
capital is made out of the present difficulties of the country and the
government', as was done after the first Acheh expedition.[174]

But politicians and journalists were far more unanimous and
reacted more belligerently to the 'treachery of Lombok' than they
had the 'treachery of Singapore' twenty years earlier. 'The nation
and the government need *new courage and new energy*. We have to
act swiftly and forcefully', commented the paper *Nieuws van den
Dag*. 'The historians of the next century may not be able to say
anything about us except this one thing; they lost a lot – but they
kept up their *courage*.' Press reactions were virtually unanimous in
this respect. Characteristically, any judgement on the relevant policies was generally reserved until after the earlier setback was remedied. The commentaries in the *Handelsblad, NRC, Standaard,
Tijd* and popular press differed only in their degree of indignation
about 'the treacherous behaviour of the Balinese', their display of
sympathy and homage towards the 'valiant fallen soldiers' and their
relatives, and their condemnation of Balinese 'misgovernment' and
the 'cruel suppression' of the Sasaks.[175] The 'treachery of Lombok'
gave cause to considerable nationalist excitement in the Netherlands, which partly arose spontaneously and was partly the result of
conscious agitation. Officers and ex-officers played an important
part in this agitation. They were the ones who often called for
volunteers to take part in the war against Lombok and who organised collections on behalf on the Red Cross and the fallen soldiers'
families. The press strongly supported such calls. All over the
country 288 local Lombok committees were set up, which – usually
under the leadership of the mayor – co-ordinated the collection
campaigns. Over 300,000 guilders were eventually collected.

173. Bergsma to Van der Wijck, 4 September 1894, Van der Wijck Collection. Cf.
Nieuws van dan Dag. 28 August 1894.
174. Fransen de Putte to Röell, 30 August 1894; Van Naamen van Eemnes to
Röell, 30 August 1894, Röell Collection, Cf. Bergsman to Van der Wijck, 4 Septem-
ber 1894, Van der Wijck Collection.
175. *Nieuws van den Dag*, 1 September 1894. Cf. *De Standaard*, 30–1 August,
Het Handelsblad, 30 August and 4 September, *De Tijd*, 1 and 10 September, *De
Telegraaf*, 1 September 1894.

Hundreds of volunteers, mostly Acheh veterans and students, applied directly or indirectly to the minister, who thanked them but declared that he would not make use of their offer for the time being. 'You understand that I have no intention of agreeing to these ill-considered plans,' he wrote to Van der Wijck, 'but as long as there is this excitement it is better not to go against it.'[176] What Bergsma found far more important was the extra drafts in Harderwijk where nearly 400 'trained soldiers' had signed up for the East Indies within a matter of days. The sudden popularity of the colonial service can be seen in the departure of the first detachment from Rotterdam, an event which attracted considerable public interest. 'Thousands and thousands flocked together . . . tonight', reported the *NRC*, which also quoted word for word the speeches of various commanders to the soldiers; 'These men are going to defend the flag of our dear fatherland in the East Indies and revenge the treachery which has been committed.' All the speeches were welcomed by the crowd with 'thunderous applause'.[177]

At the end of September all these scattered activities were brought together in a national Lombok committee, with the retired general Th. J. A. van Zijll de Jong as chairman and the president of the Dutch Bank N. P. van den Berg as vice-chairman. As the collected money already exceeded the financial needs of the victims and their families, the committee decided to set up a 'national fund' with a 'wider application' than merely Lombok. They had in mind the future victims and relatives of the 'fight against Acheh, which was still continuing, and the expeditions that went out to various parts of the Indian Archipelago from time to time'. Queen Emma sent 15,000 guilders 'directly to the national fund, as a token of her great sympathy'. Apart from the queen, the committee also received support from prominent politicians such as Mackay, Fransen van de Putte and Wertheim, as well as well-known Acheh veterans like the queen's aide-de-camp Verspeyck and the elderly Van der Heijden.[178] When the Dutch victory over Lombok became known, there were all kinds of spontaneous demonstrations in the big cities. The Leiden historian P. J. Blok interrupted his lectures to commemorate the great martial achievement, whereupon his students began

176. Bergsma to Van der Wijck, 4 September 1894, Van der Wijck Collection. For various public appeals, see *NRC* and *De Standaard*, 1–6 September 1894.

177. *NRC*, 16 September 1894; cf. 14 October for the departure of the second detachment.

178. *NRC*, 25 and 27 September 1894; cf. Van Goor, *Episode*, p. 20.

to chant the slogan *Long Live the Queen*. Queen Emma herself emphatically praised Governor-general Van der Wijck and General Vetter and generously conferred orders upon them for their victory.[179]

This nationalist climate silenced much of the criticism which the defeat of Lombok had originally caused: 'P. H. [i.e. Pijnacker Hordijk] is rearing his head again,' reported Bergsma to Van der Wijck, 'and you can already read that the government would have done better to listen to his warnings than the reckless tale of a minister who is only a few weeks old.'[180] However, the 'fierce opposition' which Bergsma was expecting for the budget debates was not as bad as he had expected. 'The atmosphere in the First Chamber is definitely friendly', he said with relief, adding that even 'P. H.' seemed to be favourably inclined towards the minister.

Criticism in the Second Chamber was limited to the initial management of the troops, which had apparently precipitated the Balinese attack by spreading the Dutch military presence too thinly. Furthermore, criticism was expressed that the Dutch government was planning direct rule in Lombok, which would be too much of a burden for the colonial administration. Such criticism came particularly strongly from the progressive Liberal leader H. Goemans Borgesius, who found Bergsma's policies too conservative in many ways. However, this was really his opinion of all the policies of the current right-wing Liberal cabinet. Most spokesmen, in fact, supported the Lombok policy, especially Cremer, Rutgers van Rozenburg, Van Vlijmen and Mackay, who repeatedly expressed their great appreciation of the governor-general's decisive action and paid tribute to the valiant Dutch East Indian army.[181] The only ones who continued to oppose the Lombok expedition were the Socialists. However, they were not represented in the Dutch Parliament and were badly divided among themselves at the time. According to Van Goor, the SDAP had considerable trouble with the nationalist

179. Bergsma to Van der Wijck, 11 December 1894, Van der Wijck Collection. Cf. *De Standaard*, *NRC*, *Het Handelsblad* and *De Tijd*, 22–3 November 1894. On Blok, see Van Goor, *Kooplieden*, p. 100.

180. Bergsma to Van der Wijck, 4 September 1894, Van der Wijck Collection. *De Amsterdammer* (daily), in particular, responded with criticism on 1 and 4 September 1894.

181. *Handelingen Tweede Kamer* (Parliamentary Reports of the Second Chamber), 16 and 20 November 1894, pp. 134–5, 138–9, 149, 151–5; ibid., *Handelingen Eerste Kamer* (Parliamentary Reports of the First Chamber), 19 September 1894, pp. 8–10; Bergsma to Van der Wijck, 30 October and 11 December 1894, Van der Wijck Collection.

excitement which burst out in connection with Lombok shortly after their formation.[182]

The Pacification of Acheh

After Lombok came Acheh. The successful subjection of Lombok prompted a number of MPs to insist on a more 'vigorous policy' in Acheh.[183] Van der Wijck had always favoured such a course of action, but he first had to persuade Bergsma who was worried about the other MPs. Meanwhile it was becoming increasingly difficult to implement the policy of concentration which had been introduced as an emergency measure in 1884.

Continuing attacks by the Achenese meant that this line gradually had to be extended: first the patrols and eventually the outstations. From 1892 onwards the governor and commander in Acheh, C. Deijkerhoff, tried to consolidate Dutch influence by supporting 'loyal' Achenese leaders against 'hostile' ones. The most important ally of the Dutch, Teuku Umar, was to receive the necessary weapons and financial assistance in exchange for his support. Van der Wijck felt that Deijkerhoff was a complete failure and that his policy was 'highly dangerous', though with regard to Acheh his hands were tied by The Hague'.[184] However, after the defeat in Lombok, Bergsma became rather concerned that Teuku Umar might turn out to be similarly treacherous. When Lombok was defeated, Van der Wijck therefore suggested 'making a definite end to the uncertain situation' in Acheh: 'The chronic bungling in Acheh is a disgrace to us, and as soon as I can come up with a well-thought-out plan that will put an end to it, I shall feel obliged to ask your permission to put it into practice.'[185] Bergsma, however, was afraid that a drastic change in the Acheh policy would cause 'a storm' in the Second Chamber, 'which would hit me first'. Van der Wijck did not get a chance until spring 1896 when Teuku Umar did indeed become disloyal and attacked the outposts, eliminating most of them. 'Deijkerhoff's house of cards has finally

182. Cf. Van Goor, *Episode*, pp. 17 and 21.
183. Particularly Rutgers van Rozenburg and Van Vlijmen, *Handelingen Tweede Kamer* (Parliamentary Reports of the Second Chamber), 16 and 20 November 1894, pp. 134 and 151.
184. Van der Wijck to Bergsma, 25 June 1894, Van der Wijck Collection; cf. Van 't Veer, *Atjeh-oorlog*, pp. 182–3.
185. Van der Wijck to Bergsma, 4 December 1894; Bergsma to Van der Wijck, 4 July and 29 October 1895, Van der Wijck Collection.

collapsed', reported Van der Wijck with malicious satisfaction; 'thank goodness he was in it himself.'[186]

The policy of concentration had always been a controversial issue in the Netherlands. Historians often give the impression that the system did not meet with fundamental criticism and rejection until Snouck Hurgronje's Acheh report of 1892 and Van Heutsz's brochure of 1893. It is indeed true that their recommendations subsequently formed the guidelines for the pacification of Acheh after 1898 – a successful endeavour, in which they played an important role themselves.[187] But the most important aims of their pacification strategy go back to 1890, when the military subjection of the whole of Acheh, the introduction of direct Dutch administration, followed by *rapprochement* towards the local leaders and continuing repression of the religious ones, had already been put forward. This had been in nine anonymous articles published by *De Standaard* under the title 'Our Duty in north Sumatra'.[188] That such a fundamental attack on the policy of concentration should have been published by this Anti-Revolutionary paper and Kuyper's mouthpiece shows that the formation of opinions in this circle had already begun to move in the direction of expansion around 1890. It is also worth noting that the anonymous author concluded his articles with a plea for a scientific study of 'local society' in Acheh which bore a resemblance to the conclusion of Snouck Hurgronje's Acheh report.[189]

Snouck Hurgronje, however, expressed himself rather contemptuously about the 'moral life of the Achinese', while at the same time rejecting the idea that their society was mainly dominated by Islam. His most outspoken pronouncements can be found in his unpublished writings, though his views were also expressed quite strongly in his publications.[190] In his survey the colonial physician J. Jacobs, on the other hand, had noted considerably more religious influence and less moral decadence in Acheh than the leading

186. Van der Wijck to Bergsma, 15 April 1896; cf. Bergsma to Van der Wijck, 4 July and 29 October 1894, Van der Wijck Collection.

187. Cf. Somer, *Korte Verklaring*, p. 241; Van 't Veer, *Atjeh-oorlog*, pp. 186ff.; Witte, *Van Heutsz*, pp. 37ff. For the published parts of Snouck's Acheh report, see *Atjehers*; for the unpublished parts, *Ambtelijke Adviezen*, I, pp. 50–116; Van Koningsveld, 'Snouck Hurgronje', pp. 774–7. Cf. Van Heutsz, *Onderwerping*, originally published as a series of articles in *Het Indisch Militair Tijdschrift*.

188. *De Standaard*, 30 July, 1, 4, 6, 8, 11, 13–15 August 1890.

189. Ibid., 15 August; cf. Gobée and Adriaanse, *Ambtelijke Adviezen* I, pp. 94–7.

190. Van Koningsveld, 'Snouck Hurgronje', pp. 775–6.

government adviser had recorded; such differences in insight and background contemporary critics were bound to notice.[191] Although Jacobs did not deny that the Achenese had unfavourable traits of character, he felt that these were largely the result of a twenty-year struggle against the Dutch. 'Is it surprising', he asked, 'that the Achenese are secretive towards us, that they cheat . . . and mistrust us? No, we are making a mistake if we judge the character of the Achenese solely on the basis of what we have seen of them.' In this connection, Jacobs pointed out the less pleasant traits of character of the Calvinist sea-beggars during the Eighty Years' War against the Spanish, and he also compared the more open, much-reviled homosexuality among some Achenese with the more secretive homosexuality among some contemporary Dutchmen.[192] So much understanding and tolerance was more than the former government adviser Van den Berg could endure. In *De Gids* he subjected Jacobs's 'ultra-newfangled theories' to a fiercely critical review, in which he repeated his earlier, drastic solution of the 'Achenese question' by colonising Acheh with Amboinese ex-soldiers from the colonial army. Because of their 'hybrid origin' Van den Berg felt that the Achenese were 'a people without future'. 'our policy should no longer be aimed at their subjection or their assimilation, but their elimination.'[193]

These debates were still resounding in people's ears when the defection of Teuku Umar became known. 'Something has finally happened which has been feared on various sides and about which we have heard repeated warnings', announced *De Telegraaf*, which was the first to publish the news this time: 'Teuku Umar has betrayed us.' Van 't Veer's remark that 'Acheh had been forgotten in the Netherlands' does not really reflect the predominant mood correctly.[194] It is true, however, that reactions were at first less indignant and aggressive than shortly before with regard to Lombok. Tak felt that after twenty years the Dutch had become used to a war which had 'gradually turned into a national institution'.[195]

Three solutions to the new situation were being discussed: with-

---

191. J. Jacobs, *Familie- en kampongleven*. Cf. Quarles van Ufford's review of the two Acheh studies, *De Economist*, 1894, II, pp. 827–46. See also A. Jacobs, *Herinneringen*, p. 133.

192. Jacobs, *Familie- en kampongleven* I, pp. 222 and 374.

193. L. W. C. van den Berg, 'De Atjehers', *De Gids*, 1894, iv, pp. 195–239. Cf. chapter III, note 197, above.

194. *De Telegraaf*, 31 March 1894. Cf. Van 't Veer, *Atjeh-oorlog*, p. 211.

195. 'Atjeh', *Kroniek*, 5 April 1896.

drawal from Acheh; subjection of the entire territory of Acheh; and the continuation of the policy of concentration. The withdrawal option was advocated, in particular, by ex-governor Pruys van der Hoeven who said that the only ones to benefit from this never-ending war were those involved in the war industry. He felt that it would be far more sensible to withdraw to the port of Acheh or Pulu Weh, possibly block the coast and wait quietly for the 'pretender' to the sultanate to put things in order. The Socialist Tak, left-wing Liberal Brooshoft and Catholic leader Schaepman expressed themselves in a similar way.[196]

Obviously, those who favoured pacification were rather scandalised by the thought of withdrawal. 'We now have to do our international duty and finally defeat that pirates' den', declared Boissevain.[197] Like a number of military publishers, Boissevain sounded 'such a highly patriotic note' that Kuyper became concerned that the 'cool and calm debate' which was required would be hampered by these strong words. For the time being Kuyper wanted to postpone the choice between withdrawal and subjection until the situation in Acheh had become more transparent, although it was obvious to him that a 'decision one way or another' had to be made. He did not feel that there was much point in restoring the status quo.[198] Many Liberals were at first rather hesitant about abolishing the policy of concentration.[199] Van Gennep, too, expressed himself in a similar vein when he questioned the minister on the Acheh issue in the Second Chamber. Bergsma, however, made it quite clear to him that 'as long as I have the honour of being Minister of the Colonies, it shall not be willing to co-operate in . . . giving up the concentrated position which we have.' Gennep felt that this was rather 'poor consolation'.[200]

During the Acheh crisis Bergsma made a weak impression on all sides. On the one hand he declared in The Hague that he would first wait for further proposals from Batavia; on the other hand, he tried to keep Van der Wijck from taking far-reaching measures, with a

196. Pruys van der Hoeven, *Laatste nieuws*. Cf. P. Brooshooft, 'De Atjeh-crisis', *De Amsterdammer* (weekly), 19 and 26 April, 3 and 10 May; *Kroniek*, 3 and 17 April, *Het Centrum*, 3 April 1896.
197. *Het Handelsblad*, 5 April; cf. 3 and 24 April 1896. Though less drastically, *De Tijd* of 1 April and the *NRC* of 1, 2, 5 and 7 April also advocated decisive action.
198. *De Standaard*, 20, 24 and 27 April 1896.
199. Cf. *Het Vaderland*, 8 May 1896.
200. *Handelingen Tweede Kamer* (Parliamentary Reports of the Second Chamber), 7 May 1896, pp. 1050–2.

view to strong opposition in the Netherlands. After the defection of Teuku Umar he allowed Van der Wijck to replace Deijkerhoff with the 'hero of Lombok', General Vetter, on condition that 'Vetter will not go any further than is strictly necessary for the consolidation of our authority in Acheh and for our prestige in the Dutch East Indies.' When Vetter's disciplinary campaign in Acheh turned out to be unexpectedly successful and there was a good deal of pressure in the Netherlands to pursue an unambiguous political line, Bergsma finally asked Van der Wijck in July to indicate clearly what the 'views of the East Indian government' were, 'in any case . . . before the discussion of the East Indian budget'.[201] The same options were discussed in Batavia as in The Hague, that is withdrawal, pacification or continuing concentration, though all the parties concerned agreed that the policy of concentration should not be resumed; according to Van der Wijck, this would be tantamount to 'an aimless dissipation and weakening of forces'. Withdrawal was advocated in the East Indian Council by the Acheh expert G. A. Scherer. However, the majority of the council followed Van der Wijck who preferred General Vetter's plan of conquering Acheh gradually. This had also been suggested by Snouck Hurgronje and Van Heutsz. Though reluctantly, Bergsma agreed, on condition that the concentrated posts would continue for the time being.[202]

When Bergsma submitted the East Indian budget, at first he broached the decision for pacification very cautiously in the Dutch Parliament, describing it as a 'continuation' of the current active policy in Acheh. However, under the influence of the military successes, many MPs had by now become convinced that it was possible to subject the whole of Acheh within a very short time. The most prominent speech in this connection was Kuyper's strong plea for a quick pacification of Acheh, without taking back any of his earlier opposition to declaration of war. 'Now is the time for us to get Acheh under control', said Kuyper, warning Bergsma of 'half-measures'. 'This is the most favourable moment, at a time when national slackness and indifference have finally made room for a national enthusiasm which the government must take advantage of.'

201. Bergsma to Van der Wijck, 23 April, 14 and 24 July 1896, Van der Wijck Collection. Bergsma was interpellated in the First Chamber about the lack of clear policy proposals by J. H. Geertsema; *Handelingen Eerste Kamer* (Parliamentary Reports of the First Chamber), 10 July 1896, pp. 436–7.
202. Van der Wijck to Bergsma, 21 July and 8 September 1896; Bergsma to Van der Wijck, 8 and 30 October 1896, Van der Wijck Collection. See also [Colijn], *Politiek beleid* I, pp. 122–4.

Kuyper then added his own 'Christian national' contribution to the policy of pacification by impressing upon the Islamic Achenese that

> a sacred awareness is gradually awakening in us, an awareness that we are not just called to round up our colonial possessions, but – and this is far more important – to take even to Acheh those blessings of security and order, blessings which the Netherlands has received by God's grace and which it has possessed ever since the light of the Gospel penetrated us.[203]

Apart from Kuyper, Cremer, Rutgers van Rozenburg and Van Vlijmen also believed that Bergsma had been far too reticent and half-hearted in his approach. Cremer wanted to know why only 300,000 guilders were added to the budget in order to pacify Acheh, a project which would probably cost three million. Van Vlijmen submitted a motion in which it was strongly recommended that the whole of Acheh should be subjected; he did not withdraw this motion until Bergsma clearly stated that this was in fact the aim of his own policy.

The only outspoken opponent of this revival of an 'agressive policy' in Acheh was Goeman Borgesius, who expressed grave concern about the dominant position which Batavia was to have in the decision-making process: 'We are constantly being given a *fait accompli*, and isn't it the same for the minister?'[204] In the First Chamber Fransen van de Putte and Pijnacker Hordijk also objected to the endeavour to subject Acheh whatever the cost. 'In my estimation, we are not fit to conquer such a country', warned Van de Putte. Most Liberals, however, had by now accepted the new Acheh policy, because, as Van Gennep put it, 'we are now sitting in this boat and the captain and navigating officer are people whom we trust.'[205] The East Indian budget was therefore accepted by both Chambers, without a division.

The change in the Acheh policy of 1896 was to be followed by new elections to the Dutch Parliament a year later. Under Van Houten's new Ballot Act the number of voters had almost doubled, so that the 'progressive' element in the Dutch government and

203. *Handelingen Tweede Kamer* (Parliamentary Reports of the Second Chamber), 17 November 1896, pp. 144–7. Cf. *De Standaard*, 4 and 24 June, 17 and 19 September.

204. *Handelingen Tweede Kamer* (Parliamentary Reports of the Second Chamber), 17 November 1896, pp. 152–3. Cf. ibid., 13 and 18 November 1896, pp. 131ff.

205. Ibid., 17 November 1896, p. 142. Cf. ibid., *Eerste Kamer* (First Chamber), 17 September 1896, pp. 11–18; ibid., 29 December 1896, pp. 93–7.

Parliament was likely to be much stronger than before. Van der Wijck therefore insisted that the new decisions should be carried out as quickly as possible: 'Once there are a new Minister of the Colonies and new Chambers, the plan might fall through.'[206] But Van der Wijck need not have worried. Although the Liberal left gained considerably and three Socialists were elected in the Second Chamber – a number that only partly reflected the actual vote for Socialist candidates – Queen Emma expressed her wish at the formation of the cabinet that the first person to be appointed should be a Minister of the Colonies 'who is favourably disposed towards Governor-general Van der Wijck's policy in Acheh'. Pierson agreed, 'not because I find that policy so admirable, but because any other choice would cause great confusion'.[207] Cremer was willing to leave his business obligations for a while to join the new Liberal 'cabinet of social justice'. Cremer, who had been returned as MP in Amsterdam with the largest majority, favoured both social legislation in the Netherlands and expansion in the East Indies. 'The most important consideration was probably that I would regret it too much if no further fruit could be picked from the advantages that have so far been achieved in Acheh', he wrote to Van der Wijck. 'Now that a few Social Democrats have joined the Second Chamber . . . there will be quite a lot of commotion there, but that obviously means very little, and it will calm the opposition in the First Chamber.'[208]

However, when the introduction of colonial administration in New Guinea was discussed, the opposition turned out to be stronger than the experienced politician Cremer had expected. Indeed, the Liberal left mainly voted against it, together with the Socialists. But Van Kol and Troelstra lashed out so vehemently against the 'Dutch annexation fanaticism' and 'colonial capital interests' of the Acheh policy that the Liberal left dissociated themselves again. The Socialist motion, which branded the Acheh War a 'national disaster', was rejected by 72 votes to 3. Apart from Van Kol and Troelstra only the Independent Socialist G. van der Zwaag had voted in favour.[209] In the First Chamber Fransen van de Putte continued to reject the

206. Van der Wijck to Bergsma, 11 December 1896, Van der Wijck Collection. Cf. Taal, *Liberalen*, pp. 432ff.

207. Pierson's diary, 15 July 1897, Pierson Collection.

208. Cremer to Van der Wijck, 2 and 12 August 1897, Van der Wijck Collection.

209. *Handelingen Tweede Kamer* (Parliamentary Reports of the Second Chamber), 19 November 1897, p. 168; cf. ibid., 16 and 17 November 1897, pp. 112ff.

Acheh policy both on pragmatic and humanitarian grounds. He felt that the Netherlands had neither the military nor the financial means to conquer Acheh, and a gradual, peaceful increase of Dutch influence should therefore be preferred. 'Let us bring civilisation to them,' he said to the new Minister of the Colonies, 'but not by means of bloodbaths! What is needed? One thing. Patience. Which is lacking.'[210]

Such criticism, which could also be heard in the Second Chamber and even in the Cabinet Council, was met by Cremer with the argument that a short but intensive war effort in Acheh would eventually be cheaper for the Netherlands – both financially and in terms of manpower – than the indefinite continuation of limited military involvement.[211] Figures soon appeared to confirm this. During the climax of the campaign in 1898 about 10,000 men were involved in Acheh. In 1899 this number could already be reduced to about 6,000 for the whole of Acheh, hardly more than the military occupation during the policy of concentration. The extra expenditure, in addition to the seven million guilders which Acheh was already costing the Netherlands every year, was estimated to be two million guilders over a period of ten years. However, after 1899, the revenues of the colonial administration in Acheh rose so much that the extra costs could partly be compensated for. It was important for the morale of the Dutch troops that the number of sick and wounded had gone down since the repeal of the policy of concentration.[212]

The decisive step in the pacification of Acheh was the expedition to Pedir in 1898, under the military leadership of Van Heutsz with Snouck Hurgronje as scientific adviser. The remote Pedir had always been a sanctuary for the Achenese war leaders of the core area of Acheh. After the subjugation of Acheh Van Heutsz and Snouck did not want to repeat Van der Heijden's mistake and allow them to gather strength again in Pedir. The expedition was prepared with close co-operation between The Hague, Batavia and Kota Radja, with more balanced mutual relations under Cremer than earlier under Bergsma. In May 1898 Van Heutsz was appointed military and civilian governor of Acheh; he was 'a good soldier, but not a militarist in a negative sense', Cremer commented. 'I am

210. *Handelingen Eerste Kamer* (Parliamentary Reports of the First Chamber), 29 December 1897, pp. 63–5.
211. Ibid., p. 66. Cf. Cremer to Van der Wijck, 3 December 1897 and 5 January 1898, Van der Wijck Collection.

expecting a lot of good from the combination of Van Heutsz and Snouck,' he wrote to Van der Wijck after the successful start of the Pedir expedition, 'and I am looking to the future with great confidence.'[213]

The successful results of the Pedir expedition during the summer meant that pragmatic opposition to the Acheh policy soon diminished. As soon as the news of the first military success had reached him, Cremer personally informed Fransen van de Putte. 'He, too, is convinced now that the only thing we can do is to take decisive action', said Cremer.[214] Shortly afterwards Teuku Umar, the symbol of resistance in Acheh, was killed. The non-military part of the pacification programme could now begin. Even Van Kol, who had condemned the Acheh War so sharply and on principle, was impressed by the 'salutary' effects of the pacification when he visited Acheh in 1902. 'We have not been masters and tyrants in recent years, but rulers', he concluded after his 'instructive talks' with Van Heutsz and a guided tour with Van Heutsz's young right-hand man, Captain H. Colijn, the future director of the Royal Dutch Oil Company, Anti-Revolutionary leader and prime minister. 'A *national war* has turned into a *gang war*,' was Van Kol's impression of the resistance movement, 'a war which we will have to continue for the time being, in order to protect the native population who are putting their trust in us.'[215]

This 'gang war' was to cost about 22,000 Achenese lives between 1899 and 1909, as well as 508 on the Dutch side. When Lieutenant Colonel G. C. E. van Daalen's bloody campaign in the Gajo and Alas areas became known, Van Kol largely withdraw his words of praise. However, this does not alter the fact that, around the year 1900, the pacification of Acheh was widely regarded as a success. Cremer and Van der Wijck were confident about its further progress, even after their forthcoming retirement. 'I am now totally convinced that, with men like Van Heusz and Snouck, you will be able to eliminate sizeable resistance in Acheh for ever and thus create the conditions for an orderly state of affairs under this administration', wrote Cremer to Van der Wijck after the conquest

212. Cf. [Colijn], *Politiek beleid* I, pp. 124–6.
213. Cremer to Van der Wijck, 4 and 28 June 1898, Van der Wijck Collection; cf. Van 't Veer, *Atjeh-oorlog*, pp. 234–7.
214. Cremer to Van der Wijck, 4 June 1898, Van der Wijck Collection. See also Toekoe Mohsin, 'Atjeh, mei 1897–September 1899', *IG*, 1900, I, pp. 56–89.
215. Van Kol, *Koloniën* I, p. 86; cf. pp. 38ff.

of Pedir. 'If people in the Netherlands . . . are still not convinced that that we have taken the only possible path towards the pacification of the Acheh, then that would be very discouraging', Van der Wijck replied.[216] At the request of the queen and her ministers, Van der Wijck had agreed to continue as governor-general for another year, so that he could supervise the final phase of the Acheh War in person. In 1899 he was able to transfer his office with a peaceful mind to his successor Rooseboom, who was not a colonial affairs expert but nevertheless a 'smart' general. Candidates who were not entirely trustworthy with regard to Acheh, such as the former vice-president of the East Indian Council and sinologist Groeneveldt, had already been put out of action by Cremer in the Netherlands.[217]

In 1901 Cremer himself was able to transfer the Colonial Department to his Anti-Revolutionary successor, Van Asch van Wijck, with complete confidence. Although Kuyper had expressed himself frequently and clearly in favour of the pacification of Acheh, Queen Wilhelmina nevertheless impressed it upon him that he was obliged to continue the current policy in Acheh.[218] The Acheh War was formally ended in 1903, when the pretender to the sultanship solemnly surrendered to Governor Van Heutsz. As a result, many believed that the pacification had been completed when Van Heutsz resigned as governor of Acheh in 1904 and temporarily returned to the Netherlands. It became a real triumphal procession, with official receptions and cheering crowds. In a specially dedicated edition of *Het Vaderland* ex-minister Cremer wrote: 'The man to whom this paper has been dedicated belongs to all parties. His valiant policy put our scaremongers to shame and strengthened our self-confidence.'[219] The celebration committee was headed by Van Heutsz' former comrade in arms, the future supreme commander during the First World War, General C. J. Snijders. Van Heutsz first went to *Het Loo*, where he discussed the pacification of Acheh

216. Van der Wijck to Cremer, 15 November 1898; Cremer to Van der Wijck, 28 June 1898, Van der Wijck Collection. For the official number of casualties and the course of Van Daalen's expedition, see Van 't Veer, *Atjeh-oorlog*, pp. 260ff.

217. Cremer to Van der Wijck, 28 May 1899; cf. Cremer to Van der Wijck, 12 September and 3 December 1897; Van der Wijck to Cremer, 15 October 1897 and 6 June 1899, Van der Wijck Collection.

218. Kasteel, *Kuyper*, p. 302.

219. *Het Vaderland*, 10 July 1904; cf. Witte, *Van Heutsz*, pp. 81–2. For the termination of the Acheh War, see ibid., pp. 73–4; Van 't Veer, *Atjeh-oorlog*, pp. 245–54.

with Queen Wilhelmina. Then he was given a warm reception by the officers and students of the Royal Military Academy in Breda. Being a Catholic Van Heutsz made a triumphal procession from Breda through the southern cities of Roozendal, Den Bosch and Nijmegen, up to Dordrecht and Rotterdam, and finally to The Hague, where he was cheered by the largest crowds. During his stay in The Hague he was appointed as the new governor-general of the East Indies by minister Idenburg.

Administrative, Economic and Cultural Expansion

The pacification of Acheh paved the way for the systematic expansion of colonial rule in the Outer Regions. Although this did not happen on a grand scale until the time of Governor-general Van Heutsz, a beginning was already made on all the large islands around 1900. This administrative expansion was not an isolated occurrence, but was accompanied by economic expansion and, to a lesser extent, cultural expansion as well. It was supported by mining and agricultural enterprises, as well as Protestant and Roman Catholic missionary activities.

In practice, these different forms of expansion overlapped quite considerably, so that the question arose as to how the establishment of Dutch rule was actually motivated – whether it was by administrative, economic or Christian interests. This question greatly occupied the minds of contemporaries and later historians. In fact, while this paragraph is being written, there is still a good deal of interesting research in progress, both with regard to administrative, economic and cultural expansion and also the actual establishment of colonial rule around 1900. I shall therefore give no more than a brief preliminary outline.

Administrative expansion consisted in continuing the general modernisation of the East Indian civil service after 1870, both in Java and also in the Outer Regions. That this resulted in the gradual growth of the Outer Regions can be gathered from an increase in the number of *controleurs* (controllers), the 'field workers' of the civil service. By 1880 a hundred of them were active in Java and 116 in the Outer Regions; in 1900 there were 115 in Java and as many as 142 in the Outer Regions.[220] However, the more populous Java

220. De Kat Angelino, *Staatkundig beleid* II, p. 91; cf. chapter H in *Koloniale Verslagen* (Colonial Reports).

remained the centre of gravity of the colonial administration. Apart from establishing Dutch authority in the Outer Regions, Van der Wijck also paid a great deal of attention to the reform of sugar cultivation, the increase of irrigation and the curbing of opium use in Java. The welfare programmes of the 'Ethical Policy' were at first directed to an even greater extent at Java.[221] But around the turn of the century the colonial administration began to concentrate mainly on the Outer Regions. The successful pacification of Acheh played an important role, with regard to both quantity and quality. With regard to quantity, it set free a large number of troops and financial resources that could now be used for other parts of the Outer Regions. As for quality, the pacification of Acheh was used as a model for establishing Dutch rule in other parts, a task that was often undertaken by civilian and military 'Acheh men'. The subjection of local rulers and elites to Dutch authority often took place after the so-called 'Short Declaration'; this was the model contract which Van Heutsz and Snouck Hurgronje had developed, in the first instance, for the dependencies of Acheh. According to Van der Wijck, the declaration was to eliminate once and for all the 'unfavourable consequences of the Nisero issue'. In 1898 the Short Declaration was chosen as the rule for all 'native self-government' in the Outer Regions, although often an even more direct form of colonial rule was adopted. The declaration was short indeed, but it firmly established Dutch authority over local rulers and elites. Major Colijn, who became responsible for the implementation of the Short Declaration in the Outer Regions, under governor-general Van Heutsz, by persuasion when possible and by force if necessary, therefore dated the final end of the policy of absention in 1898.[222]

As part of his pacification policy in Acheh, Van Heutsz promoted European agriculture and mining in particular, with the idea that this would increase both the welfare of the local population and also the revenue of the colonial administration.[223] European agricultural and mining enterprises, in turn, were equally keen to benefit from the pacification of north Sumatra. The Royal Dutch Oil Company had struck its first wells in 1892 in Langat, an unstable border area between Siak and Acheh. In 1894 there had been an attack of an

221. Locher-Scholten, *Ethiek*, pp. 186–90. Cf. W. M., 'Java en Madoera contra de Buitenbezittingen', *IG*, 1905, I, pp. 505–46.

222. [Colijn], *Politiek beleid* I, p. 198; cf. Somer, *Korte Verklaring*, pp. 252ff. See also Van der Wijck to Cremer, 12 December 1898, Van der Wijck Collection.

223. Cf. Witte, *Van Heutsz*, pp. 66ff.; Landhout, *Staatkunde*, pp. 176ff.

Achenese war party on the wells. In 1897 a strong expansion of activities and profits was anticipated in the annual report 'now that the East Indian administration is establishing Dutch authority so efficiently and energetically in northern Sumatra, and our valiant army can see its feats of arms crowned with success'. That the interests of this company were not simply allowed to gain the upper hand but were weighed seriously can be seen in the well-known conflict between Van Heutsz and the Royal Dutch Oil Company over the Perlak oil wells. Van Heutsz refused to grant the company permission to build a pipeline for the processing of oil outside Perlak, as the local population would then not be able to profit. In Batavia, however, Van der Wijck eventually decided in favour of the pipeline. 'The general interest of the East Indies at large demanded such a step', Gerretson was to comment later.[224]

According to Gerretson, the idea of a general interest in the promotion of trade and industry and the revenue of the colonial administration also dominated the new mining law, introduced to Parliament by Cremer in 1899. On the one hand, to allow for the possibility of state-run mines, this bill reinforced the position of the state in controlling the land and the granting of concessions. On the other hand, private mining companies were assured of profitable business opportunities by means of a limited fixed entitlement and no more than a 2 per cent on gross proceeds. For new oil-concessions a taxfree period of three years was proposed. When Cermer gave in to a parliamentary committee and raised this tax to 4 per cent, Van Kol and the left-wing Liberals Pyttersen and J. M. Pijnacker Hordijk (brother of the former governor-general) put forward various amendments aimed at greater increases. However, their motions were defeated by varying majorities, and the entire bill was finally passed with 64 votes to 9. As well as the Socialists, several Liberals and Anti-Revolutionaries had voted against.[225] 'The only difficult thing to endure were those long-winded speeches of Van Kol', wrote Cremer, who was still suffering from headaches, to Van der Wijck.

Apart from economic development, Cremer felt that his mining law would also be of great importance to the expansion of the colonial administration. 'The more that development in the Outer

---

224. Gerretson, *Geschiedenis* II, p. 145; cf. Van Tijn, 'Nabeschouwing', p. 85.
225. Wellenstein, *Mijnbouwvraagstuk*, pp. 53ff.; cf. Idema, *Geschiedenis*, pp. 122–9.

Regions is brought about by agriculture and the mining industry, the easier it will be to follow the policy which I have outlined, as this will benefit the revenue of the treasury', he told Van der Wijck in confidence. 'It therefore seems right to me that we should continue on the path we have taken and encourage private industry wherever possible . . . If we ever get a chance to acquire a good mine, then the interests of the general public will be served well enough.'[226]

These considerations affected not only the mining industry. Cremer also ensured that the concession for the Royal Packet Company was extended in 1899, and indeed with conditions that were very advantageous to the company. After all, not only had the KPM given effective help in promoting the economic development of the Archipelago, but it had also rendered important services to the colonial administration, particularly by transporting quick military reinforcements to Lombok in 1894 and Acheh in 1896.[227]

Partly due to preferential treatment by the administration, private investment in the Outer Regions, both in agriculture and in the mining industry, showed a strong increase around 1900. Van Tijn, for example, has pointed out that there was an increase in the number of Amsterdam-based agricultural companies and their sub-scribed capital. During the 1890s the number of these companies outside Java effectively grew from 9, with a capital of 8.5 million guilders in 1890, to 58, with a capital of 49.2 million guilders in 1900. Investment in the mining industry was even greater, but subject to considerable fluctuation. In a peak year such as 1897 five million guilders was channelled into the gold mines of the Celebes and Borneo, and no less than 31.5 million guilders into the 16 petroleum companies active in the East Indies.[228] The share of products from the Outer Regions in the strongly increasing East Indian exports rose from 20 per cent in 1890 to nearly 50 per cent in 1913. Not only in the Outer Regions but also in Java there was a steady increase in Dutch investment, especially after the inter-national abolition of protective laws on sugar beet by the 1904 Brussels Convention. According to various estimates, the total

226. Cremer to Van der Wijck, 28 June 1898, Van der Wijck Collection.
227. *Halve Eeuw*, pp. 88–94.
228. Van Tijn, 'Nabeschouwing', pp. 83–4. Cf. 'Staat van alle te Amsterdam gevestigde Nederlandsch-Indische Cultuur- en Landbouw-Maatschappijen sedert 1870 opgericht', *Verslag Kvk Amsterdam* (Report of the Amsterdam Chamber of Commerce) 1900.

Dutch investment doubled between 1900 and 1913, from 750 million guilders or 7.5 per cent of all Dutch investments (domestic and foreign) in 1900, to 1.5 billion or 10 per cent in 1913. Their lucrative nature can be gathered from the fact that issues from Dutch companies in the East Indies were effectively 325 million guilders between 1904 and 1914: that is 30 per cent of all domestic issues of Dutch enterprises.[229] Foreign investments in the Outer Regions increased also, particularly British and American investments in Deli and surrounding areas, although Dutch capital remained predominant. In 1897 the British Shell Company started oil exploitation in Borneo, which was successfully expanded. In 1907 the Royal Dutch Oil Company and Shell amalgamated, with a majority position for Royal Dutch. In 1912 even Standard Oil was finally admitted to the East Indies.

In 1903, there were about 65,000 Europeans and Eurasians living in the East Indies, 50,000 in Java and 15,000 in the Outer Regions. Out of a population of over 35 million Indonesians, of which 28 million lived in Java and 7 million in the Outer Regions, 446,000 were 'indigenous Christians'; they were mainly Protestants, Roman Catholics numbering only 28,000. Protestant missions, in particular, had stepped up their activities quite considerably around the year 1900. In 1904 there were over 150 missionaries in the Archipelago, compared to about 100 in 1897. Nearly half of them, however, were members of the German Rhineland Mission, rather than the various Dutch missionary organisations. Protestant missionary activities clearly benefited from the administrative and economic expansion in the Archipelago. Cremer saw missionaries as 'a way . . . of spreading culture, promoting welfare and establishing law and order': a statement by the Liberal minister which was appropriately welcomed by the Christians.[230]

As early as 1888, when Cremer was still an MP, he had spoken strongly in favour of admitting Dutch missionaries to the Batak areas, accompanied by one or two commissioners, in order to curb the proselytising zeal of the Muslims coming from Acheh. 'If civil servants and missionaries go there, then the simple-minded Bataks

229. Burger, *Geschiedenis* II, p. 83; cf. the entry 'Rechten (in-, uit- en doorvoer)' [Rights (import, export and transit)] in the *ENI*.
230. Memorandum of a reply, *Bijlagen Handelingen Tweede Kamer* (Parliamentary Reports of the Second Chamber, Appendix) 1897–8, p. 4. Cf. the entries 'Zending' (Protestant mission) and 'Christengemeenten' (Christian communities) in *ENI*.

can form a bulwark against Acheh; if not, then they will feel compelled to join our enemies', reasoned Cremer, who was also thinking of the safety of nearby Deli.[231] In 1892 a commissioner in charge of Batak affairs was appointed, though for the time being no permanent colonial post was set up. Through the mediation of Cremer, however, the Dutch Missionary Society was permitted to set up a missionary station in the Batak area, which was temporarily funded entirely by the Deli Company. This Dutch Batak mission turned out to be extremely successful and helped to pave the way for a permanent colonial post. In central Celebes, in the 1890s, A. C. Kruyt played a similar mediating role between the population and the colonial administration.[232] The work of the Utrecht missionaries in New Guinea benefited very strongly from the opening of a KPM steamship line in 1891, set up through the mediation of the colonial administration. The arrival of the commissioners and thus the direct establishment of a colonial post was welcomed at the missionary stations with great celebrations because they had been requesting this for quite some time.[233]

As we have seen before, apart from the interest of the missionaries, the colonial post in New Guinea was mainly motivated by foreign politics. Even Van Kol had to admit that economic interests hardly played any role at all, though he felt that New Guinea was an exception in this respect – a conclusion which seems to have been confirmed by more recent historical research.[234] Administrative expansion in northern Celebes was apparently directed primarily at the promotion and control of the gold industry. Several members of the colonial administration and East Indian Council developed business connections with the mining companies.[235] The oil industry, which was looking for oil not only in northern but also in central Sumatra, especially in Djambi, was even more promising. Disruptions to the oil industry therefore led directly to the military

231. *Handelingen Tweede Kamer* (Parliamentary Reports of the Second Chamber), 16 November 1888, pp. 194–5; cf. *Mededeelingen van het Nederlandsch Zendelinggenootschap*, 1891, pp. 43–68 and 309–412; ibid. 1893, pp. 406–7.

232. Arts and Van Beurden, *Goud*, pp. 90–3.

233. *Berigten Utrechtsche Zebndingsvereeniging*, 1899, pp. 117–19.

234. *Handelingen Tweede Kamer* (Parliamentary Reports of the Second Chamber), 19 November 1897, pp. 76–7.

235. Former Minister of the Colonies Sprenger van Eyck acted as the commissioner of one of the affected mining companies. From 1894 to 1897, he had been Minister of Finance under Röell-Van Houten. Cf. Arts and Van Beurden, *Goud*, pp. 19ff.

annexation of the sultanate by the colonial administration in 1901.

In The Hague minister Van Asch van Wijck defended this action with the ethical argument that the population had to be protected from the sultan's 'misgovernment'. Van Kol could brush aside this argument quite easily, pointing to 'the powerful influence of the capital which dominates agriculture, mining and industry at the expense of the interests of the indigenous population'. Locher-Scholten's research has so far shown that, in the final analysis, administrative interests and motives were the decisive factors. For the colonial administration Djambi was offering the first opportunity outside Acheh to put its new principles into practice. The establishment of Dutch authority was both the starting point and the final aim and therefore more important than any other considerations, whether economic or ethical.[236] At the end of the chapter, where we will be looking at the imperialism debate in the Netherlands around 1900, we shall come back to this configuration of interests and motives.

The Reaction to the Boer War

New Holland under Pressure

While opinions in the Netherlands were extremely divided as to whether the establishment of Dutch rule in the Indonesian Archipelago should be called imperialist, there was unanimous consent about the British subjection of the South African Boer republics. Only a small number of contemporaries seem to have realised that the aim of a 'New Holland' in the Transvaal – which was abruptly ended by the British annexation – also had imperialist features. This aim had already come under increasing pressure before the Boer War, not only from the British side but also from the 'kinsmen' of the Dutch, the Boers. During the 1890s several Dutch friends of the Transvaal, especially Kuyper, increasingly reverted to their pursuit of a Dutch South Africa. Nevertheless, this did not diminish their indignation at British imperialism and their concern for the fate of the Boers.

Van Winter has pointed out that Dutch interest in South Africa

---

236. Locher-Scholten, *Motieven*. Cf. *Handelingen Tweede Kamer* (Parliamentary Reports of the Second Chamber), 20 and 21 November 1901, pp. 103–4 and 120–1.

reached a climax around 1890.[237] At the time, it seemed as if a 'New Holland' might have a real chance of being established – with the NZAV as an active pressure group in the Netherlands; with Dutchmen like Leyds and Mansvelt in key positions within the SAR; and with the NZASM paving the way for further Dutch influence in South Africa. The most prominent opponent on the side of the Afrikaners, Du Toit, seemed to have completely lost his influence in the Transvaal and finally returned to the Cape Colony. Like Leyds before, Kuyper now began to see his former ally as a dangerous henchman of British imperialism. He had already been suspicious of Du Toit's language policy for a long time. Kuyper saw Afrikaans as a Dutch dialect like Frisian or Limburg Dutch and felt it would therefore not be able to stand up to the linguistic influence of English. He strongly advised against an Afrikaans Bible translation.[238] Neither Kuyper nor Leyds were able to see any authentic, viable elements in Afrikaner nationalism, as proclaimed by Du Toit, J. H. Hofmeyer and other leaders of the Afrikaner Bond. For these Cape Afrikaners cultural unity and autonomy were more important than national independence; they were so important, in fact, that they could on the whole support Rhodes's plans to set up a united, bilingual South Africa under British supremacy.[239]

Kuyper saw the co-operation between Du Toit and Rhodes as no more than 'the terrible danger which . . . lurks in any contact with Mammon', and merely repeated his plea for a Dutch South Africa – an idea which had only alienated Du Toit. Kuyper stated with regret that through the loss of the Cape and the cession of the Gold Coast the Netherlands could now no longer play any direct role 'in the great steeplechase of the great powers for the possession of the Black Continent'. But the Netherlands could at least use its 'indirect influence' in South Africa as much as possible. On the one hand, it was of course important that the political independence of the SAR and the Orange Free State should be respected.

And on the other hand we regard it as equally indisputable that the Transvaalers cannot possibly hold their own against the Anglo–Saxon race unless they do their utmost to reach that higher level of linguistic and cultural development which has been achieved by their kinsmen on the rivers Schelde and Rhine.

237. Van Winter, *Hollanders* II, p. 13.
238. *De Standaard*, 24 April 1884. Cf. Van Koppen, *Kuyper*, pp. 58–9.
239. Davenport, *Afrikaner Bond*, Chapter 8.

Indeed, the continuation of Dutch support was made dependent on this point. 'If there were the prospect that the Transvaal would become a British protectorate again after a few years, then why should we make any sacrifice?' wondered Kuyper as early 1890.[240]

Such remarks caused great protests not only among the more cultured Afrikaners but also among the Transvaal Boers, whose traditional rejection of Dutch arrogance and greed was also rekindled by the gradual growth of Dutch influence after 1884. Kruger's counter-candidate for the presidential elections, P. J. Joubert, was swift to make use of the many disparate grievances against Kruger's *Hollandpolitiek*. In 1893 Kruger defeated Joubert with a very close majority of 7,881 votes to 7,009, having beaten him with 4,483 votes to 834 in 1888. Joubert's Progressive Party subsequently extended its influence in the Parliament of the SAR even further, until it had 11 out of 26 seats in 1895, as opposed to 9 Kruger supporters and 6 independents.[241] The Dutch Friends of the Transvaal still celebrated Kruger's victory, though it soon became obvious that Kruger was distancing himself from the Dutch.

State concessions were increasingly given to other foreigners, and an increasing number of well-qualified Cape Afrikaners were admitted into the civil service apparatus. With its high fares, the NZASM had been causing more and more irritation in the Transvaal and was no longer assured of Kruger's protection when the new Parliament of the SAR began to urge nationalisation. Meanwhile the chaotic – and at times corrupt – financial administration of the SAR had also caused consternation in the Netherlands. 'Sadly, I must admit that I have not succeeded in organising our system of finance and taxation in accordance with the principles of correctness . . . that I have learnt', Leyds confided to Pierson, who had taught him these principles. However, even Leyds caused suspicion in the Netherlands. 'The way in which you were talked about', warned Moltzer, 'no longer exuded the same total and complete trust in your integrity.'[242] At the same time Leyds increasingly became the centre of hatred towards the Dutch in the Transvaal. Leyds had already said in 1892, when he was reappointed Secretary of State, 'The Dutch are welcome as long as they are needed, but not because

240. *De Standaard*, 30 May 1890; cf. 5 May.
241. Gordon, *Growth*, pp. 213 and 239. For Kruger's *Hollanderpolitiek* as an 'issue', see ibid., pp. 126–39; Schutte, *Hollanders*, chapter 6.
242. Moltzer to Leyds, 25 November 1892; Leyds to Pierson, 19 September 1891, Leyds Collection.

they are loved.' Even Kruger was now less willing than before to leave governmental matters in Leyds's hands.[243]

However, now that it seemed as if the Transvaal and the Netherlands were going to have opposing interests in the railway issue, Leyds unambiguously decided in favour of the Transvaal. 'Nationalisation is bound to happen sooner or later,' he warned Beelaerts in the Netherlands, 'and this is largely the fault of the NZASM itself.'[244] At the end of 1893 Leyds travelled to Europe to help the NZASM acquire the Portuguese railway concession to Delagoa Bay. Although there was a good deal of communication, with many issues being clarified during the Amsterdam transactions, there remained a certain distance between Leyds and the Dutch parties concerned. 'It is unwise to give preference to an unsuitable Dutchman rather than a suitable foreigner', he remarked on Dutch pressure when a director of the National Bank was appointed.[245]

Through his loyal attitude Leyds managed to maintain Kruger's trust and, in the course of the 1890s, was able to help Dutch interests after all. For the time being the danger of a nationalised NZASM had been averted. And when the Delagoa line was opened in 1895, the credit balance of the company in the SAR increased again. Leyds strongly recommended sending 'a smart cruiser' on this occasion, to clearly emphasise Dutch interests in South Africa, and the Dutch government did indeed sent the brand-new *Koningin Wilhelmina* from the East Indies. Unfortunately, however, one of the Dutch naval officers spoilt the effect again when he remarked about the Transvaal, 'After all, this *is* the finest of all our colonies.'[246]

The opening of the Delagoa railway line also attracted attention in the Netherlands, and indeed 'not merely because of traditional kinship'. 'The sincere co-operation of an efficient and enterprising Dutch element with the citizens of the South African Republic can be very fruitful', concluded F. V. Engelenburg in *De Gids*. The

243. Leyds to E. Everwijn Lange, 10 July 1892; cf. Leyds's diary entry on Kruger of 17 September 1892, Leyds Collection.
244. Leyds to Beelaerts, 6 May 1893. Beelaerts, on the other hand, felt that nationalisation would be 'a disaster'; Beelaerts to Leyds, 15 June 1893, Leyds Collection.
245. Leyds to Beelaerts, 13 May 1894, Leyds Collection. Cf. Van Winter, *Hollanders* II, pp. 147–9.
246. Schutte, *Hollanders*, p. 25. Cf. Leyds to Beelaerts, 30 December 1894, Leyds Collection.

orders for railway material placed by the NZASM in the Netherlands underlined his words, totalling nearly six million guilders'
worth from Werkspoor and another two million from other Dutch
companies.[247] The new consul-general in Pretoria, F. J. Domela
Nieuwenhuis, expressed himself very positively about Dutch trading prospects in South Africa, now that the Delagoa line had been
completed and the Transvaal economy was recovering from a
temporary slump. Along with several Amsterdam companies, he
strongly recommended that a direct steamship link should be
opened between the Netherlands and Delagoa Bay, although trade
with the SAR remained in fact rather too insignificant and one-sided
for such a step.[248]

Apart from the NZASM, which had about 1,500 Dutch employees in 1898, the most important source of Dutch influence was
still education. Under the energetic leadership of Superintendent
Mansvelt, a number of measures were taken to strengthen the
position of the Dutch language and Dutch teachers in the SAR. A
new Education Act in 1892 increased the government subsidy and
improved the system of school inspections, as well as setting up a
'model state school' and a grammar school in 1893, and a mining
school in 1897. Out of 836 teachers in the Transvaal, about 300
came from the Netherlands. The number of Dutch civil servants had
also increased from 160 in 1892 to 306 in 1898. However, as the
overall civil servant apparatus had also grown quite considerably,
the Dutch share had in fact gone down from 18.5 to 17.1 per
cent.[249]

During Leyds's last term of office in South Africa, Dutch interests therefore continued to be in good hands, although 'New
Holland' was not mentioned as frequently and passionately as it
used to be. In 1897 Leyds was re-elected as Secretary of State by the
Parliament of the SAR. He was staying in Europe at the time, where
he was being treated for a serious throat problem. It was a handicap
which rather impeded his ability to speak in public and eventually
led to his early resignation as Secretary of State in 1898. But there
were also important political reasons for his return to Europe. The

247. F. V. Engelenburg, 'De wording van den Delagoabaai-spoorweg', *De Gids*,
1895, i, p. 71. Cf. Schotanus, *Betrekkingen*, p. 123.
248. *Consulaire verslagen* (Consular Reports) 1895, pp. 211–13; ibid. 1896, pp.
651–64. Cf. *Verslag Kvk Amsterdam* (Report of the Amsterdam Chamber of Commerce) 1895, pp. 29–30; ibid. 1896, p. 189.
249. Schutte, *Hollanders*, pp. 49 and 51–52.

attempts of British 'foreigners' to gain suffrage in the Transvaal resulted in increasing British pressure on the republic, first by Rhodes from Cape Town and then Chamberlain from London. Again and again Leyds saw himself confronted by 'further evidence that Albion is as perfidious as ever'. In Europe he had already frequently stated that the aged Beelaerts van Blokland was no longer very effective as a diplomatic representative of the threatened republic. 'He is a diplomat of the old school; the sort of person who always makes a mysterious face and never says anything', Leyds wrote after a talk at the German Foreign Office in Berlin.[250] After Beelaerts's death in 1898 Leyds was to become his official successor as the SAR ambassador in Europe. Meanwhile he had already functioned as such when the Jameson Raid had brought about an international crisis at the end of 1895 and beginning of 1896 – first in relations between Britain and the Transvaal and then between Germany and Britain.

From the Jameson Raid to the Peace Conference

When Jameson raided Johannesburg with about five hundred mounted policemen, the Boer leaders closely attached themselves to Kruger, and Dutch interest in South Africa increased again. However, the unsuccessful Jameson raid only temporarily delayed the end of the SAR British pressure on the republic was soon to increase again very quickly, due to Britain's suzerainty claims based on the 1884 convention. This meant that the SAR became more and more isolated in international politics. Having come to an agreement with Britain in 1898 on the possible partitition of the Portuguese colonies, Germany now pursued a policy of aloofness, although the Kaiser had explicitly given his support to Kruger in 1896. The diplomatic isolation of the SAR could be seen especially clearly at the Peace Conference in The Hague in 1899, when neither the South African Republic nor the Orange Free State were invited because of British participation. The exclusion of the two Boer republics, which was the responsibility of the Dutch Minister for Foreign Affairs De Beaufort, almost led to a domestic crisis in the Netherlands.[251]

250. Leyds's diary entry of 29 December 1895; cf. Leyds to Beelaerts, 28 April 1895, Leyds Collection.
251. Cf. Pakenham, *Boer War*, pp. 9–61; Porter, *Origins*, chapters 3–8; Marais, *Fall*, chapters 3–6.

This 'buccaneer attack on the Transvaal', as Boissevain called the Jameson raid, caused extremely strong feelings in many circles.[252] For L. Penning, an ordinary travelling trade representative and fundamentalist Christian with nationalist leanings, New Year's Eve 1896 was to be 'the turning point' of his life. 'I could not sleep that night', he later wrote in his memoirs; 'my nerves were in a terrible state. And when I finally fell asleep, I was woken by a nightmare about Jameson and the Boers.' Penning then wrote a poem about the Boer victory over the 'arch-bandit' Jameson, but this only calmed him down for a little while. This was followed by a series in a local Christian paper and eventually, during the actual Boer War, Penning became a 'famous popular author'.[253] Kuyper responded far more cautiously to the Jameson Raid than many other rank-and-file Calvinists. Eventually, however, he also welcomed the victory of the Boers 'with unfeigned joy', while strongly condemning Rhodes's and Jameson's 'dark plot' and rejecting British suzerainty claims as a manifestation of 'false jingoism'. At the beginning, he felt that the Transvaal was apparently making 'too little effort to fend off "British culture" and it would do better to strengthen its ties with traditional Dutch development'. 'It's the curse of gold', said Kuyper.[254]

Though for different reasons, the Catholic magazine *Tijd* was equally sceptical:

As long as Garibaldi is still revered as a knightly hero by the vast majority of those who are currently getting steamed up about the cause of the Boers, we cannot see anything of what we would like to see in all this display of indignation about Britain's perfidy; that is, evidence of advanced public morality and a victory of people's sense of justice.[255]

The Socialist publicist Tak also described reactions in the Netherlands as 'exaggerated', even though he himself rejected British power politics and approved of Kruger's 'shrewd' policy towards foreigners as being 'aimed at self-preservation'.[256] Especially among Liberals there was plenty of indignation at the 'perfidious Albion' while at the same time they were paying homage to the 'heroic Boers'. The well-known telegram of the German Kaiser was gener-

252. *Het Handelsblad*, 3 January 1896.
253. Penning, *Leven*, pp. 134ff.
254. *De Standaard*, 1, 4, 7 and 8 January 1896.
255. *De Tijd*, 8 January 1896.
256. 'Engelsche politiek', *De Kroniek*, 12 January 1896.

ally welcomed. 'Unfortunately', stated the *NRC* with regret, 'we do not have a fleet, an army or any authority with which we might actively help the Boers against a great power.'[257]

The NZAV leadership used the alternative weapons of a small state by invoking international law in their manifesto 'To the British People'. Gunning and Spruyt warned the 'blinded' British that 'only strict observance of the principles of *law* and *morals* can restore the shaken confidence and secure the gradual development of South Africa.' This manifesto certainly seemed to speak to the Dutch public, and indeed so strongly that the NZAV decided to set up a 'Language Fund for the preservation and promotion of Dutch as the national language in the Boer republics of South Africa', so that the Boers could at least have an 'intellectual sword'. As a result of the Jameson Raid the NZAV, which had become somewhat apathetic, received fresh vigour, and its membership rose from 800 in 1895 to more than 1,800 in 1896. In the following years the older, more idealistic generation of board members was succeeded by a new generation of men who had a more prosaic interest in South Africa: H. P. G. Quack, who was interested both in railways and 'the dream of the Greater Netherlands', acted as chairman until the managing director of the NZASM, Middleberg, returned from South Africa.[258]

The old defensive concept of a 'New Holland' in the Transvaal had indeed made room for a new, ambitious idea of a 'Greater Netherlands', in which somehow or other the Netherlands, Flanders and South Africa would be united. After the Jameson Raid an appeal had already been published under the title 'The Dutch Lion' in the weekly paper *De Amsterdammer*, calling for the formation of 'a big, powerful Dutch Alliance' in order to get closer to such a lofty goal.[259] In the summer of 1896, at the 23rd Conference of Dutch Language and Literature in Antwerp, it was decided to set up a General Dutch Alliance (Algemeen Nederlands Verbond, ANV) that would give more concrete substance to the 'Greater Netherlands idea', at least culturally. All three great political and ideological groups in the Netherlands were represented in the cultural nationalism of the ANV: the Catholic leader Schaepman, who had

257. *NRC*, 5 January 1896; cf. *Nieuws van den Dag, De Telegraaf, Het Vaderland* and *Het Handelsblad* of 3 January 1896.
258. *Nederland–Zuid-Afrika*, pp. 110–14; *Verslag NZAV* (NZAV Report) 1895–6, pp. 8–14. Cf. Quack, *Herinneringen*, p. 496.
259. *De Amsterdammer* (weekly), 12 January and 2 February 1896.

helped to found the society as a prominent poet, became vice-chairman, while both Prime Minister Pierson and the leader of the opposition, Kuyper, joined the Advisory Council. President Kruger became honorary chairman of the South African division.[260] As before, only the Socialist weekly *De Kroniek* spoilt it all, and Tak treated the ANV with mild mockery. All this enthusiasm over the spreading of the Dutch language in Belgium, South Africa and the East Indies made him think rather irreverently of genteel ladies knitting 'for the bare buttocks of the Firelanders'. But according to Frank van der Goes all the 'cant' of the 'Greater Netherlands' merely concealed the profit motive of the NZASM and other Dutch capital interests in South Africa.[261]

For the time being, Dutch foreign politics were to remain safe from this revival of Greater Dutch interest in South Africa. 'And what about Holland?' Kruger had asked Consul-general Domela Nieuwenhuis, when he received the telegram from the German Kaiser. After the Jameson Raid Domela advised sending a Dutch warship to Lorenço Marques, with a view to 'our interests here'. But minister Röell felt that showing the flag was 'not desirable in the very first months', because of the tensions between Germany and Britain. The Dutch government decided to wait for another week before sending its carefully worded congratulations to Kruger. Röell could assure Queen Emma that 'this telegram cannot give offence to the British government, either in content or in tendency, while at the same time it shows that we are sympathetic.'[262]

The British government, however, did not leave him in peace but asked for clarification when an innocent extradition treaty had been concluded between the Netherlands and the SAR – a treaty which, according to the 1884 convention, had to be submitted to Britain for approval. Röell saw the SAR as a 'sovereign state', though both he and the Minister of Justice, W. van der Kaaij, realised that the Transvaal itself had accepted British authority over its treaties with other countries. There was therefore a great temptation to leave the whole question entirely to the British and Transvaal governments. On the other hand, however, the British request for clarification could hardly be denied. 'What would we say if Britain took such a view towards semi-sovereign states in the East Indies which have

260. *Neerlandia*, May 1897.
261. *De Kroniek*, 9 February 1896; cf. Tak, 'Het Algemeen Nederlandsch Verbond', ibid., 18 December 1898.
262. Woltring, *Bescheiden* VI, no. 120; cf. nos 116 and 123.

also ceded to us their right to conclude treaties', Van der Kaaij said in this connection. Röell therefore decided to pass the requested information to the British ambassador, pointing out emphatically that the Netherlands did not wish to reinterpret the 1884 convention.[263]

Minister De Beaufort could not get out of it quite so easily when, during preparations for the Peace Conference at the beginning of 1899, the decision had to be made whether the Boer republics should be invited. In retrospect, De Beaufort was criticised for simply accepting the list of invitations submitted to him by the Russian Foreign Minister; this list included neither the Boer republics nor the pope, because they were not represented in St Petersburg. De Beaufort was well aware that his Russian colleague had put him in a rather critical position. De Beaufort had learnt through the Dutch and foreign ambassadors that Britain and Italy would not take part in the conference if the Boer republics or the pope were invited. If even one of the great powers refused to participate, the conference would have failed before it had even started. De Beaufort could of course have tried to elicit an official declaration from the British government, as his German colleague Von Bülow suggested, but this could be viewed as implicit recognition of British suzerainty over the Boer republics.

De Beaufort then tried to ask one of the great powers – Germany – to advise the SAR and the Orange Free State to follow the example of the other African and South American states and to refrain from applying. But Von Bülow showed no interest, so that De Beaufort was finally confronted with South African applications after all, which he then had to reject.[264] De Beaufort could in fact have been less cautious towards Britain on this issue. At an earlier stage he had already made some careful enquiries with the British ambassador about a possible invitation for the Boer republics, but when the ambassador failed to answer him in a direct way, De Beaufort decided to let the matter rest. Official approaches need not have included the question of recognising British suzerainty if he had followed Röell and made it clear that the Netherlands had its reservations in this matter. However, this would have meant greater risks for the Netherlands. And such approaches could hardly have prevented the British veto.[265]

---

263. Ibid., nos 218–218A; cf. nos 191, 199 and 212.
264. De Jong, *De Beaufort*, pp. 43–8; Smit, *Nederland*, pp. 35–7; Dülffer, *Regeln*, pp. 63–5.
265. Smit, *Bescheiden* I, nos 25 and 76; cf. De Jong, *De Beaufort*, pp. 45–6.

It is certainly not true that De Beaufort acted out of indifference towards the fate of the Boer republics, as Kuyper suggested later. In 1881 he had been one of the founders of the NZAV and he continued as one of the board members until 1897. He had frequently crossed swords with Kuyper, among others within the NZAV in 1882, before the latter interpellated him in the Second Chamber about the exclusion of the Boer republics. Apart from personal animosity, Kuyper also seems to have seen a political opportunity to cause embarrassment to the Liberal government. Van Koppen – and with him many observers at the time – felt that there was 'something insincere, something sly' about Kuyper's indignation.[266]

Kuyper criticised De Beaufort for not having ascertained whether the Boer republics could actually be invited at all; if not, then the Russian proposal to hold the Peace Conference in The Hague should have been turned down. Meanwhile, however, he had let every opportunity pass when he could have pointed out this possibility to the government at an early stage. Although he was now criticising De Beaufort for collaborating in the 'international ostracism' of the 'ethnically and linguistically related republics', he himself had regularly expressed his doubts about their right of existence during the past years, on the grounds that they were making too little effort to resist British influence. This criticism, in turn, was totally contradicted by his recent recommendation of the United States as a country for Dutch emigrants, especially Protestants, even though this would mean far-reaching adaptation to an English-speaking environment.[267] Kuyper's interpellation therefore seems to have been directed mainly at the public gallery, which was indeed 'full to overflowing' with interested persons from the Netherlands and abroad, as De Beaufort had to admit. Although De Beaufort rejected Kuyper's proposal to find out whether the Boer republics could be invited after all, Kuyper did not succeed in bringing about a parliamentary ballot on this occasion.[268]

Indirectly, the interpellation was to cause great embarrassment to De Beaufort, because the Dutch ambassador in St Petersburg,

266. Van Koppen, *Kuyper*, p. 141. 'We regret that Dr Kuyper will be the interpellant', wrote *De Amsterdammer* (weekly) on 30 April 1899, also strongly condemning the exclusion of the Boer republics.
267. *De Standaard*, 13 and 15 March 1899.
268. *Handelingen Tweede Kamer* (Parliamentary Reports of the Second Chamber), 2 May 1899, pp. 950–6. Cf. *De Standaard*, 17 April and 5 May 1899; De Beaufort, *Vijftig jaren* I, pp. 207–8.

Wttewaal van Stoetwegen, gave vent to his feelings by writing a violent attack on Kuyper in the *NRC*. The diplomat apparently felt offended by Kuyper's criticism that Dutch diplomacy had already failed towards the Russian government at an early stage, and he characterised Kuyper's interpellation as a 'web of heresies as regards international law, interwoven with untrue facts, false premises, incorrect allegations and illogical conclusions, giving proof of phenomenal ignorance of the sphere of diplomacy'. This grotesque intervention, which according to Tak aroused 'convulsions of laughter' in many circles, gave Kuyper an excellent opportunity to repeat with great sarcasm his scepticism about the functioning of Dutch diplomacy.[269] When Prime Minister Pierson, to his 'horror', saw this 'preposterous and peculiarly clumsy letter' printed in the *NRC*, he felt that this ambassador could no longer be supported. De Beaufort and other ministers agreed, and in an icy letter De Beaufort notified the belligerent ambassador of his dismissal.[270]

But more cold-blooded diplomats than Wttewaal also felt scandalised by Kuyper's interpellation. Van Goltstein in London warned that, with regard to South Africa, domestic politics should not start dominating foreign affairs in the Netherlands. Van Goltstein expressed concern not only about Kuyper's 'political manoeuvre', but also about the stamina of some ministers, particularly Pierson, although Pierson was very much on his guard against 'thoughtlessness' towards Britain.[271] Indeed, during the Peace Conference, the situation in South Africa deteriorated even further. In December 1899, while the foreign affairs budget was being discussed and during the final debate on the Peace Conference, the Boer War was already at its height. The cautious attitude of non-interference which the Dutch government had adopted towards the conflict aroused indignation on all sides.

Kuyper did not put forward many new arguments on the issue of invitations, though he did submit a motion stating that 'on the occasion of the Peace Conference not as much was done on behalf of the republics in South Africa, to whom we are ethnically related,

269. *NRC*, 11 May 1899; cf. *De Standaard*, 13 and 15 May 1899; *De Kroniek*, 26 November 1899.
270. See De Beaufort's draft letter to Wttewaal, De Beaufort Collection; cf. Pierson's diary, 12 May 1898, Pierson Collection.
271. Van Goltstein to De Beaufort, 20 May 1899; Pierson to De Beaufort, 30 April 1899, De Beaufort Collection. Cf. Pierson's diary, 27 April and 5 May 1899, Pierson Collection.

as might have been done.' It seemed at first that the motion would also be supported by Catholics and left-wing Liberals: the former, because the pope had been passed over in the Peace Conference; and the latter partly because of De Beaufort's conservative attitude in home affairs. The Catholics, however, dropped out when Kuyper refused to condemn the exclusion of the pope and De Savornin Lohman openly offended the feelings of the Roman Catholic part of the population. The Liberal-Democratic Chamber Club did not withdraw its support for Kuyper's motion until Pierson asked for a vote of confidence. In the end, the motion was rejected by 71 votes to 21, and only the Anti-Revolutionaries and Socialists voted in favour.[272] Domestic politics had not gained the upper hand of Dutch foreign affairs after all.

The Initial Phase of the Boer War

The long-expected war between the Boers and the British finally broke out on 11 October 1899. The Boers had set Britain an ultimatum to remove its reinforcements from their borders, and when this was ignored, the South African Republic and the Orange Free State declared war. The Boers attacked the Cape Colony and Natal and initially achieved one success after another. However, the Boer generals made no use of their victories and as soon as the British armed forces had been strengthened by new reinforcements, the tables were turned. During the 1900 the British conquered first Bloemfontein, then Johannesburg and Pretoria.

In May the formal annexation of the Orange Free State was declared, and in September that of the SAR. The Boers now began a guerilla war which the British could not possibly win by military means. President Kruger had already left South Africa on board a Dutch warship and taken up residence in the Netherlands.[273] By sending the *Gelderland*, the Dutch government had met with pressure from the general public which had become more and more impatient with Dutch aloofness and passivity. The Liberal Pierson government was put in an awkward position by the Boer War: on the one hand, with a view to the East Indies, they did not want to jeopardise their good relations with Britain; on the other hand, British behaviour towards Dutch subjects and the ethnically related

272. *Handelingen Tweede Kamer* (Parliamentary Reports of the Second Chamber), 5 and 6 December 1899, pp. 595–622. Cf. Pierson's diary, 10 December 1899.
273. Cf. Pakenham, *Boer War*, pp. 61ff.; *Gedenkboek*, pp. 84ff.

Boers in South Africa had generally caused great consternation in the Netherlands.

Although some observers were critical towards the Boers' final ultimatum on 9 October, everyone in the Netherlands agreed that the British were responsible for the ensuing war. After all, ever since the Jameson Raid it had become increasingly obvious that Chamberlain and his representative in Cape Town, the British High Commissioner Miller, would only be satisfied with totally British rule, 'Imperialism has become an *idée fixe*', said Kuyper in his 1898 annual report with regard to British government policies and public opinion. Moreover, when the news had leaked out that Britain and Germany had concluded a secret agreement about the possible partitioning of Portuguese colonies in Southern Africa, it became obvious to Kuyper 'that the free Dutch republics can now abandon any hope of moral support from Germany, if John Bull continues his perfidious policies.'[274] During the Peace Conference in 1899, when Britain continued its 'perfidious policy' in South Africa by making new, far-reaching demands on the SAR, the absence of German 'moral support' had already become apparent. 'It will be a terrible struggle', predicted Kuyper, who seems to have had very few illusions about the chances of survival for the Boer republics. At first, when war had broken out, he left the condemnation of Britain and the encouragement of the Boers to other contributors to *De Standaard*, such as Lionel Cachet.[275]

Finally, however, Kuyper also made his contribution to the international Boer propaganda by writing an incensed protest article for the French paper *Revue de deux mondes*. In this article, which was also published as a brochure in the Netherlands, Kuyper discussed, among other things, the religious side of the 'crisis in South Africa'. He fiercely attacked the justification of British action in the interests of the black population by the missionaries and their spokesmen in Britain: 'The Christian tint of imperialism is the worst danger.' True Christianity, he felt, was represented by the Boers: 'an entire nation, father, sons and grandsons, who shed their blood in the name of the Lord for their own country and who show so much moral power that the whole world is shaken by it'. Despite all the temptations of gold, said Kuyper, the Boers had kept their *Geuzen* blood.[276] As soon as the war had broken out, there were

274. *De Standaard*, 5 and 12 January 1899.
275. *De Standaard*, 20 September, 4, 9 and 16 October 1899.
276. Kuyper, *Crisis*, pp. 57 and 59.

some very belligerent reactions from Kuyper's rank and file. A number of Amsterdam teachers and Christian ministers took the initiative to form a Christian National Boer Committee and made extensive use of the *Geuzen* metaphor in their publication *Voor de Boeren* (For the Boers). Penning had sleepless nights again and started working on *De leeuw van Modderspruit* (The Lion of Modderspruit) as his contribution to 'national Christian consciousness'. This appeared as the first book in a popular Dutch series.[277]

Liberal reaction was vehement, too, and often contained a strong element of nationalism. The Dutch paper *De Amsterdammer* exhorted its readers with the words, 'Netherlands, now that your kinsmen and also your own sons are falling on the field of honour, arise. Don't just reach into your pocket but give something of your ability to work and think.' When the negotiations between Milner and Kruger were still in process in Bloemfontein, the radical paper was already explaining that general suffrage in South Africa meant something totally different to that in the Netherlands. Suffrage for the 'floating' foreigners in the Transvaal would only be of benefit to the British imperialists and capitalists, whereas the black population would never even be considered.[278] In the *Handelsblad* Boissevain, too, held his own, commenting on the war under headings such as 'Chamberlain's war', 'Blood and thunder','The weeping women of Pretoria' and 'The heroic Dutchmen'. Around Christmas he wrote an 'Open letter to the Duke of Devonshire', in which he strongly argued against the duke's conceited remarks about the Boers and their supporters in Europe.[279] The *NRC* and the *Vaderland* also condemned British action as 'flagrant injustice', but these Liberal papers showed a greater awareness of the 'incongruous relationship between *wanting to* and *being able to* do anything', a dilemma which was threatening to develop for the Netherlands with regard to South Africa.[280] The British ambassador Howard later recorded how leading Liberals had even confided in him 'in a "please don't say I told you" manner' that they would not think it quite such a horrible disaster if the backward Kruger government was replaced by a modern British one. However, Prime Minister Pierson's com-

---

277. Penning, *Leven*, pp. 142–4. For the foundation of a Christian National Boer Committee see *De Standaard*, 9 November 1899. Cf. *Voor de Boeren*, 4 and 11 May, 6 July and 21 October 1901.
278. *De Amsterdammer* (weekly), 18 June, 3 and 8 October, 29 November 1899.
279. *Het Handelsblad*, 7 January 1900; cf. 1, 4, 13, 22, 25 and 27 October 1899.
280. *NRC*, 25–6 November 1899; *Het Vaderland*, 5 October.

ment in his diary at the outbreak of the war was perhaps far more representative: 'If the Transvaal wins, it will be a victory for conservatism, and if Britain wins, it will be a victory for arrogance.'[281]

Catholics and Socialists, too, found the conservatism of the Boers difficult at first: Catholics for religious reasons and Socialists more from an economic point of view. Nevertheless, this did not keep either of the two groups from condemning British action. The Catholic leader Schaepman, who spoke at a number of Transvaal meetings said, 'The world empire which so many us, despite all sin and misery, still see as the firm stronghold of freedom and justice, this world empire has turned out to be a robber state, and its people cheer their approval.'[282] But for many Catholics this was far from obvious at first. 'Surely we cannot be expected at this moment to raise our voices in support of the Boers in the Transvaal, together with those who have welcomed the unjustified suffering that has been inflicted on our friends', commented *De Tijd* bitterly. Nevertheless, as in 1881, the same paper called upon Dutch Catholics to follow 'the voice of the blood' and to gather behind the national call of their kinsmen, the Boers: 'We, the Dutch, feel these days that regardless of religious affiliations, political parties or social classes we all form a single nation together.' In a reply to an indignant letter, *De Tijd* pointed out consolingly that, when it came to it, the Boers were far more Christian than Chamberlain or Rhodes, 'or the Prince of Wales who is known to be a great dignitary in freemasonry'.[283]

Socialists did not find the Boer War any less complicated. Whenever British imperialism was condemned, this was accompanied by a number of qualifying remarks. In *De Kroniek* W. A. Bonger, who later became a famous criminologist, argued that the war was obviously based on British capital interests but that British capitalists could speed up the development of South Africa more quickly than the archaic Boers.

This does not mean that anyone should have participated in bringing about this war; but now that it has started, it is desirable for progress and thus for social democracy that British capital should have a free hand. It's hard for the Boers, but money doesn't care about that.

281. Pierson's diary, 2 October 1899, Pierson Collection. Cf. Smit, *Bescheiden* VI, no. 115.
282. *Het Centrum*, 20 October 1899. Cf. Van Wely, *Schaepman*, pp. 562–3.
283. *De Tijd*, 25 August, 5 and 7 November, 16–17 December 1899.

Jos Loopuit in *De Sociaal-demokraat* expressed himself in similar terms.[284] Such views, however, were strongly rejected by prominent Socialists. Tak, who had little sympathy for the naive ruthlessness of young Marxist intellectuals, pointed out to Bonger that the expectations aroused by the scientific analysis of capitalist development in the long term, must not hinder a social democrat from trying to mitigate the direct consequences of capitalist development, especially whenever 'cannons and guns' were called to assist. Bonger and Loopuit's views were rejected on strictly theoretical grounds in *De Nieuwe Tijd*. Van der Goes and Roland Holst felt that Marx's analysis of the German–Danish War as a war of the 'progressive' Prussians against the 'backward' Danes could not be applied to the war in South Africa: after all, British capitalism had become parasitical and imperialist, whereas the Boer republics also included modern, progressive forces. They agreed with Tak that, in the case of the Boers, the principle of nationality should be 'recognised and defended'. 'Social democracy is for the Boers,' *De Sociaal-demokraat* commented succinctly, 'not for the sake of the Boers, but because it breathes and lives in and through the struggle against capitalism.'[285]

All the participants in this internal socialist debate agreed, however, that the chauvinistic excitement which had got hold of the Dutch bourgeoisie must be rejected. 'A warlike spirit has pervaded Holland', said the *Sociaal-demokraat*; 'the most peaceful lamb-like disposition among large numbers of the bourgeoisie, whose only weapons are innocent scissors for cutting coupons, swells up dangerously with spite against the cursed British.' The Social Democrat leader Troelstra therefore refused to take part in the umbrella Committee for the Transvaal which had been formed in 1899 and which was to co-ordinate the material and intellectual help of the different associations and committees.[286] The respected Liberal member of the First Chamber, J. E. N. Baron Schimmelpenninck van der Oye, became chairman; J. Th. de Visser, a conservative Protestant member of the Second Chamber, was made secretary; while the board of managers was formed by the NZAV

284. *De Kroniek*, 12 November; *De Sociaal-demokraat*, 26 August 1899.

285. *De Kroniek*, 12 November 1899; *De Sociaal-demokraat*, 18 and 20 November 1899. Cf. Van den Goes, 'Voor of tegen Transvaal?', *De Nieuwe Tijd*, 1899–1900, pp. 356–71. Roland Holst, 'De balans van den Zuid-Afrikaanschen oorlog'; ibid. 1900, pp. 257–65.

286. *De Sociaal-demokraat*, 18 November 1899; cf 26 August.

chairman Middelberg, ANV chairman Kern and representatives of the Liberal, Protestant and Catholic parties and trade unions.[287]

In the meantime the NZAV had written another manifesto *To the People of Great Britain*, which was signed within a very short time by 140,000 Dutch. However, the moderate, conciliatory tone of this manifesto did not go far enough for many Dutch people. The criticism in *De Amsterdammer* was typical of the fiercely nationalist, anti-British mood at the time, when it spoke of 'the *unworthy, childish, faint-hearted* and *insincere* language which the NZAV makes our people use'. The left-wing Liberal paper had more respect for the belligerent 'Greater Netherlands' solidarity which set the tone of the ANV.[288] The ANV literally saw the Transvaal movement as 'an opportunity to prove their right to exist'. Together with Leyds, the ANV secretary and grammar school teacher Kiewiet de Jonge set up a press office in Dordrecht and published as their first piece of propaganda an *Appel aux nations représentées à la conférence de la Haye*.[289] However, the Boers received the most active and tangible support from the NZAV, who organised a national collection for the benefit of war victims; together with local authorities, businesses and the academic world a total of 1.3 million guilders was raised.[290]

Although the Dutch Red Cross – one of the organisations that were sent out with this money – had quite a few problems, the Dutch government was mainly concerned about the more intellectual anti-British propaganda. During the summer De Beaufort had followed Von Bülow's request and taken a number of steps to make the Transvaal government more moderate and accommodating towards Britain. De Beaufort emphatically pointed out that if war broke out the Boer republics would receive no international support; furthermore, Pierson was very much in agreement with some of the domestic reforms which Britain was demanding of the Transvaal. As for Transvaal sovereignty, however, both Dutch ministers agreed with Leyds; in August, after mutual consultation, it was decided that Pierson should write to the British minister Goschen as a friend and ask him to try to understand the Transvaal

287. Kröll, *Buren-Agitation*, p. 146.

288. *De Amsterdammer* (weekly), 20 August and 15 October 1899. For the NZAV manifesto, see *Nederland–Zuid–Afrika*, pp. 114–15.

289. *Neerlandia*, September 1899; cf. October–December. For the Kiewiets press office, see Kröll, *Buren-Agitation*, pp. 176ff.

290. Ibid., pp. 147–51.

point of view.[291] De Beaufort assented to a similar letter which Queen Wilhelmina was to write to Queen Victoria in September.[292]

On the eve of the war De Beaufort himself informally submitted a Dutch proposal for arbitration to the British government. But before the British could reply, Kruger had already delivered his ultimatum.[293] It would therefore be wrong to say that the Dutch government did not want to help the Boers. According to the Dutch ambassador in London, the government had departed much further from their policy of aloofness towards South Africa than was justified. 'Should we risk our friendly relationship with it [the British government] for the sake of a small state which is blessed with a backward administration? I think it would be foolish', said Van Goltstein. When the war had become inevitable, he said that he would much rather stay on his country estate in the Netherlands than receive a 'mocking reply' to a Dutch declaration of neutrality from the British government. De Beaufort, however, instructed the ambassador to interrupt his furlough and return to his post, in the interests of the SAR, 'whose inhabitants are linked to us in such close kinship'. Van Goltstein returned to London again, though he also handed in his resignation because of the 'emotional policies' with regard to South Africa.[294]

It was by no means easy for the Dutch government to find the right form of aloofness in the conflict, an aloofness which – according to all the parties concerned – was demanded because of the colonial interests that were at stake in relation to Britain. The British government did indeed refuse to accept a declaration of neutrality, as it regarded the Boer republics as rebellious vassals. Following the example of other powers, the Netherlands therefore dropped this declaration.[295] Many Dutch people felt that, with this passive attitude, their government had in fact deserted the Boers, just as they had done earlier at the Peace Conference. Left-wing Liberals, in particular, were now openly urging De Beaufort to resign.[296] Meanwhile, the anti-British demonstrations in the

291. Pierson's diary, 23 July, 4 August 1899, Pierson Collection; Leyds, *Correspondentie 1899*, nos 101 and 152. Cf. Smit, *Nederland*, pp. 52–54.

292. Smit, *Bescheiden* I, no. 91; cf. Van Raalte, *Staatshoofd*, pp. 169–79.

293. Smit, *Bescheiden* I, nos 107, 113 and 115.

294. Ibid., no. 117; cf. nos 106, 113 and 118. See also Van Goltstein to De Beaufort, 11 October 1899, De Beaufort Collection.

295. Smit, *Bescheiden* I, nos 121–4 and 143. Cf. Smit, *Nederland*, pp. 56–8.

296. *De Amsterdammer* (weekly), 2 October, 26 November and 3 December 1899.

Netherlands were causing great concern in government circles. In London not only Van Goltstein but also Lord Reay warned that the 'unbridled passions in the Netherlands' would have a counter-productive effect on the British government and public opinion. As Reay put it in a concerned letter to De Beaufort: 'Professor Blok wrote to me that a lot of Dutch people would love to send a declaration of war to Britain!'[297]

The British authorities, on the other hand, caused continuous embarrassment to De Beaufort by their aggressive behaviour towards Dutch subjects and property, such as the confiscation of 'contraband goods' on Dutch ships and the internment of the NZASM staff.[298] While the Boers were still gaining victories, attention was somehow diverted from these incidents and the cautious Dutch reactions to them. This soon changed, however, when at the beginning of 1900 the war began to turn against the Boers. After the surrender of General Cronjé and his 4,000 men, President Steyn of the Orange Free State and Kruger sent a peace offer to Britain that was aimed at independence. At the same time they also asked a number of other powers, including the Netherlands, to intervene in the matter. Britain, however, simply rejected the peace offer, making it quite clear that it would not accept intervention from any country. Queen Wilhelmina even sent a personal request to the German Kaiser to develop an initiative for intervention, quite probably with De Beaufort's full knowledge. When Kaiser Wilhelm II declined, however, De Beaufort advised against sending such a letter to the tsar. It had become quite obvious by now that none of the great powers would want to defy Britain in South Africa.[299]

The reaction of the Dutch general public can be seen very clearly in the enthusiastic reception of the Transvaal deputation, consisting of Fischer, Wessels and Wolmarans, who had travelled to Europe to find support for the South African peace offer and for their request for intervention. The secretary-general of the Foreign Affairs Department, L. H. Ruyssenaers, stated that everyone in the Netherlands was in an anti-British mood, 'more or less from top to bottom', and he felt that this could no longer be ignored. The deputation was therefore given a warm welcome by Queen Wilhel-

---

297. Reay to De Beaufort, 8 November 1899, De Beaufort Collection; Smit, *Bescheiden* I, no. 130.

298. Cf. Smit, *Nederland*, pp. 58–62.

299. Ibid., pp. 62–4. Cf. De Jong, *De Beaufort*, pp. 88–9; Van Raalte, *Staatshoofd*, pp. 181–90.

mina, despite a great number of diplomatic risks. 'It is really not easy for the Queen', commented Ruyssenaers on her vulnerable position. Due to the Boer War Prince Alexander of England was no longer considered to be a prospective husband for Wilhelmina.[300]

The evasive attitude which De Beaufort had adopted towards the request for intervention and the arrival of the deputation obviously caused great consternation. When the bill for Dutch participation in the arbitration agreements of the Peace Conference was discussed, Kuyper and the Liberal Democrats Pyttersen and Veegens strongly condemned De Beaufort's policy. However, the bill was still passed by a majority of 65 votes to 20.[301]

After the British eviction of the NZASM staff and the internment of the members of the Dutch Red Cross during the conquest of the Orange Free State and the SAR, virtually everyone in the Netherlands was critical of De Beaufort's careful policy. De Savornin Lohman wrote to De Beaufort that he would refrain from any public criticism, 'but I would never have thought that any Foreign Minister could set aside his own convictions so completely just because he is afraid of Britain'.[302] Even Blok, who as a historian and Liberal was very close to De Beaufort and 'fully' understood his difficult position, felt that the Netherlands could not simply ignore such 'a blatant insult to our national feelings' as the discharge of the NZASM staff.[303] De Beaufort also received a number of anonymous letters in which a declaration of war against the 'hereditary enemy' was demanded, he was described as a 'coward', and his resignation was demanded because of his 'damned stick-in-the-mud policies'.[304]

In the autumn of 1900 feelings were running so high that it became questionable whether the government could continue in power. *De Telegraaf* and *De Amsterdammer* called upon the Dutch nation to put pressure on the government. Britain, they said, should be asked to account for its recent humiliation of the Dutch nation. De Louter in the *Utrechtsch Dagblad* described De Beaufort's foreign policies as 'pernicious' – both with regard to international law and the position of the Netherlands as a small state. The

300. Smit, *Nederland*, p. 73. Cf. Ruyssenaers to De Beaufort, 15 April 1900, De Beaufort Collection.

301. *Handelingen Tweede Kamer* (Parliamentary Reports of the Second Chamber), 30 March and 3 April year, pp. 1360–78.

302. Lohman to De Beaufort, 25 April 1899, De Beaufort Collection.

303. Blok to De Beaufort, 23 July 1900, De Beaufort Collection.

304. Book jacket 'curiosa' under no. 33, De Beaufort Collection.

criticism of this prominent Liberal was of course grist to the mill of the Christian opposition press: 'a sign of life', as *De Standaard* put it.[305] Blok and Van Naamen van Eemnes warned De Beaufort 'as friends' that the Transvaal movement was threatening to get out of hand; 'hot-headed' people were planning a demonstration outside the British embassy, a strongly worded petition to Queen Victoria and a national petition against the policy of the Dutch government. Blok felt that 'the very existence of the government is being seriously threatened.'[306] Pierson was therefore very concerned about the imminent opening of the Dutch Parliament, because 'the nation has reached boiling point with regard to the Transvaal.' Even De Beaufort was eventually persuaded that something had to be done in order to prevent undesirable 'demonstrations' directed against Britain. And so Minister of the Navy J. A. Röell had the brilliant idea of sending the cruiser *Gelderland* to Lorenço Marques. The *Gelderland*, which was in the Red Sea at the time on its way to the East Indies, was to pick up the exiled President Kruger and offer him passage to Europe. This was obviously rather risky with regard to Britain, but 'we *had to* do something that would calm down the people here at home', said Pierson.[307]

As soon as the decision had been taken, De Beaufort notified the British ambassador, of course, though ambassador Howard and he took great pains to explain to him that sending the *Gelderland* was not directed against Britain. 'He understood very well that we had done this for the sake of public opinion in our own country and said with a laugh, "Ça vous fera beaucoup de bien ici" [That'll certainly do you good here].'[308] By sending the *Gelderland* the government did indeed succeed in soothing people's hot tempers. The decision was welcomed almost unanimously. Only Fransen van de Putte expressed his view that, so far as he was concerned, the *Gelderland* should have been left to proceed to the East Indies.[309]

Kuyper, however, declared: 'Just as strongly and sharply as we

305. *De Standaard*, 17 September 1900; *Het Utrechtsch Dagblad*, 14 September. Cf. *De Amsterdammer* (weekly), 2 September, and *De Telegraaf*, 18 September 1900.

306. Blok to De Beaufort, 12 and 13 September 1900, cf. Van Naamen to De Beaufort, 7 September 1899, De Beaufort Collection.

307. Pierson's diary, 15 and 25 September 1900, Pierson Collection. Cf. De Beaufort to Blok, 14 September 1899, De Beaufort Collection.

308. Quoted from De Beaufort's notes by De Jong, *De Beaufort*, p. 93. Cf. De Beaufort, *Vijftig jaren* I, pp. 234–42.

309. *Handelingen Eerste Kamer* (Parliamentary Reports of the First Chamber), 20 September 1900, p. 10.

rejected the attitude of the cabinet with regard to the Transvaal during the Peace Conference and also when the deputation was put off, so we can now express our heartfelt joy about the decision which has been made.' Kuyper, too, seems to have been rather concerned at the strong feelings which had got hold of the Transvaal movement, and he warned his rank and file 'not to throw suspicion on the seriousness of his protest' and told them to welcome Kruger, that 'profoundly grieved old man', with dignity – 'no throngs, no impetuousness, no clamorous uproar'. At the same time, however, Kuyper could not help asking De Beaufort whether Kruger was to be met as a 'friendly head of state' or as a 'private individual'.[310]

The Final Phase of the Boer War

The sending of the *Gelderland* only gave De Beaufort a temporary respite from his problems. When Kruger was taken on board, the reception was unemotional but cordial and appropriate to his position as the exiled president of an ethnically related nation. Subsequently, however, the Dutch government did its utmost to prevent the voyage from becoming a political demonstration. When the *Gelderland* arrived in Marseilles, Leyds and the leaders of the Transvaal deputation were expressly forbidden access.[311]

But the government could not prevent Kruger from being given a very enthusiastic welcome in The Hague, both by the masses of people who had flocked together and also by the queen and influential political circles. On this third and last visit to the Netherlands, after fruitless trips to Paris and Berlin to obtain support for the Boer republics, Kruger was to make a profound impression on the Dutch people. 'The enthusiasm in the streets was simply beyond description', reported *De Standaard*. 'It was moving enough to see those thousands of people so deeply touched and gazing at that sturdy old man who was completely calm and, in turn, gazing peacefully at the tempestuously emotional multitude.'[312] The experienced diplomat and privy councillor Asser, who was among the crowds, was 'deeply moved' by this experience: 'I had trouble holding back my tears.'

De Beaufort was equally touched by Kruger and his fate. How-

310. *De Standaard*, 28 September and 2 October 1900; cf. 18 September, 1 October and 13 November.
311. Smit, *Bescheiden* I, nos 325 and 327.
312. Leyds, *Correspondentie* IV, no. 43. Cf. *De Standaard*, 12 December 1900.

ever, the anti-British incidents that occurred during the reception also convinced him that Kruger could not stay in the capital.[313] The Dutch government was greatly embarrassed when the *NRC* published a confidential letter of welcome from Van Naamen van Eemnes as chairman of the First Chamber. In it he reassured Kruger that his Chamber was

> in complete agreement with your noble pursuit of justice so that the unjust war, which has been imposed on you in such a barbarian way, may be ended and so that the freedom and independence of the two republics, which is desirable from all points of view, can be maintained and secured for all times.

Questioned by London, the government denied all responsibility for this letter, even though it had agreed, in good faith, that the chairmen of both Chambers should write a word of welcome.[314] After a trip around the Netherlands, which caused large masses of people to gather everywhere, Kruger finally followed the recommendation of the government and settled down in Utrecht. There he was to receive many admirers, including Penning, before his death in 1904.[315]

Meanwhile the mood in the Netherlands remained strongly anti-British. Characteristically, when King Edward VII arrived in Flushing at the beginning of 1901, he was given a hostile reception by the crowds who spontaneously began to sing the Transvaal national anthem as soon as the royal yacht came to anchor – 'the most disgraceful scene I ever witnessed in my life', said the British ambassador Howard.[316] As the position of the Boers became more and more precarious, De Beaufort began to receive suggestions from Britain about how he might move the Transvaal leaders to surrender in an honourable way. But with a view to public opinion in the Netherlands, De Beaufort refused to take any such steps. He did help to set up a telegraph link between the deputation in Europe and the temporary government in the Transvaal, as it might contribute to the opening of peace negotiations with Kitchener. However, not much of this initiative was fruitful.[317] Paradoxically enough, it

313. De Beaufort, *Vijftig jaren* I, pp. 244–6.
314. Smit, *Bescheiden* I, no. 347; Pierson's diary, 9 December 1900, Pierson Collection. Cf. *NRC*, 8 December 1900.
315. Penning, *Leven*, pp. 145–54.
316. Smit, *Bescheiden* VI, no. 118; cf. De Beaufort, *Vijftig jaren* I, pp. 247–8.
317. Smit, *Nederland*, pp. 68–9; De Jong, *De Beaufort*, pp. 100–1.

was in fact Kuyper – now prime minister – who made an important contribution to a peace in which the Boers lost their political independence. But Kuyper was still regarded as a trusted friend of the Transvaal and an outspoken critic of British imperialism, and according to some aggrieved Liberals this was why he won the 1901 elections.[318]

De Beaufort as well as many diplomats and the Dutch court were therefore rather concerned about the prospect of Kuyper as head of government. 'Kuyper has been too active in South African affairs to remain entirely passive at this stage,' wrote De Beaufort in his notes, 'and there can be no doubt that he now has a moral obligation towards his voters as well as the South Africans.'[319] 'Throughout my entire service no Foreign Minister has ever been faced with such difficult issues as you,' Tets assured De Beaufort, 'and your successor, under theocratic inspiration, will have to side with the Maccabees in South Africa.'[320] When Kuyper took office, Queen Wilhelmina asked for an explicit guarantee that 'the Netherlands would remain a neutral power with regard to events in South Africa'. Kuyper did not hesitate to give this guarantee, though his only reservation was the – theoretical – possibility 'that stronger powers might eventually intervene'.[321]

Van Koppen, whose study will serve as a key for the following passages, has correctly pointed out that there was indeed very little cause for concern. Despite all the dissonant notes which he was still sounding, Kuyper had adopted a far more cautious approach at this stage, and indeed even before the outbreak of the Boer War he had ceased to regard South Africa as the main area of Dutch expansion. Once the war had begun, he seems to have had virtually no illusions about the chances of survival of the Boer republics, in view of the unfavourable international situation and because there had been no general rebellion among the Afrikaners living in the Cape Province or Natal. Even at the turn of the century, 1899–1900, when Dutch public opinion generally believed in a military victory of the Boers, Kuyper did not commit himself.[322] When the tables had turned and various sides demanded support for the peace offer and the request

318. Goeman Borgesius to De Beaufort, 25 September 1901; Van Houten to De Beaufort, 24 August 1901, De Beaufort Collection.
319. Quoted by De Jong, *De Beaufort*, p. 101.
320. Tets to De Beaufort, 17 June 1901, De Beaufort Collection.
321. Van Koppen, *Kuyper*, pp. 174–5.
322. Kuyper, *Crisis*, pp. 58–9.

for intervention by the SAR and the Orange Free State, Kuyper pointed out quite emphatically that the Netherlands could only play a limited role in this respect, and urged his rank and file to be careful. Even during the 1901 election campaign he abandoned his outbursts against Britain, his criticism of De Beaufort and his homage to the Boers and wrote moderate leading articles for *De Standaard*.[323]

Once he had become head of government, Kuyper soon made it quite clear that no radical changes were to be expected with regard to Dutch policies towards South Africa. 'What has been done we cannot undo, and what has been left undone we cannot do at this stage', he said at the debate on the new government's declaration of policy. 'For the time being the government will persist with the policy of neutrality', he assured the Liberal opposition, but

> no one can demand that we should lose sight of the kinship between our people and the people of those two states. The government will therefore always take care not to miss an opportunity . . . to contribute within its limited means to the upholding of international law and the restoration of peace.[324]

At the turn of year 1901–2 Kuyper did indeed respond to Britain's latest request to persuade the Boers that an honourable peace was the best solution, if necessary at the expense of losing their independence. The decisive factor seems to have been the situation in South Africa itself. The Boers were waging a desperate guerilla war that could have continued for a good many years but which they would never have won. In their merciless fight against the guerillas, the British destroyed many farms of the Boers and interned their wives and children under deplorable conditions in improvised concentration camps. Towards the end of the war about 27,000 internees had died, of whom the majority were children. According to Kuyper the Boers were thus threatened with physical extinction. Furthermore Kuyper now saw the future prospects of the Boer nation within the British Empire far more positively than previously, partly because of the moral strength which the Boers had shown during the war.[325]

Before Kuyper's offer of mediation in January there had also been

---

323. Van Koppen, *Kuyper*, pp. 171–2.
324. Ibid., p. 175.
325. Ibid., pp. 150–1. Cf. Pakenham, *Boer War*, pp. 503ff.; *Gedenkboek*, pp. 421ff.

steps by private British persons, particularly the Liberal Quaker F. W. Fox and the former military attaché in The Hague, Ch. à Court Repington. Despite objections from his Foreign Minister Melvil van Lynden, Kuyper decided to agree to these steps, as they clearly indicated that both camps were ready for peace. However, the draft memorandum which Kuyper had compiled in consultation with Asser and Melvil van Lynden contained the suggestion 'that independence will be forfeited', and being under considerable pressure from Leyds, who wanted to fight to the 'bitter end', the Transvaal deputation found this point insurmountable at first.

Van Lynden was therefore extremely cautious when he took diplomatic steps in London, and they would probably never have led to an official offer of mediation if Kuyper had not secretly called in the help of Lord Reay. The latter approached the British government who very much appreciated the offer but turned it down. Kuyper, however, decided to go ahead anyway and secured the co-operation of Wolmarans who made it known that he was speaking on behalf of the other members of the deputation. Only then did Kuyper inform Van Lynden of his personal initiatives. Instead of resigning, Van Lynden gave in and obediently saw to it that the official offer of mediation was submitted in London. As would be expected, the British government rejected the offer and preferred direct negotiations between Kitchener and the Boer leaders in South Africa.[326]

Leyds felt that Kuyper had, intentionally or unintentionally, allowed himself to be used by the British government who wanted to sow discord among the Boer leaders and undermine the morale of the commanding officers.[327] Boissevain, too, rejected the idea of Dutch mediation, though without doubting Kuyper's good intentions: 'Our government has given Britain *le beau rôle* by asking a question which they knew would be answered in the negative. They made it all too easy for Britain.'[328] Most national newspapers, however, were supportive of Kuyper's peace initiative. 'There is no denying that Kuyper has made himself popular with this note', said Mees in a letter to De Beaufort, who felt unable to see more than a political manoeuvre in it.[329] *De Standaard* regarded the offer of

326. Van Koppen, *Kuyper*, pp. 182–8; cf. Smit, *Nederland*, pp. 69–73.
327. Leyds, *Correspondentie* IV, xvii–xviii.
328. *Het Handelsblad*, 7 February 1902.
329. Mees to De Beaufort, 8 March 1902, De Beaufort Collection. Cf. De Jong, *De Beaufort*, pp. 102–3; Van Koppen, *Kuyper*, p. 192.

mediation in itself as a resounding success. After all, the British government had responded with words of appreciation and expressed itself leniently about the Boers. Moreover, 'our voice is being listened to in the world again.' 'The international respect for what our government has done . . . increases our own national pride', commented *De Standaard*; 'More than ever, we feel that we are children of forefathers who made their word heard in world politics, a word which was frequently of great moment, and who saw to it that the Dutch flag was greeted with due reverence on all the oceans.'[330]

Having rejected Dutch mediation, the British government informed the Boer leaders in South Africa of the offer, as evidence that it was pointless to continue the war any further. When Kuyper's offer of mediation contributed indirectly to the surrender of the Boers at the Peace of Vereeniging on 31 May 1902, Kuyper apparently had no regrets. After all, nothing could be heard in South Africa 'but the death cries of the dying and the desperate screams of the suffering'. Kuyper felt that the peace would open the path to the restoration and possibly even final victory of the Boer nation, and he therefore addressed an urgent plea to the Dutch nation to 'offer a helping hand' to the much-tested Boers after the end of the war.[331] Although many were at first unable to see the peace in such positive terms, the Dutch public nevertheless heeded the exhortations of Kuyper and other friends of the Boers. 'It was a violent and bitter disenchantment', commented *De Gids*; 'Now that we have slowly begun to recover, we are able to judge more fairly.'[332] The NZAV, the Christian National Boer Committee and other organisations continued to give material support for a number of years. The ANV and the Educational Fund of the NZAV also continued to be devoted to the promotion of the Dutch language in South Africa. With the support of NZAV loans, even emigration to South Africa started again.[333]

But the old enthusiastic pursuit of a 'New Holland' or the 'Greater Netherlands' in South Africa had definitely been lost. The NZASM had been nationalised by the British authorities in 1900, and the expropriation could no longer be reversed. There were to be difficult negotiations between the Netherlands and Britain about the

330. *De Standaard*, 6 February 1902.
331. Van Koppen, *Kuyper*, pp. 192–3.
332. W. F. Andriessen, 'De vrouwen der Boeren', *De Gids*, 1903, i, p. 65.
333. *Nederland–Zuid–Afrika*, pp. 117–24. Schotanus, *Betrekkingen*, pp. 50ff.

indemnification of the company.[334] Apart from the railway service, the administrative apparatus of the Transvaal and the Free State had of course also ceased to exist as potential employers. This led to a rather defeatist attitude in the Netherlands, of which Quack's reaction seems to have been typical. Quack, the prominent social scientist and former director of the state railway company in the Netherlands, who resigned from all NZAV functions in 1902, commented in his memoirs:

> We abandoned the illusion of the Greater Netherlands in Africa for the time being. It was hard to behold the victory of power over justice. It was extremely sad to see the dead old Kruger being transferred to the country which was no longer his own country. However, it had become a duty for all of us to remain silent for the sake of the higher interests of our country. One could still think about it, but not express one's thoughts.[335]

The Imperialism Debate around 1900

Acheh and the Transvaal

The reaction to the Boer War was strongly dominated by what Kossman rightly called 'pure Dutch nationalism'; this was a nationalism that was often overtly vehement, though it became more reserved and covert after the war, as illustrated in Quack's *Herinneringen* (Reminiscences). With regard to South Africa, Dutch nationalism very clearly displayed 'the touchiness of a small nation with a great past', as the Amsterdam historian G. W. Kernkamp so aptly characterised the spirit of 1901.[336] With this pattern of reactions the current interests of the Netherlands as a small nation eventually outweighed the memories of the great past or the wishful dreams of a 'Greater Netherlands' of the future which had been triggered off by British actions in South Africa.

Nor was De Beaufort himself immune to such historical thinking. 'Twice this century the Dutch race has been cut short in its development as a state by the force of events', he stated 'with regret' in his notes on the British annexation of the Boer Republics: 'Belgium has officially become a French country, with French as the official

334. Smit, *Nederland*, pp. 47–51.
335. Quack, *Herinneringen*, p. 497.
336. Blaas, 'Prikkelbaarheid', p. 284; cf. Kossmann, *Lage landen*, p. 322.

language, and has therefore been separated from developments in the Netherlands. The South African republics will henceforth become British states to an even greater extent and form part of the great British Empire.' But because of the considerable Dutch interests that were at stake in relation to Britain, De Beaufort had to remain a 'mere observer' as Foreign Minister and was unable to prevent the downfall of the ethnically related republics.[337] Even a politically committed university professor such as Blok – whose nationalist historiography displayed very clearly that touchiness which Kernkamp described – admitted in a letter to De Beaufort that 'we must be careful with Great Britain if we do not suddenly want to face some grave complications.' He felt that 'a cautious policy . . . is extremely important for our future as a colonial power.'[338]

As early as in 1896, after the Jameson Raid, Minister Röell had explicitly given priority to 'keeping and further developing the East Indies', rather than to the promotion of Dutch or ethnically related interests in South Africa. Indeed all Dutch cabinets, including those of Kuyper and De Beaufort, saw restraint towards British expansion in South Africa as the necessary condition for Dutch expansion in the Indonesian Archipelago. In an international context where security depended partly on informal British protection, Dutch expansion in the Archipelago around 1900 was also coupled with a good deal of Dutch nationalism. With regard to the East Indies, Dutch nationalism developed even more freely and became more permanent than it did regarding South Africa. This was because the Netherlands could act more successfully towards the 'indigenous enemy' whose 'treachery' aroused the colonial variant of nationalism, than towards British imperialism, on which it continued to be dependent. Many contemporaries, however, refused to acknowledge this, and they certainly did not recognise the connection between Acheh and the Transvaal, the Netherlands and Britain. Boissevain, for example, argued against British action in South Africa with the same inflated nationalism with which he applauded Dutch action in the Archipelago.

Kossman felt that this paradoxical reaction pattern was quite representative of Dutch public opinion in general: 'Incidentally, it never occurred to anyone that the Netherlands itself was waging an

---

337. De Beaufort, *Vijftig jaren* I, p. 236.
338. Blok to De Beaufort, 17 August 1900 and 1 August 1901, De Beaufort Collection.

imperialist war in Acheh that was in many ways similar to the one in the Transvaal.'[339] However, nationalist blindness did not go quite as far at the time. The Socialists, in particular, did not miss the opportunity to criticise the Dutch bourgeoisie by repeatedly comparing Acheh and the Transvaal as well as Dutch and British imperialism. In this way they certainly succeeded in provoking nationalist journalists such as Boissevain to even greater fury and indignation.

Exasperation at the chauvinistic 'Transvaal fever' of the Dutch bourgoisie undoubtedly played an important role in the Socialist attitude. 'There is an epidemic. Feverish people like Mr Boissevain are already delirious, and the public at large is also beginning to show some dangerous symptoms', said Bonger, who was prompted to advocate a British victory in the Boer War for fear that *De Kroniek*, 'which otherwise looks at everything from an intellectual point of view', might get carried away by the prevailing pro-Boer nationalism. In his reply to Bonger, Tak pointed out that 'for the same reasons which he himself has given, one could also justify the Acheh War – something which his party comrades are not in the habit of doing.'[340] Dutch Socialists had indeed criticised the Acheh War from the very beginning as a 'passion for annexation', a 'policy of robbery' and – more recently – 'imperialism'. Now the Dutch bourgeoise, which had always supported the Acheh War, was condemning British action in South Africa in very similar terms. Indignant at so much 'hypocritical integrity towards foreigners', Van Kol emphasised in the Second Chamber the points which the two wars had in common:

> *Both* are unjust wars, waged against a weaker nation and motivated purely by greed and a hunger for power. *Both* were made possible by the attitude of a large part of the press, the government and Parliament. *Both* wars were caused by lust for profit; and in *both* countries the armed forces had a special interest in the war, which enabled them to enjoy promotion and distinction. In *both* countries there was only a small minority who showed any resistance to the conflict.[341]

Obviously the analogy was disputed by everybody else. Minister Cremer, who had reminded the Chamber a little earlier that the

339. Kossmann, *Lage landen*, p. 322.
340. *De Kroniek*, 12 November 1899.
341. *Handelingen Tweede Kamer* (Parliamentary Reports of the Second Chamber), 22 November 1899, pp. 415–16.

Netherlands had 'an enormous field to work' in the East Indies, denied the alleged 'capitalist aims' in the pacification of Acheh. The Liberal Verhey pointed out the fundamental difference between the Boers, 'a nation which granted others access to European civilisations and industry', and the Achenese, 'a nation . . . who are barbarians in their behaviour, who have been pirates in the past and who only cause trouble for us'. Van Vlijmen also added the difference in skin colour between the Boers and the Achenese. Himself a Roman Catholic and former officer in the Dutch East Indian army, he indignantly rejected Van Kol's allegations about the army, while in the same breath extolling its military feats under Van Heutsz who had made 'the coronation year of our honourable queen . . . a year of establishing Dutch authority in the coastal areas of Acheh'.[342]

Van Kol and Van der Zwaag then tried to involve Kuyper in the debate, because he had once compared the Dutch annexation of Acheh with the British annexation of the Transvaal in 1877. Since then, however, Kuyper's view of the Dutch side in this comparison had changed, so that Van Kol and Van der Zwaag's attempts were in vain. Without coming back to his initial opposition to the declaration of war, Kuyper now made it clear to the Socialists in a *Standaard* article that 'we cannot just stand and watch while the social conflagration which was caused through our own fault continues to burn. It is absolutely imperative that we should extinguish this fire.'[343] When Van Kol raised the comparison between Acheh and the Transvaal again during the budget debate in 1900, Kuyper in fact criticised him for doing 'the same as the Jingoes', that is, 'maligning the Boers' and 'arousing animosity against us in the whole of Europe'.[344] As we have seen above, Van Kol was to moderate his view on the pacification of Acheh quite considerably after he had gathered the relevant information from Van Heutsz and Colijn in Acheh itself. The Socialist daily *Het Volk*, however, consistently continued to compare Acheh with the Transvaal as well as the Netherlands with Britain. Boissevain, in particular, came under a good deal of criticism. 'When he shouted *Transvaal!*, we shouted, *Acheh!*', said Troestra sarcastically:

342. Ibid., pp. 422ff.; ibid., 23 November 1899, pp. 439–40.
343. *De Standaard*, 6 December 1899.
344. Handelingen Tweede Kamer (Parliamentary Reports of the Second Chamber), 21 and 22 November 1900, pp. 385 and 396.

When he poured out the phials of his wrath on *Chamberlain*, we called out, *Cremer!* When he talked about *gold* and *diamonds*, we drew his attention to *tobacco* and *petroleum*; when he accused Britain of *burning down farms*, we accused the Netherlands of *burning down kampongs*. And the most odious thing of all was that when he called Britain's reason for its war a *pretext*, we did the same with the Acheh War and showed that it was just as much a function of *capitalist greed* as the war in the Transvaal.[345]

The editor-in-chief of *Het Handelsblad* put up with these sneers and deliberate provocations for over a year. And at the end of 1901, when he could no longer contain his anger and spoke out against 'sly innuendo' and 'malicious aspersions', he did so to preserve the 'honour of the country' rather than with a view to his own person. Supported by the colonial affairs correspondent of *Het Handelsblad*, the ex-officer and former MP Kielstra, Boissevain took up the fight against socialist allegations. Before long the controversy came to a head, concentrating mainly on the causes of the Acheh War. Boissevain and Kielstra argued that the war had been forced on to the Netherlands at the time, because Acheh had stubbornly refused to put an end to piracy and slavery in its waters, while at the same time seeking support from foreign powers. This had nothing to do with economic interests; after all, the complications in Acheh had started a long time before the first tobacco had been planted in Deli. 'We trust that by pointing out the above facts we have aroused the conviction in our readers that all comparisons between South Africa and Acheh are totally futile', concluded Kielstra. 'We did not declare war on Acheh for mercenary reasons, as servants of Mammon; this war was forced on us by the behaviour of the Achehnese government.'[346]

Socialist journalists, on the other hand, could easily show that north Sumatra had raised high expectations of profit for some time, while it was undeniable that tobacco had already been grown in Deli in 1873, when the Netherlands declared war.[347] But the more they studied the matter, the more Dutch Socialists, too, came across elements which could not simply be squared with Marxist theory.

345. *Het Volk*, 10 November 1901; cf. 31 March, 23 June, 3 July, 21 and 31 December 1900; 27 July, 11 August and 29 October 1901.

346. Kielstra, 'De Atjeh-oorlog verdedigd', *Indisch Nederland*, pp. 179–97, originally published in *Onze Eeuw*, 1901. Cf. *Het Handelsblad*, 4, 15 and 16 November 1901.

347. *Het Volk*, 14, 18 and 20 November 1901.

The comparison between Acheh and the Transvaal as well as between the Netherlands and Britain prompted all parties concerned to take a closer look at the Dutch position with regard to imperialism and to define it more closely.

Pursuit of Profits and Moral Calling

There was relatively little controversy about the general features of imperialism, which was seen as the violent manifestation of capitalist endeavours to acquire new markets and to make greater profits. There was also unanimous agreement with regard to the accompanying phenomena, such as the social Darwinist disrespect of justice and the jingoistic hysteria of the masses. Moreover, all parties concerned saw imperialism chiefly, though not exclusively, as an overseas phenomenon. That military aggression and capitalist expansion should largely be directed at non-white peoples was certainly not regarded as a fundamental feature.

According to socialists, capitalism was 'colour-blind' whenever new markets were to be acquired and greater profits were to be made. Non-socialist observers even preferred to reserve the term imperialism for aggression against weaker white nations, in the first place, for the British subjection of the Boer republics; Roman Catholics also used the term to describe the American conquest of the Spanish colonies; and several Liberals thought the term could be used to describe the Russian suppression of Finland and Poland. It was typical of this great consensus about imperialism as a general phenomenon that Hobson's *The War in South Africa* was reviewed in almost identical terms by *Het Handelsblad* and *Het Volk* – almost identical, because the Liberal paper regarded almost the whole world, in addition to South Africa, as territory for the new form of imperialism, with the exception of the Dutch East Indies, whereas the Socialist paper concluded: 'What we saw happening in South Africa, happens wherever the modern capitalist spirit has ensconced itself. It happened in Java, it is happening in Acheh, in the Congo and on Madagascar.'[348] The manner in which the Netherlands expanded, particularly in the Indonesian Archipelago, but also elsewhere, formed the crux of the imperialism debate in the Netherlands. This expansion was characterised as capitalist and militarist by Socialists, whereas non-Socialists preferred a milder

348. Ibid., 15 July 1900; cf. *Het Handelsblad*, 15 January and 11 August 1900.

terminology using words, such as 'development' and 'extending Dutch authority'.

'If there is over-production, there must necessarily be an expansion of export markets. Only the acquisition of new colonies and the conquest of larger areas can halt the approaching demise of capitalist society', reasoned Van Kol in the traditional Marxist manner in his article on 'The imperialism of the Netherlands' in *De Nieuwe Tijd*. The Netherlands, too, he argued, was 'willy-nilly swept along by the flow of time'. But he had difficulty identifying the appropriate motives in a number of expeditions and annexations, that is, 'the profit motive of the big capitalists'. In a number of cases, in particular those of Bali and Lombok and parts of Borneo and Celebes, Van Kol described military and administrational forms of profit seeking, whereas he could describe the more recent establishment of Dutch rule on a shipping route to New Guinea as no more than a 'precursor of imperialism and capitalism'.[349]

Henriëtte Roland Holst took over Van Kol's analysis of imperialism in her *Kapitaal en arbeid* (Capital and Labour), though with considerably more emphasis on the special features and conditions that applied to the Dutch situation. She felt that, compared with other imperialist powers, industrial capitalism was still rather underdeveloped in the Netherlands, and the same could therefore be said for the first capitalist function of the colonies – the expansion of consumer markets for industrial products. The other two reasons for the existence of colonial possessions were therefore seen as even more important, that is, 'to provide the sons of the bourgeoisie with civilian and military offices', and 'to serve as a sphere of exploitation for capitalists, lured by the prospect of consistently higher profits'. But in her elaboration of the latter, central motive of the new imperialism Roland Holst stated a number of further limitations. Obviously, the alliance between the old trading capital and the new colonial capital, symbolised by Cremer's Deli Company, could hardly count as a fully fledged variant of that monopolist fusion between banking and industrial capital which most Marxist theorists regarded as the main feature of the imperialist phase of modern capitalism. Moreover, Dutch capitalism had so far not succeeded in developing the entire Archipelago for the purpose of exploitation, but was mainly directed at Java, followed

349. Van Kol, 'Het imperialisme van Nederland', *De Nieuwe Tijd*, 1902, pp. 1–17, 67–8.

by Sumatra.[350] Roland Holst, incidentally, was one of the few Socialist authors who included not only the East Indies in her analysis of Dutch capitalist expansionism but also South Africa. In J. Visscher's study of the Boer republics – a study which is very worthwhile in itself – the NZASM, for example, was seen as a political bulwark against British imperialism rather than a combination of rival Dutch and German capital interests.[351]

The Socialist contribution to the imperialism debate was marked by a good deal of one-sidedness and exaggeration. According to Van Kol, all non-economic reasons for the recent colonial expansion, such as 'political interests', 'humanitarian considerations' and 'national honour', were no more than pretexts for the one true motive: 'the greed for profit that characterises large-scale capitalism'.[352] But many of his opponents were equally one-sided as they totally disregarded any economic interests in the expansion whatsoever. In defending their position they confined themselves mainly to reiterating the reasons which Van Kol had called pretexts. As a result, the debate soon became trivial, in the same way that the controversy over the parallels between Acheh and the Transvaal in *Het Volk* and *Het Handelsblad* had lost its significance. After each new expedition in the Archipelago Van Kol and the other colonial experts performed the same sham fight in the Second Chamber, continually repeating the same old arguments again and again.[353]

The discussion between Van Kol and Kuyper was far more exciting. Kuyper was one of the few non-Socialists who had developed a more or less coherent vision of modern imperialism and the position of the Netherlands within it; his vision, with different emphasis, took both economic and non-economic factors into account, while the latter were hardly recognised at all by Van Kol and other Socialists. Kuyper, at any rate, was also one of the few who brought forward arguments as to why Dutch expansion in the Archipelago could not be regarded as imperialist, as the Socialists contended. Kuyper had clearly identified economic motives in the emergence of modern imperialism as early as the 1880s. Commenting on the 'imperialist policies' of the great powers, he noticed

350. Roland Holst, *Kapitaal* I, pp. 151–8.
351. *Idem*, 'De Balans van den Zuid-Afrikaanschen oorlog', *De Nieuwe Tijd*, 1900, pp. 261–52. Cf. Visscher, *Ondergang*, pp. 94–7.
352. Van Kol, 'Imperialisme', pp. 73–8.
353. Cf. *Handelingen Tweede Kamer* (Parliamentary Reports of the Second Chamber), 10 November 1901, pp. 98ff.

that the 'sphere of conflicts has been narrowed down in recent years to the single question of commercial interests'. However, Kuyper felt that imperialism was more than an unintentional consequence of 'a commercial dispute, the peaceful *struggle for life*'; especially with regard to Britain he showed that there were certain forces at work which were aimed quite purposefully at violent expansion, such as jingoism, militarism and social Darwinism. In the final analysis, imperialism was 'the policy of Caesarism'; that is, it 'poses as the *most important power in the whole world* and presumes that, wherever it rules, it has a right to dominate every living creature that has breath'. Kuyper therefore criticised Socialists for being 'utterly absurd' in speaking of 'imperialist policies in their proper sense' when referring to 'a small power like Belgium in the Congo or the Netherlands in the Archipelago'. 'This is an incorrect use of a term', he said, 'which has a completely different meaning.'[354]

On the other hand, Kuyper was far less reluctant to apply the terms 'expansion' and 'moral calling' to 'our little country', provided they were stripped of the evil power-political and 'pantheistic' connotations which they had acquired through the behaviour of the great powers. After all, the colonial possessions of the Netherlands had also frequently been acquired 'by means of immoral, unjust actions'. 'However, in retrospect, it has turned out that it was our moral duty to settle down in the Archipelago and that our supremacy was a blessing for the Archipelago.' Kuyper therefore suggested that 'it is and remains our moral duty to bring more and more parts of the Archipelago under our authority, even if by means which cannot stand the test of justice.'[355]

In a direct debate with Van Kol Kuyper expressed himself even more clearly. He agreed that Cremer's nomination as Minister of the Colonies was the 'product of the industrial movement' in the Netherlands and the East Indies. But, unlike Van Kol, Cremer's 'socio-economic view' of colonial affairs should be assessed positively. He felt that Van Kol was 'not sufficiently sensitive to the historical origins of the situation' and reasoned 'as if one could make everything *tabula rasa*'.

According to Kuyper, 'the first and greatest problem' was that of the 'relationship between highly developed and underdeveloped races'. 'We must accept one of the following systems', he said:

354. *De Standaard*, 6 December 1899; cf. 12 January.
355. Ibid., 24 May 1899; cf. 25 January.

'Either we simply leave the higher and lower developed races . . . to themselves', or we should acknowledge that 'the higher races have a moral duty towards the lower ones.' In such a case, however, even Van Kol would have to 'take into account the consequences which are bound to occur as a result of contact between the different races'. Would it not follow from the inability of the 'natives' to exploit, for instance, their minerals that 'these *must* be brought to the surface by others for the sake of world life?'[356] Van Kol, incidentally, was criticised in similar terms by other Socialists, particularly the strict Marxist J. Saks, who felt that only capitalist exploitation could bring about the development of the Archipelago and thus eventually socialism.[357]

But such words from Kuyper's mouth sounded to Van Kol like 'imperialism of the first water', especially when Kuyper's moral calling also seemed to include the acquisition of Dutch outposts outside the Archipelago, for example in China.[358] In his pursuit of overseas expansion Kuyper did indeed repeatedly put forward arguments which he himself would probably have branded as imperialist, jingoist or social Darwinist if they had come from Britain. Typical in this respect was his abandonment of South Africa as an area for Dutch expansion even before the Boer War had broken out. When he felt that the ethnically related Boers failed to defend Dutch heritage against the predominance of British influence, particularly with regard to the language, his support became rather more qualified. Kuyper's theories of linguistic, that is, national development displayed quite a few social Darwinist features, as Van Weringh has shown.[359] As a good Calvinist Kuyper rejected Darwin's explanation of the origins of mankind, God's creation, but he accepted the relevance of Darwinist ideas on the subsequent evolution of mankind. Kuyper was thus convinced that 'an odd dialect' like Afrikaans was doomed and only Dutch, which was 'more highly developed', could stand against the powerful English language 'one and same everywhere in the world'. It was for similar reasons that the Betuwe dialect of the Dutch immigrants to the United States was gradually getting lost. However, unlike

356. *Handelingen Tweede Kamer* (Parliamentary Reports of the Second Chamber), 22 November 1900, pp. 395–6.
357. Cf. Tichelman, *Sdap*, pp. 14–27.
358. *Handelingen Tweede Kamer* (Parliamentary Reports of the Second Chamber), 22 November 1899, p. 415; ibid., 22 November 1900, p. 407.
359. Van Wehring, *Maatschappijbeeld*, pp. 131–3.

British imperialism in South Africa, American political culture was so open to Calvinist influences from the Netherlands that Kuyper could whole-heartedly recommend the United States as an alternative emigration target. During his visit to the United States in 1898–9 Kuyper himself met with sufficient interest in the Dutch language among 'our kinsmen' in the United States to help in setting up a branch of the ANV.[360]

Ethical Imperialism?

More often than not, Kuyper's arguments were noticeable because of their peculiar logic, but he was not the only one putting them forward in the Netherlands at the time. In many circles and different spheres a strong sense of moral mission began to emerge around the turn of the century, and under the influence of current events this sense of mission changed from having a moderate and defensive tone to a more radical and aggressive one. When, before the Boer War, Minister De Beaufort made enquiries about the ANV and its aims outside the Netherlands, its chairman Kern was in a position to reassure him that 'chauvinistic aims' were totally alien to their idea of the 'Greater Netherlands'. 'If there is any fighting at all,' he said, 'then it is mainly against ourselves and against the spirit of discouragement and apathy.'[361]

However, once the Boer War had broken out, the nationalist zeal began to gain so much ground that some spokesmen of the ANV were satisfied with nothing less than the elimination of all British influence in South Africa. 'There will be the united states of South Africa, a Dutch confederacy as big as half of Europe . . . and there will be the Netherlands . . . both of them complementing each other', predicted J. B. Schepers in an article on the 'future of the Dutch race in the twentieth century'.[362]

'No chauvinism' were also the words of Prof. Kalff, but he went on to say that 'there should be none of that narrow-minded scornfulness towards one's own country and people, that spineless way in which some dwell on our own weakness.' These were the considerations he had in mind when he took the initiative to set up the association Volksweerbaarheid (Popular Defence), which was at first widely supported, among others by the leaders and members of

360. *De Standaard*, 13 and 15 March 1899.
361. Kern to De Beaufort, 26 February 1899, De Beaufort Collection.
362. *De Amsterdammer*, 15 October 1899.

the Liberal and Christian trade union movement. Before long, however, the meetings of the association were dominated so much by 'the military interpretators of the national interest' that the workers stayed away – obviously to the satisfaction of the Socialists. *De Kroniek* printed an ironical report of a 'thunderous speech' in which a highly committed officer demanded that everyone should stand up firmly for 'God, the Netherlands and the House of Orange': 'It was too overpowering to endure.'[363]

Defence in the Netherlands, however, never became very popular, and indeed the armed forces had more reason to complain about anti-militarism than the Socialists about militarism. Nevertheless, in view of military operations in South Africa and the Indonesian Archipelago, the relationship around 1900 was the exact opposite. In the latter case the belligerent mood, brought about in the Netherlands by the 'treachery' of Lombok and Acheh, was further intensified by the unexpectedly quick large-scale victories of the Dutch East Indian army that were soon reported. To obtain support for further military actions, political leaders often appealed to the Dutch sense of moral mission towards the indigenous population, in whose interest intervention was thought to be necessary.

After a while, however, this ethical justification was felt to be incompatible with the actual use of violence. At first Van Heutsz's policy of pacification was very popular because it seemed to be both successful and humane. Indeed, one of the reasons for Boissevain's indignation was the comparison of Van Heutsz with Kitchener in *Het Volk*, with headlines such as 'Kitchener in Acheh', 'Kitchener's successor' and 'Worse than Kitchener'.[364] Van Kol only supported Van Heutsz's policy of pacification because he believed that the Achenese population would benefit. But when it became known in 1904 that 3,000 villagers, including 1,200 women and children, had been killed during Van Daalen's 'excursion' through the Gayo and Alas areas, with only 26 members of the military police dying, Van Kol and many others changed their views again.

In particular, the enlightened Roman Catholic Victor de Stuers complained to the Dutch Second Chamber about this 'murderous' episode in which over a quarter of the local population had been killed. 'What makes me feel uneasy is that we are moving in a militarist atmosphere at this time', said De Stuers, pointing out that

363. *De Kroniek*, 27 October 1900, cf. notes 12 and 49 above.
364. *Het Volk*, 21 December 1900, 29 October 1901 and 6 February 1902.

the Minister of the Colonies Idenburg, Governor-general Roosen-boom and his successor Van Heutsz were all servicemen, and that Van Daalen had already been designated by Van Heutsz as new governor of Acheh, before he carried out his pacification action. Liberal speakers also felt that Van Daalen had been too ruthless, but they did not question the necessity of military force as such. Most Christian spokesmen, especially Van Vlijmen, emphatically distanced themselves from De Stuers and unambiguously expressed their appreciation of the policy of pacification. This time there was no ethical justification whatever. 'In situations like this weak sur-geons cause stinking wounds', Kuyper declared on behalf of the government. De Savornin Lohman also felt that

> there can never be a good conclusion in these lands unless we take decisive action, for the simple reason that the people who live there will not recognise any authority which does use weapons to assert itself . . . You may call this imperialism or not, but there is no other way.[365]

As we saw at the beginning of this chapter, the Dutch effort to strengthen international law was also accompanied by a strong sense of moral mission. Here, too, under the influence of current affairs, the defensive and pragmatic view of international law gradually turned into the active and idealistic concept of 'the task of the small state'. 'It should be everybody's desire to show what a small state can do and how such a state – as the Netherlands itself once showed – can serve as an example and a driving force to the whole of Europe', Boissevain declared as early as 1900.[366] This 'idea of a guiding nation (*Gidslandgedachte*)' – before the term itself had been invented – was subsequently further elaborated and underpinned by the Utrecht professor in international and East Indian law, De Louter, and his Leiden colleague, van Vollenhoven. Like Boisse-vain, they thought that the lofty international duty of the Nether-lands derived not only from its disinterested position in the world as a small state, but also from the success of the 'Ethical Policy' and the pacification of the Dutch East Indies. Van Vollenhoven in particu-lar, who undoubtedly used extremely outspoken and high-flown words to express the 'calling of the Netherlands' in this context, praised the 'hard and beneficial hand' in Lombok and Acheh. 'At

---

365. Tillema, *De Stuers*, pp. 61–6; Idema, *Geschiedenis*, pp. 177–80. Cf. Van 't Veer, *Atjeh-oorlog*, pp. 267–73.
366. *Het Handelsblad*, 12 August 1900.

last', he declared proudly in 1913, 'the policy of Lombok and the new Acheh policy have been extended to include the rest of Sumatra as well as Borneo, Celebes, Ceram, Timor and Bali.' Calling the Netherlands 'the Joan of Arc' among nations, Van Vollenhoven made a passionate plea for his country to be given the role of an international police force within the future legal order of the world.[367]

Boogman therefore correctly described Van Vollenhoven as an 'ethical imperialist', and his theories as 'a striking expression of ethical imperialism'.[368] However, the views of Van Vollenhoven, De Louter and other kindred spirits were not supported very widely and, as Kossmann and Kamphuis have shown, had no direct influence on Dutch foreign policies.[369] The Dutch Foreign Ministers and their advisers on international law considered the Netherlands as having a more modest and pragmatic role in the international legal order. At the international Peace Conference in 1899 they still felt a bit uncomfortable about this role, because of the exclusion of the Boer republics, but then they took great pleasure in acting as host nation at the Second Peace Conference in 1907. At these conferences they were above all concerned with the promotion of international arbitration and the law of the sea – concrete issues which directly affected the Netherlands as a small maritime and commercial nation.[370] According to Wels, both Dutch neutrality and the promotion of an international legal order continued as pragmatic policies until the First World War, and it was only after the war that these policies became independent and turned into rigid principles of foreign affairs.[371]

It therefore seems that the term 'ethical imperialism' is more typical and representative of Dutch colonial affairs than foreign affairs around the year 1900. In this context Van 't Veer was already talking about a 'missionary imperialism' which developed in conjunction with economic expansion. According to Kossmann, the 'Ethical Policy' itself was largely identical with 'capitalist imperialism'. Locher-Scholten believes that the term 'ethical imperialism' can mainly be applied to the period between 1894 and 1905, the first phase of the 'Ethical Policy'.[372]

However, this interpretation may well need a number of marginal

367. Van Vollenhoven, *Eendracht*, pp. 52–7.
368. Boogman, 'Netherlands', p. 496; 'Achtergronden', p. 26.
369. Kossmann, *Lage landen*, p. 318; Kamphuis, *Vredebond*, pp. 25–6.
370. Smit, *Nederland*, pp. 39–41 and 125–38.
371. Wels, *Aloofness*, pp. 19–20.
372. Locher-Scholten, *Ethiek*, pp. 194–9; Kossmann, *Lage landen*, p. 302; Van 't

notes. The motives of Governor-general Van der Wijck, who took the initiative for expansion with his Lombok expedition of 1894, were ethical too, but mainly of an administrational kind. Minister Bergsma's contribution to this policy was neither ethical nor imperialist, whereas Cremer's could easily be summed up quite simply as capitalist imperialism. Among the spokesmen of the ethical trend itself after 1900, Van Kol was the only one who criticised imperialism with any consistency, apart from his short-lived enthusiasm for Van Heutsz's policy of pacification. In 1904 Van Kol even suggested selling part of the Outer Regions to other countries in order to implement the 'Ethical Policy' more fully in Java and Sumatra. Other ethicists rejected this idea out of hand, as did Van Kol's Marxist critics.[373]

However, not all Liberal and Anti-Revolutionary ethicists welcomed Dutch expansion in the Archipelago with the same enthusiasm. The Liberal Van Deventer preferred to be occupied with the welfare policy in Java. The programme that Van Deventer outlined for Java, as a special adviser of minister Idenburg, called for 'education, irrigation and emigration'. For the latter policy, the emigration from populous Java, the Outer Regions were vital. So Van Deventer accepted the necessity of extending Dutch colonial control in the Archipelago, though the military expeditions filled him with 'melancholy' and the 'crude violence' of a modern colonial army against a primitive indigenous enemy distressed him.[374] The Anti-Revolutionary ethical Van Idenburg, a former colonial officer, spoke a somewhat different language. When the government of Kuyper – a person with whom he felt great affinity – came to power, Idenburg said as an MP: 'Rather than imputing imperialist aims to our government, I would be inclined to criticise it for being too worried about a possible image as evil imperialism and therefore being too reluctant to interfere in the affairs of those territories which have not yet come directly under our rule.'[375]

Once he had joined the cabinet, he helped to change this state of affairs very quickly. Idenburg felt that Dutch authority had first of all to be very firmly established before the ethical policy of develop-

Veer, 'Machthebbers', pp. 45–6.

373. Van Kol, 'Inkrimping onzer koloniën', *De Nieuwe Tijd*, 1904, pp. 247–63. Cf. Locher-Scholten, *Ethiek*, p. 199; Tichelman, *Sdap*, p. 16.

374. Colenbrander and Stokvis, *Van Deventer* I, pp. 302–4; ibid. III, p. 121.

375. *Handelingen Tweede Kamer* (Parliamentary Reports of the Second Chamber), 21 November 1901, p. 110.

ment could be carried out. Governor-general Rooseboom, he thought, was not sufficiently ethical with regard to Java and not energetic enough in the Outer Regions. When De Savornin Lohman dropped out, Idenburg regarded Van Heutsz as his most suitable successor. Together with Van Heutsz he set up an ambitious programme for the expansion of the colonial administration and socio-economic development as well as an increase in missionary activities – ideas which were energetically put into practice in the East Indies by Van Heutsz.[376] Defending Van Heutsz's military actions in the Outer Regions Idenburg once pointed out to the Second Chamber that 'the use of the sword' could be 'the highest demand of love for one's fellow men'. In general, it is certainly correct to speak of 'ethical imperialism' in Dutch colonial affairs from 1894 onwards, but it seems to me that the expression describes most fittingly Idenburg's and Van Heutsz's terms of office between 1902 and 1909.

Questions of power and justice occupied the minds of Dutch contemporaries around 1900 quite considerably, and situations of 'power above justice' always caused great indignation. Virtually everyone perceived the Boer War in this way, but in many cases people's sense of justice was rather more selective, depending on their political and philosophical convictions. Foreign examples of 'power above justice' were often remembered much longer and more vividly than similar examples in the Netherlands itself or its colonies. In his memoirs, the former Socialist Prime Minister W. Drees (1948–58), gave an interesting and detailed account of the Boer War and the Dreyfus Affair. The Dutch Dreyfus Affair, the Hoogerhuis Affair, not a case of anti-Semitism but of class justice, was also mentioned. But the pacification of Acheh seems to have failed to make an impression on Drees during his late childhood.

The Boer War prompted Drees at the age of 13 and 14 to read the newspapers, so that he quickly became familiar with terms such as capitalism and imperialism. The Boer generals were the heroes of his youth and when the aged Kruger visited Amsterdam, the young Drees 'cheered him passionately'. Nor did he ever forget the Dreyfus Affair and the anti-Semitism that was connected with it. 'That my youthful spirit rebelled against imperialist aggression and anti-Semitic injustice . . . may explain the awakening of an inner urge to fight against any form of injustice', Drees concluded sixty years later. This shows that the pacification of Acheh was apparently not

376. Van 't Veer, *Atjeh-oorlog*, pp. 252–9; Witte, *Van Heutsz*, pp. 82–90; Brouwer, *Houding*, pp. 20–1.

a very formative youthful experience for him. Instead, Drees felt that the 'emerging imperialism' around 1900 was a practice of the great powers and that it was directed mainly towards Africa.[377]

377. Drees, *Zestig jaar*, pp. 3–18.

Conclusion

As the preceding chapters have been largely descriptive, their connection with the theoretical and historiographic introduction has not always been very obvious. This was done deliberately in order to avoid colouring the description with existing views and explanations which might then have dominated it. In this conclusion the results of the descriptive analysis will be explicitly related to theoretical and historiographic concepts – though without losing sight of facts that are divergent and specific and which do not tie up with current Dutch or foreign literature on the subject.

The main question of this conclusion is therefore: how far does the Netherlands fit into the general pattern of the rise of modern imperialism? In other words, what are the similarities and differences when compared with other countries?

There are a number of obvious answers which should be avoided. If we were to apply mechanically the general explanations offered for other countries, we could easily over-emphasise the similarities between them and the Netherlands. If, however, we merely followed studies which concentrate entirely on the Netherlands, we might over-emphasise the differences. But it would be even more unsatisfying to present a seemingly qualified view of the type 'on the one hand – on the other hand', where it is a foregone conclusion that the truth will be in the middle. The format of this chapter has been designed to avoid such pitfalls. First of all, we shall establish the basis on which the Dutch position in the emergence of modern imperialism can be regarded as comparable with that of other countries. It can then be compared in concrete terms with Britain, Portugal and Belgium.

The Dutch Pattern of Expansion and Reaction

The Use of the Term Imperialism in the Netherlands

The use of the term *imperialism* in the Netherlands may give us a first indication of the Dutch situation. On the face of it, it seems as if the term was adopted rather gradually. It was not used explicitly in the Netherlands until about 1880, and even then only occasionally, to refer to British colonial expansion under Disraeli. However, Koebner has shown in his well-known study that even in Britain itself the term 'imperialism' was not used for overseas expansion until Disraeli's policy gave occasion for its adoption. Until then imperialism was used as a synonym for Caesarism or Bonapartism in the European context.[1]

However, the charge of a 'greed for annexation' or a 'policy of conquests', which the Dutch opposition frequently put before the government after the outbreak of the Acheh War, often had the same connotations, and references to the two Napoleons and Bismarck in 1873–4 were made frequently. Those who defended the Dutch policy in Acheh regularly pointed to the example of British colonial expansion in Central Asia, Oceania and West Africa. This changed, however, when British expansion under Disraeli started to spread more widely and Dutch interests in Borneo and South Africa were being jeopardised. 'There's nothing more natural', said the chairman of the Peace Alliance, Van Eck, in 1877, 'than annexing the Achenese, the natives of the South Sea islands; they plot evil against others and are guilty of murder, robbery and plundering. But the population in the Transvaal has been behaving in an orderly and peaceful way. They're just a bit too religious.'[2] This supposed difference between Dutch action in Acheh and British action in South Africa subsequently continued to dominate the formation of Dutch views on modern imperialism.

As early as 1879 the Dutch ambassador Van Bylandt explained the new British 'Imperial Policy' in terms of economic factors, a policy which he believed to be mainly directed at Africa:

Britain's gigantic industry is having more and more of its markets disputed by continental European and American industry. It is therefore a matter of survival for this industry to acquire new markets. Africa is the

1. Koebner and Schmidt, *Imperialism*, chapters 1 and 2.
2. Kamphuis, *Vredebond*, p. 123.

last continent which can still be conquered for trade and industry. This is the reason why Britain must endeavour to seize as much control of that continent as possible.[3]

During the 1880s many Dutch observers applied this analysis to the 'new colonial policies' of other European powers, especially Germany, but not the Netherlands. After all, after the cession of Elmina the Netherlands no longer entertained any territorial ambitions in Africa, and after its disastrous war in Acheh it seemed to have great difficulties maintaining its position in the Indonesian Archipelago. Dutch capitalists were hardly able to overcome the consequences of the sugar crisis in Java or develop the Archipelago any further – let alone help the development of the ethnically related republics in South Africa. Both politically and economically, it seemed as if the overseas position of the Netherlands in the 1880s was considered largely a matter of concentration rather than expansion. Only a small number of radical and Socialist journalists dared to compare the position of the Netherlands with the imperialism of other countries. The well-known journalist Frans Netscher felt that anti-imperialism in the Netherlands was even less deeply rooted than imperialism itself. In France, after the bloody Tonkin expedition, the electorate had at least voted Ferry out of office, and the masses had chanted *A bas Ferry! A bas le Tonkinois!* But in the complacent Netherlands there had been no loud cry: *Down with Fransen van de Putte! Down with the Achenese!*[257]

This situation had almost certainly changed in the course of the 1890s, and around the year 1900 the term 'imperialism' seemed to be just as widespread in the Netherlands as it was elsewhere. This was partly due to American action during the Spanish–American War and to the British conquest of the ethnically related Boers in South Africa, though some of the general public were also influenced by the Dutch pacification of Acheh. The imperialism debate around the turn of the century has been discussed in detail in the previous chapter. In this context, it is particularly important to investigate to what extent this debate was kindled by opinions in other countries, as described by Koebner and Etherington.[5]

On the whole, with regard to its timing and political develop-

---

3. Woltring, *Bescheiden* II, no. 396.
4. Netscher, *Parlement*, pp. 157–9; cf. Ganiage, *Expansionism*, pp. 140–2.
5. Cf. Koebner and Schmidt, *Imperialism*, chapters 9–10; Etherington, *Theories*, chapters 1–2.

ment, the imperialism debate in the Netherlands was parallel with the corresponding international discussion. Its content, however, clearly differed in two respects. Firstly, most commentators still saw a considerable difference between other – imperialist – countries and the non-imperialist Netherlands. This image had emerged earlier and now continued undiminished. Unlike in the United States and Britain where many politicians, journalists and entrepreneurs openly and quite literally advocated imperialism, the word never acquired a positive meaning in the Netherlands. Those who favoured the fast and decisive subjection of Acheh reacted with great indignation when it was suggested that they were imperialists. Their Socialist accusers, however, had great difficulties in providing a satisfactory foundation for a theory of Dutch imperialism. Foreign theoreticians directly or indirectly linked aggressive overseas behaviour of a country with its industrialisation, the formation of monopolies and the increase of surplus capital in the mother country. Around the year 1900 such conditions seemed to be almost totally absent in the Netherlands.

Before we proceed from a description of the historical situation to a historiographic analysis of modern imperialism we must add a few notes on the realism of the Dutch self-image. After all, the tendency to see other countries as imperialist and the Netherlands as non-imperialist was a result of 'the touchiness of a small nation with a great past'.[6] This defensive attitude towards Britain overseas and Germany in Europe had given rise to a new, nationalist form of expansionism which was at first mainly directed at South Africa, and later at the Indonesian Archipelago. When this expansionism became successful in the Archipelago around the turn of the century, it was definitively thwarted in South Africa. The British conquest of the Boer republics made it impossible to use the word 'imperialism' in any positive sense in the Netherlands. Furthermore, the refusal to talk about 'imperialism' in connection with the Netherlands became a positive matter of principle under the influence of the 'Ethical Policy'. The predominant climate after 1900 was such that the contrast between foreign, imperialist powers and the ethical, non-imperialist Netherlands was firmly established not only in people's views on colonial affairs, but also in historiography.[7]

The Socialist viewpoint was not entirely free from ideological prejudice either – neither in its polemical emphasis on shared

6. Blaas, 'Prikkelbaarheid', pp. 284 and 292–3.
7. Cf. Van Goor, *Kooplieden*, pp. 134–5.

features with other countries, nor in its reluctant admission of differences. In the latter case, an adherence to dogmatic Marxist theories sometimes diverted the attention of Socialists from the actual developments that were taking place in the Netherlands. The formal criteria of the imperialist phase of capitalism may have been lacking in the Netherlands, but Dutch investments in the East Indies were greatly increasing, in particular in the Outer Regions. Later, in *Kapitaal en Arbeid* (Capital and Labour) part two of 1932, Henriëtte Roland Holst apparently attached far more importance to this spectacular growth in colonial investment than she had in part one. Indeed, she felt that 'obvious imperialist tendencies' only began to be clearly predominant after the publication of part one in 1902.[8] There still has not been any satisfactory research into the extent to which economic factors were determinant in the expansion of Dutch power in the Archipelago around 1900, although there can be no doubt that such factors did play a considerable role.

The Applicability of the Term Imperialism

Obviously, critical remarks about the historical self-image of the Netherlands as a nation distinguishing itself from other countries by its lack of imperialism do not in themselves prove that the opposite is true. Whenever Dutch expansion in the Archipelago was discussed by traditional colonial historiographers, their writings were still largely dominated by this ideological image.

More recently, however, Schöffer's and Wesseling's emphasis on the distinct position of the Netherlands within modern imperialism has displayed a different historiographic approach. Implicitly or explicitly, they refer to the findings of modern, international and mostly comparative studies of modern imperialism.[9] And in more recent surveys the Netherlands is indeed discussed as a separate case and a pre-imperialist colonial power, though we noted in the introduction that such characterisations were often made either *a priori* or casually or on the basis of rather dated handbooks. It is therefore certainly worthwhile to take another look at the views on modern imperialism that were discussed in the introduction and to compare these systematically with the Dutch situation once more.

8. Roland Holst, *Kapitaal* II, pp. 20–9; cf. ibid. I, pp. 151–9.
9. Cf. Schöffer, 'Dutch "expansion"', pp. 79–80; Wesseling, 'Dutch Historiography', pp. 138–9.

Gollwitzer gave the Netherlands as an example to show that a small European power was unable to conduct an imperialist world policy.[10] However, it seems that the common ground which he identified in the *weltpolitisches Denken* (world-political thinking) of the great powers could, to a greater or lesser extent, also be applied to the Netherlands. Gollwitzer's first category, the social Darwinist world-view, was not seen in the Netherlands in terms of *Weltmacht oder Niedergang* (world power or decline), but in terms of the possible loss of the East Indies or even independence in Europe and also in terms of the possible restoration of historical greatness in the East Indies and South Africa. So although the scope was different, the core of the matter – defensive expansionism – was the same in both cases. This nuclear mechanism also shows two further tendencies listed by Gollwitzer. Both of them can be applied to the Netherlands and other countries; they are the fear of traditional enemies (projected particularly on Britain in this case), and the attraction of pan-ideologies, such as the concept of a 'New Holland' in South Africa and the idea of the 'Greater Netherlands'. However, with regard to rivalry and co-operation, the Netherlands as a small power remained largely dependent on the goodwill of Britain. The special position of the Netherlands as a small European power but a large-scale colonial one is also clearly reflected in the other tendencies. After all, economic expansionism, racial and geopolitical thinking and the sense of a moral mission were aimed increasingly at the Dutch East Indies, despite expansionist attempts in South Africa and other parts of the non-Western world. And indeed Gollwitzer himself mentions that it was in the Netherlands that the term *ethical imperialism* was coined, and that its 'Ethical Policy' served as an example for some great powers, in Gollwitzer's view particularly Germany.[11]

Gollwitzer's analysis mainly concerns imperialist philosophy, whereas Betts's and Baumgart's studies and the collection of essays *Expansion and Reaction* (Leiden) also refer to the practice of modern imperialism. Among these approaches it seems to me that Betts's ideas, in particular, clarify the Dutch situation. We saw in the introduction that, according to Betts, the rise of modern imperialism was mainly determined by two factors: the mechanism of pre-emption, that is preventive occupation resulting from political,

10. Gollwitzer, *Geschichte*, p. 19.
11. Ibid., p. 78.

economic and ideological rivalry; and the contiguity factor, that is expanding geographical borders.[12] Particularly for the European powers who had established themselves overseas at the beginning of the nineteenth century, this last factor points to the continuity in colonial expansion. The mechanism of pre-emption, on the other hand, marks the discontinuity in this expansion. In the case of the Netherlands this mechanism began, with the increase in overseas rivalry, to play an important and often dominant role in the course of the 1870s, culminating in the external consolidation of the East Indies and the pacification and exploitation of the Outer Regions during the 1890s and the first decade of the twentieth century. To adapt Rosebery's 'pegging' phrase to the Dutch situation: long existing, but vague and reticent claims turned indeed into new, active ones for the future. In my view, the factors of contiguity and pre-emption explain much in the development of Dutch expansion, as long as we bear in mind that the Netherlands was a small European power but a rather large colonial power, that was already well established in Java before 1870.

After the Napoleonic Wars the Netherlands had managed to keep its possessions both in Africa and in Asia. But in view of its limited means and dependence on Britain, it was understandable with regard to contiguity that it deliberately chose to cede Elimina and to expand in Sumatra. The element of pre-emption subsequently played a decisive role in the outbreak of the Acheh War, when potential rivals such as the United States and Italy had to be excluded. It therefore seems to be sensible and justified to date the rise of Dutch imperialism at the outbreak of this war in 1873.

However, it seems to have been not only an early start but also a false one. The war was already directly impeding Dutch expansion in other parts of the Archipelago, and during the 1880s the subjection of Acheh itself seems to have exceeded the capacities of the Netherlands. In 1884, when the scramble for colonies had clearly become an international phenomenon and all kinds of conflicts with Britain seemed imminent in the Archipelago, the Netherlands decided to concentrate its forces in Acheh to a considerable extent. Meanwhile, the pre-emptive element continued to play a role in a number of colonial outposts, but the Dutch government did not go to any extremes. For example, the outpost in the disputed border area of northern Borneo, which had been set up so proudly in the

12. Betts, *False Dawn*, pp. 81–2.

1880s, was quietly abandoned again in a border agreement with Britain ten years later.

In the 1880s, generally considered the beginning of world-wide imperialism, the Netherlands did indeed form an exception – though not entirely, because the 1880s was also the time when nationalist ambitions for a 'New Holland' in South Africa began to emerge. However, it would be wrong to speak of fully-fledged imperialism in this context, because the ethnically related republics were jealously guarding their independence, acquired with such great difficulty, on all sides, and the Dutch government carefully avoided giving any active support to Dutch expansionists.

During the Boer War the government remained as aloof as possible, despite pressure from public opinion. The same was true for the international complications in China and Venezuela in which the Netherlands was involved. However, the border delimitations of the 1890s gave the Dutch a good basis for considerable expansion in the Indonesian Archipelago. The first initiatives were taken by the East Indian colonial administration in Lombok in 1894 and in Acheh in 1896. This new pacification policy was increasingly supported by the government and encouraged by the Dutch Parliament and public opinion. Also, Dutch entrepreneurs were showing more and more interest in the Outer Regions, and the government created the conditions for lucrative investment in a variety of different areas. Even if we follow Etherington in defining modern imperialism as a specific form of aggressive state action, dating from 1895, aimed at securing new investment opportunities, Dutch expansion in the Archipelago around 1900 fits a more general pattern.[13]

But also when the other current concepts of modern imperialism are applied, the Netherlands displays no fundamental divergences from them, except during the 1880s. All the factors which Baumgart, for instance, has identified for Britain and France, were also present in the Netherlands, albeit often to a lesser extent, on a smaller scale and with differing proportions. Just like Schöffer and Wesseling, Baumgart himself characterised Dutch expansion in the Archipelago as a 'peripheral', administrative form of imperialism. Local factors were indeed important for Dutch expansion in Indonesia, but no more than for British or French expansion in Africa, if we are to believe Robinson and Brunschwig.[14] Baumgart's 'real'

13. Etherington, *Theories*, pp. 273–5.
14. Baumgart, *Imperialismus*, p. 30. Cf. the contributions by Schöffer, Robinson and Brunschwig in: Wesseling, *Expansion and Reaction*.

European factors of imperialism were, however, important in Dutch expansion in the Archipelago: there was the factor of international power politics in pre-emptive occupation and diplomatic agreements, and of mass nationalism at the beginning of the Acheh War, during the Lombok expedition and at the end of the Acheh War. If we also take expansionism in South Africa into account, then this last factor also played a role during the intervening period. Baumgart generally felt that socio-economic factors were less important for modern imperialism than political ones – an assessment which is doubtful not only for Britain and France but also for the Netherlands. Although economic considerations were nearly always present in the extension of colonial rule in the Outer Regions, they were hardly ever decisive in the short term. Only social imperialism seems to be largely absent in the case of the Netherlands; although such notes were sounded with regard to the East Indies and South Africa, they were ignored in actual policy.

The relative significance of different Dutch, local and international factors will be discussed in greater detail below. But if we look at the pattern of expansion and reaction which has just been described, we can certainly conclude that the most important historiographic concepts of modern imperialism can indeed be applied to the Netherlands. But in applying the term, we can also gain a clearer picture of the differences, or rather the special features, of the Dutch position. The Dutch variant of imperialism was that of a small European nation that had already established itself overseas and displayed certain differences compared with other countries at a time, mainly during the 1880s, when modern imperialism was beginning to dominate international relations. The international context and foreign relations were therefore of strategic importance for the position taken by the Netherlands during the rise of modern imperialism.

The Significance of International Relations

The significance of international relations for modern imperialism is often seen in connection with the scramble for colonies which took on spectacular proportions, especially during the partition of Africa. The Netherlands generally kept aloof from this competitive struggle, and even ceded its last possession on the eve of the partition, as Wesseling noted correctly.[15] However, as we saw

---

15. Wesseling, 'Dutch Historiography', p. 139.

above, this aloofness – or indeed withdrawal – was closely related to the extension and defence of Dutch possessions in the Indonesian Archipelago. In this way international rivalry was in a position to promote Dutch imperialism – an imperialism, however, that was more selective and indirect than that of the greater powers. Whenever matters in this respect were determined by Dutch policies, they were always the outcome of co-operation between the Dutch Foreign Affairs Department and the Department of the Colonies. Although their political aims sometimes differed, they were usually determined by a number of regular considerations: first of all, there was the question of how significant the various overseas interests actually were; secondly – and this was often decisive – there were the status and actions of the foreign powers concerned; and finally there were the reactions of the Dutch Parliament, pressure groups and public opinion in the Netherlands.

During the rise of modern imperialism there was always a great deal of consensus between the Foreign Ministers and the Ministers of the Colonies. Priority was nearly always given to 'the keeping and further developing of the East Indies', as Minister Röell put it in 1896. Within the East Indies Java and Sumatra clearly came first, followed by Borneo and Celebes, the Moluccas and the small Sunda Islands, and finally New Guinea. Importance was also attached to the maintenance and further development of Dutch possessions in the West Indies, as was demonstrated in the case of the Antilles during the Venezuela crises around 1870 and 1900, and with regard to Surinam in the so-called Coolie Treaty with Britain and the border conflict with France.

Africa was clearly assigned the least important position by Dutch ministers, so that they were only too happy to cede Elmina. During the partition of Africa they resolutely rejected the option of new colonial outposts and preferred to limit themselves to defending free trade which offered protection to the large-scale, well-established trading interests of the Netherlands. But whenever East Indian interests were indirectly at stake, the ministers became more involved, for example by taking an active part in the management of the Suez Canal and by showing special reserve during the two Boer Wars. In Asia, too, East Indian interests played a role, with regard to the Muslim pilgrimages to Mecca and the import of contract labour from China, but any territorial aspirations were rejected.

Moreover, the overseas activities of the Netherlands were largely determined by the kind of foreign powers it was dealing with, that is, Western or non-Western, large or small. Britain and Germany always continued to be the most important ones for the Netherlands. On the occasion of the 1884 Berlin conference Minister Van der Does de Willebois described the Dutch position: 'After all, we must clearly bear in mind that . . . on the continent we will always be the weaker neighbour of a powerful Germany and that we continuously rub shoulders with Great Britain in the Indian Archipelago where we might have permanent problems.'[16] With regard to Germany, the East Indies were considered vital for the independence of the Netherlands, although this was never said explicitly in public.

During the rise of modern imperialism relations with Britain clearly posed a dilemma for the Netherlands: on the one hand, Britain remained the most important ally of the Netherlands on which it depended if it was to maintain the East Indies; on the other hand, Britain appeared to be the most important rival of the Netherlands in a number of overseas interests. During the Nisero issue and the Suez Convention Minister Van der Does tried to obtain German support against Britain, but Britain's sharp reaction soon put an end to this experiment. Even during the British conquest of the ethnically related Boer republics the Dutch government wanted to avoid everything that might put its good relations with Britain at risk. But when dealing with non-Western or weaker European countries, Dutch ministers often took more liberties. This could be seen particularly clearly in the aggressive actions towards Acheh and, to a lesser extent, Venezuela, as well as in the Dutch participation in international interventions in Japan and China, and its occasional pressure on Portugal.

Obviously, the colonial and diplomatic priorities of the Dutch ministers were not always shared by the Dutch Parliament, interest groups and public opinion in the Netherlands. There was particularly strong opposition when Dutch interests were given up in Africa. This opposition came to the fore during the cession of Elmina around 1870, the violation of Dutch trade interests in the Congo Free State around 1890 and, above all, during the British conquest of the Boers and the Dutch in South Africa around 1900. Also with regard to the East Indies there was often pressure in the Netherlands to take more forceful action regarding Britain. After the Nisero issue and the Boer War several MPs and journalists

16. Woltring, *Bescheiden* III, no. 511.

openly advocated active co-operation with Germany against Britain. The Dutch Ministers of the Colonies and Foreign Ministers nearly always took domestic opposition into account, but they hardly ever gave in to it. Nevertheless, there were some instances of successful domestic pressure on overseas policies, as for example in the rejection of the Siak Treaty by the Second Chamber in 1871; the setting-up of a colonial outpost in Batu Tinagat in Borneo in 1883; the stubborn defence of Dutch trade interests in the Congo at the Brussels conference in 1890; and the sending of the *Gelderland* to bring President Kruger to the Netherlands in 1900. In most cases, however, the majority of MPs as well as public opinion followed governmental policies, albeit with some obvious reluctance at times. Apparently, when it came to it, Dutch parliamentarians had to acknowledge the same circumstances as the Dutch ministers.

Inevitably, however, these circumstances changed between 1870 and 1900. Having to decide between different overseas interests as well as foreign and domestic relations, the Dutch ministers were increasingly confronted with the rise of modern imperialism in their choice of policies. These choices ranged from withdrawal or aloofness to the threat or use of violence. At first, during the 1870s, the international situation still offered the Dutch government a good deal of freedom in their decision making. The cession of Elmina and Dutch freedom of action in north Sumatra were the result of Dutch initiatives and were handled in the traditional way, that is in consultation with Britain. The introduction of free trade in the East Indies provided a further guarantee of British support. However, the Dutch declaration of war on Acheh was largely motivated by its fear of foreign interference, particularly from hitherto unknown and unpredictable powers such as the United States and Italy. At the same time, in the West Indies, the Netherlands strongly opposed Venezuelan claims on Curaçao, partly because it was concerned about foreign – American or German – interference.

During the 1880s, when international rivalry was moving more and more outside Europe and the scramble for colonies was in full swing, Dutch policies were generally far more reserved. The change in the British attitude, in particular, filled The Hague with growing concern. At first the Dutch government responded actively to British expansion in Borneo with real counteractions. But after the Nisero issue, when Britain had indeed almost intervened in Acheh, the Dutch ministers were rather more cautious. The alternative – active co-operation with Germany or France – was considered, but quickly discounted. In general, the Netherlands kept as aloof as possible from the mutual rivalry between the great powers. In itself, this was not very difficult, because this rivalry was mainly concerned with Africa. However, the new criteria for colonial possession caused concern because of their possible implications for the East Indies. After all, effective Dutch occupation was still missing in large parts of the Archipelago, and even the formal borders had still not been established satisfactorily.

At the end of the 1880s and beginning of the 1890s the Dutch government concentrated on the international borders of its colonial possessions. For the sake of security it was quite willing to make concessions, as with the cession of Batu Tinagat in the border agreement with Britain. When setting up the Timor Treaty with Portugal, the Netherlands certainly acted rather less modestly. But as soon as problems with the great powers were imminent, such as the Surinam border conflict with France or the issue of the *Costa Rica Packet*, The Hague preferred international arbitration.

The external protection of the East Indies was not only a matter of diplomacy but also economics. Generally speaking, other countries continued to have free access to East Indian trade and industry, but certain key sectors such as intra-insular shipping and the oil industry were reserved for Dutch companies. And towards the end of the century, when the focal point of modern imperialism moved from Africa to the Far East, the Dutch also took the necessary military precautions, by strengthening their navy in the East Indies, in particular. In this way Dutch expansion in the Indonesian Archipelago could proceed without the threat of direct interference. When a large number of colonial outposts were set up after the Lombok expedition in 1894, fear of foreign threats receded into the background. But Dutch aloofness during the Boer War continued to be a painful reminder of the fact that the Netherlands was a small power which depended on the great powers to keep its colonies.

In all, it seemed that the existing power relations had a determining influence on the position of the Netherlands during the emergence of modern imperialism. But a number of specifically Dutch elements can also be discerned which were described by Boogman as the 'Holland tradition' and 'commercial-maritime tendencies'.[17] Boogman's terms drew attention to the elements of free trade and

17. See Boogman, 'Achtergronden', 'Netherlands' and 'Tradition'. Cf. 'Holland's Foreign Policy Traditions', in Voorhoeve, *Peace*, pp. 42–55.

territorial concentration as well as aloofness and international law in the overseas policies of the Netherlands. However, they do not take account of the regularly recurring elements of territorial expansion and economic constraints as well as aggression and power politics in Dutch relations with non-Western or weak European powers overseas.

In general, however, foreign policies were mainly determined by family tradition and aristocratic mentality rather than the clear historical tradition that went back to the seventeenth century. Combined with the continuity which characterised the international position of the Netherlands after 1830, the continuity of Ministers for Foreign Affairs never led to anything more than a certain political tradition – the Dutch version of 'masterly inactivity'. In this sense we can follow Brands, who spoke of 'patrician' policies which were temporarily challenged by a broad 'plebeian' opposition during the Boer War around the turn of the century.[18]

Between 1870 and 1900 the international position of the Netherlands, particularly in the European context, meant that it had to put a special emphasis on aloofness, free trade and international law in its foreign affairs. And as modern imperialism was largely the result of mutual rivalry between the great European powers, these elements also affected the overseas policies of the Netherlands. Each time the Netherlands was confronted with European rivalry outside Europe, such as the partition of Africa and the complications over China, the Dutch Foreign Ministers insisted on restraint. But as soon as the obstacle had become less prominent, the minister's freedom of movement increased again; his colleague, the Minister of the Colonies, could assert himself; and overseas interests and local power relations came to the fore again in the various policies. In Europe, the Netherlands remained a relatively small nation, but outside Europe the Netherlands was a great colonial power. Even the Amsterdam merchant and aristocrat Hartsen, who followed the 'Old Holland' tradition more than any of the other ministers, was firmly convinced of the 'great political importance' of the East Indies. 'However small our country may be,' he said in 1888, 'our East Indian dominions give us a position which is often underestimated.'[19] And yet it was difficult to bridge the gap between the European and the non-European position of the Netherlands.

18. Brands, 'Elementen', p. 60.
19. Woltring, *Bescheiden* IV, no. 266.

Although colonial possessions gave it more status, they did not give a guarantee of a firm place as a 'middle power' in the international order. European power relations continued to be dominant, even during the First World War. Moreover, even outside Europe the Netherlands was confronted with the insecure and transitory character of its mid-position.[20]

The development of Dutch relations with Japan during the rise of modern imperialism was indicative in this respect. Despite its traditional ties of friendship, the Netherlands took an active part in the system of armed interventions and unequal treaties practised by the Western powers during the opening of Japan in the 1850s and 1860s. In the 1870s and 1880s, during the negotiations aimed at dismantling this system after the Meiji restoration, the Netherlands tried to establish itself as 'the first among the powers of the second rank', as the Dutch representative put it at the time.[21] But the new rulers in Japan quickly put the Netherlands out of action and twice declared an immodest Dutch representative *persona non grata*. In the 1890s, when the Netherlands finally resumed negotiations with Japan, the tables had turned completely. Japan had become a new great power and, in the new trade agreement, was able to wrest significant concessions in the East Indies from the Netherlands. Around 1900 Japan was seen by many observers as the most dangerous threat to Dutch possessions in the East Indies.

The Interaction between Dutch and Local Factors

To sum up, the international factor therefore functioned as a cause for Dutch imperialism in the Indonesian Archipelago, while at the same time preventing it elsewhere. At first, particularly when the Acheh War had just broken out, this factor was a direct cause, though it then became a more indirect one in the sense that it created the external conditions for Dutch expansion in the Archipelago around the turn of the century. This strategic but partial significance of the international factor raises the question about the influence of other factors again, that is, of Dutch and local factors. It is a question which can be narrowed down to Dutch expansion in the Indonesian Archipelago and then supplemented and compared with the issue of limited Dutch expansion in South Africa.

While international relations reinforced the element of 'pre-

20. Vandenbosch, *Foreign Policy*, pp. 214–17; cf. Wight, *Power Politics*, pp. 63–5.
21. Woltring, *Bescheiden* IV, no. 201A, note 3.

emption' in connection with certain Dutch factors, local factors pointed to a permanent element of 'contiguity', that is geographical and historical continuity of Dutch expansion in the Archipelago. Before 1870 interaction between the colonial administration and local princes had formed the most important cause of Dutch expansion. The Hague generally adhered to a strict policy of abstention but was often presented with a *fait accompli*. However, from 1850 onwards there was a gradual increase of Dutch interest in the Outer Regions, especially the promising island of Sumatra. From 1865 the Liberal Ministers of the Colonies Fransen van de Putte, De Waal and Van Bosse developed initiatives that were aimed at bringing that 'den of robbers', Acheh, under Dutch control. These resulted from a combination of strategic and economic considerations, such as the opening of the Suez Canal, the fight against piracy and the development of nearby Deli.

The Conservative Governor Mijer did not favour more forceful action very much, whereas his Liberal successor Loudon listened enthusiastically to such ideas from the Netherlands, where quite a few were advocating and indeed anticipating a violent conquest. Minister Fransen van de Putte, on the other hand, preferred a peaceful solution. However, when foreign interference became imminent, he no longer followed his own line with any consistency and did nothing to restrain Loudon. Realising that he now had a free hand, Loudon then declared war on Acheh.

Once the war had broken out, it had a crippling effect on the Dutch and local factors for expansion. Between 1873 and 1885 the war claimed some 10 to 15 per cent of the East Indian budget, and between a quarter and a third of the Dutch forces were tied to Acheh. Under these circumstances The Hague kept to its policy of abstention as much as possible, and Batavia had no scope to deviate in any way. When, in 1884, it became obvious that neither a military nor a political solution to the Acheh War was realistic, the Dutch government decided that their military presence in Acheh should be concentrated on a limited area, with a view to reducing costs. This concentration increased the opportunities for expansion in the other parts of the Archipelago again. At the same time an interesting connection emerged between economic and administrational expansionism, of which the tin expedition to Flores formed the most notorious, though not the only, example. Around 1890 the Dutch Parliament and public opinion were still very reticent towards an expansion of colonial administration in the Outer Regions, although the policy of abstention had in principle already been abandoned by minister Mackay.

But when Governor-general Van der Wijck took the initiative in the Lombok expedition, prompted mainly by administrative motives, the response in the Netherlands was unexpectedly enthusiastic. The nationalist reaction to the initial defeat contributed to the decisive action of the colonial administration and the Dutch East Indian army. The same pattern was more or less repeated in Acheh in 1896, and Van Heutsz's pacification around 1900 was given great support in the Netherlands. The Dutch East Indian army received reinforcements and a quarter was temporarily deployed in Acheh again.[22] But even before the official end of the Acheh War in 1903 troops and financial resources were made available for new activities in the Outer Regions. Not only administrative motives but also economic motives often played an important role in this connection, and around the turn of the century Dutch investment in the Outer Regions increased considerably. Minister Cremer strongly promoted economic expansion, especially through the Mining Act. Between 1902 and 1909 the subjection and development of the Archipelago were systematically brought to completion under Idenburg as Minister of the Colonies and Van Heutsz as governor-general.

Of the different Dutch and local political and economic motives for expansion the latter, in particular, have until now only been examined very sketchily. Etherington's suggestion that more attention be paid to the area of government contracts, apart from trade and direct investment, is no doubt of relevance here.[23] This relevance is obvious in the case of the KPM, but it should also be examined further for the supply of equipment and provisions for the Acheh War and other expeditions, or indeed for a whole series of concessions in agriculture, forestry and mining. Moreover, it seems to me that the relative significance of the economic factor can be measured not only by the short-term motivation of certain colonial actions; the 'spirit of the colonial administration' asserted itself most strongly in such areas of practical policy making. But the private correspondence between ministers and governor-generals also included suggestions for the realisation of general, long-term economic objectives. The plans which Cremer and Van der Wijck

22. See appendix 4.
23. Etherington, *Theories*, p. 270.

had developed around 1900 for the 'spiritual and material development of the populations in our Archipelago' were certainly of a largely capitalist kind.[24] The functions which they had in Dutch cultivation, trade, banking and industry before and after their terms of office suggest this even more strongly.[25]

In all, economic causes seem to have had a less direct but more permanent influence than political and administrational causes, which were often seriously weakened by the unfavourable course of the Acheh War. In traditional colonial historiography the impression is often given that the war could have come to an end far more quickly if the far-sighted administrators in Batavia and the resolute commanding officers in Kota Radja had not been repeatedly kept back by The Hague.[26] However, the results of the present study suggest that there was interaction rather than antagonism between the different administrative centres.

When the most important decisions were being made, such as the annexation of Acheh in 1874, the introduction of the policy of concentration in 1884 and its cessation in 1896, the same options were under discussion in The Hague, Batavia and Kota Radja. In the end, decisions were indeed made in a formal and hierarchical way, because considerable political and financial interests were at stake in the Acheh War. Obviously, the personalities of the minister, the governor-general and the governor of Acheh also played a role. But even a 'strong' governor such as Van der Wijck was not given free reign by the 'weak' minister Bergsma until the Second Chamber had clearly decided in favour of pacification. Meanwhile Governor Deijkerhoff had already disappeared from the scene, and every time there was a change of policy the 'man on the spot' was the first to get the sack. If Van Heutsz and Snouck Hurgronje had a considerable degree of autonomy in the pacification of Acheh, this was

24. Cremer to Van der Wijck, 28 June 1898, Van der Wijck Collection (ARA), Cf. Fasseur, *Geest*.

25. Before Cremer became Minister of the Colonies in 1897, he had played leading roles in the Deli Company, the Deli Railways Company, the large cultivation bank Netherlands–Indies Agriculture Company working mainly in Java, the Royal Packet Company, the machinery and railway material company Werkspoor and its connected shipbuilding company, all based in Amsterdam. After his term of office Cremer was president of the powerful Netherlands Trading Company between 1907 and 1912. Before Van der Wijck was appointed governor-general in 1893, he had been a member of the Royal Packet Company's board of managers, and after his resignation he became chairman of the board of managers of the Royal Dutch Oil Company and a board member of a large number of cultivation companies.

26. Cf. Somer, *Korte Verklaring*, pp. 183–4 and 204ff.

based largely on a broad consensus in the Netherlands.

Generally speaking, Dutch policies with regard to the East Indian Outer Regions were more systematic than external overseas policies, which were largely decided *ad hoc*. Whenever there was a political change, the various options were subject to the same policies or strategies as before. And so the colonial administration, the colonial army and the Dutch court preferred on the whole a rather formal and territorial kind of imperialism, with a tendency towards military pacification and direct rule – a more aggressive strategy that was supported by a growing majority of the Liberal and Christian parties in the Netherlands. The most important alternative option was seen in a 'pacifist' policy of abstention, which had been promoted by the Conservatives mainly on pragmatic grounds, although some Liberals and Socialists continued to defend it on principle. Finally, there was also an intermediate strategy of a more informal, maritime kind of imperialism, aimed at indirect rule and economic expansion. This more defensive strategy was favoured by a number of governmental and naval circles and supported by a declining majority of the Liberal and Christian parties. Their spokesman was Fransen van der Putte, who always advocated a peaceful and gradual expansion, following the Siak model, and who actively helped to promote Dutch naval interests in the East Indies. After 1870 this strategy repeatedly dominated Dutch policies, especially during the first phase of the Acheh War and the introduction of the system of concentration. Around the year 1890 it still seemed as if this would continue to be the Netherlands' most important expansion strategy in the entire Archipelago. In Acheh Colonel Clarksen's maritime policy was still being tried out, after it had been recommended to the colonial administration by minister Van Dedem, while Fransen van der Putte as chairman of a state committee was preparing a further extension of naval duties in the East Indies.[27] But the course of events in Lombok and Acheh meant that the offensive strategy of the armed forces, the colonial administration and the court eventually gained the upper hand.

This analysis merely differs in emphasis from Fasseur's view of Dutch expansion in his article on the Dutch East Indies in the new *General History of the Netherlands* (*AGN*), also published in

27. For Clarkson's note and Van Dedem's recommendations of 10 February 1890 and 25 November 1891, see Pijnacker Hordijk Collection (ARA). Cf. the *Rapport aan de Koningin-Weduwe, Regentes van de Commissie, benoemd bij Koninklijk Besluit van 31 juli 1889* . . . 's-Gravenhage 1891.

Overzee.[28] He puts more weight than before on the political and economic expansionism in the Netherlands which indirectly led to the Acheh War. 'But the Acheh War', says Fasseur, 'did not form a definitive break with the policy of abstention. It was only when abstention threatened to lead to a vacuum which might then be filled by other Western powers that there was any willingness on the level of government to proceed with intervention.'[29] This external, power-political factor did indeed still play an important role in setting up colonial outposts in Borneo and New Guinea after the Acheh War in the 1880s and 1890s. Pre-emption also motivated certain economic strategies, in particular the grant of a permanent maritime monopoly to the Dutch KPM in the East Indies and the exclusion of American Standard Oil from the East Indies until 1912. Even in the reinforcement of the navy and the establishment of new telegraph links, pre-emption can be detected. The element of pre-emption may well have gained new significance by the Japanese–Russian War in 1904–5, when the Christian government even feared for a sudden British attack on Puluh Weh and the resistance in Acheh flared up again. But the sudden change in favour of expansion which took place in the Netherlands between the 1894 Lombok expedition and the Japanese–Russian War was largely autonomous in character: apart from administrative initiatives and military successes in the East Indies this change was mainly caused by nationalist impulses and economic developments in the Netherlands. Obviously, as Van Goor has pointed out correctly, the power vacuum which Fasseur had in mind consisted of *de facto* independent Indonesian societies. Indonesian initiatives, such Achehnese diplomacy after 1870, the attempts of the Sasaks to obtain help, the Balinese counteractions in Lombok after 1890 and the defection of Teuku Umar in 1896, should therefore be regarded as inducements rather than causes of Dutch imperialism; the decisive steps were taken in Batavia and, in the final instance, in The Hague.[30]

As imperialism was eventually becoming the predominant policy in the Dutch East Indies, the Netherlands continued to follow a strict policy of non-involvement and neutrality in South Africa. Here the most important cause of Dutch expansion came from the growing nationalism within Dutch society during the 1880s and 1890s. The Dutch Transvaal movement was not so much geared

28. Fasseur, 'Nederland'.
29. Ibid., p. 176; cf. Fasseur, 'Koloniale paradox', p. 179.
30. Van Goor, *Kooplieden*, p. 137.

towards territorial expansion, even though this element was not entirely absent in the concept of a 'New Holland' in South Africa. In accordance with the wishes of the Transvaal government, which was formally independent but in practice rather dependent, the movement aimed at a strengthening of the Dutch element in the administration, education and economy of the SAR.

Despite the abstention of the Dutch government and opposing interests in the Dutch business world, some steps towards informal imperialism were taken around 1890 by the Dutch Transvaal movement, the Dutch railway company and the Dutch administrators in the government of the SAR. However, as a result of pressure from public opinion in the Transvaal, Dutch influence was curbed again during the 1890s. This meant that Dutch endeavours to achieve a 'New Holland' disappeared into the background again, even though economic contacts with South Africa were on the increase. The nationalist reaction to the Jameson Raid and the Boer War temporarily brought these aspirations to the fore again. However, after the British conquest of South Africa, any Dutch expansion in South Africa had definitely come to an end.

We saw in the introduction that post-war historiography had a strong tendency to describe the development of nineteenth-century Dutch society as being extremely different from that of other countries, especially in areas which could either promote or prevent imperialism. As a temporary conclusion and a starting point for a more specific comparison with other countries, we shall briefly examine how the perceived pattern of expansion and reaction compares with such concepts of the Netherlands as a special case. In our discussion of international relations we noted the unmistakable influence of commercial and maritime tendencies on Dutch overseas policies. However, apart from free trade, territorial concentration, abstention and international law, this policy also showed elements of territorial expansion, economic coercion, aggression and power politics. Of the different fixed and variable factors which Wels distinguished for the formation of Dutch foreign policies, the element of tradition certainly played no dominant role whatever.[31] Instead, policies were generally decided *ad hoc* and on the basis of Dutch interests overseas, external power relations and the domestic reactions which affected the various ministers. Obviously, their perception of these interests, power relations and reactions played

31. Wels, 'Historicus', p. 23.

an important part in their final choice of policies. But this perception seems to have been governed by current circumstances and personal qualities rather than implicit or explicit historical traditions. Within the continuity of the Dutch position as a small European nation and a great colonial power, these political choices therefore displayed a certain amount of variation.

Economically, too, the Netherlands was strongly oriented towards trade and the colonies. Although industrialisation increased, it remained limited compared with other countries. Nevertheless, the Dutch economy was already rather modern around 1870: as Griffith put it, it was 'different', and in some respects 'behind', but certainly not 'backward' compared with other countries.[32] For branches of industry which were industrialised, such as Twente textiles, overseas markets had already become important; the same applied to a number of new industries around 1900, like machinery and railway material. In particular shipbuilding, so strategic for overseas trade, had recovered much ground since 1870. But most shipping and trade took place fairly near home, via the German hinterland. After the introduction of free trade in 1874 the share of the East Indies in Dutch trade even decreased, particularly in Dutch exports, although Dutch imports from the East Indies recovered and Dutch imports from other overseas markets even increased.[33] Free trade and an open door to foreign investments was the price the Netherlands had to pay to other, larger countries for the undisturbed possession and exploitation of the Indonesian Archipelago. And in view of the enormous growth of East Indian production and trade, this price was rather small and easy to pay. The contribution of the East Indies to the growing national income of the Netherlands increased from 2–3 per cent in 1870 to 5 per cent in 1890 and at least 10 per cent in 1913. The growth of Dutch investments in the East Indies emphasised by Van Tijn and the increasing economic autonomy of the East Indies emphasised by à Campo did not exclude each other. It follows that economically, too, the Netherlands had the position of a small European and a great colonial power during the rise of modern imperialism.[34]

The international position of the Netherlands also influenced domestic relations. It was no obstacle to the emergence of a power-

32. Griffiths, *Achterlijk*.
33. See appendix 3.
34. Cf. à Campo, 'Orde', pp. 178–9; Van Tijn, 'Nabeschouwing', pp. 82–4. See also De Jonge, *Industrialisatie*, pp. 355–7.

ful nationalist current, though it did prevent Dutch nationalism from being implemented it its foreign affairs. During the Boer War both tendencies – nationalist agitation among the general public and the restraint of the government – demonstrated themselves very clearly. After the British victory in South Africa the Netherlands as a small nation could not afford any irredentism or policy of revenge, so that public interest in South Africa quickly waned again after 1902. In the East Indies, on the other hand, nationalist expansionism found a more durable and less hazardous target. On the domestic front 'pillarisation' certainly did not form an obstacle to overseas nationalism. The outspokenly nationalist behaviour of Christian leaders such as Kuyper and Schaepman were particularly significant in this respect. In colonial affairs and within the Transvaal Movement institutional pillarisation remained rather limited. Ideologically, however, overseas nationalism complemented domestic 'pillarisation' rather than presenting a valid alternative, so that Anti-Revolutionaries, Roman Catholics and Liberals all developed their own special brands of nationalism.[35]

There are still considerable gaps in our knowledge of the intellectual origin and the social basis of *fin de siècle* nationalism. Kossmann's reference to the educational reform of the 1860s and 1870s certainly deserves closer attention.[36] While 'pillarisation' did not form an obstacle to nationalist expansionism, the political system and social relations did not really generate many impulses for social imperialism. Writing from a comparative point of view, Schöffer has correctly pointed out the gradual and moderate character of political and socio-economic developments in the Netherlands.[37]

The Dutch Position Compared with Other Countries

The Dutch Position Between Britain and Portugal

It should have become clear by now that during the rise of modern imperialism the Netherlands occupied the position of a small European power as well as a large, established colonial power. However, without an explicit comparison such a statement must remain vague

35. Cf. Van Wehring, *Maatschappijbeeld*, pp. 129–38; Bornewasser, 'Katholieken', pp. 593–605; Kossmann, *Lage landen*, pp. 306 and 318.
36. Ibid., p. 311; cf. Gellner, *Nations*, chapter 3.
37. Schöffer, 'Dutch "expansion"', pp. 80–1.

and unsatisfactory. Undoubtedly many readers will be asking themselves whether the glass is half-empty or half-full. For a further definition of European and non-European factors in the pattern of expansion and reaction we will find some useful starting points when we compare the Netherlands with Britain and Portugal.

Britain has always had a prominent place in the formation of theories on modern imperialism, and most of the general approaches shown in the introduction were implicitly or explicitly based on Britain as an example of the first and greatest imperialist power in the world. Small and weak Portugal, on the other hand, forms an obvious contrast. However, the Netherlands shared a number of more general starting points with both Britain and Portugal. Traditionally, all three had always been 'commercial-maritime' nations which had already established themselves overseas a long time before the rise of modern imperialism. During the emergence of modern imperialism, however, they displayed great differences in power and development. So which country did the Netherlands, in practice, resemble most? This was a question which many Dutch contemporaries regularly asked themselves – with different tendencies and divergent conclusions.[38]

At first, during the first half of the nineteenth century, the Netherlands had frequently been in the company of Portugal, rather than Britain. Between 1815 and 1870 Britain was, comparatively speaking, at the height of its political and economic power. The industrial revolution and free trade were promoting British overseas expansion throughout the world, and, where necessary, the *Pax Britannica* was enforced by the Royal Navy. In Africa, Latin America and the Far East expansion was largely limited to informal imperialism, and no more than a limited number of strategic points were occupied. In many cases, according to Platt, particularly in Latin America, this did not even amount to informal imperialism.[39] But in Oceania and the Indian subcontinent British expansion had already acquired a largely formal and territorial character. British dominion in India was further consolidated by the suppression of the Great Rebellion in 1857–8. However, India's open borders were

38. After the British ultimatum to Portugal in 1890 both Kuyper and Van Bylandt wondered if the Netherlands could now expect a similar ultimatum in Borneo. In 1898 the Portuguese celebrations in memory of Vasco da Gama were reported with self-satisfied condescension in the *NRC* of 17 May. Cf. *De Standaard*, 22 January 1890; Woltring, *Bescheiden* IV, no. 413.

39. Platt, *Finance*, pp. 310–12 and 360–2; cf. Eldridge, *Victorian Imperialism*, chapter 2.

still a problem, and the element of 'pre-emption' played a role in the annexation of north-west India as early as the 1840s. In particular, the 'Great Game' – Britain's rivalry with Russia in Central Asia, as an extension of the Eastern question – continued to motivate defensive expansion.[40]

In 1815 both the Netherlands and Portugal were strongly dependent on Britain, which showed itself, among other things, in the abolition of the slave trade. But whereas the Netherlands managed to restore its political and economic independence very quickly, Portugal remained a semi-developed client state of Britain throughout the nineteenth century. The establishment of British hegemony during the Napoleonic Wars had permanently disrupted the Portuguese economy. Between 1820 and 1825 Portugal finally lost control over Brazil, the largest and richest of its colonies. The remaining colonies in Africa and Asia were exploited in a traditional way, often by means of slave labour. Although British pressure achieved the abolition of the slave trade in 1815 and the abolition of slavery in 1858, forced labour and the export of labourers continued to be the most important source of revenue for Portuguese Africa. With the exception of the small colony of Sao Tomé, Portugal's system of exploitation yielded very little profit. By the end of the nineteenth century the trade enclave of Goa in India was still more profitable for the Portuguese state than Angola or Mozambique. Portugal's actual rule therefore remained limited to small coastal strips.[41]

The Netherlands fared much better after 1815. Its unification with the southern Netherlands had already given it a more powerful position and greater economic potential. Although both were partly lost again after the separation of Belgium in 1830, the Netherlands managed to make a lasting recovery, but this recovery was at first very slow in the remaining colonies. Surinam's plantation economy, in particular, continued to stagnate after Britain had successfully imposed the abolition of the slave trade on the Netherlands in 1815. Dutch dominion in Java was only established after a war of attrition, the Java War of 1825–30. However, Java became a very profitable colony for the Netherlands again when the system of forced cultivation was introduced and free trade, which had been of considerable benefit to Britain, was abolished. Compared with the Portuguese system of state monopoly and forced labour, the Dutch

40. Cf. Gillard, *Struggle*, chapters 3–4; Yapp, *Strategies*, parts 2–3.
41. Marques, *History* I, pp. 458–62; ibid. II, pp. 80–1. Cf. Hammond, *Portugal*, chapters 1–2.

system not only yielded more profit for the treasury but was also more beneficial for Dutch industry, and even for the local population. Although there were important pre-colonial and continuing colonial differences, the Dutch system of state cultivation in Java may have had metropolitan and local results similar to the British – formally free – market economy and various land rent systems in Northern India before 1870.[42] We have already noted that Dutch control had gradually spread over some parts of the Archipelago before 1870. As in British India, the initiative in this 'frontier' imperialism was often taken by local government officials and the military. And whenever there was an external threat, such as Brooke's activities in northern Borneo during the 1840s, even The Hague departed from its policy of abstention. However, compared with Britain's territoral expansion in India, Dutch expansion outside Java remained very limited and rather informal in character.[43]

Although by 1870 there were already great differences between Britain, the Netherlands and Portugal with regard to their power, development and colonial possessions, their responses to the rise of modern imperialism also showed a number of similarities. The expansionism of these established colonial powers was rather defensive in character and was largely aimed at rounding off and consolidating their existing colonies. Indeed, the contrast with the preceding p   od was most conspicuous in Britain. In 1872, when Disraeli was leader of the Conservative opposition, he announced his future 'Imperial Policy', even though in the past he had described the colonies as 'deadweights' and 'millstones'. But according to Robinson and Gallagher, this policy was no more than the continuation of Britain's previous overseas expansion. Eldridge has shown convincingly that, if there was any change at all, it was more a matter of ideology than practical politics.[44] Although Gladstone remained an avowed opponent of colonial expansion, his Liberal government became increasingly involved in local overseas crises between 1868 and 1874, such as problems on the Gold Coast. Disraeli's 'Imperial Policy' between 1874 and 1880, on the other hand, was partly mere rhetoric. A number of annexations and wars which were ascribed to his personal ambitions were in fact due to

42. Fasseur, *Kultuurstelsel*, pp. 35–6 and 40–2. Cf. Bayly, *Rulers*, p. 262; Charlesworth, *British Rule*, pp. 17–21.
43. Fasseur, 'Koloniale paradox', pp. 174–84; cf. Yapp, *Strategies*, pp. 540–58.
44. Cf. Eldridge, *Victorian Imperialism*, pp. 92–111; idem, *England's Mission*, passim.

the initiatives of local proconsuls.

Nevertheless, colonial expansionism increased quite considerably in Britain under Disraeli. This was due to the economic crisis and reinforced by the Eastern question. For Disraeli, the security of British India was a top priority. The strategic interests of India were a central factor in the Afghan and Burmese wars, and played an indirect role in the establishment of British control over the Suez Canal as well as British expansion in South Africa. By offering Queen Victoria the Empress's crown, Disraeli made British India the symbol of imperial pride – 'the secret of the mastery of the world'.[45]

In 1880, after a fierce campaign against Disraeli's overseas adventures, Gladstone became prime minister again. His government reversed the annexation of the Transvaal, but was compelled to occupy the whole of Egypt. International rivalry inevitably involved Britain in the partition of Africa. However, many British, including an increasing number of Liberals, found Gladstone's policies far too restrained and half-hearted. Between 1885 and 1903 one prime minister after another followed a consistent policy of colonial expansion – in either a Conservative, Unionist or Liberal fashion. 'We are all imperialists now', declared Gladstone's successor Rosebery in 1899. Frequently the chartered companies acted as pacemakers in the process of expansion, supported by local proconsuls. The government in London then ensured further international steps.[46]

From 1895 to 1903 Chamberlain, as Secretary of the Colonies, systematically promoted British expansion from London. In Africa his aggressive policy led, among other things, to the Fashoda Crisis with France and finally to war with the Boer republics. Chamberlain's Conservative colleagues, the foreign affairs secretaries Salisbury and Landsdowne, also cast their eyes on Asia where Russia was making further advances in the area around India and the Far East.[47] The vigorous development of British imperialism around 1900 was due to a number of different factors, the most central one being the assurance of new investment opportunities and foreign

45. Gollwitzer, *Geschichte*, pp. 93ff. Cf. Eldridge, *Victorian Imperialism*, pp. 110–20; Hynes, *Economics*, chapter 3; Lowe, *Reluctant Imperialists*, chapter 4.

46. Cf. Eldridge, *Victorian Imperialism*, chapter 5; Lowe, *Reluctant Imperialists*, chapters 6 and 8; Hynes, *Economics*, chapters 4–7; Schreuder, *Scramble*, chapters 8–9.

47. Gillard, *Struggle*, chapter 8; cf. Lowe, *Reluctant Imperialists*, chapters 9–10; Porter, *Origins, passim*.

markets – 'pegging out claims for the future', in Roseberry's words. This economic expansionism was reinforced by international rivalry, domestic nationalism and social imperialism. However, Chamberlain's concepts of an 'Imperial Federation' and 'Imperial Preference' also pointed to a continuing defensive undercurrent in British imperialism. Furthermore, the Boer War was followed by a strong anti-imperialist reaction.[48]

The Dutch pattern of expansion and reaction clearly showed similarities with the British pattern, especially around 1870 and 1900. The Acheh War showed roughly the same combination of local and metropolitan factors as the Ashanti war and also a similar combination of 'contiguity' and 'pre-emption' as the Afghan war, although in both cases the British government withdrew its forces more easily than the Dutch, without any annexations. Around the turn of the century Dutch expansion in the Archipelago also showed an interaction between financial interests, military aggression and nationalism. But on the international scene, in particular, there were now considerable differences between the imperialism of Britain as a great power and that of smaller powers, such as the Netherlands. Dutch policies began to concentrate even more strongly on the East Indies than British policies on India. Like Britain during the partition of Africa, the Netherlands continually took its Asian possessions into account. But the difference was that Britain annexed nearly half the continent in the course of the partition, whereas the Netherlands actually ceded its last African possessions and remained as aloof as possible, despite its trading interest in the Congo and nationalist interest in South Africa.

Furthermore, Dutch expansion in the Indonesian Archipelago around 1870 was finally catching up with British expansion in India, which had already nearly reached completion. This process was slowed down again by the unfavourable course of the Acheh War, and it took the Netherlands until the turn of the century to achieve the same level of internal and external consolidation in the Archipelago as Britain had attained in India. This parallel was reflected in a number of basic figures. Around 1900 Britain had about 40 million inhabitants and British India approximately 285 million; the Indian army had 280,000 troops. In the same year the Netherlands only had five million inhabitants, and the Dutch East Indies about 35

48. Eldridge, *Victorian Imperialism*, pp. 193–5 and 233–5. Cf. Semmel, *Imperialism*, pp. 83–98 and 160–6; Kennedy, *Rise*, pp. 307–11; Porter, *Origins*, pp. 267–77; Edelstein, *Overseas Investment*, pp. 301–6.

million, of whom 28 million lived in Java. The Dutch East Indian army had about 40,000 men. But around 1900 the share of British investments in India was already declining to 10 per cent of all capital exports in 1913, while Dutch investments in the East Indies were increasing to 30 per cent of all capital exports in 1913. The Outer Regions offered Dutch investors new opportunities within the East Indies, which British investors increasingly sought outside India, particularly in South Africa.[49]

Portugal, too, had about five million inhabitants around 1900, though the total population of its colonies was probably even smaller, and its colonial army only had 10,000 men. Being nearly bankrupt, Portugal was hardly able to afford private and public investments on a large scale.[50] According to Hammond, the most important author in this field, Portuguese expansion in Africa was therefore a typical example of 'uneconomic imperialism'. Although this theory, too, has now been disputed, the criticism of his thesis seems more convincing for the eventual exploitation of the Portuguese colonies than for the territorial expansion that preceded it.[51] At first, Portuguese expansion was rather defensive in character, but it became intensified by military and administrative ambitions, nationalism and economic protectionism. Internationally, the Portuguese response to the rise of modern imperialism was in some ways similar to that of the Netherlands. In 1875, seeking international arbitration in a dispute with Britain, Portugal had managed to obtain the recognition of its sovereignty over Delagoa Bay by the French president. When international interest in Africa increased even further, Portugal tried to secure its colonial possessions with the help of British patronage. Traditionally, it had always claimed the Congo estuary, and in 1884 it obtained British support for its ambitions. But during the Berlin Conference, which had been called as a result of the British–Portuguese treaty, Britain dropped Portugal again in favour of Leopold's Association.[52]

The Portuguese government then opted for an alternative strategy, which the Netherlands only followed occasionally and

49. Cf. Charlesworth, *British Rule*, pp. 44 and 51–5; De Jonge, *Industrialisatie*, pp. 306–7; Wesseling, 'Koloniale oorlogen', p. 480.

50. Marques, *History* II, p. 83. In 1884 the number of inhabitants in the Portuguese colonies was estimated to be about three million. *De Economist*, 1884, II, p. 807.

51. Hammond, *Portugal*, pp. 335–6; cf. Clarence-Smith, 'Myth'. See also Marques, *History* II, chapters 1–2 and 5.

52. Hammond, *Portugal*, chapters 3–4; cf. Anstey, *Britain*, chapters 5–8.

even then only very cautiously: it dissociated itself from Britain and openly began to seek *rapprochement* with Germany and France. In 1886, in its frontier settlements with the two great powers, it made considerable concessions in Africa so that it could, if necessary, maintain their support. Portugal then tried to establish a link between Angola and Mozambique, which was bound to thwart the British 'Cape to Cairo' ambition. In 1890 the British government therefore demanded in an ultimatum that Portugal should relinquish all claims in Central Africa, thus pre-empting an effective occupation. When no support was given by Germany or France, the Portuguese government had no choice but to give in to British demands, despite vehement opposition from the Portuguese Parliament. In the British–Portuguese border treaty of 1891 Angola and Mozambique were given definitive territorial borders.[53]

During the 1890s Portugal's foreign debts reached crisis point, and foreign intervention was being threatened on all sides. Operating from Tanganyika, Germany simply occupied a strategic border area in Mozambique in 1894. Even the Netherlands put some pressure on Portugal in order to obtain preferential rights to Portuguese Timor in the Timor Treaty. In 1898 Britain and Germany agreed on the distribution of Portuguese colonies in the event that Portugal should no longer be able to meet its financial obligations. The end of Portugal as a colonial power seemed to be at hand. Ironically, however, British imperialism in South Africa gave Portugal a certain amount of leeway again. In 1899, in order to secure passive Portuguese support in the Boer War, Britain gave Portugal new guarantees for its colonies. Meanwhile the Portuguese colonial administration had already started the internal pacification of Angola and Mozambique in 1891. In Angola the pacification was completed shortly after 1900, but indigenous resistance in Mozambique was not quelled until the eve of the First World War. To achieve economic development the colonial administration engaged colonists and Portuguese or foreign charter companies, though this yielded very few concrete results before 1900.[54]

A comparison of the Netherlands, Portugal and Britain shows that in the rise of modern imperialism general factors such as 'contiguity' and 'pre-emption' could mean very different things for greater and the smaller powers as well as for African and Asian

53. Hammond, *Portugal*, chapters 5–6.
54. Ibid., chapters 7–9.

territories. The British response to imperialism included both the completion of colonial expansion in Asia and its continuation in Africa. Portugal was in the doubly unfavourable position of being a small European power and being entirely dependent on Africa for its colonial expansion, where the scramble for colonies was most intense. In this respect the Netherlands had a much easier job in South East Asia, where international rivalry remained limited at first. While Portugal never succeeded in establishing a link between its African colonies, the Netherlands managed to extend control over nearly the entire Indonesian Archipelago, which offered more fertile soils and even more lucrative minerals than Central Africa.

But the relative success of Dutch colonial expansion and the relative failure of Portuguese attempts were not just the result of different geographical conditions. As a small European power, the Netherlands was economically and politically far more developed than Portugal, where the modernisation process proceeded only haltingly. According to all the usual indicators of modernisation – communications, industrialisation, national product, literacy and level of organisation – the Netherlands was closer to Britain than Portugal. In 1900, for example, 46.3 per cent of the working population in Britain and 32.2 per cent in the Netherlands were involved in industry, whereas in Portugal the figure seems to have been nearer 10 per cent. Of the Portuguese population 75 per cent were still illiterate at the time, as compared to 10–20 per cent in Britain and the Netherlands.[55]

The Netherlands had as many inhabitants around the turn of the century as Portugal, but its colonies had about 35 million, whereas in the Portuguese colonies there were only five million inhabitants at the most. Because of its greater wealth and higher level of development the Netherlands was far more capable of colonial expansion than Portugal. The vast differences between their respective colonial armies as well as their colonial investment showed this very clearly. Furthermore, because of its domestic development as well as its extensive colonial possessions, the Netherlands occupied a more prominent place among the European powers of the second rank. This difference in international status in turn affected their colonial expansion, as illustrated by the different results of thier respective confrontations with Britain in the rise of modern imperialism.

55. Marques, *History* II, pp. 6, 27 and 30. Cf. Kossmann, *Lage landen*, pp. 310–15; De Jonge, *Industrialisatie*, p. 223; Read, *England*, pp. 220–1 and 282–5.

Both in its domestic process of modernisation and also the nature and extent of its colonial expansion, the Netherlands showed more similarities with Britain than with Portugal. And yet internationally, compared with Britain, the Netherlands always remained a second-rate power. The fact that the Netherlands achieved no lasting expansion in South Africa showed that it was more than a matter of pure quantitative differences. In determining the position of the Netherlands in the rise of modern imperialism, its direct neighbour, Belgium, is perhaps more comparable than Britain or Portugal.

The Netherlands and Belgium

What makes a comparison between the Netherlands and Belgium so interesting is that there are so many small but characteristic differences between the two countries, despite their many similarities with regard to geographical position, size, number of inhabitants, state of internal modernisation and international status. Eventually their overseas expansion also proceeded along very similar lines. Nevertheless, both countries had completely different starting points, with lasting effects on the course which their expansion was to take.

While the Netherlands had achieved independence at a very early stage and had become an established 'commercial-maritime' nation, Belgium was a much younger state with a more 'continental' orientation, a country which had not yet established itself overseas when modern imperialism began. Indeed, Belgium's colonial expansion was almost entirely the work of an ambitious king and his closest associates. Formally, there was no more than a personal union between Belgium and the Congo, and Belgium did not become a colonial power until it took over the Congo in 1908. King Leopold II's imperialism was caused by Belgium's fate as a kingdom of permanently secondary importance within Europe. It was a rather recent political construction and internally far from homogeneous and stable. Unlike the Netherlands, Belgium had not chosen international neutrality of its own free will; neutrality had been formally imposed on it. Due to its strategic position between France and Germany, it was even more vulnerable as a small country than the Netherlands. Furthermore, it did not have any colonies, which gave the Netherlands an extra bonus of wealth and prestige. Leopold's hunger for overseas possessions – Stengers even called it gluttony –

was therefore strongly compensatory in character: by acquiring an overseas province, he was hoping to enhance the national and international status of the Belgian monarchy.[56]

Leopold drew his inspiration from the Dutch system of forced cultivation in Java. As crown prince he had been deeply impressed by the colonial profits which the system had yielded for the Dutch state. After his accession to the throne in 1865 Leopold therefore first travelled to Asia to find his own Java.[57] Only when the Netherlands had declined his offer to buy Borneo, and Spain had declined his offer to buy part of the Philippines, did Leopold turn towards Africa. When Portugal did not show much inclination to sell – for example – Mozambique, he finally cast his eye on the unoccupied Congo area. Sensitive to the spirit of the time, he presented himself as a philanthropist with humanitarian and scientific interests, without territorial aspirations.

In 1876 an international geographical conference was held in Brussels, followed by the foundation of the Association Internationale du Congo in 1877. Thus Leopold was able to engage the services of the famous explorer Stanley, who explored the Congo area and concluded contracts with the local chiefs. Behind the scenes Leopold subsequently managed to make good use of the growing British–French rivalry in Africa. At the Berlin Conference it seemed that his international association was the ideal alternative to Portuguese rule over the Congo area under British patronage. Supported by Bismarck, Leopold's Association was granted sovereignty over the Congo in 1885, on condition that the Congo remained internationally neutral and that free trade would continue.[58]

As sovereign of the new Congo state, Leopold continued to cultivate his enlightened image, partly by fighting the Arab slave trade. This enabled him at the same time to avoid his obligation to promote free trade, and so reduce Dutch trade on the Congo, which he accomplished at the 1890 Brussels conference, while showing more consideration for British trade. In reality, however, Leopold introduced a perverted version of the Dutch system of forced cultivation. After the entire area had been stripped of most of its ivory, the local population was violently forced to adopt rubber

56. Stengers, 'Leopold's Imperialism', p. 249; cf. Kossmann, *Lage landen*, pp. 281–5.

57. Stengers, 'Léopold II'.

58. Kossmann, *Lage landen*, pp. 285–9; cf. Stengers, 'King Leopold'.

cultivation. Belgian charter companies were used for trade, the railway system and the exploitation of minerals. This uncontrolled and destructive exploitation of humans and resources was further corroborated by the financial problems of the Free State. At first the Congo cost King Leopold more than it yielded. The pacification of the enormous territory was difficult, and it took until 1900 to get rid of Arab warlords such as Tippu Tip.[59] Leopold soon had to apply to the Belgian government for financial assistance. In 1895 the government proposed a formal take-over of the Congo, with favourable financial terms for the king. However, this proposal seemed to meet with so much resistance in the Belgian Parliament that it was hastily withdrawn again. Belgian capitalists, too, had their doubts about the Congo, especially the powerful Société Générale. In 1895 less than 7 per cent of Belgian capital exports went to the Congo and more than 25 per cent to Latin America. Only a handful of statesmen, military leaders and financiers within the immediate entourage of the court were fully supportive of Leopold's African project.[60]

Compared with the Netherlands, colonial expansion was at first hardly popular at all in Belgium. From the very beginning Leopold had to make a considerable effort to obtain domestic support for his African initiatives. He held out the prospect of a large mission field to Roman Catholics, while pointing out to Liberals that the area was important for trade, science and education. However, they remained extremely reluctant, both in 1876 and in 1885. Socialists in Belgium rejected Leopold's colonial adventures and a possible annexation of the Congo out of principle. And unlike their political kinsmen in the Netherlands they were represented by a parliamentary party at a much earlier stage, winning 28 out of 152 seats in the Chamber of Deputies in 1894. Most Liberals, too, opposed colonial expansion, though for more pragmatic reasons. Only Roman Catholics increasingly supported a Belgian take-over of the Congo, partly in the interest of their missionaries. This support eventually turned out to be decisive, as Roman Catholics had a parliamentary majority between 1894 and 1914.[61]

The major impulse for a Belgian take-over of the Congo, however, came from outside. After 1900, foreign protests against Leo-

59. Gann and Duignan, *Rulers*, pp. 53–58 and 116–141.
60. Kurgan-Van Hentenryk, *Léopold II*, pp. 45 and 54; cf. Kossmann, *Lage landen*, p. 290.
61. Ibid., pp. 291–4; cf. Wils, 'Politieke ontwikkeling', pp. 186–95 and 395–409.

pold's exploitation of the Congo had increased considerably, particularly after the revelations of the British journalist E. D. Morel. When in 1904–5 official steps against the Free State were being threatened by Britain and the United States, public opinion in Belgium was suddenly in favour of annexation. Difficult negotiations with Leopold followed, as he wanted to sell the Congo as profitably as possible. Between 1906 and 1908 Belgian politics were strongly dominated by the Congo question. Finally King Leopold had to give in to the will of the Belgian Parliament.

When the appropriate bill was dealt with, the Roman Catholics voted *en bloc* in favour of the Belgian annexation of the Congo, the Socialists voted *en bloc* against it, and the Liberals were divided on the issue.[62] Belgium's first Minister of the Colonies, the progressive Roman Catholic J. Renkin, made sure that Belgian rule in the Congo was immediately organised along modern lines. On the eve of the First World War the Congo was in some respects as important to Belgium as the East Indies was to the Netherlands. Although the Belgian colony probably had no more than 10 million inhabitants and the Dutch East Indies already had over 40 million. Belgian investments had increased considerably, with the support of the Société Générale, especially in the profitable area of mining. The Belgian Catholics found indeed a large missionary field in the Congo. One indication of the importance of the Congo was also the strength of Belgium's *force publique*, a colonial army of 17,000 men in 1910 – more than Germany's colonial army in Africa.[63]

Dutch and Belgian colonial expansion took place in different parts of the world: in South East Asia and Central Africa, respectively. In some areas, however, both Dutch and Belgian interests were involved, particularly in South Africa and China. In both cases it was Leopold once again who acted as the pacemaker of Belgian expansionism. In the context of his large-scale African project Leopold had become interested in South Africa during the 1870s. After the visit of the president of the Transvaal, Burgers, he saw good opportunities for Belgian involvement in South African railway projects. He immediately tackled the matter with great enthusiasm and appointed a professional consul to Pretoria even before the Netherlands. However, after the British annexation of the Transvaal in 1877 and the First Boer War of 1880–1, Leopold was a little more

62. Ibid., pp. 412–16; cf. Kossmann, *Lage landen*, pp. 294–300.
63. Gann and Duignan, *Rulers*, pp. 67 and 79; cf. ibid., chapters 5–6.

cautious. To avoid giving offence to Britain, Belgium did not resume diplomatic relations with the SAR until 1884; though, again, this was before the Netherlands.[64]

Leopold subsequently tried to support the Société Générale in order to obtain the rights for the Delagoa line, but this concession remained firmly in the hands of the Dutch–German syndicate. Leopold then quickly lost interest in South Africa. Meanwhile, however, a romantic form of nationalism had arisen within the Flemish Movement. The First Boer War and Kruger's visit in 1884 provided a link between South Africa and the emerging Flemish nationalism. However, compared with the NZAV, the significance of the Flemish Transvaal Movement remained limited.[65] After the Jameson Raid and during the Boer War Flemish interest in South Africa was rekindled again, partly under the influence of the ANV's ambitions for a Greater Netherlands. Among Walloons, too, the mood was mainly pro-Boer and anti-British. But like their Dutch neighbours, the Belgian government also exercised great restraint towards public opinion within the country and maintained a strict policy of neutrality.[66]

In China Leopold paid less attention to British feelings. On his initiative Belgian railway licencees and financiers participated in the construction of the strategic Peking–Hankow railway line from 1895 onwards. This joint French–Belgian project met with a great deal of opposition from the British side.[67] First Leopold had started his quest for colonies with a futile attempt to acquire Formosa, and he now used the financial and international facilities of his Congo state in order to create a Belgian sphere of influence in China. The degree to which he was still entertaining territorial ambitions could be seen during the Boxer Rebellion of 1900. While the Dutch government was reluctantly responding to the German initiative for international intervention, Leopold was, as it were, kicking his heels with impatience and wanted to be involved. He was already calling for volunteers to take part in an expedition corps, but Wilhelm II of Germany vetoed the participation of neutral Belgium.[68] Neither did the French government feel very enthusiastic about a joint French–Belgian military police force to protect the Peking–Hankow line.

64. Goris, *België*, chapter 5.
65. Ibid., pp. 233–7 and 280–4.
66. Ibid., pp. 403–8.
67. Kurgan-Van Hentenryk, *Léopold II*, chapter 2.
68. Ibid., pp. 379–82.

And an attempt to follow in Russia's footsteps and acquire a Belgian extra-territorial concession in Tientsin eventually also failed.[69] Economically, however, Leopold's Chinese initiatives were very successful. Typical in this respect was the participation of the powerful Société Générale in the Chinese banking project of 1901. In all, we can certainly conclude with Kossmann that Belgian expansion in China was strongly 'continental' in its orientation, while the character of the Dutch presence was mainly 'commercial-maritime'.[70]

The Netherlands generally displayed a far more balanced pattern of expansion and reaction during the rise of modern imperialism than Belgium. In Belgium colonial expansion only ever had one important centre, the Belgian court, while the other sections of Belgian society reacted far more slowly and reluctantly than in the Netherlands. The Dutch court, however, was equally strongly in favour of decisive action. Writing about her youth, Queen Wilhelmina commented in her memoirs, 'I began to dream of great deeds very early'; and, 'the weak spirit of the time' aroused in her 'a not inconsiderable dissatisfaction'; while her 'zest for action' was greatly stimulated by the 'military operations of the Dutch East Indian army in Lombok and Acheh'.[71]

Like Queen Emma, Wilhelmina actively helped to promote colonial expansion, but in the Netherlands her efforts remained strictly within constitutional boundaries and within the territorial borders of the East Indies. Leopold, on the other hand, succeeded in acquiring considerable domestic scope until after 1900 by playing off the government against the Belgian Parliament, and the different parliamentary parties and factions against each other. He used this scope above all for his diplomatic and colonial activities. Paradoxically, though, this royal activism compensated for a number of 'structural' handicaps that resulted from the external position of Belgium compared with that of the Netherlands. Thus Leopold created an important Belgian colony out of nothing and was able to be active in European diplomacy until about 1904.[72]

These vigorous activities were to some extent facilitated by the

69. Ibid., pp. 382–91.
70. Kossmann, *Lage landen*, p. 320; cf. Kurgan-Van Hentenryk, *Léopold II*, pp. 401ff.
71. Wilhelmina, *Eenzaam*, pp. 76–7.
72. Kossmann, *Lage landen*, pp. 155–6, 283–4, 324–5, See also Lademacher, *Belgische Neutralität*, pp. 274ff.

formal neutrality of Belgium and its initial lack of colonial possessions. As the head of state of a small, neutral and non-colonial power Leopold was able to present himself as an innocuous alternative, particularly in the Congo issue. And so he co-operated alternately with each of the great powers that were at loggerheads with each other. In the long term, however, this policy was in danger of antagonising all the great powers: first, and indeed permanently, Germany; occasionally also France; and finally even Britain.[73] The foreign policies of the Dutch governments, by contrast, were far more humdrum, but at the same time also less hazardous. Structural and personal elements were more naturally related in the Netherlands: with Kuyper as a temporary exception, there was no dominating figure such as the king of Belgium. Due to its strategically less vulnerable position in Europe and its rich colonies outside Europe the Netherlands had a far better starting point in the rise of modern imperialism than Belgium. Dutch ministers endeavoured to extend and consolidate this position. Their version of 'free hand politics' can in fact be summarised as passive aloofness in Europe and an informal alliance with Britain outside Europe. But taking into account their different starting points and objectives the cautious policies of the Dutch governments were no less successful than the daring ones of King Leopold.

Dutch expansionism showed itself not so much on the international scene as within its territorial borders. Indeed, domestically and in the Dutch colonies this expansionism was far more advanced and varied in its development than in Belgium. Again, these differences were almost certainly the result of the existing 'commercial maritime' tendencies of the Netherlands and the 'continental' industrial tendencies of Belgium. There could be no doubt that, compared with Belgium, the Netherlands was less industrialised and more oriented towards trade with the colonies; in 1900 43.9 per cent of the working population in Belgium and 32.2 per cent in the Netherlands were involved in industry. But the 'commercial-maritime' tendencies of the Netherlands and the 'industrial-continental' tendencies of Belgium were noticeable both inside and outside Europe.

After 1870 Dutch trade and shipping were increasingly directed at the German hinterland, whereas Belgian industrialists, financiers and railway licencees had already been active in overseas markets

73. Ibid., pp. 382–94; cf. Willequet, *Congo Belge*, pp. 22–6.

before Leopold acquired the Congo.[74] In the Netherlands, on the other hand, there were stronger motives for expansion – particularly political ones. Unlike their spiritual kinsmen in Belgium, the majority of Dutch Liberals had always been in favour of colonial expansion. The Socialist opponents of expansion were represented in the Belgian Parliament at a much earlier stage and in larger numbers than in the Dutch Parliament. Among the Catholic party the change in favour of colonial expansion took place about the same time as among the other Christian parties in the Netherlands, showing also a tendency towards 'ethical imperialism'.

But the presence of established colonial interests and traditions was not the only reason why Dutch expansionism was stronger. Another element that was much more developed in the Netherlands than in Belgium was modern mass nationalism. In Belgium the initial striving for unity was increasingly thwarted by sharp linguistic and class antagonisms. Inasmuch as Leopold's initiatives in Central Africa met with the approval of the Walloon and Flemish middle classes, it was precisely because of their international character, and not their national significance. And Flemish interest in South Africa was completely without that expansionism which so strongly coloured Dutch interest.[75] By comparison, it therefore seems that nationalism was the most typical feature of the Dutch position in the rise of modern imperialism. Dutch nationalism had ethical rather than jingoistic overtones; in the light of Kennedy's comparative structural analysis, however, it displayed quite a few similarities with British nationalism, as regards its defensive origins, support among the elites and the middle classes and its influence on colonial affairs.[76]

Outside the colonies, however, Dutch nationalism was subject to far more restrictions than its British counterpart, as could be seen very clearly during the Boer Wars in South Africa and the arms race in Europe. In words and literature, nationalism in Portugal was no less developed than in the Netherlands. But its internal basis and external power position were much weaker. Finally, compared with neighbouring Belgium, nationalism in the Netherlands had a longer historical tradition, was more widespread among broader sections

74. Kossmann, *Lage landen*, pp. 310–17.
75. Goris, *België*, pp. 402–4. Cf. Kossmann, *Lage landen*, pp. 150–1 and 350–8; Wils, 'Politieke ontwikkeling', pp. 424–30.
76. Kennedy, *Rise*, chapter 18; cf. Kennedy's introduction to Kennedy and Nicholls, *Movements*.

of the population and so played a greater and more permanent role in overseas expansion.

Concluding Remarks

The Netherlands displayed both similarities and differences with other European countries during the rise of modern imperialism. It has been pointed out by Heldring, among others, that countries form collectivities which are of a fundamentally different order than individuals, even though we constantly personify them in our description. But Heldring also points out that relations between states – just like relationships between people – are largely based on 'the differences between one another' and 'assertive contrasts'.[77]

However, our comparison of the Netherlands with Britain, Portugal and Belgium shows that the significance of special and characteristic differences is partly dependent on the existence of certain general similarities. The most important common feature was obviously the emergence of a general international phenomenon such as modern imperialism, which confronted all the countries concerned in one way or another. While countries are tangible communities, a phenomenon like modern imperialism remains to some extent a historical abstraction, although it was real enough for many people in Western and non-Western countries. As modern imperialism occurred both within and outside the boundaries of a particular country, contemporaries often tended to ascribe the causes and less pleasant consequences of the phenomenon to the other countries. This was particularly true for the Netherlands, a small European power which already possessed rich colonies and where people loved to take pride in free trade, aloofness and international law whenever the occasion arose.

As for the external position of the Netherlands during the rise of modern imperialism, its historical self-image was still quite accurate. Internationally, the difference when compared with other countries was indeed noticeable. In its relations with the great powers the Netherlands was even more cautious and restrained than Portugal. Röell's rule of 1896, that 'we must concentrate on *keeping* and further developing the East Indies and that we must not take on any other task', was in fact shared by all Dutch Foreign Ministers. Occasionally, however, territorial expansion seemed necessary for

---

77. Heldring, *Verschil*, pp. 9–17.

the maintenance and further development of the East Indies, as in the case of Acheh around 1870. And with regard to the pacification of Acheh and other parts of the Outer Regions within the international borders of the Dutch East Indies, Röell's pronouncement was undoubtedly a euphemism . In the colonial sphere the Dutch subjection and exploitation of the Indonesian Archipelago only differed in scale from British imperialism in Asia and Africa – including South Africa in some respects. Röell's recommendation of the racist, social Darwinist strategy, developed for Acheh by the former government adviser Van den Berg, proves that one cannot merely rely on the modest and ethical aspects of the Dutch self-image.[78]

Around the turn of the century, particularly during the Boer War, nationalist arguments in the Netherlands consistently went hand in hand with a serious warning against 'misplaced chauvinism' and 'false jingoism'. In support of a more appropriate form of patriotism Queen Wilhelmina was often quoted as saying that the world should be made to see 'where a small nation can be great'; that is in the spheres of art, culture and science. As for the colonies, Melchior Treub's work for the Botanical Gardens in Batavia was often mentioned, as was the Siboga expedition, a scientific voyage of exploration on board one of the latest warships.[79] But, as we have seen, the queen's national pride and indeed that of many of her subjects also included military operations in Lombok and Acheh. The poet Charles Boissevain even put the pacification of Acheh on the same level as 'the pumping-out of the Zuiderzee'.[80] Partly under the influence of the belligerent, nationalist reaction in the Netherlands to the 'treachery' of Lombok in 1894 and the 'treachery' of Teuku Umar in 1896, the policy of abstention was finally replaced by a policy of systematic pacification of the Outer Regions. Dutch rule certainly ended or reduced traditional practices such as piracy, slavery, widow-burning and cannibalism, as far as they existed. But the spread of Dutch rule did have its human costs too. Between 1873 and 1909, 60–70,000 Achenese and 2,000 members of the colonial army were killed in Acheh; 10,500 members of the colonial army, 25,000 Javanese forced labourers and an unknown number of Achenese died of illness, exhaustion or hunger. Starting with Lombok in 1894, the military actions in other parts of the Outer Regions

78. See above, chapter 2, notes 197–8, and chapter 3, notes 123 and 193.
79. A. A. W. Hubrecht, 'De Siboga-expeditie', *De Gids*, 1898, iv, pp. 274–6.
80. *Het Handelsblad*, 5 April 1896.

caused the additional deaths of 10–15,000 local inhabitants and about 500 members of the colonial army. Some of the scenes of heavy fighting, in particular Lombok, Banjarmasin and Flores, were of little interest to either entrepreneurs or missionaries – Dutch, foreign or Indonesian.

Was there an alternative to this rather formal, territorial and agressive kind of imperialism? In a situation of increasing economic and cultural contacts in many parts of the Outer Regions, it became indeed more difficult to maintain the policy of abstention for any length of time. The sale of large parts of the Outer Regions to other countries in order to implement the 'Ethical Policy' more fully in Java and Sumatra, as Van Kol suggested, was only for international reasons already impossible. Around 1900, however, there was still room for an intermediate strategy of a more informal, maritime and defensive kind of imperialism, although such a compromise also had its contradictions. We have seen that Fransen van de Putte, in particular, frequently advocated such a gradual, relatively peaceful expansion. Even when he failed to implement it fully as the Minister of the Colonies responsible for the Dutch declaration of war on Acheh and its annexation, van de Putte's favoured example had been the treaty with the Sultan of Siak, a very indirect form of colonial rule. He felt that the subsequent development of Deli formed a decisive economic argument, although he opposed the disciplining of contract labour by the 'penal sanction' enforced by the colonial administration. According to van de Putte the flexible use of the navy should provide the appropriate means for the external defence of the East Indies, the containment of Acheh and applying pressure in other, more relevant places, if necessary supplemented by the restrained deployment of military forces. All this, of course, in close co-operation with both humanitarian and pragmatic administrators of the old school and with the new merchant navy of the Royal Packet Company.

Van de Putte died in 1902, 'in the harness', on his seat in the First Chamber. But former Minister of Foreign Affairs Van Karnebeek may have had Van de Putte's ideas in mind when, commenting on Van Daalen's pacification campaign in the Gajo and Alas areas in 1904, he said in the Second Chamber that it signalled the end of 'an old tradition of our administration in the East Indies', whereby one sought to establish 'contacts with the population and its leaders', and indeed to do so gradually. This policy, he said, was increasingly being replaced by 'the rather simple method of armed force; it is a fact that the sword is drawn far more readily than it used to be, at the orders of the colonial administration.'[81]

In 1849 the conservative Minister of the Colonies Baud had pointed out to the Liberal Prime Minister Thorbecke the 'heterogeneity' that existed between the Dutch and the Indonesians in a large number of areas. 'This heterogeneity includes a seed of disintegration within itself', he warned; 'This is bound to happen sooner or later. Wisdom and caution can postpone such a point in time, but recklessness and rigidity will hasten it.'[82] This awareness of the temporary and relative nature of the Dutch presence in the Indonesian Archipelago still had not disappeared completely half a century later, but it had rather been pushed into the background. At the same time, however, the systematic subjugation and economic exploitation of the Indonesian Archipelago was to create the conditions for the emergence of a modern mass movement of Indonesian nationalism. The obstinacy of Dutch resistance to Indonesia's independence seems to have been largely the continuation of the imperialist mentality which had emerged around the turn of the century. It is often said, in the Netherlands and in other countries, that the Netherlands has always been a nation of merchants and ministers. This book provides sufficient evidence for such an observation. But it cannot be denied that the Netherlands became, towards the Indonesian Archipelago, a nation of soldiers and investors as well, and remained so for a considerably long time.

81. Idema, *Geschiedenis*, p. 177.
82. Alberts, *Baud*, p. 172.

Appendix 1

Foreign Ministers, Ministers of the Colonies and Governor-generals of the Dutch East Indies

Foreign Ministers

T. M. Roest van Limburg (8 June–12 December 1870)

J. L. H. A. Baron Gericke van Herwijnen (18 January 1872–27 August 1874)

Jonkheer P. J. A. M. van der Does de Willebois (27 August 1874–3 November 1877)

W. Baron van Heeckeren van Kell (3 November 1877–19 August 1879)

C. T. Baron van Lynden van Sandenburg (19 August 1879–15 September 1881)

Jonkheer W. F. Rochussen (15 September 1881–23 April 1883)

Jonkheer P. J. A. M. van der Does de Willebois (23 April 1883–1 November 1885)

Jonkheer A. P. C. van Karnebeek (1 November 1885–21 April 1888)

Jonkheer C. Hartsen (21 April 1888–21 August 1891)

G. van Tienhoven (21 August 1891–21 March 1894)

Jonkheer J. Röell (8 May 1894–27 July 1897)

W. H. de Beaufort (27 July 1897–1 August 1901)

R. Melvil Baron van Lynden (1 August 1901–9 March 1905)

Ministers of the Colonies

E. de Waal (2 June 1868–16 November 1870)

P. P. van Bosse (4 January 1871–6 July 1872)

I. D. Fransen van de Putte (6 July 1872–27 August 1874

W. Baron van Goltstein van Oldenaller (27 August 1874–11 September 1876)

F. Alting Mees (11 September 1876–3 November 1877)

P. P. van Bosse (3 November 1877–21 February 1879

O. van Rees (12 March 1879–20 August 1879)

W. Baron van Goltstein van Oldenaller (20 August 1879–1 September 1882)

Jonkheer W. M. de Brauw (1 September 1882–23 February 1883)

F. G. van Bloemen Waanders (23 April 1883–25 November 1883)

A. W. P. Weitzel (25 November 1883–27 February 1884)

J. P. Sprenger van Eyk (27 February 1884–21 April 1888)
L. W. C. Keuchenius (21 April 1888–24 February 1890)
Ae. Baron Mackay (24 February 1890–21 August 1891)
W. K. Baron van Dedem van Vosbergen (21 August 1891–May 1894)
J. H. Bergsma (9 May 1894–27 July 1897)
J. T. Cremer (27 July 1897–1 August 1901)
Jonkheer T. A. J. van Asch van Wijck (1 August 1901–9 September 1902)
A. W. F. Idenburg (25 September 1902–13 August 1905) (28 May 1908–16 August 1909)

Governor-generals of the Dutch East Indies

P. Mijer (28 December 1866–1 January 1872)
J. Loudon (1 January 1872–26 March 1875)
J. W. van Lansberge (26 March 1875–12 April 1881)
F. 's Jacob (12 April 1881–20 January 1884)
O. van Rees (11 April 1884–29 September 1888)
C. Pijnacker Hordijk (29 September 1888–17 October 1893)
Jonkheer C. H. A. van der Wijck (17 October 1893–3 October 1899)
W. Rooseboom (3 October 1899–1 October 1904)
J. B. van Heutsz (1 October 1904–18 December 1909)

Appendix 2

Distribution of Political Parties in the Second Chamber of the Dutch Parliament

	Liberals		Conservative Liberals	Conservatives	Protestants			Roman Catholics	Socialists			Total
	Liberal Union[a]	Radical VDB[b]	Free Liberals[c]		ARP[d]	CHU[e]	Independent		SDB[f]	SDAP[g]	Independent	
1868	36		10	20	4			5				75
1871	43		4	15	5			13				80
1874	45		3	7	9			16				80
1878	51			8	10			17				86
1883	45			5	18			18				86
1887	48			–	19			19				86
1888	45			1	27			26	1			100
1891	53	1			21			25				100
1894	55	3			17			25				100
1897	35	4	13		17	6		22		2	1	100
1901	18	9	8		23	9	1	25		6	1	100
1905	25	11	9		15	8		25		6	1	100

Notes: The headings at the top of the table represent the traditional, not yet formally organised parties, and they also note the general continuing trends. At the bottom of the table are the names of the new parties.

Political orientation:
a Mainstream
b Left wing
c Right wing
d Calvinist
e Dutch Reformed
f Socialist-anarchist
g Social democrat

Sources: Van Tijn, 'The Party Structure of Holland and the Outer Provinces in the Nineteenth Century', in *Vaderlands Verleden in Veelvond. 31 opstellen over de Nederlands geschiedenis na 1500*, 's-gravenhage 1975, pp. 560–90; S. Stuurman, *Verzuiling, kapitalisme en patriarchaat. Aspecten van de ontwikkeling van de moderne staat in Nederland*, Nijmegen 1983, p. 259.

Appendix 3

Overseas Trade

	Dutch East Indies	Asia	Africa	South America	Overseas total
Imports of consumer goods (in million guilders)					
1865	73.5 (18.2)	3.0 (0.7)	3.0 (0.7)	11.8 (2.9)	91.3 (22.5)
1870	81.0 (15.9)	10.7 (2.1)	2.4 (0.5)	8.9 (1.8)	103.0 (20.3)
1875	77.2 (10.7)	27.2 (3.8)	3.3 (0.5)	11.2 (1.6)	118.9 (16.6)
1880	56.1 (6.7)	28.5 (3.4)	7.0 (0.8)	10.5 (1.2)	102.1 (12.1)
1885	97.0 (9.6)	45.6 (4.1)	6.8 (0.6)	19.7 (2.2)	169.1 (16.5)
1890	159.5 (12.3)	44.0 (3.4)	9.8 (0.7)	21.6 (1.6)	234.9 (18.0)
1895	202.4 (14.0)	67.6 (4.7)	6.9 (0.5)	46.6 (3.2)	323.5 (22.4)
1900	272.5 (13.8)	46.8 (2.4)	9.5 (0.5)	116.6 (5.9)	445.4 (22.5)
1905	399.6 (15.5)	74.3 (2.9)	11.9 (0.5)	114.9 (4.4)	600.7 (23.3)
Exports from free traffic (in million guilders)					
1865	27.0 (7.8)	3.1 (0.9)	0.4 (0.1)	5.9 (1.7)	36.4 (10.5)
1870	31.6 (7.9)	3.5 (0.9)	0.7 (0.2)	4.7 (1.2)	40.5 (10.2)
1875	40.9 (7.8)	3.8 (0.7)	0.8 (0.1)	3.2 (0.6)	48.7 (9.2)
1880	46.8 (7.4)	0.9 (0.1)	1.5 (0.2)	3.2 (0.5)	52.4 (8.2)
1885	45.2 (5.0)	3.1 (0.4)	2.8 (0.3)	2.3 (0.3)	53.4 (6.0)
1890	53.2 (4.9)	9.6 (0.9)	5.0 (0.5)	6.3 (0.6)	74.1 (6.9)
1895	52.0 (4.4)	7.7 (0.7)	5.0 (0.4)	7.0 (0.6)	71.7 (6.1)
1900	63.8 (3.8)	8.9 (0.6)	4.7 (0.3)	8.4 (0.5)	85.8 (5.2)
1905	70.5 (3.5)	16.8 (0.8)	9.6 (0.5)	16.6 (0.8)	113.5 (5.6)

Note: Figures in parenthesis are percentages.
Sources: *Statistiek voor den handel en scheepvaart* (Statistics for Trade and Shipping) and *Statistiek van de in-, uit- and doorvoer* (Statistics of Imports, Exports and Transit).

Appendix 4

Military Presence in the Dutch East Indies

	Land forces		Navy		(Auxiliary
	Total	Acheh	Total	Ships	Squadron)
1870	27,200		4,000	31	(7)
1873	29,000	(3,400)[a]	2,900	24	(3)
1874	29,300	(7,500)[b]	3,800	26	(4)
1875	29,800	6,300	3,500	29	(4)
1878	33,800	8,000			
1879	36,600	10,600			
1880	31,500	7,500	3,600	28	(4)
1885	30,400	5,300	3,800	28	(4)
1890	32,500	6,000	3,100	26	(4)
1895	34,600	5,800	3,800	26	(4)
1896	40,200	8,200			
1897	41,200	8,000			
1898	41,200	8,100			
1900	39,400	7,200	3,400	23	(6)
1905	36,900	5,700	3,900	22	(5)

[a] 1st expedition.
[b] 2nd expedition.
Note: Figures refer to the actual presence at the end of each year; in 1878, 1896 and 1898 about 10,000 troops were deployed in Acheh. Between 1870 and 1905 the share of the European element in the colonial army gradually declined from nearly 50 per cent to less than 40 per cent. See also Teitler, 'Manpower Problems'.
Source: Colonial Reports.

Abbreviations

AG	Aardrijkskundige Genootschap (Geographical Society)
AGN	*Algemene Geschiedenis der Nederlanden* (General History of the Netherlands)
AHV	Afrikaansche Handelsvereeniging (African Trade Association)
ANV	Algemeen Nederlandsch Verbond (General Dutch Alliance)
AP	*Acta Politica*
ARA	Algemeen Rijksarchief (General National Archive)
ARP	ARP Anti-Revolutionaire Partij (Anti-Revolutionary Party)
BMGN	*Bijdragen en Mededelingen betreffende de Geschiedenis der Nederlanden* (Contributions and Information on the History of the Netherlands)
BMHG	*Bijdragen en Mededelingen van het Historisch Genootschap* (Contributions and Information of the Dutch Historical Society)
CHU	Christelijk Historische Unie (Christian Historical Union)
EcHR	*Economic History Review*
ENI	*Encyclopaedie van Nederlandsch-Indië* (Encyclopaedia of the Dutch East Indies)
HAL	Holland-America Line
IG	*Indische Gids* (East Indian Journal)
JCH	*Journal of Contemporary History*
KB	Koninklijke Biblioteek (Dutch Royal Library)
KPM	Koninklijke Paketvaart-Maatschappij (Royal Packet Company)
KvK	Kamer van Koophandel (Chamber of Commerce)
NAHV	Nieuwe Afrikaansche Handelsvennootschap (New African Trade Company)

Abbreviations

NHM	Nederlandsche Handel-Maatschappij (Dutch Trading Company)
NIL	Nederlandsch-Indisch Leger (Dutch East Indian army)
NRC	*Nieuwe Rotterdamsche Courant*(New Rotterdam Daily)
NZASM	Nederlandsch Zuid-Afrikaansche Spoorweg-Maatschappig (Dutch South-African Railway Company)
NZAV	Nederlandsch Zuid-Afrikaansche Vereeniging (Dutch South-African Association)
RKSP	Rooms-Katholieke Staatspartij (Roman Catholic State Party)
SAR	South African Republic
SDAP	Sociaal Democratische Arbeiderspartij (Social Democratic Workers' Party)
SDB	Sociaal Democratische Bond (Social Democratic Union)
TAG	*Tijdschrift van het Aardrijkskundig Genootschap* (Journal of the Geographical Society)
TG	*Theoretische Geschiedenis* (Theoretical History)
TvG	*Tijdschrift voor Geschiedenis* (Journal of History)
TNI	*Tijdschrift voor Nederlandsch-Indië* (Journal for the Dutch East Indies)
VDB	Vrijzinnig-Democratische Bond (Liberal Democratic Alliance)
VOC	Verenigde Oost-Indische Compagnie (Dutch East Indian Company)

Bibliography

UNPUBLISHED SOURCES

Algemeen Rijksarchief 's-Gravenhage (The General National Archive of 's-Gravenhage)

Parliamentary Reports of the Second Chamber, in closed session, 13 June 1884
Private Collections of:
T. M. C. Asser
W. H. de Beaufort
I. D. Fransen van de Putte
A. R. W. Gey van Pittius
W. J. Leyds
J. Loudon
Ae. Mackay
D. J. Mackay (Lord Reay)
C. Pijnacker Hordijk
J. Röell
A. Schimmelpenninck van der Oye
D. A. W. Tets van Goudriaan
E. de Waal
C. H. A. van der Wijck

Koninklijke Bibliotheek, 's Gravenhage (Royal Library, s' Gravenhage)

L. W. C. Keuchenius's private collection
F. 's Jacobs's correspondence (loose sheets 76 B 57)

Universiteitsbibliotheek Amsterdam (University Library, Amsterdam)

N. G. Pierson's private collection

Bibliography

Archief Nederlands-Zuidafrikaanse vereniging Amsterdam
(Archive of the Dutch–South African Association, Amsterdam)

Minutes of the NZAV management meetings

PUBLISHED SOURCES

Parliamentary Reports (*Handelingen van de Eerste en Tweede Kamer der staten-generaal, met Bijlagen*) (Reports of the First and Second Chamber of Parliament, with Appendices)

Daily Papers

Het Algemeen Handelsblad
De Amsterdammer
De Arnhemsche Courant
Het Centrum
Het Dagblad von Zuid-Holland en 's-Gravenhage
De Maasbode
Het Nieuws van den Dag
De Standaard
De Telegraaf
De Tijd
Het Utrechtsch Provinciaal- en Stedelijk Dagblad
Het Vaderland
Het Volk

Periodicals

De Amsterdammer
Berigten van de Utrechtsche Zendingsvereeniging
De Economist
De Gids
De Indische Gids
De Katholiek
De Kroniek
Mededelingen van het Nederlandsch Zendelingsgenootschap
De Nederlandsche Industrieel
Neerlandia
Recht voor Allen
De Sociaal-demokraat
Tijdschrift van Aardrijkskundig Genootschap
Tijdschrift voor Nederlandsch-Indië
Voor de Boeren
Vragen des Tijds

Bibliography

Serial Works

Consulaire verslagen en berichten (Consular Reports)
Handelingen en geschriften van het Indisch Genootschap (Reports and Writings of the East Indian Society)
Jaarcijfers van het Koninkrijk der Nederlanden (Annals of the Kingdom of the Netherlands)
Levensberichten van de Maatschappij der Nederlandsche Letterkunde (Biographical Notes of the Society of Dutch Literature)
Statistiek van de in-, uit- en doorvoer (Statistics of Imports, Exports and the Transit)
Verslagen van de Kamer van Koophandel voor Amsterdam (Reports of the Amsterdam Chamber of Commerce)
Verslagen van de Kamer van Koophandel voor Rotterdam (Reports of the Rotterdam Chamber of Commerce)
Verslagen der Nederlandsch Zuid-Afrikaansche Vereeniging (Reports of the Dutch–South African Association)

BOOKS AND OTHER PRINTED SOURCES

Aa, P. J. B. C. van der, *Afrikaansche Studiën, Koloniaal bezit en particuliere handel op Afrika's Westkust*, 's-Gravenhage 1871
Abdullah, Taufik, 'Impacts of Colonial Policy on Sumatra', in Haryati Soebadio and C. A. du Marchie Sarvaas (eds), *Dynamics of Indonesian History*, Amsterdam 1978, pp. 207-21
Alberts, A., *Baud en Thorbecke 1847–1851*, Utrecht 1939
Alfian, Teuku Ibrahim, 'Acheh Sultanate under Sultan Mohammad Daud-syah and the Dutch War', in Sartono Kartodirdjo (ed.), *Profiles of Malay Culture, Historiography, Religion and Politics*, Jakarta 1976, pp. 147-67
Anderson, M. S., *The Eastern Question 1774–1923*, London 1972
Anstey, R., *Britain and the Congo in the Nineteenth Century*, Oxford 1962
Araki, T. J., *Geschichte der Entstehung und Revision der ungleichen Verträge mit Japan (1853–1894)*, Marburg 1959
Arts, J. and Beurden, N. van, *Goud en Geloof. De invloed van de goud-mijnbouw en de zending op het moderne imperialisme in Celebes 1880–1994*, doctoral thesis, Utrecht 1982
Asser, T. M. C., *Het bestuur der buitenlandsche betrekkingen volgens het Nederlandsche staatsrecht*, Amsterdam 1860
Baesjou, R. (ed.), *An Asante Embassy on the Gold Coast. The Mission of Akyempon Yaw to Elmina 1869–1872*, Leiden 1979
Bartstra, J. S., *Geschiedenis van het moderne imperialisme (tijdvak ca. 1880–ca. 1906)*, Haarlem 1925
Baumgart, W., *Der Imperialismus. Idee und Wirklichkeit der englischen und französischen Kolonialexpansion 1880–1914*, Wiesbaden 1975
Bayly, C. A., *Rulers, Townsmen and Bazaars. North Indian Society in the*

Age of British Expansion, 1770–1870, Cambridge 1983

Beaufort, J. A. A. H. de, *Vijftig jaren uit onze geschiedenis, 1868–1918*, 2 volumes, Amsterdam 1928

Betts, R. F., *The False Dawn. European Imperialism in the Nineteenth Century*, Minneapolis 1975

Beunders, H. J. G., *Weg met de Vlootwet! De maritieme bewapeningspolitiek van het kabinet-Ruys de Beerenbrouck en het successvolle verzet daartegen in 1923*, Bergen 1924

Blaas, P. B. M., 'De prikkelbaarheid van een kleine natie met een groot verleden: Fruins en Bloks nationale geschiedschrijving', *TG* 9 (1982), pp. 271–304

Blom, J. C. H. *Verzuiling in Nederland, 1850–1925*, Amsterdam 1981

Boer, M. G. de, *Honderd jaar Nederlandsche scheepvaart*, Amsterdam 1939

Boogman, J. C., 'Achtergronden, tendenties en tradities van het buitenlandse beleid van Nederland (eind zestiende eeuw-1940)' in: *Nederlands buitenlandse politiek. Heden en verleden*, Baarn 1978, pp. 9–29

Boogman, J. C., 'The Netherlands in the European Scene, 1813–1913' in: *Vaderlands Verleden*, pp. 481–97

Boogman, J. C., 'Die holländische Tradition in der niederländischen Geschichte' in: *Vaderlands Verleden*, pp. 89–105

Boon, M., *J. W. van Lansberge en de praktijk van art. 4 van de geheime instructie van 5 juni 1855*, Utrecht 1943

Bornewasser, J. A., 'De Nederlandse katholieken en hun negentiende-eeuwse vaderland', *TvG* 95 (1982), pp. 577–605

Bos, R. W. J. M., *Brits-Nederlandse handel en scheepvaart, 1870–1914. Een analyse van machtsafbrokkeling op een markt*, Tilburg 1978

Bosscher, Ph. M., 'Oorlogsvaart', in *Maritieme Geschiedenis der Nederlanden* IV, Bussum 1978, pp. 315–59

Brands, M. C. 'Modernisering. Een bruikbaar begrip voor historici?', *TG* 2 (1975), pp. 118–26

Brands, M. C. 'Patricische en plebejische elementen in de Nederlandse buitenlandse politiek. Heldrings paradoxen' in: *Deze jaren. Buitenlands beleid en internationale werkelijkheid*, Baarn 1982, pp. 58–74

Broeke, W. van den, *The 'Koninklijke' and 'Biliton': two Dutch concerns in Indonesia at the Time of Modern Imperialism 1890–1914*. Paper delivered to the Second Indonesian–Dutch Historical Conference. Ujang Pandang 22 to 30 June 1978

Broersma, R., *Oostkust van Sumatra I. De ontluiking van Deli*, Batavia 1919

Brouwer, B. J., *De houding van Idenburg en Colijn tegenover de Indonesische Beweging*, Kampen 1958

Brugmans, I. J., *Paardenkracht en mensenmacht. Sociaal-economische geschiedenis van Nederland 1795–1940*, 's-Gravenhage 1961

Bibliography

Brugmans, I. J., *Van Chinavaart tot Oceaanvaart. De Koninklijke Java-China-Japanlijn – Konijklijke Java-China Paketvaart-lijnen 1902–1952*, Amsterdam 1952

Brunschwig, H., 'French Expansion and Local Reactions in Black Africa in the Time of Imperialism (1880–1914)', in Wesseling (ed.), *Expansion and Reaction*, pp. 116–41

Brunschwig, H., *Mythes et réalités de l'impérialisme colonial français 1871–1914*, Paris 1960

Burger, D. H., *Sociologisch-economische geschiedenis van Indonesia*, 2 volumes, Wageningen 1975

Burr, R. N., *By Reason of Force. Chile and the Balancing of Power in South America 1830–1905*, Berkeley 1967

Cairns, H. A. C., *Prelude to Imperialism. British Reactions to Central African Society 1840–1890*, London 1965

Campo, J. à, 'Orde, rust en welvaart. Over de Nederlandse expansie in de Indische Archipel omstreeks 1900', *AP* 15, 1980, pp. 145–89

Charlesworth, N., *British Rule and the Indian Economy 1800–1914*, London 1982

Cittert-Eymers, J. G. van and Kipp, P. J. (eds), *Pieter Harting 1812–1885. Mijne Herinneringen*, Amsterdam 1961

Clarence Smith, W. G., 'The Myth of Uneconomic Imperialism: the Portuguese in Angola, 1836–1926', *Journal of Southern African Studies* 5, 1979, pp. 165–81

Colenbrander, H. T., *Koloniale geschiedenis*, 3 volumes, 's-Gravenhage 1925–1926

Colenbrander, H. T. and Stokvis, J. E., *Leven en arbeid van Mr. C. Th. van Deventer*, 3 volumes, Amsterdam 1916–1917

[Colijn, H.], *Politiek beleid en bestuurszorg in de buitenbezittingen*, 4 volumes, Batavia 1907–1909

Coolhaas, W. Ph., 'De Nisero-kwestie, Professor Harting en Gladstone', *BMHG* 78 (1964), pp. 271–325

Coolsma, S., *De zendingseeuw voor Nederlandsch Oost-Indië*, Utrecht 1901

Coombs, D., *The Gold Coast, Britain and the Netherlands 1850–1874*, London 1963

Corporaal, K. H., *De internationaal-rechtelijke betrekkingen tusschen Nederland en Venezuela 1816–1920*, Leiden 1920

Cremer, J. T., *Een woord uit Deli tot de Tweede Kamer der Staten-Generaal*, Amsterdam 1976

Creutzberg, P. (ed.), *Changing Economy in Indonesia*, II, *Public Finance 1816–1939*, 's-Gravenhage 1976

Daalder, H., 'The Netherlands: Opposition in a Segmented Society', in R. A. Dahl (ed.), *Political Opposition in Western Democracies*, New Haven 1966

383

Davenport, T. R. H., *The Afrikaner Bond. The History of a South African Political Party, 1880–1991*, Cape Town 1966

Davenport, T. R. H., *South Africa. A Modern History*, London 1977

Dobson, J. M., *America's Ascent. The United States Becomes a Great Power, 1880–1914*, DeKalb 1978

Dongen, F. van, *Tussen neutraliteit en imperialisme. De Nederlands-Chinese betrekkingen van 1863 to 1901*, Groningen 1966

Doorn, J. van, *The Engineers and the Colonial System. Technocratic Tendencies in the Dutch East Indies*, Rotterdam 1982

Drees, W., *Zestig jaar levenservaring*, Amsterdam 1962

Dülffer, J., *Regeln gegen den Krieg? Die Haager Friedens-Konferenzen von 1899 und 1907 in der internationalen Politik*, Frankfurt 1981

Dunk, H. W. von der, 'Conservatisme in vooroorlogs Nederland', *BMGN* 90, 1975, pp. 15–38

Dunk, H. W. von der, *Die Niederlande im Kräftespiel zwischen Kaiserreich und Entente*, Wiesbaden 1980

Dyserinck, J., *P. N. Muller*, Amsterdam 1909

Edelstein, M., *Overseas Investment in the Age of High Imperialism. The United Kingdom, 1850–1914*, London 1982

Eldridge, C. C., *England's Mission. The Imperial Idea in the Age of Gladstone and Disraeli 1868–1880*, London 1973

Eldridge, C. C., *Victorian Imperialism*, London 1978

Encyclopaedie van Nederlandsch-Indië, 8 volumes, 's-Gravenhage 1917–1940

Encyclopaedie van Nederlandsch West-Indië, 's-Gravenhage and Leiden 1914–1917

Etherington, N., *Theories of Imperialism. War, Conquest and Capital*, London and Canberra 1984

Fasseur, C., *De 'geest' van het gouvernement*, Leiden 1977

Fasseur, C., *Kultuurstelsel en koloniale baten. De Nederlandse exploitatie van Java 1840–1860*, Leiden 1975

Fasseur, C., 'Een koloniale paradox. De Nederlandse expansie in de Indonesische archipel in het midden van de negentiende eeuw (1830–1870)', *TvG* 92 (1979), pp. 162–87

Fasseur, C., 'Nederland en Nederlands-Indië 1795–1914', in *Overzee*, pp. 166–94

Fasseur, C. 'Van suikercontractant tot kamerlid. Bouwstenen voor een biografie van Fransen van de Putte (de jaren 1849–1862)', *TvG* 88, 1975, pp. 333–55

Fasseur, C., 'Suriname en de Nederlandse Antillen 1795–1914', in *Overzee*, pp. 194–201

Fieldhouse, D. K., *Economics and Empire 1830–1914*, Ithaca and London 1973

Fieldhouse, D. K., 'Imperialism: an Historiographical revision', *EdHR* 2nd series 14, 1961, pp. 187–210

Bibliography

Fievez de Malines van Ginkel, H., *Overzicht van de internationaal-rechtelijke betrekkingen van Nederlandsch-Indië (1850–1922)*, 's-Gravenhage 1924

Fisch, J., *Die europäische Expansion und das Völkerrecht*, Wiesbaden 1984

Fruin, R., 'Een Hollandsch woord over de Transvaal- Quaestie', in *Verspreide Geschriften X*, 's- Gravenhage 1905, pp. 402–19

Gallagher, J. and Robinson, R., 'The Imperialism of Free Trade', *EcHR* 2nd series 6, 1953, pp. 150–68

Ganiage, J., *L'expansion coloniale de la France sous la Troisième République (1871–1914)*, Paris 1968

Gann, L. H. and Duignan, P., *The Rulers of Belgian Congo, 1884–1914*, Princeton 1979

Gedenkboek van het Algemeen Nederlandsch Verbond bij gelegenheid van zijn 25-jarig bestaan 1898–1923, Amsterdam 1923

Gedenkboek van Nederlandsch-Indië 1898–1923, Amsterdam 1923

Gedenkboek van den Oorlog in Zuid-Afrika, Sneek 1904

Geertz, Cl., *Negara. The Theatre State in Nineteenth-Century Bali*, Princeton 1980

Gellner, E., *Nations and Nationalism*, Oxford 1983

Gerretson, C., *Geschiedenis der Koninklijke*, 3 volumes, Haarlem 1932–1937

Giele, J. J., *De eerste internationale in Nederland. Een onderzoek naar het ontstaan van de Nederlandse arbeidersbeweging van 1868 tot 1876*, Nijmegen 1973

Gifford, P. and Louis, W. R. (eds), *Britain and Germany in Africa. Imperial Rivalry and Colonial Rule*, New Haven and London 1967

Gifford, P, and Louis, W. R. (eds), *France and Britain in Africa. Imperial Rivalry and Colonial Rule*, New Haven and London, 1967.

Gillard, D., *The Struggle for Asia 1828–1914*, London 1977

Gobée, E. and Adriaanse, C. (eds), *Ambtelijke Adviezen van C. Snouck Hurgronje 1889–1939*, 3 volumes, 's-Gravenhage 1957–1962

Goedemans, A. J., *Indië in de branding. Een diplomatiek steekspel. 1840–1843*, Utrecht 1953

Gollwitzer, H., *Die gelbe Gefahr. Geschichte eines Schlagworts*, Göttingen 1962

Gollwitzer, H., *Geschichte des weltpolitischen Denkens*, II, *Zeitalter des Imperialismus und der Weltkriege*, Göttingen 1982

Goor, J. van, *An Episode in Dutch Imperialism: the Lombok Expedition of 1894*. Paper delivered to the Second Indonesian–Dutch Historical Conference, Ujung-Pandang, 22–30 June 1978

Goor, J. van, *Kooplieden, predikanten en bestuurders overzee. Beeldvorming en plaatsbepaling in een andere wereld*, Utrecht 1982

Gordon, C. T., *The Growth of Boer Opposition to Kruger (1890–1895)*, London 1970

Goris, J. M., *België en de Boerenrepublieken. Belgisch–Zuid–Afrikaanse*

Bibliography

betrekkingen (ca. 1835–1895), Louvain 1982

Goslinga, C. Ch., *Curaçao and Guzmán Blanco. A Case Study of Small Power Politics in the Carribean*, 's-Gravenhage 1975

Goudsblom, J., 'De Nederlandse samenleving in een ontwikkelingsperspectief', *Symposium* 1, 1979, pp. 8–28

Gould, J. W., *Americans in Sumatra*, 's-Gravenhage 1961

Griffiths, R. T., *Achterlijk, Achter of Anders? Aspecten van de economische ontwikkeling van Nederland in de 19e eeuw*, Amsterdam 1980

Groen, P. M. H., '"Soldaat" en "bestuursman": Het Indisch Leger en de Nederlandse gezagsvestiging op Ceram: een case study', *Mededelingen van de sectie militaire geschiedenis landmachtstaf 5*, 1982, pp. 203–45

Halve Eeuw paketvaart 1891–1945, Eene, Amsterdam 1941

Hamel, J. A. van, *Nederland tusschen de Mogendheden. De hoofdtrekken van het buitenlandsch beleid en de diplomatieke geschiedenis van ons vaderland sinds deszelfs onafhankelijk volksbestaan onderzocht*, Amsterdam 1918

Hammond, R. J., *Portugal and Africa 1815–1910. A Study in Uneconomic Imperialism*, Standord 1966

Headrick, D. R., *The Tools of Empire. Technology and European Imperialism in the Nineteenth Century*, Oxford 1981

Heldring, J. L., *Het verschil met anderen*, Amsterdam, undated

Helten, J. J. van, 'German Capital, the Netherlands Railway Company and the Political Economy of the Transvaal 1886–1900', *Journal of African History 19*, 1978, pp. 369–90

Hemels, J. M. H. J., *Op de bres voor de pers. De strijd voor de klassieke persvrijheid*, Assen 1969

Henssen, E., *Gerretson en Indië*, Groningen 1983

Heutsz, J. B. van, *De onderwerping van Atjeh*, 's-Gravenhage and Batavia 1893

Hofdijk, W. J., *Prins Hendrik der Nederlanden 1820–1879*, Zaltbommel 1880

Honoré Naber, S. P. l' (ed.), *Het leven van een vloothouder, Gedenkschriften van M. H. Jansen*, Utrecht 1925

Hood, M., *Gunboat Diplomacy 1895–1905. Great Power Pressure in Venezuela*, London 1983

Hopkins, A. G., *An Economic History of West Africa*, London 1973

Hynes, W. G., *The Economics of Empire. Britain, Africa and the New Imperialism 1870–95*, London 1979

Idema, H. A., *Parlementaire geschiedenis van Nederlandsch-Indië 1891–1918* 's-Gravenhage 1924

Iriye, Akira, *Pacific Estrangement. Japanese and American Expansion, 1897–1911*, Cambridge, Mass. 1972

Irwin, G., *Nineteenth-Century Borneo. A Study in Diplomatic Rivalry*, 's-Gravenhage 1955

Jaarsveld, F. A. van, Rensburg, A. P. J. and Stals, W. A. (eds), *Die eerste*

Bibliography

Vrijheidsoorlog 1880–1881, Pretoria and Cape Town 1980

Jacobs, Aletta, *Herinneringen*, Amsterdam 1924

Jacobs, J., *Het familie- en kampongleven op groot-Atjeh. Eene bijdrage tot de ethnographie van Noord-Sumatra*, 2 volumes, Leiden 1894

Japikse, N., *Staatkundige geschiedenis van Nederland van 1887–1917*, Leiden 1918

Jobse, P. J., 'De tin-expedities naar Flores 1887–1891. Een episode uit de geschiedenis van Nederlands-Indië in het tijdperk van het moderne imperialisme', *Utrechtse Historische Cahiers* 1, 1980, no. 3

Jong, W. M. C. de, *De Beaufort, de Boerenrepublieken en de Nederlandse buitenlandse politiek, 1897–1901*, doctoral thesis, Utrecht 1983

Jonge, J. A. de, *De industrialisatie in Nederland tussen 1850 en 1914*, Amsterdam 1968

Jungslager, G., *Een halve eeuw Koninklijke Marine. Schets van het maritiem-strategische denken in Nederland, de daaruit voortvloeiende vlootplannen en de organisatievormen der koninklijke marine gedurende de eerste helf der 20e eeuw*, thesis of the Koninklijk Instituut der Marine (Dutch Royal Naval Institute), Den Helder 1972

Jurriaanse, M. W., *De Nederlandse Ministers van Buitenlandse Zaken 1813–1900*, 's-Gravenhage 1974

Kamerbeek, E., 'Geschiedenis op school. Drie discussies in de onderwijspers gedurende de tweede helft van de negentiende eeuw over het vak geschiedenis op de lagere scholen in Nederland', *Utrechtse Historische Cahiers* 4, 1983, no. 2

Kamphuis, P. H., *Het Algemeene Nederlandsche Vredebond 1871–1901. Een verkennend onderzoek over dertig jaar ijveren voor een vreedzame internationale samenleving*, 's-Gravenhage 1982

Kartodirdjo, Sartono, *The Peasants' Revolt of Banten in 1888. Its Conditions, Course and Sequel*, 's-Gravenhage 1966

Kasteel, P., *Abraham Kuyper*, Kampen 1938

Kat Angelino, A. D. A. de, *Staatkundig beleid en bestuurszorg in Nederlandsch-Indië* II, 's-Gravenhage 1930

Kemp, A. F., *De standvastige tinnen soldaat, 1860–1960. N. V. Billiton-Maatschappij*, 's-Gravenhage 1960

Kennedy, P. M., *The Rise of Anglo-German Antagonism, 1860–1914*, London 1980

Kennedy, P. M. and Nicholls, A. (eds), *Nationalist and Racialist Movements in Britain and Germany before 1914*, Oxford 1981

Kern, J. H. C., *Verspreide Geschriften* IV, 's-Gravenhage 1917

Kielstra, E. B., *Indisch Nederland*, Haarlem 1910

Kiernan, V. G., *European Empires from Conquest to Collapse, 1815–1960*, Leicester 1982

Kleffens, E. N. van, *De internationaal-rechtelijke betrekkingen tusschen Nederland en Japan (1605-heden)*, Leiden 1919

Klerck, E. S., *De Atjeh-oorlog* I, 's-Gravenhage 1912

387

Koebner, R. and Schmidt, H. D., *Imperialism. The Story and Significance of a Political Word, 1840–1960*, Cambridge 1960

Kol, H. van, *Uit onze koloniën*, 2 volumes, Leiden 1903

Koningsveld, P. S. van, 'Snouck Hurgronje zoals hij was', *De Gids* 143, 1980, pp. 763–85

Koppen, C. A. J. van, *Abraham Kuyper en Zuid-Africa*, doctoral thesis, Utrecht 1981

Kossmann, E. H., *De lage landen 1780–1940. Anderhalve eeuw Nederland en België*, Amsterdam and Brussels 1976

Kraan, A. van der, *Lombok: Conquest, Colonization and Underdevelopment 1870–1940*, Singapore 1980

Kröll, U., *Die internationale Buren-Agitation 1899–1902. Haltung und Agitation zugunsten der Buren in Deutschland, Frankreich und den Niederlanden während des Burenkrieges*, Münster 1973

Kuiper, D. Th., *De Voormannen. Een sociaal-wetenschappelijke studie over ideologie, konflikt en kerngroepvorming binnen de gereformeerde wereld in Nederland tussen 1820 en 1930*, Meppel 1972

Kuitenbrouwer, M., 'De Nederlandse afschaffing van de slavernij in vergelijkend perspectief', *BMGN* 93, 1978, pp. 69–101

Kuitenbrouwer, M., 'N. G. Pierson en de koloniale politiek, 1860–1909', *TvG* 94, 1981, pp. 1–29

Kurgan-Van Hentenryk, G., *Léopold II et les groupes financiers belges en Chine. La politique royale et ses prolongements (1895–1914)*, Brussels 1971

Kuyper, A., *Ons Program*, Amsterdam 1879

Kuyper, A., *De crisis in Zuid-Afrika*, Amsterdam 1900

Lademacher, H., *Die belgische Neutralität als Problem der europäischen Politik 1830–1914*, Bonn 1971

Langer, W. L., *The Diplomacy of Imperialism 1890–1902*, New York 1968, 2nd impression

Langhout, J., *Economische staatkunde in Atjeh*, 's-Gravenhage 1923

Leeuw, A. S. de, *Nederland in de wereldpolitiek van 1900 tot heden*, Zeist 1936

Lehmann, J., *The First Boer War*, London 1972

Leyds, W. J., *Eenige correspondentie uit 1899*, 's-Gravenhage 1919

Leyds, W. J., *Tweede, derde en vierde verzameling correspondentie (1899–1902)*, 's-Gravenhage 1930–1934

Leyds, W. J., *Onze eerste jaren in Zuid-Afrika, 1884–1889* Dordrecht 1938

Lijnkamp, H. A. F., *De 'Japannerwet'. Onderzoek naar de wording*, Utrecht 1938

Lijphart, A., *Verzuiling, pacificatie en kentering in de Nederlandse politiek*, Amsterdam 1968

Lion-Cachet, F., *De worstelstrijd der Transvalers aan het volk van Nederland verbeeld*, Amsterdam 1882

Lith, P. A. van der, 'Pieter Johannes Veth', in *Jaarboek van de Koninklijke Akademie van Wetenschappen 1896*, Amsterdam 1897

Locher-Scholten, E., *Ethiek in fragmenten. Vijf studies over koloniaal denken en doen van Nederlanders in de Indonesische Archipel 1877–1942*, Utrecht 1981

Locher-Scholten, E., *Motieven voor het optreden tegen het sultansbestuur van Jambi in 1901*. Paper for the symposium 'Imperialisme in de marge', Utrecht, 18 January 1984

Louis, W. R., 'The Berlin Congo Conference', in Gifford and Louis (eds), *France and Britain*, 1967, pp. 167–221

Louis, W. R. (ed.), *Imperialism. The Robinson and Gallagher Controversy*, New York 1976

Louter, J. de, *Handleiding tot de kennis van het staats- en administratief recht van Nederlandsch-Indië*, 's-Gravenhage 1884, 3rd impression

Louter, J. de, *De taak van een kleinen staat*, Utrecht 1900

Lowe, C. J., *The Reluctant Imperialists*, I, *British Foreign Policy 1877–1902*, London 1967

Mansvelt, W. M. F., *Geschiedenis der Nederlandsche Handel-Maatschappij*, 2 volumes, Haarlem 1924

Marais, J. S., *The Fall of Kruger's Republic*, Oxford 1961

Marks, H. J., *The First Contest of Singapore, 1819–1824*, 's-Gravenhage 1959

Marques, A. H. de Oliveira, *History of Portugal*, 2 volumes, New York 1976

Mees, W. C., *Man van de daad. Mr Marten Mees en de opkomst van Rotterdam*, Rotterdam 1946

Miers, S., *Britain and the Ending of the Slave Trade*, London 1975

Miller, S. C., *'Benevolent Assimilation'. The American Conquest of the Philippines 1899–1903*, New Haven and London 1982

Minderaa, J. T., 'De politieke ontwikkeling in Nederland 1887–1914', in *AGN* 13, Haarlem 1979, pp. 431–79

Mommsen, W. J., *Der europäische Imperialismus. Aufsätze und Abhandlungen*, Göttingen 1979

Mommsen, W. J., *Theories of Imperialism*, Chicago 1980

Mulders, A., *De missie in tropisch Nederland*, 's-Hertogenbosch 1940

Muller, H., *Muller. Een Rotterdams zeehandelaar. Henrik Muller Szn. (1819–1898)*, Schiedam 1977

Muller, H. P. N., *Land und Volk zwischen Sambesi und Limpopo*, Leipzig 1894

Multatuli, *Verzameld Werk* V, Amsterdam 1973

Nederland-Zuid-Africa. Gedenkboek uitgegeven door de Nederlandsch-Zuid-Afrikaansche Vereeniging 1881–1931, Amsterdam 1931

Netscher, F., *Uit ons parlement. Portretten en schetsen uit de Eerste en Tweede Kamer*, Amsterdam 1890

Bibliography

Nieuw Nederlandsch Biografisch Woordenboek, 10 volumes, Leiden 1911–1937

Nieuwenhys, R., *Oost-Indische Spiegel. Wat Nederlandse schrijvers en dichters over Indonesië hebben geschreven vanaf de eerste jaren der Compagnie tot op heden*, Amsterdam 1973, 2nd impression

Nijpels, G., *Japan-Nederland in Oost-Azië. Eene militaire studie*, Haarlem 1899

Noer, Deliar, *The Modernist Muslim Movement in Indonesia 1900–1942*, Kuala Lumpur 1973

Nusteling, H. P. H., *De Rijnvaart in het tijdperk van stoom en steenkool 1831–1914*, Amsterdam 1974

Obieta, J. A., *The International Status of the Suez Canal*, 's-Gravenhage 1960

Officieele bescheiden betreffende het ontstaan van den Oorlog tegen Atjeh in 1873, 's-Gravenhage 1881

Oosterwijk, B., *Vlucht na victorie. Lodewijk Pincoffs (1827–1911)*, Rotterdam 1979

Overzee. Nederlandse koloniale geschiedenis 1590–1975, Haarlem 1982

Owen, R., and Sutcliffe, B. (eds), *Studies in the Theory of Imperialism*, London 1972

Pakenham, Th., *The Boer War*, London 1979

Pelzer, A. N., 'Die erkenning van de Suid-Afrikaanse Republiek deur Nederland', in *Hertzog Annale van die Suid-Afrikaanse Akademie vir Wetenskap en Kuns* 13, 1964, pp. 49–59

Penning, L., *Uit mijn leven*, Zwolle, undated

Platt, D. C. M., *Finance, Trade and Politics in British Foreign Policy 1815–1914*, London 1968

Plesur, M., *America's Outward Thrust. Approaches to Foreign Affairs 1865–1890*, DeKalb 1971

Ploeger, J., *Onderwys en onderwysbeleid in die Suid-Afrikaanse Republiek onder ds. S. J. du Toit en dr. N. Mansvelt (1881–1900)*, Pretoria 1945

Pluvier, J. M., 'Internationale aspekten van de Nederlandse expansie', *BMGN* 86, 1971, pp. 26–72

Porter, A. N., *The Origins of the South African War. Joseph Chamberlain and the Diplomacy of Imperialism 1895–1899*, Manchester 1980

Pruys van der Hoeven, A., *Het laatste nieuws uit Atjeh*, place of publication unknown, 1896

Quack, H. P. G., *Herinneringen uit de levensjaren van Mr H. P. G. Quack 1834–1913*, Amsterdam 1913

Raalte, E. van, *Staatshoofd en ministers. Nederlands constitutionele monarchie historisch-staatsrechtelijk belicht*, Zwolle 1971

Ramm, A., 'Great Britain and France in Egypt, 1876–1882', in Gifford and Louis (eds), *France and Britain*, 1967, pp. 73–121

Read, D., *Engeland 1868–1914. The Age of Urban Democracy*, London 1979

Bibliography

Reid, A., *The Contest for North Sumatra. Acheh, the Netherlands and Britain, 1858–1898*, Kuala Lumpur 1969

Reid, A., 'Indonesian diplomacy. A documentary study of Achehnese foreign policy in the reign of Sultan Mahmud, 1870–1874', *Journal of the Malaysian Branch of the Royal Asiatic Society* 42, 1969, pp. 70–114

Resink, G. J., *Indonesia's History between the Myths. Essays in Legal History and Historical Theory*, 's-Gravenhage 1968

Reynolds, Ch., *Modes of Imperialism*, Oxford 1981

Ricklefs, M. C., *A History of Modern Indonesia, c. 1300 to the Present*, London 1981

Ritter, P. H. (ed.), *Eene halve eeuw 1848–1898. Historisch Gedenkboek*, 2 volumes, Amsterdam 1898

Robinson, R. and Gallagher, J., with A. Denny, *Africa and the Victorians. The Official Mind of Imperialism*, London 1961

Robinson, R., 'Non-European Foundations of European Imperialism: Sketch for a Theory of Collaboration', in Owen and Sutcliffe (eds), *Studies*, 1972, pp. 117–43

Robinson, R., 'European Imperialism and Indigenous Reactions in British West Africa, 1880–1914', in Wesseling (ed.), *Expansion and Reaction*, 1978, pp. 141–67

Roland Holst, H., *Kapitaal en arbeid in Nederland*, 2 volumes, Amsterdam 1902–1932

Romein, J., *Op het breukvlak van twee eeuwen*, 2 volumes, Leiden and Amsterdam 1967

Roo de la Faille, P. de, 'Herdenking', in *Gedenkschrift uitgegeven ter gelegenheid van 75-jarig bestaan van het Koninklijk Instituut voor de Taal-, Land- en Volkenkunde van Nederlandsch-Indië*, 's-Gravenhage 1926, pp. 1–36

Ru, A. de, 'Het beeld van de Zuid-Afrikaanse geschiedenis in Nederland 1899–1956', in *Hertzog Annale van die Suid-Afrikaanse Akademie vir Wetenskap en Kuns* 9, 1960, pp. 74–117

Ryxman, A. S., *A. C. Wertheim, 1832–1897. Een bijdrage tot zijn levensgeschiedenis*, Amsterdam 1961

Schaper, B. W., 'Nieuwe opvattingen over het moderne imperialisme', *BMGN* 86, 1971, pp. 4–21

Scheffer, H. J., *Henry Tindal. Een ongewoon heer met ongewone besognes*, Bussum 1976

Schneider, M. and Hemels, J., *De Nederlandse krant 1618–1978. Van 'niewstydinghe' tot dagblad*, Baarn 1979

Schöffer, I., 'Het politiek bestel van Nederland en maatschappelijke verandering', in *Vaderlands Verleden*, 1975, pp. 622–44

Schöffer, I., 'Dutch "Expansion" and Indonesian Reactions: Some Dilemmas of Modern Colonial Rule (1900–1942)', in Wesseling (ed.), *Expansion and Reaction*, 1978, pp. 78–100

Schotanus, F. B., *De internationale betrekkingen tussen Nederland en*

Zuid-Afrika, 1890–1910, Langbroek 1979

Schreuder, D. M., *Gladstone and Kruger. The Liberal Government and Colonial Home Rule, 1880–1885*, London 1969

Schreuder, D. M., *The Scramble for Southern Africa, 1877–1895. The Politics of Partition Reappraised*, Cambridge 1980

Schutte, G. J., *De Hollanders in Krugers Republiek, 1884–1899*, Pretoria 1968

Schutte, G. J., 'Nederland en de eerste Transvaalse Vrijheidsoorlog, 1880–1881', *TvG* 94, 1981, pp. 565–95

Semmel, B., *Imperialism and Social Reform. English Social-Imperialist Thought 1895–1914*, London 1960

Smit, C., *Diplomatieke geschiedenis van Nederland inzonderheid sedert de vestiging van het koninkrijk*, 's-Gravenhage 1950

Smit, C. (ed.), *Bescheiden betreffende de buitenlandse politiek van Nederland 1848–1919. Derde periode 1899–1919*, 6 volumes, 's-Gravenhage 1957–68

Smit, C., *Nederland in de eerste wereldoorlog, I, Het voorspel (1899–1914)*, Groningen 1971

Smit, H. J. and Wieringa, W. J. (eds), *Correspondentie van Robert Fruin, 1845–1899*, Groningen 1957

Snouck Hurgronje, C., *De Atjehers*, 2 volumes, Batavia and Leiden 1893–4

Snouck Hurgronje, C., *Mekka*, 2 volumes, 's-Gravenhage 1888–9

Somer, J. M. *De Korte Verklaring*, Breda 1934

Spanjaard, L., *Nederlandsche diplomatieke en andere bescherming in den Vreemde 1795–1914*, Amsterdam 1923

Spies, F. J. du Toit, *'n Nederlander in diens van die Oranje-Vrystaat. Uit die nagelate papiere van Dr Hendrik P. N. Muller*, Amsterdam 1946

Stapel, F. W., *Geschiedenis van Nederlandsch-Indië*, V, Amsterdam 1940

Stengers, J., 'King Leopold and Anglo-French Rivalry, 1882–1884', in Gifford and Louis (eds), *France and Britain*, 1967, pp. 121–67

Stengers, J., 'King Leopold's Imperialism', in Owen and Sutcliffe (eds), *Studies*, 1972, pp. 248–77

Stengers, J., 'Léopold II et le modèle colonial hollandais', *TvG* 90, 1977, pp. 46–72

Storry, R., *Japan and the Decline of the West in Asia 1894–1943*, London 1979

Sturler, J. E. de, *Het grondgebied van Nederlandsch Oost-Indië*, Leiden 1881

Stuurman, S., *Verzuiling, kapitalisme en patriarchaat. Aspecten van de ontwikkeling van de moderne staat in Nederland*, Nijmegen 1983

Suttorp, L. C. Jhr., *Mr Alexander Frederik de Savornin Lohman 1837–1924*, 's-Gravenhage 1948

Swellengrebel, J. L., *In Leydeckers voetspoor. Anderhalve eeuw bijbelkunde en taalkunde in de Indonesische talen*, I, 's-Gravenhage 1974

Swieten, J. van, *De waarheid over onze vestiging in Atjeh*, Zaltbommel 1879

Taal, G., *Liberalen en Radicalen in Nederland. 1872–1901*, 's-Gravenhage 1980

Tamse, C. A., *Nederland en België in Europa (1859–1871). De zelfstandigheidspolitiek van twee kleine staten*, 's-Gravenhage 1973

Tamse, C. A. (ed.), *Memoires van een enfant terrible. Politieke herinneringen van de Zeeuwse liberale afgevaardigde Mr Daniël van Eck aan vijfendertig jaar kamerlidmaatschap 1849–1884*, place of publication unknown, 1975

Tamse, C. A., 'Liberale ministeries 1868–1874', in *AGN* 12, Haarlem 1977, pp. 424–49

Tamse, C. A., 'De politieke ontwikkeling in Nederland 1874–1887', in *AGN* 13, Haarlem 1979, pp. 207–25

Tamse, C. A., 'The Netherlands Consular Service and the Dutch Consular Reports of the Nineteenth and Twentieth Centuries', in *Business History* 23, 1981, pp. 271–6

Tarling, N., *British Policy in the Malay Peninsula and Archipelago 1824–1871*, London 1969

Teitler, G., *The Dutch Colonial Army in Transition: the Militia Debate, 1900–1921*, Rotterdam 1980

Teitler, G., 'Manpower Problems and Manpower Policy of the Dutch Colonial Army, 1860–1920', *AP* 14, 1979, pp. 71–94

Thompson, R. C., *Australian Imperialism in the Pacific. The Expansionist Era 1820–1920*, Melbourne 1980

Tichelman, F., *De Sdap en Indonesië, 1897–1907. Enkele gegevens en problemen*, place of publication unknown, 1968

Tichelman, F., *Stagnatie en beweging. Sociaal-historische beschouwingen over Java en Indonesië in Aziatisch verband*, Amsterdam 1975

Tijn, Th. van, *Twintig jaren Amsterdam. De maatschappelijke ontwikkeling van de hoofdstad van de jaren '50 der vorige eeuw tot 1876*, Amsterdam 1965

Tijn, Th. van, 'Een nabeschouwing', *BMGN* 86, 1971, pp. 79–90

Tijn, Th. van, 'Op de drempel van een nieuwe tijd: Nederland omstreeks 1870', in *Vaderlands Verleden*, 1975, pp. 497–529

Tijn, Th. van, 'The Party Structure of Holland and the Outer Provinces in the Nineteenth Century', in *Vaderlands Verleden*, 1975, pp. 560–90

Tillema, J. A. C., Victor de Stuers. *Ideeën van een individualist*, Assen 1982

Tinker, H., *A New System of Slavery. The Export of Indian Labour Overseas 1830–1920*, London 1920

Vaderlands Verleden in Veelvoud. 31 opstellen over de Nederlandse geschiedenis na 1500, 's-Gravenhage 1975

Vandenbosch, A., *Dutch Foreign Policy since 1815. A Study in Small Power Politics*, 's-Gravenhage 1959

Vatikiotis, P. J., *The History of Egypt from Muhammed Ali to Sadat*, London 1980, 2nd impression

Veer, P. van 't, 'Het einde van een eeuw. Ir. Henri Hubertus van Kol, 1852–1925' in: id., *Geen blad voor de mond. Vijf radicalen uit de negentiende eeuw*, Amsterdam 1958, pp. 183–218

Veer, P. van 't, *De Atjeh-oorlog*, Amsterdam 1969

Veer, P. van 't (ed.), *Maar Majesteit! Koning Willem III en zijn tijd. De geheime dagboeken van minister A. W. P. Weitzel*, Amsterdam 1969

Veer, P. van 't, 'De machthebbers van Indië', *BMGN* 86, 1971, pp. 40–7

Verkade, W., *Thorbecke als Oost-Nederlands patriot*, Zutphen 1974

Veth, P. J., *Atchin en zijne betrekkingen tot Nederland. Topographisch-historische beschrijving*, 2 volumes, Leiden 1873

Veth, P. J., *Ontdekkers en onderzoekers*, Leiden 1884, 2nd impression

Veth, P. J. (ed.), *Midden-Sumatra. Reizen en Onderzoekingen der Sumatra Expeditie, uitgerust door het Koninklijk Nederlandsch Aardrijkskundig Genootschap*, 9 volumes, Leiden 1881–1897

Veur, P. W. van der (ed.), *Documents and Correspondence on New Guinea's Boundaries*, 's-Gravenhage 1966

Veur, P. W. van der, *Search for New Guinea's Boundaries. From Torres Strait to the Pacific*, 's-Gravenhage 1966

Visscher, J., *De ondergang van een wereld. Historisch-oeconomische studie over de oorzaken van den Anglo-Boer Oorlog (1899–1902)*, Rotterdam, undated

Vlekke, B. H. M., 'Indonesië en de publieke opinie in de Verenigde Staten', *Indonesië* I, 1947–1948, pp. 397–408

Vlekke, B. H. M., *Nusantara. A History of Indonesia*, 's-Gravenhage 1965, 2nd impression

Vollenhoven, C. van, *De eendracht van het land*, 's-Gravenhage 1913

Voorhoeve, J. J. C., *Peace, Profits and Principles. A Study of Dutch Foreign Policy*, 's-Gravenhage 1979

Vreede, G. W., *Hoofdartikelen van wijlen professor Vreede, overgedrukt uit het Utrechtsch Dagblad, 1869–1880*, Leiden 1906

Vries, J. de (ed.), *Herinneringen en dagboek van Ernst Heldring 1871–1954*, 3 volumes, Utrecht 1970

Waal, E., de, *Onze Indische Financiën. Nieuwe Reeks Aanteekeningen*, 10 volumes, 's-Gravenhage 1876–1907

Wal, S. L. van der, 'De Nederlandse expansie in Indonesië in de tijd van het moderne imperialism: de houding van de Nederlandse Regering en de politieke partijen', *BMGN* 86, 1971, pp. 47–55

Wanjon, D., *Geschiedenis van den Nederlandschen handel sedert 1795*, Haarlem 1900

Wehler, H.-U., *Der Aufstieg des amerikanischen Imperialismus. Studien zur Entwicklung des Imperium Americanum 1865–1900*, Göttingen 1974

Wehler, H.-U., *Bismarck und der Imperialismus*, Cologne 1969

Bibliography

Wehler, H.-U., 'Industrial Growth and Early German Imperialism', in Owen and Sutcliffe (eds), *Studies* 1972, pp. 71–93

Wehler, H.-U., *Das Deutsche Kaiserreich 1871–1918*, Göttingen 1973 (Eng edn: *The German Empire, 1871–1918*, trans. Kim Traynor, Leamington Spa and Dover NH 1985)

Wehler, H.- U., *Modernisierungstheorie und Geschichte*, Göttingen 1975

Wellenstein, E. P., *Het Indische Mijnbouwvraagstuk* 's-Gravenhage 1918

Wels, C. B., *Aloofness and Neutrality. Studies on Dutch Foreign Relations and Policy-Making Institutions*, Utrecht 1982

Wels, C. B., 'De historicus en de constanten in het buitenlandse beleid' in: *Lijn in de buitenlandse politiek van Nederland*, 's-Gravenhage 1984, pp. 9–29

Wely, J. van, *Schaepman. Levensverhaal*, Bussum 1954

Weringh, J. van, *Het maatschappijbeeld van Abraham Kuyper*, Assen 1967

Wertheim, W. F., 'Counter-Insurgency Research at the Turn of the Century: Snouck Hurgronje and the Acheh War', *Sociologische Gids* 19, 1972, pp. 320–8

Wesseling, H. L. (ed.), *Expansion and Reaction. Essays on European Expansion and Reactions in Asia and Africa*, Leiden 1978

Wesseling, H. L., 'Expansion and Reaction: Some Reflections on a Symposium and a Theme', in *idem* (ed.), *Expansion and Reaction*, 1978, pp. 2–17

Wesseling, H. L., 'Koloniale corlogen en gewapende vrede, 1871–1914. Een terreinverkenning', *TvG* 91, 1978, pp. 474–90

Wesseling, H. L., *Myths and Realities of Dutch Imperialism: Some Preliminary Observations*. Paper delivered to the Second Indonesian–Dutch Historical Conference, Ujang Pandang, 22 to 30 June 1978

Wesseling, H. L., 'Dutch Historiography on European Expansion since 1945', in *Wesseling and Emmer* (eds), *Reappraisals*, 1979, pp. 122–40

Wesseling, H. L., 'Nederland en de Conferentie van Berlijn, 1884–1885', *TvG* 93, 1980, pp. 559–77

Wesseling, H. L., 'Post-imperial Holland', *JCH* 15, 1980, pp. 125–43

Wesseling, H. L. and P. C. Emmer (eds), *Reappraisals in Overseas History. Essays on Post-war Historiography about European Expansion*, Leiden 1979

Wesseling, H. L. and Emmer P. C., 'What is Overseas History? Some Reflections on a Colloquium and a Problem', in Wesseling and Emmer (eds), *Reappraisals*, 1979, pp. 3–21

Westermann, J. C., *Gedenkboek Kamer van Koophandel en Fabrieken voor Amsterdam*, I, *Het tijdvak 1811–1922*, Amsterdam 1936

Wight, M., *Power Politics*, Harmondsworth 1979

Wilhelmina, *Eenzaam maar niet alleen*, Amsterdam 1959

Willemsen, G., *Koloniale politiek en transformatie processen in een plantage-economie. Suriname 1873–1940*, Amsterdam 1980

Bibliography

Willequet, J., *Le Congo Belge et la Weltpolitik (1894–1914)*, Brussels 1962

Wils, L., 'De politieke ontwikkeling in België 1870–1914', in *AGN* 13, Haarlem 1979, pp. 165–207, 395–431

Winter, P. J. van, *Onder Kruger's Hollanders. Geschiedenis van de Nederlandsche Zuid-Afrikaansche Spoorweg-Maatschappij*, 2 volumes, Amsterdam 1937–8

Winter, P. J. van, *Dr Leyds en Zuid-Afrika. Willem Johannes Leyds*, Leiden 1942

Witte, J. C., *J. B. van Heutsz. Leuen en Legende*, Bussum 1976

Woltring, J. (ed.), *Bescheiden betreffende de buitenlandse politiek van Nederland 1848–1919. Tweede Periode 1871–1898*, 6 volumes, 's-Gravenhage 1962–72

Yapp, M. E., *Strategies of British India. Britain, India and Afghanistan 1798–1850*, Oxford 1980

Zijl, M. C. van *Die Protesbeweging van die Transvaalse Afrikaners (1877–1880)*, Pretoria and Cape Town 1979

Index

397

Index

Index

Index

Index

Index

Index

Index

social Darwinism, 14, 16–17, 171, 214, 229, 315, 318–19, 332, 367
social democracy, 298
Social Democratic Alliance, 223
Social Democratic Workers' Party, 222, 223, 224, 226
social imperialism, 8–9, 15–16, 21, 211, 335, 349, 354
socialism, 5–6, 19 149, 211, 215, 226, 232, 259, 265, 297–8, 312, 314–17, 319, 321, 329–31
Société Générale, 360, 361, 362, 363
Soest, G. H. van, 48, 142
Soeterwoude, P. J. Elout van, 42, 95
South Africa (New Holland in)
  kinship discovery, 189–95
  Netherland and, 208–13
  towards New Holland, 202–8
  Transvaal deputation, 195–202
South African Republic, see Transvaal
South America
  colonies without trade, 84–7
  intervention, 243–6
sovereignty, 46, 82, 233, 247, 355, 359
  dilemma of Outer Region, 113, 120
  origins of Acheh War, 92–3, 95–7
  rights, 139, 142–3, 157, 160, 168, 172, 173
Transvaal, 299
Spain, 238
  colonial rivalry, 134, 135
  –American War, 1, 5, 239, 243–4, 256, 329
Spruyt, C. Bellaer, 191, 203, 209, 223, 289
Standard Oil, 239, 252–3, 280, 346
Stapel, F. W., 18
Stengers, J., 358–9
Steyn, President M. T., 301
Stoetwegen, E. W. F. W van, 78, 293
Stork, C. T., 69, 75, 80
Straits settlements, 35
Stuers, A. L. F. de, 150–1
Stuers, Victor de, 321–2
Stuurman, S., 218, 220
Suez Canal, 53–6, 67, 73–4, 82, 342, 353
Suez Convention, 25, 151, 337
suffrage, 217, 219, 296
Sugar Convention (1903), 251–2
Sultan of Acheh, 33, 35, 92, 96–7, 103, 215
Sultan of Deli, 114–15
Sultan of Siak, 35, 61, 368

Sultan of Turkey, 94, 107
Sumatra, 60–1, 63, 65–7, 333, 338, 342
  Treaty, 89–92, 98–101, 106, 114
Surinam, 146, 150–2, 154
suzerainty claims, 287, 288, 291
Swieten, General J. van, 46, 48, 102–5, 107, 109, 110, 116, 167, 176

Tak, P. L., 226, 235, 239, 253, 269, 288, 293, 298, 312
Tamse, C. A., 47
tariffs, 65, 67, 71, 78, 91, 183
Teuku Umar, 266, 268, 270, 274, 346, 367
Thiers, President Louis A., 108
Thorbecke, J. R., 43, 61, 197, 369
Tichelman, F., 24, 27
Tienhoven, G. van, 221, 256
Tijn, Th. Van, 22, 24, 59, 279, 348
Timmer, H. H., 193, 197
Timor Treaty, 256, 339, 356
Tippu Tip, 360
Tirpitz, Admiral Von, 230
Toit, S. J. Du, 196–201, 204, 206, 283
trade
  comparative values of imports and exports of major trading partners (table), 249
  overseas trade (appendix), 374
Trade Politics Committee, 225, 237
Transvaal
  Acheh and, 310–15
  annexation, 82–4, 189–91, 282, 310, 313, 353, 361
  Boer War, see main entries
  deputation, 195–202, 204
  movement, 27, 197, 201–2, 346–7, 349, 362
  New Holland, 189–95, 202–8, 282–7, 332, 334, 347
  support committees, 190–1, 194–5, 208, 224, 298
Treub, M. W. F., 231, 367
triple alliance, 227, 228
Troelstra, P. J., 226, 272, 298, 313
Tromp, Th. M., 83, 195
Turkish Empire, 239–40

Ufford, J. K. W. Quarles van, 51, 123, 164–5
United States, 22–3, 148, 238, 252–3
  intervention in South America, 243–5
  Spanish–American War, 1, 5, 239,

Index